The Beta Sigma Phi
INTERNATIONAL

HOLIDAY COOKBOOK

NEW YEAR'S EV INCOLN'S BIRTHDAY
EASTER VALENTINE
WASHIN ST. PATRIC
WEDDIN H OF JULY
THANK RISTMAS

Congratulations and Thank You...

to each Beta Sigma Phi whose recipe was selected for this outstanding cookbook.

It is a privilege indeed to introduce this exciting collection of holiday recipes to homemakers everywhere. This Holiday Cookbook is a remarkable assemblage of holiday ideas. It contains favorite recipes and ideas that will make your holidays brighter and more exciting throughout the year.

From New Years to Christmas — you will find great recipes, unusual menus, a treasury of ideas for entertaining family and friends for every festive occasion. And homemakers can prepare each recipe with confidence, knowing that each one has been tested and proven by a Beta Sigma Phi.

Beta Sigma Phi is an international sorority offering opportunities for friendship, development of cultural appreciation, and community service. Founded in 1931 by Walter W. Ross, the organization has grown rapidly. Beta Sigma Phi is the largest, most outstanding women's organization of its kind in the world.

Today there are 200,000 Beta Sigma Phis dedicated to the belief that the only right they have is the right to be useful. Organized into approximately 9,000 chapters, the membership represents every state in the United States, every province in Canada, and fourteen other countries. Kansas City, Missouri is the location of the international headquarters.

The Beta Sigma Phi International Cookbooks are very meaningful to the communities of participating members. The profit on each cookbook goes directly to the individual chapters who use these funds for their current local service projects.

Bill Ross

WALTER W. ROSS III
President
International Executive Council
of Beta Sigma Phi
Kansas City, Missouri

Favorite Recipes Press ©MCMLXXI
Box 77 Nashville, TN 37202
Library of Congress Card Catalog No. 79-157863

Preface

This is a book about holidays and, more specifically, about delightful holiday foods. About the food served on those very special occasions when the ordinary, day-to-day world stops and holiday magic takes over.

This is a book in which hundreds of women share their all-time favorite holiday recipes with you. These are the recipes they serve on festive holiday occasions when nothing but the very finest food will do.

Every homemaker knows the pleasure of working with a recipe until each ingredient is right ... until the proper combination of seasonings blend for an unforgettable taste treat. The recipes in this book have been developed with this loving care and have won acclaim for the women who now share them with you.

Added to these marvelous recipes are ideas to make every holiday a gala occasion. A Fourth of July Reunion with all-American Fried Chicken and Fresh Peach Pie ... a St. Valentine's Day Gourmet Dinner for Two with Broiled Lobster-Tails ... an English Christmas Dinner featuring a Standing Rib Roast and Yorkshire Pudding.

Ideas for these and many more holiday happenings fill the pages of this book. In every section, you'll find ideas to give holidays a special flair. This is a book that shows you just how much fun a holiday can be!

Contents

Abbreviations, Substitutions, and Cooking Guides

IN MEASURING, REMEMBER. . . .

3 tsp. = 1 tbsp.
2 tbsp. = 1/8 c.
4 tbsp = 1/4 c.
8 tbsp. = 1/2 c.
16 tbsp. = 1 c.
5 tbsp. + 1 tsp. = 1/3 c.
12 tbsp. = 3/4 c.
4 oz. = 1/2 c.
8 oz. = 1 c.
16 oz. = 1 lb.
1 oz. = 2 tbsp. fat or liquid
2 c. fat = 1 lb.
2 c. = 1 pt.
2 c. sugar = 1 lb.
5/8 c. = 1/2 c. + 2 tbsp.
7/8 c. = 3/4 c. + 2 tbsp.
1 oz. butter = 2 tbsp.
1 lb. butter = 2 c. or 4 sticks
2 pt. = 1 qt.
1 qt. = 4 c.
A few grains = less than 1/8 tsp.
Pinch = as much as can be taken between tip of finger and thumb
Speck = less than 1/8 tsp.

WHEN YOU'RE MISSING AN INGREDIENT . . .

Substitute 1 teaspoon dried herbs for 1 tablespoon fresh herbs.

Try 1 cup minus 2 tablespoons all-purpose flour as a substitute for 1 cup cake flour.

Add 1/4 teaspoon baking soda and 1/2 cup buttermilk to equal 1 teaspoon baking powder. The buttermilk will replace 1/2 cup of the liquid indicated in the recipe.

Use 3 tablespoons dry cocoa plus tablespoon butter or margarine instead of 1 square (1 ounce) unsweetened chocolate.

Make custard with 1 whole egg rather than 2 egg yolks.

Mix 1/2 cup evaporated milk with 1/2 cup water (or 1 cup reconstituted nonfat dry milk with 1 tablespoon butter) to replace 1 cup whole milk.

Make 1 cup of sour milk by letting stand for 5 minutes 1 tablespoon lemon juice or vinegar plus sweet milk to make 1 cup.

Substitute 1 package (2 teaspoons) active dry yeast for 1 cake compressed yeast.

Add 1 tablespoon instant minced onion, rehydrated, to replace 1 small fresh onion.

Substitute 1 tablespoon prepared mustard for 1 teaspoon dry mustard.

Use 1/8 teaspoon garlic powder instead of 1 small pressed clove of garlic.

Substitute 2 tablespoons of flour for 1 tablespoon of cornstarch to use as a thickening agent.

Mix 1/2 cup tomato sauce with 1/2 cup of water to make 1 cup tomato juice.

Make catsup or chili with 1 cup tomato sauce plus 1/2 cup sugar and 2 tablespoons vinegar.

WHEN YOU NEED APPROXIMATE MEASUREMENTS . . .

1 lemon makes 3 tablespoons juice
1 lemon makes 1 teaspoon grated peel
1 orange makes 1/3 cup juice
1 orange makes about 2 teaspoons grated peel
1 chopped onion, medium makes 1/2 cup pieces
1 pound unshelled walnuts makes 1 1/2 to 1 3/4 cups shelled
1 pound unshelled almonds makes 3/4 to 1 cup shelled
8 to 10 egg whites make 1 cup
12 to 14 egg yolks make 1 cup
1 pound shredded American cheese makes 4 cups
1/4 pound crumbled blue cheese makes 1 cup
1 cup unwhipped cream makes 2 cups whipped
4 ounces (1 – 1 1/4 cups) uncooked macaroni make 2 1/4 cups cooked
7 ounces spaghetti make 4 cups cooked
4 ounces (1 1/2 – 2) uncooked noodles make 2 cups cooked

OVEN TEMPERATURES

Temperature Fahrenheit	*Term*
250-300	Slow
325	Moderately slow
350	Moderate
375	Moderately quick
400	Moderately hot
425-450	Hot
475-500	Extremely hot

MEAT THERMOMETER TEMPERATURES

Beef	
Rare	140°
Medium	160°
Well-done	170°
Fresh Pork	170 - 185°
Smoked Pork	
Fully Cooked	130°
Cook before eating	160°
Veal	170°
Lamb	175 - 180°

MAKE 1 CUP OF FINE CRUMBS WITH . . .

28 saltine crackers
4 slices bread
14 square graham crackers
22 vanilla wafers

ABBREVIATIONS

Cup	c.
Tablespoon	tbsp.
Teaspoon	tsp.
Pound	lb.
Ounce	oz.
Package	pkg.
Gallon	gal.
Quart	qt.
Pint	pt.
Dozen	doz.
Large	lge.
Small	sm.

Wonderful New Year's Eve — the time when balloons, confetti, laughter, music, good friends, and loved ones combine for really great parties. A time to share memories of the passing year and hopes for the new one. And a perfect time to entertain and shine as a hostess! Perhaps you'll want to capitalize on the elegance of formal balls and plan an after-the-ball party. Or you may prefer casual gatherings around a blazing fireplace. Whatever your preference, you'll want to plan a party that's fun for everyone and easy for you!

Try a buffet! Buffet parties are a welcome change from the delicious — but heavy — dinner parties which fill everyone's holiday calendar from Thanksgiving until after Christmas. And a buffet party is so easy on you. You can prepare the foods you are going to serve hours — or even days — in advance. Everyone serves himself from a gaily decorated holiday party table — it's so much fun for your guests and so little work for you, the happy hostess!

New Year's Eve

Here's our idea of a truly elegant — and easy — New Year's Eve buffet for eight. The menu we've suggested contains dishes that will serve either a formal party or a casual gathering. Your guests will delight in taste-tempting Party Steak Bits — bite-sized pieces of tender sirloin marinated in a tangy mixture of oil, spices, and herbs and served in its own rich sauce. Complement this with another main dish, fabulously tasty Lobster-Artichoke Newburg. An unusual blend of fruit and vegetable flavors make Confetti Salad Mold a welcome and appropriate addition to your taste-tempting menu. Top this meal with Cranberry-Nut Bread — a delicious blend of cranberry, orange, and walnut flavors — and you'll have your guests raving about your culinary skill!

These dishes are easy to make and contain that all-important make-ahead quality. Prepare tangy Party Steak Bits the morning of your party. Marinate a 2-inch thick round or sirloin strip steak in 1/2 cup of wine vinegar, 1/4 cup salad oil, and garlic to taste. Let it stand for at least one hour. Then broil it rare (8 minutes each side), and cut it into 1/2-inch strips or squares. Reserve the meat drippings. In a bowl, mix 1/4 cut butter, 1/4 cup olive oil, 1 tablespoon dry mustard, 1/2 teaspoon minced garlic, 1 teaspoon Worcestershire sauce, and a dash each of nutmeg, angostura bitters, and freshly-ground black pepper. Add the drippings from the steak. Pour this sauce over the meat. This can be served immediately or kept in the refrigerator until time for the party. If you do chill this dish, be sure to reheat thoroughly before serving. It looks scrumptious and stays warm when served from a chafing dish!

Lobster-Artichoke Newburg can be made the morning of your party, too, and baked that evening. Drain one 13-ounce can of artichoke hearts, and cut them into bite-sized pieces. Melt 3 tablespoons butter, and add 1 tablespoon paprika, 1/8 teaspoon pepper, 1/2 teaspoon salt, and 1/4 cup flour. Stir ingredients together over medium heat until they are blended and the mixture forms tiny bubbles around the edges. Remove from heat and gradually add 1 cup milk. Return to heat and cook over low heat

Serve Buffet Style for New Year's Eve

until the sauce is thickened, stirring constantly. Add 1 cup cottage cheese, 3 hard-cooked eggs cut into quarters, and the artichoke hearts. Drain a 6 1/2-ounce can of lobster, and cut the meat into bite-sized pieces. Add to artichoke mixture. Pour into a buttered 1 1/2-quart casserole, and arrange strips of pimento on top. This dish may be refrigerated until about an hour before your party. Then take it out of the refrigerator, let it warm to room temperature (about 1 hour), and bake it at 350 degrees for 25 minutes. Serve it buffet-style in its casserole. Your guests will be able to handle this delicious entree more easily if you offer pastry shells or toast points to hold the Newburg.

Confetti Salad Mold adds a bright and light taste to your buffet. And it's easy to make! In a saucepan, sprinkle two envelopes of unflavored gelatin on 3/4 cup of water. Add 1/2 cup of white wine vinegar, 2 tablespoons of sugar, 2 teaspoons of seasoned salt, and 4 drops of hot sauce. Heat, stirring constantly, until gelatin dissolves. Remove from heat, and add 1 34-ounce can of pineapple juice. Chill the mixture until it is partially set. Add 1 cup shredded cabbage, 1 cup shredded carrots,

1/2 cup finely chopped mixed celery and radishes, 1 tablespoon finely chopped green onion, and 2 tablespoons chopped pimento; stir. Spoon into individual molds and chill until firm. Unmold onto crisp salad greens. Serve with side dishes of mayonnaise, tangy French dressing, and other dressings, to taste.

To cap this elegant meal, Cranberry-Nut Bread! It can be baked several days ahead without losing its freshness. Sift together 4 cups all-purpose flour, 1 1/2 cups sugar, 1 tablespoon baking powder, 1 teaspoon salt, 1 teaspoon soda. Add 2 cups of cranberries, halved, 1 cup of chopped walnuts, and 2 teaspoons grated orange rind. In another bowl, beat 2 eggs and add 1 1/2 cups of orange juice and 1/2 cup salad oil. Add to dry ingredients, stirring just enough to moisten. Pour mixture into two greased and floured 8 x 4 x 2 1/2-inch loaf pans. Bake at 375 degrees for 50 minutes or until a toothpick inserted into loaves comes out clean.

This elegant holiday menu deserves decorations to match. You might decide to play up the New Year's Eve theme with masses of bright balloons, crepe paper streamers, confetti, and party hats.

Or add a seasonal touch — fragrant bunches of greenery with red and silver accents. And if you're lucky enough to have a fireplace, be sure to have plenty of firewood on hand. Some hardware stores sell treated discs which turn your flames into multicolored splendor — a nice touch for this holiday.

The traditional "time" motif is always fun to use. A clock-face cake would make a nice centerpiece. Or you could cluster small hourglasses among greens.

If you want to try something really different, explore the new color schemes. Nothing brightens a midwinter party quicker than the vibrant pinks, burning blues, and metallic greens of the "mod" spectrum! To complement these colors let masses of great fat candles of bright hues lighten your buffet table.

Whatever your theme, here's a particularly elegant touch. Put a drop of your perfume on each lightbulb in the rooms where you are going to have the party. (Be sure the bulbs are turned off when you put on the perfume, as liquid on a hot light bulb may make it explode.) When you turn on the lights, the perfume will scent the air as the bulbs warm up.

When you get everything done, stop and look around. Your best dishes are quietly elegant. Your buffet table is ready for the evening. In the refrigerator, the main dishes — and platters of delightful side dishes — are ready for your guests' enjoyment. By planning ahead, you are ready hours ahead of time for a great party. Relax and get set to enjoy a truly memorable gathering, secure in the knowledge that your New Year's Eve buffet will be remembered for years to come by you and your guests.

HOLIDAY APPETIZER DIP

1 8-oz. package cream cheese
2 tbsp. milk
3/4 c. finely snipped dried beef
2 tbsp. instant minced onion
2 tbsp. finely chopped green pepper
1/8 tsp. pepper
1/2 c. sour cream
Chopped walnuts

Soften cream cheese; blend cream cheese and milk. Stir in dried beef, onion, green pepper and pepper; mix well. Stir in sour cream and walnuts. Place in small shallow baking dish or 8-inch pie plate. Bake at 350 degrees for 15 minutes. Serve hot with assorted crackers.

Mrs. Andy Rognlien
Xi Psi X2968, Eau Claire, Wisconsin

MUSHROOM CANAPES

1 lb. fresh mushrooms
2 tbsp. butter
1 tsp. lemon juice
1 pt. sour cream
Paprika
1 loaf party rye bread

Clean mushrooms; cut in small pieces. Saute mushrooms in butter for about 10 minutes; add lemon juice, sour cream and enough paprika to tint pink. Mix well. Place 1 teaspoon mixture on each piece of bread. Broil for 5 to 10 minutes or until lightly browned. Serve hot. Yield: 40 canapes.

John Chopchinski
Theta Delta, Amherst, Ohio

HOT CRAB MEAT APPETIZER

1 8-oz. package cream cheese
1 6 1/2-oz. can crab meat
2 tbsp. finely chopped onion
1 tbsp. milk
1/2 tsp. salt
Dash of pepper
1/3 c. sliced toasted almonds

Soften cream cheese; drain and flake crab meat. Combine all ingredients except almonds in bowl; mix until well blended. Spoon into 8-inch baking dish. Sprinkle with almonds. Bake in 375-degree oven for 15 minutes. Serve hot with cauliflowerets, carrot and celery sticks and cherry tomatoes for dipping.

Vera Mohan
Xi Tau X351, Pittsburgh, Pennsylvania

BRANDY-CHEESE BALL

12 oz. cream cheese
12 oz. Old English cheese
6 oz. blue cheese
1 tbsp. Worcestershire sauce
1 tsp. hot sauce
1 lge. grated garlic clove
3 tbsp. brandy or whiskey
Chopped nuts
Parsley

Blend cheeses together; add Worcestershire sauce, hot sauce, garlic and brandy. Combine nuts and parsley. Roll cheese ball in mixture; chill until firm.

Barbara R. Rehm
Xi Eta Eta X3292, Palatine, Illinois

TERIYAKI STEAK APPETIZERS

1 1/2 lb. sirloin steak
1/4 c. salad oil
1/4 c. soy sauce
1/4 c. honey
1/2 c. finely chopped onion
1 crushed garlic clove
1/2 tsp. ginger

Cut steak across grain into long thin strips. Combine remaining ingredients in large flat pan; add steak strips. Marinate for several hours. Lift strips out of marinade; shake to remove excess. Thread strips on metal skewers. Place on charcoal grill; broil over medium coals just until well browned, turning and brushing with marinade. Serve hot.

Grace-Anne Risedorf
Xi Kappa X848
Nanaimo, British Columbia, Canada

PICKLED SHRIMP HORS D'OEUVRES

2 lb. cooked med. shrimp
2 lb. onions, sliced lengthwise
Bay leaves
1/2 c. lemon juice
1/2 c. vinegar
1 c. French dressing
1 box pickling spice

Remove shells from shrimp; devein. Arrange layers of shrimp, onion slices and 5 or 6 bay leaves in crock. Repeat layers until shrimp and onions are used. Combine lemon juice, vinegar, French dressing and pickling spice; pour over shrimp and onions. Cover; refrigerate. Do not mix for 24 hours. Stir once a day for 3 or 4 days. Serve shrimp and onions with toothpicks for spearing.

Mrs. Johnnie Rowe
Psi Mu No. 5667, Chula Vista, California

RIPE OLIVE CHILI

2 1-lb. cans kidney beans
1/2 lb. lean ground beef
1 tbsp. cooking oil
1 1 5/8-oz. package chili seasoning mix
1 1-lb. can stewed tomatoes
1 8-oz. can tomato sauce
1/2 tsp. salt
1 1/2 c. canned pitted ripe olives

Drain and rinse kidney beans. Brown beef lightly in oil. Add kidney beans, chili seasoning mix, tomatoes, tomato sauce and salt; simmer for 10 minutes. Drain olives; add to beef mixture. Heat for several minutes longer. Serve as dip with tortillas. Yield: 6 servings.

CHAFING DISH MEATBALLS AND FRANKS

2 lb. ground chuck
1 egg, slightly beaten
1 lge. grated onion
Salt to taste
1 bottle chili sauce
1/2 lge. jar grape jelly
Juice of 1 lemon
2 lb. frankfurters

Combine chuck, egg, onion and salt; shape into 50 to 60 small balls. Combine chili sauce, jelly and lemon juice in skillet. Simmer meatballs in mixture until brown. Slice frankfurters 1/2 inch thick diagonally; add to meatball mixture. Serve from chafing dish. May be frozen.

Pauline Bonavire
Preceptor Delta XP655, Natick, Massachusetts

MOLDED VEGETABLE SALAD

1 c. shredded cabbage
1/2 c. shredded carrot
1/2 c. diced celery
1/2 c. shredded green pepper
Thinly sliced cucumber
Thinly sliced radishes
1 3-oz. package celery-seasoned gelatin
1 c. boiling water
1 c. cold water
2 tsp. vinegar

Toss cabbage, carrot, celery and green pepper together; place in mold. Arrange cucumber and radish slices on top. Dissolve gelatin in boiling water; add cold water and vinegar. Pour over vegetables; chill until firm.

Marilyn Eck
Rho No. 7692, Bethel Park, Pennsylvania

JELLIED COTTAGE CHEESE AND SALMON LOAF

2 env. unflavored gelatin
1/4 c. cold milk
1/4 c. hot milk
3 c. small curd cottage cheese
1/4 tsp. grated onion
1/4 tsp. salt
2 c. flaked red salmon
1 c. mayonnaise
1/2 c. finely chopped celery
1 tbsp. lemon juice

Soften 1 envelope gelatin in cold milk; dissolve in hot milk. Add cottage cheese, onion and salt. Chill until partially set. Pour into wet mold; chill until firm. Combine salmon, mayonnaise, celery and lemon juice. Soften remaining gelatin in 1/4 cup cold water; dissolve over hot water. Stir into salmon mixture; cool. Pour over cottage cheese mixture in mold. Chill until set. Unmold onto platter. Surround with watercress, lettuce and sliced tomatoes if desired.

Mary A. Jones
Xi Eta, Red Deer, Alberta, Canada

CINNAMON-APPLESAUCE MOLDED SALAD

1/3 c. cinnamon candies
1/2 c. water
1 pkg. lemon gelatin
2 tbsp. lemon juice
1 sm. can crushed pineapple
1/4 tsp. nutmeg
1 med. can applesauce

Bring cinnamon candies and water to a boil in saucepan; stir until candies are dissolved. Add gelatin; stir until dissolved. Add lemon juice, pineapple, nutmeg and applesauce; pour into mold or 8 x 8 x 2-inch pan. Chill until firm. Yield: 8-12 servings.

Mrs. Richard McQueen
Xi Alpha Rho X1417, Lansing, Michigan

CRAB LOUIS

1 c. salad dressing
1/4 c. heavy cream, whipped
1/4 c. chili sauce
1/4 c. chopped green pepper
1/4 c. chopped onions and tops
1 tsp. lemon juice
Dash of salt
1 lge. head lettuce
3 c. chilled crab meat
2 lge. tomatoes
2 hard-cooked eggs
Salt to taste
Paprika

Combine first 7 ingredients; mix well. Chill. Line 4 large plates with lettuce leaves; shred remaining lettuce. Arrange shredded lettuce on leaves. Remove pieces of shell from crab meat. Arrange crab meat on lettuce. Cut tomatoes and eggs into wedges; arrange around crab meat. Sprinkle with salt. Pour 1/4 cup cream mixture over each salad; sprinkle with paprika. Pass remaining cream mixture. Yield: 4 servings.

Duveene McDonald
Eta Gamma No. 5991, Liverpool, New York

TUNA POLYNESIAN

1/3 c. mayonnaise
1/2 tsp. curry powder
1 tbsp. chopped onion
2 7-oz. cans tuna
1 1/2 c. pineapple chunks
1 c. sliced celery

Combine mayonnaise, curry powder and onion; let stand to blend flavors. Drain tuna and pineapple; break tuna into bite-sized pieces. Combine tuna with pineapple and celery. Toss with mayonnaise mixture; serve in lettuce cups. Yield: 4-6 servings.

Maye Grow
Rho No. 240, Peoria, Illinois

COACH HOUSE PLATTER

2 15-oz. cans red kidney beans
1 4-oz. can whole mushrooms
1 12-oz. can whole kernel corn
1 4-oz. can pimento
1 1/2 c. diagonally sliced celery
2 tbsp. finely chopped onion
1/4 c. finely chopped parsley
2 tbsp. capers
1/2 tsp. salt
1/4 tsp. pepper
2/3 c. Cheddar 'n Wine Dressing
12 slices cold roast beef
Salad greens

Drain beans, mushrooms, corn and pimiento well. Combine celery, kidney beans, mushrooms, corn, onion, half the pimiento, 2 tablespoons parsley and 1 tablespoon capers in mixing bowl. Sprinkle with salt and pepper. Add dressing; toss to mix well. Chill. Fold slices of roast beef; arrange along sides of platter at serving time. Place salad greens at ends of platter; spoon salad mixture in mound in center. Garnish with additional dressing and remaining pimiento, parsley and capers. Yield: 6 servings.

ROCK LOBSTER CURRY AFRIKAANS

1 green apple
1/4 c. butter or margarine
1 sm. onion, chopped
1 clove of garlic, chopped
1 ripe banana, thinly sliced
1/4 c. flour
1 c. light cream
1 c. milk
1 tbsp. curry powder
3 8-oz. packages frozen South African rock lobster-tails
Salt to taste

Peel, core and chop apple. Melt butter; saute apple, onion, garlic and banana until very soft but not brown. Stir in flour; add cream and milk gradually, stirring constantly. Add curry. Cook over low heat, stirring constantly, until sauce bubbles and thickens. Parboil frozen rock lobster-tails by dropping into boiling salted water. Bring to a boil again; drain immediately. Drench with cold water. Cut away underside membrane with scissors and carefully pull out lobster meat in one piece. Reserve empty shells to use for serving condiments. Cut lobster into 1/2-inch crosswise slices; add to sauce. Season with salt. Simmer for 5 minutes. Serve over rice and with condiments such as carrot chutney, salted peanuts, sliced bananas, chopped cucumber, pineapple chunks, coconut and avocado slices. Yield: 6 servings.

SUPER LASAGNA

1 8-oz. package lasagna
1 1/2 lb. ground beef
1/2 tsp. olive oil
1/4 c. chopped onion
1 clove of garlic, crushed
2 6-oz. cans tomato paste
2 8-oz. cans tomato sauce with mushrooms
1 tsp. dried crushed sweet basil
1 tsp. dried parsley flakes
1 tsp. salt
1/2 tsp. oregano
1 bay leaf
1/4 tsp. pepper
1 1/2 c. water
2 c. creamed cottage cheese

1 egg, well beaten
2 8-oz. packages mozzarella cheese

Cook noodles according to package directions; drain. Brown beef in large skillet in oil with onion and garlic. Add tomato paste, tomato sauce, basil, parsley, 1/2 teaspoon salt, oregano, bay leaf, 1/8 teaspoon pepper and water; simmer for 1 hour. Combine cottage cheese, egg, remaining salt and remaining pepper. Grate mozzarella cheese. Arrange layers of noodles, cottage cheese mixture, beef mixture and cheese in 12 x 8-inch baking dish, ending with cheese on top. Bake at 350 degrees for 30 minutes. Remove from oven; let stand for 15 minutes before serving. Serve with garlic bread and salad if desired. Yield: 6-8 servings.

Patricia Diane Steward
Psi Phi No. 6150, Midland, Texas

CRAB-ARTICHOKE CASSEROLE

1/4 c. butter
1/4 c. flour
2 tsp. salt
1/8 tsp. pepper
1 tsp. paprika
1 tsp. minced onion
3 1/4 c. milk
2 7 1/2-oz. cans crab meat
1 1/4 c. macaroni shells
1 8 1/2-oz. can artichoke hearts
1/3 c. dry sherry
1/4 c. grated sharp Cheddar cheese

Melt butter in skillet; stir in flour, salt, pepper and paprika until smooth. Add onion; stir in milk gradually. Bring to a boil, stirring constantly, until smooth and thickened. Reduce heat; simmer for 5 minutes. Flake crab meat. Cook macaroni according to package directions. Drain artichoke hearts. Combine crab meat, sherry, macaroni and artichoke hearts with sauce; place in 2 1/2-quart casserole. Sprinkle with cheese. Bake in 350-degree oven for about 20 minutes. Yield: 6-8 servings.

Mrs. Robert Waltlich
Theta Eta No. 5649, Flouissant, Missouri

SEAFOOD CASSEROLE

1 can crab meat, drained
1 can tuna, drained
1 lb. cooked shrimp
2 c. cooked rice
1 sm. grated onion
1 c. diced celery
1 pimento, diced
1 sm. can mushroom pieces
1 can mushroom soup
1/2 c. diced green pepper
1/2 c. grated Cheddar cheese
2 c. thin white sauce
Bread crumbs

Mix all ingredients lightly except white sauce and crumbs. Pour into baking dish. Pour white sauce over top; sprinkle with bread crumbs. Bake for 1 hour at 350 degrees.

Mrs. Louis P. Rohls
Upsilon Preceptor, Eldon, Missouri

MEATBALLS AND SCALLOPED POTATOES

1 lge. can evaporated milk
1 egg, slightly beaten
1 1/2 lb. ground beef
1/2 c. cracker crumbs
1 1/2 tsp. salt
1/8 tsp. pepper
1 tsp. dry mustard
1/4 c. chopped onion
1/2 c. diced green pepper
6 c. thinly sliced potatoes
1 can cream of celery soup
Chili or barbecue sauce

Combine 2/3 cup milk, egg, beef, crumbs, seasonings, onion and green pepper; blend well. Shape into balls. Cook potatoes in boiling water to cover for 5 to 8 minutes or until partially tender; drain. Spread potatoes in 2 baking dishes. Combine remaining milk with soup; pour over potatoes. Arrange meatballs on top. Brush with chili sauce. Bake for 30 to 45 minutes at 350 degrees.

Mrs. Sheila Row
Xi Beta Gamma X2346, Curries, Ontario, Canada

PARTY CHICKEN CASSEROLE

1 4-lb. stewing chicken
1 qt. water
Salt
1/4 tsp. pepper
1 clove of garlic, sliced
1 c. diced celery
1 green pepper, chopped
1 med. onion, chopped
2 tbsp. olive oil
1 No. 2 1/2 can tomatoes
1/2 tsp. curry powder
1 8-oz. package noodles
1/2 c. blanched chopped almonds
1 c. sliced mushrooms
1 c. ripe olives
2 c. whole kernel corn, drained
1 c. grated cheese

Disjoint chicken; combine chicken, water, 1 1/2 teaspoons salt and pepper in large kettle. Simmer until tender; reserve broth. Remove meat from bone; dice. Mash garlic with 1 teaspoon salt. Fry garlic, celery, green pepper and onion in skillet in olive oil until soft, but not browned. Add tomatoes and curry powder. Simmer, uncovered, for about 30 minutes or until thickened. Cook noodles in reserved broth until tender; drain. Combine tomato mixture, chicken, noodles, almonds, mushrooms, olives and corn. Season to taste. Place in 9 x 13 x 2-inch casserole. Sprinkle with cheese. Bake at 300 to 325 degrees for 1 hour to 1 hour and 15 minutes. Yield: 10-12 servings.

Felix Rise
Preceptor Zeta No. 508, Fayetteville, Arkansas

FESTIVE PINEAPPLE-CHICKEN CASSEROLE

2 cooked chicken breasts
1 19-oz. can pineapple chunks
1 can cream of chicken soup
1 can cream of mushroom soup
2 c. chopped celery
Chow mein noodles

Preheat oven to 350 degrees. Remove meat from chicken breasts; cut in large chunks and place in casserole. Drain pineapple, reserve juice. Add soups, pineapple and celery to chicken; pour in 1/4 cup reserved juice. Place casserole in oven. Bake for 30 minutes. Add thick covering of noodles; bake for about 10 minutes longer or until noodles are brown.

Mrs. Dianne B. L. Bryant
Tau No. 5596, Canora, Saskatchewan, Canada

SHERRIED BEEF NUGGETS

1 lb. ground beef
1/2 c. corn flake crumbs
1 1/2 c. evaporated skimmed milk
1/4 c. finely cut onion
1/4 c. chili sauce
1 tsp. salt
2 1/2 tsp. Worcestershire sauce
2 tbsp. flour
2 tbsp. shortening
1 can cream of mushroom soup
1 tbsp. sherry

Combine beef, crumbs, 1/2 cup milk, onion, chili sauce, salt and 1 teaspoon Worcestershire sauce in 2-quart bowl. Shape into 18 balls. Roll in flour. Heat shortening in 10-inch skillet; brown meatballs. Drain off drippings; push meatballs to one side of skillet. Combine remaining milk and Worcestershire sauce with remaining ingredients; add to skillet. Heat until steaming, but not boiling.

PEANUT-Y TEA RING

1 can refrigerator biscuits
1/4 c. melted butter or margarine
1 c. finely chopped peanuts
1/2 c. powdered sugar
1 tbsp. water

Separate biscuits. Dip both sides in melted butter, then in peanuts, coating well. Arrange in overlapping circle on greased baking sheet. Bake at 425 degrees for 10 to 15 minutes or until golden brown. Mix powdered sugar and water. Drizzle over hot tea ring. Slide onto serving plate; serve warm. Yield: 6-8 servings.

FILLED COFFEE CAKE

1/4 c. butter
1 c. sugar
2 eggs, separated
2 tsp. baking powder
1 tsp. salt
1/2 c. milk
1 1/2 c. flour
1 tsp. vanilla

Cream butter and sugar together until fluffy; add egg yolks, blending well. Add baking powder, salt, milk, flour and vanilla. Beat egg whites until stiff; fold into mixture.

Filling

1 tbsp. flour
1/2 c. brown sugar
1 tsp. cinnamon
1 tbsp. butter
1/2 c. pecans
Chopped dates

Combine all ingredients. Fill greased 7 x 11-inch pan 2/3 full with batter. Pour Filling over mixture; add remaining batter. Bake at 350 degrees for 45 minutes.

Cheryl Morse
Eta Eta No. 3336, Morris, Illinois

APRICOT-NUT BREAD

2 1/2 c. sifted flour
1 c. sugar
2 tsp. salt
3 tsp. baking powder
1/4 c. shortening
1/2 c. chopped nuts
1 c. diced dried apricots
2 eggs, well beaten
1 c. milk
Cream cheese, softened

Sift flour, sugar, salt and baking powder together; cut in shortening until mixture resembles coarse meal. Add nuts and apricots. Combine eggs and milk; add to dry ingredients, stirring until just dampened. Spoon batter into greased loaf pan. Bake for 1 hour at 350 degrees. Spread with cream cheese.

Mrs. Edward J. Folton
Delta Lambda No. 7399, Johnstown, Pennsylvania

HONEY TWIST

2 pkg. yeast
1/4 c. butter, softened
1/2 c. sugar
1 tsp. salt
1 c. milk, scalded
2 eggs, well beaten
6 c. sifted flour
Honey Topping
Chopped nuts
Chopped candied cherries

Dissolve yeast in 1/4 cup lukewarm water. Combine butter, sugar and salt in mixing bowl; pour hot milk over mixture, stirring until butter is melted. Cool to lukewarm. Add yeast and eggs. Beat in flour to make soft dough; turn out on floured board. Knead until smooth. Form into ball; place in greased bowl. Cover; let rise until doubled in bulk. Shape into long roll about 1-inch in diameter. Coil roll in greased cake pan, beginning at outside edge and coiling to center. Brush with Honey Topping. Let rise until doubled in bulk. Sprinkle with nuts and cherries. Bake in 375-degree oven for 25 to 30 minutes.

Honey Topping

1/4 c. butter
2/3 c. confectioners' sugar
1 egg white
2 tbsp. honey, warmed

Cream all ingredients together.

Mrs. Annetta Godochik
Gamma Upsilon No. 6437, Weirton, West Virginia

LEMON MUFFINS

2 c. self-rising flour
1 box lemon pudding mix
2 tbsp. sugar
1/4 c. oil
1 1/3 c. milk
Confectioners' sugar

Stir flour, pudding mix and sugar together in mixing bowl. Combine oil and milk; blend into flour mixture all at once. Stir only until moistened. Fill greased muffin cups 2/3 full. Bake at 425 degrees for 20 to 25 minutes. Sprinkle with confectioners' sugar. Yield: 1 1/2 dozen.

Jeanne DeGrella
Gamma Rho No. 5296, Warner Robins, Georgia

COFFEE AND CREAM FLOAT

1/2 c. sugar
2 c. water
Dash of salt
1 1/2 tbsp. instant coffee
Ice cream
1 bottle ginger ale

Combine sugar, water and salt in saucepan; simmer for 5 minutes. Add coffee; stir and chill. Pour into 4 chilled 10-ounce glasses; add 1 tablespoon ice cream to each glass. Fill almost to top with ginger ale; add scoop of ice cream to each glass. Yield: 4 servings.

Marianne LaVick
Xi Kappa X-1068, Menomonie, Wisconsin

ANISE COFFEE WITH CHICORY

Coffee with chicory
1/2 tsp. aniseed
8 stemmed red maraschino cherries
8 green maraschino cherries
16 pineapple chunks
1 c. sweetened whipped cream (opt.)

Brew 8 cups coffee with chicory, adding aniseed to coffee grinds. Arrange cherries and pineapple chunks on 8 skewers. Place in coffee cups. Fill with coffee; top with whipped cream. Yield: 8 servings.

NEW YEAR'S EVE COFFEE PUNCH

1 1/2 c. instant coffee
1 c. sugar
5 1/2 gal. vanilla ice cream
1 pt. whipped cream

Mix 1/2 gallon hot water and instant coffee; chill well. Pour coffee into large punch bowl; add sugar. Stir well until dissolved. Spoon or scoop in ice cream; add whipped cream. Mix until ice cream is partially melted and mixture is frothy. Yield: 50 servings.

"Pinky" Rerucha
Beta Chi No. 3156, Cypress Gardens, Florida

CRANBERRY SPARKLE

1/2 c. whole cranberries
1 6-oz. can frozen orange juice
3 pt. cranberry juice cocktail
1/2 c. lemon juice
2 1-pt. 12-oz. bottles ginger ale

Fill 5-cup ring mold with whole cranberries and 4 1/2 cups water or enough water to come to top of mold. Freeze. Prepare orange juice according to package directions; chill juices for several hours before serving. Pour juices into punch bowl. Dip frozen mold into warm water for 1 minute; unmold. Float ring in punch; add ginger ale. Yield: 20 servings.

Rita A. Roycraft
Xi Delta X-114, Wheaton, Illinois

HOLIDAY NECTAR

1 qt. milk
1/3 c. confectioners' sugar
1/2 c. grenadine syrup
Dash of salt
1/4 tsp. mace
Red food coloring
1 c. whipping cream, whipped

Combine milk, 3 tablespoons sugar, grenadine syrup and salt in saucepan. Heat gently; do not boil. Stir in mace and desired amount of food coloring. Sweeten whipped cream with remaining sugar. Pour milk mixture into cups; top with whipped cream. Yield: 6 servings.

Mary Ann Calley
Tau Chapter No. 2041, Butte, Montana

MULLED GRAPEFRUIT CIDER

1 c. sugar
1/2 c. water
12 whole cloves
2 1/2-in. pieces of stick cinnamon
1 48-oz. can grapefruit juice
1 qt. sweet cider

Combine sugar, water and spices in saucepan; simmer for 10 minutes. Strain. Combine with grapefruit juice and cider. Reheat; serve hot from punch bowl. Yield: 22 servings.

Sylvia Stenbol
Theta Kappa Chap., Escanaba, Michigan

After the wonderful excitement of New Year's Eve, New Year's Day stands out as an island of quiet. It's a day of football games, drop-in visits, and memories of the marvelous holiday season now passing so quickly.

New Year's Day is also a time for delicious food — nothing too heavy after the parties of the previous night, but something special, nonetheless. With the breathtaking excitement of pre-game football parades — from the Orange Bowl all the way West to the Rose Bowl — you'll be hard-pressed to get your family away from the television set. Why not plan a brunch they can enjoy *with* their parades? Here's an exciting menu for four, planned especially for TV-tray eating!

Elegant Oysters á la Rockefeller are mildly flavored and wonderfully delicious — just what you need to wake up those sleepy New Year's late-morning appetites. Satisfy your family's hunger with tangy Caesar salad

1 New Year's Day

— an unusual blend of flavors — and piping-hot Braided Onion Bread. A great brunch like this deserves a great dessert — Lemon Fruitcake, an old favorite with a new twist. Add coffee, and your family will be comfortably satisfied and ready to settle down for a long afternoon of football.

To prepare Oysters á la Rockefeller, drain and chop 1/2 cup cooked spinach. Melt 8 tablespoons butter in a saucepan. Remove from heat and add the chopped spinach, 2 tablespoons minced onion, 2 teaspoons minced celery, 3 tablespoons fine dry bread crumbs, 1/4 teaspoon herb blend for fish, 1/4 teaspoon anchovy paste, 1/4 teaspoon salt, and pepper to taste. Mix well. Remove 24 oysters from their shells, setting the oyster meat aside. Scrub the shells and boil any sand

away. Spread rock salt into four pie pans. In each pan, press six oyster half shells lightly into the salt. Place one oyster in each shell, put pans under the broiler, and broil for 5 minutes. Remove and place one spoonful of the spinach mixture on each oyster. Broil until thoroughly heated. Remove from heat and serve immediately.

Caesar Salad with its hearty flavor and blend of tastes is a special favorite of the men in the family. And it's easy to prepare, too! Trim four slices of white bread and spread them with butter. Then cut them into cubes and place on a baking sheet. Bake at 350 degrees for 10 to 15 minutes. Cut three heads of romaine lettuce crosswise into 1/2-inch strips. Cut one medium onion into thin slices and separate the slices into rings. Dice one green pepper. Place romaine, onion rings, and green pepper in a salad bowl. Place dampened towel over bowl and refrigerate until ready to use. When you are ready to serve this salad, add the croutons and sprinkle with 1/2 cup Parmesan cheese. Season with 1/2 teaspoon of garlic salt and freshly ground pepper to taste. To prepare the fabulous dressing that adds so much to this salad, mix 3/4 cup of salad oil, 1 tablespoon Worcestershire sauce, the juice of two lemons, and 1/8 teaspoon garlic powder. Pour over the salad. Break a raw egg over the salad and toss thoroughly. Add crumbled bleu cheese to taste and chopped

Begin the New Year with Flair

anchovy fillets if desired. Toss together, serve . . . and wait for the compliments you're sure to get!

This tasty meal deserves an equally-tasty bread — what else but Braided Onion Bread. Sprinkle one package yeast over 1/4 cup warm water. In another bowl, combine 1 cup sour cream, 1 envelope onion soup mix, 1/4 teaspoon baking soda, 2 tablespoons sugar, 2 tablespoons salt, 2 tablespoons butter or margarine, 2 beaten eggs, and 1 cup water. Stir in softened yeast until mixture is smooth. Gradually add enough flour to make a stiff dough (6 1/2 to 6 3/4 cups). Knead well. Place in well-greased mixing bowl and turn once to bring greased side up. Cover bowl with towel and let bread rise in warm place until it doubles in bulk. Punch down and divide into six strips each about 15 inches long. Braid three strips together, sealing ends. Place loaves on cookie sheet, and let rise until they have doubled in bulk. Brush braids with one beaten egg, and sprinkle with sesame seeds. Bake at 350 degrees until golden brown.

Lemon Fruitcake will be the perfect ending to a perfect brunch. To prepare it, chop 1/4 pound candied red cherries, 1/4 pound candied green cherries, 1/2 pound candied pineapple, and 1 pound pecans. Toss with 2 cups of flour. Cream 1 pound butter and 1 pound brown sugar together. Add 6 eggs, one at a time, beating well after each addition. Add 2 cups flour to butter, egg, and sugar mixture and beat well. Add fruit mixture and 2 tablespoons lemon extract; mix well. Pour batter into a greased and floured angel food cake pan and bake at 250 degrees for 2 hours and 30 minutes to 3 hours.

After the excitement of day-long football, your family will be more than ready for an old-fashioned New Year's Day family dinner. This is the last meal you'll share during the holidays. Tomorrow will bring the mad scramble of work, classes, meetings, etc. So why not make this a dinner you'll all remember for the entire year. Here's a hearty dinner for six.

Your dinner begins with French Onion Soup, sharply flavored and absolutely delicious. Roast Pork — flavored with an unusual blend of soy sauce and maple syrup — is a memorable main dish. Orange-Candied Sweet Potatoes, Good Luck Black-eyed Peas, and Spinach-with-Sour Cream Casserole add their individual charm to your dinner. Another taste note is provided by Spicy Peach Salad with Poppy Seed Dressing. Everyone's favorites, Butterhorn Rolls, will be a welcome addition. And for dessert, try sweet and filling, Pecan Pie. With all these delicious taste treats, you'll be sure to have a meal your entire family will enjoy and remember for a long time.

French Onion Soup is easy to prepare. Slice thinly four large onions and brown them lightly in 2 tablespoons butter or margarine. Add 4 cups brown stock or bouillon, 1 teaspoon Worcestershire sauce, 1/2 teaspoon salt, and 1/8 teaspoon pepper. Cook this mixture over medium heat for about 15 to 20 minutes. While it is cooking, cube and toast two French rolls. When the soup is cooked, place the toasted cubes in individual soup bowls, and pour soup over them. Sprinkle each serving with Parmesan cheese, and listen to your family's ooh's and aah's.

Pork Roast is also easy to prepare. You'll need a 4- to 6-pound pork loin roast. Dry it with paper toweling and place it fat side up on the rack of a roasting pan. Roast at 350 degrees for 20 to 30 minutes per pound or until it is done. After 1 hour and 30 minutes of cooking time have elapsed, baste it with about half of a 1/3-cup measure of soy sauce. Mix remaining sauce with 2 tablespoons maple syrup. Ten minutes before removing roast from oven, cover it with the soy sauce-maple syrup mixture. After taking it out of the oven, let the roast stand for 15 minutes before slicing.

Serve this tasty roast with three vegetable dishes, and everyone in your family is sure to find his favorite. To prepare Orange-Candied Sweet Potatoes, peel 8 cooked medium-sized sweet potatoes and cut them in half. Arrange them in a shallow baking dish. In a saucepan combine 2 tablespoons butter or margarine, 1 tablespoon grated orange rind, 3/4 cup dark corn syrup, and 1/4 teaspoon of salt. Bring the mixture to a boil. Pour it over the potatoes and bake them at 350 degrees for 30 minutes, basting occasionally.

Good Luck Black-eyed Peas are a traditional New Year's Day dish, especially among Southern families. Chop four strips of bacon and fry until slightly brown. Add 1/2 cup chopped onions. Saute the mixture for about 15 minutes or until golden. Then add 1/2 cup chopped bell pepper. Cook for another 10 minutes. Pour in two cans black-eyed peas, and simmer for about 30 minutes.

Spinach-with-Sour Cream Casserole is another sure-to-please dish. To prepare it, cook three 10-ounce packages frozen chopped spinach according to the package directions. Add one envelope dry onion soup mix and 2 cups sour cream. Pour the mixture into a greased 1 1/2-quart casserole. Top with 1 cup herb-seasoned stuffing mix and 2 tablespoons melted butter. Bake at 400 degrees for 15 to 20 minutes.

Spiced Peach Salad makes a festive addition to your family dinner table. Drain one jar spiced peaches and reserve 1 cup liquid. Remove the seeds. Mix one 3-ounce package of cream cheese and 1/2 cup chopped pecans. Fill the peach cavities with the cheese-and-pecan mixture. Place the stuffed peaches in muffin tins or custard cups. Dissolve one 3-ounce package orange-flavored gelatin in 1 cup boiling water. Add reserved peach liquid, mixing well. Pour gelatin over peaches; chill until set.

To top this tasty salad, try Poppy Seed Dressing. Beat together 1 cup honey, 1 cup salad oil, 2 tablespoons poppy seeds, 1/2 teaspoon salt, 1/4 teaspoon dry mustard, and 1/3 cup vinegar. Beat for two minutes. Serve with Spicy Peach Salad.

Butterhorn Rolls are everyone's favorites. To prepare, soften one package yeast in 1/4 cup warm water. Combine 3/4 cup scalded milk, 1/2 cup shortening, 2/3 cup sugar, and 1 teaspoon salt. Cool to lukewarm and add yeast mixture. Mix well. Add three beaten eggs; blend well. Add 4 1/2 cups sifted flour and mix to a smooth, soft dough. Knead lightly on floured surface. Place dough in greased bowl, turning once to grease surface. Cover. Let rise until doubled in bulk. Divide dough in thirds. Roll each third on a lightly-floured surface to a 9-inch circle. Melt 4 tablespoons butter. Brush rolls with part of melted butter. Cut each circle in 12 to 16 wedge-shaped pieces; roll each wedge, starting with wide end and rolling to the point. Arrange rolls in greased baking pan; brush with melted butter. Cover; let rise until doubled in bulk. Bake at 400 degrees for 15 minutes.

The meal-topper for this family occasion is Pecan Pie — rich but oh-so-delicious. Beat three eggs with a fork or whisk. Add 1 cup white corn syrup, 1/2 cup maple-flavored syrup, 1/2 cup soft butter or margarine, 1/3 cup brown sugar, and 1/2 teaspoon salt. Mix well. Add 1/2 cup finely chopped pecans. Pour mixture into a 9-inch pie shell, and arrange

1 cup pecan halves in a circular pattern on top. Bake at 425 degrees for 10 minutes. Reduce oven temperature to 350 degrees; bake for one hour longer.

Two menus — two great family meals. Perhaps your family has found its own special dishes over the years. On the pages that follow, you'll find a collection of all-time favorite recipes for appetizers, salads, meat, seafood, vegetables, breads, and desserts. Browsing through these home-tested recipes is sure to stir your imagination. Before you know it, you'll find yourself mixing and matching these recipes to produce meals, not just for New Year's Day, but for every extra-special family meal throughout the new year.

PEANUT-Y SOUP

2 tbsp. butter or margarine
1/4 c. chopped onion
1/2 c. chopped celery
1 c. smooth peanut butter
3 vegetable bouillon cubes
4 c. boiling water
1 1/2 tsp. lemon juice
Watercress

Melt butter in saucepan; add onion and celery. Cook until tender. Blend in peanut butter. Dissolve bouillon cubes in boiling water; add gradually to peanut butter mixture, blending well. Stir in lemon juice; heat to serving temperature. Garnish with watercress. Yield: 6 servings.

Photograph for this recipe on page 23.

CREME VICHYSSOISE

4 med. potatoes
4 green onions, chopped
1 med. onion, chopped
6 tbsp. butter
1 qt. water
4 chicken bouillon cubes
4 c. coffee cream
Salt and pepper to taste
1 pt. sour cream

Peel and quarter potatoes. Saute onions in butter in large kettle; add potatoes, water and bouillon cubes. Bring to a boil; boil rapidly for 30 minutes. Mash vegetables well. Add cream, salt and pepper; bring to a boil. Cool; add sour cream. Chill. Serve ice cold. Yield: 6 servings.

Mrs. Earl Ellis
New Summerfield, Texas

SENEGALESE SOUP

2 cans cream of chicken soup
3 c. milk
1/2 tsp. curry powder
2 tbsp. toasted coconut

Combine soup, milk and curry powder in medium saucepan; cook over medium heat until just bubbly. Beat with rotary beater until creamy and smooth. Pour into 8 small bowls or cups. Sprinkle with coconut. Yield: 8 servings.

Mrs. Claire M. Evangelista
Xi Eta Nu X-3543, Westlake, Ohio

CREAM OF OYSTER SOUP

1/4 c. butter
2 tbsp. flour
1 qt. milk
1 tsp. salt
1/4 tsp. celery salt
Dash of pepper
1/2 pt. oysters

Melt butter in saucepan over low heat; blend in flour until smooth. Add milk gradually; cook, stirring constantly, until sauce boils and thickens. Add seasonings. Chop oysters; add with oyster liquor to hot mixture. Heat thoroughly until oysters curl. Serve hot with crisp crackers or buttered toast strips. Yield: 6 servings.

Clara May Dunn
Phi Gamma Iota, Pittsburgh, Pennsylvania

LOBSTER STEW

3 tbsp. butter or margarine
2 c. cooked lobster meat
1 qt. milk
1 1/2 tsp. salt
1 tsp. paprika
1/8 tsp. pepper
Dash of cayenne

Heat butter in small skillet; saute lobster meat for about 5 minutes. Scald milk in saucepan; season with salt, paprika, pepper and cayenne. Add lobster meat; simmer for 5 minutes. Let stand for several minutes before serving.

Anita Brown
Groton Beta Epsilon, Noank, Connecticut

TURTLE SOUP

1 soft-shelled turtle
2 onions, chopped
6 cloves
1 tsp. ground allspice
4 tbsp. butter
3 tbsp. flour
1 No. 1 can tomatoes, sieved
1 sm. lemon, sliced
2 sliced hard-boiled eggs
1/4 c. sweet cream

Cut turtle into small pieces. Combine turtle, onions, cloves and allspice in 3 quarts water. Cook until tender. Melt 3 tablespoons butter in skillet; add flour, stirring until smooth. Add small amount of broth, stirring constantly, until smooth. Spoon flour mixture into broth, mixing well. Add tomatoes; salt to taste. Simmer for 30 minutes. Place lemon, remaining butter, eggs and cream in large tureen; pour in soup

Mrs. A. W. Noland
St. Francisville, Louisiana

MAJESTIC POTATO SALAD

2 env. unflavored gelatin
1 qt. tomato juice
1 tbsp. lemon juice
6 c. cold cubed cooked potatoes
1/4 c. oil and vinegar dressing
1 c. salad dressing
1 c. sliced celery
1/2 c. finely chopped onion
1/2 c. sliced stuffed olives
1/4 c. chopped parsley

Soften gelatin in 1 cup tomato juice; dissolve over hot water. Add to remaining tomato juice. Stir in lemon juice, 1/4 teaspoon salt and dash of pepper. Pour into 1-quart ring mold; chill until firm. Marinate potatoes in oil and vinegar dressing for 1 hour. Add salad dressing, celery, onion and olives; toss lightly. Season with salt and pepper. Unmold aspic on lettuce-lined platter. Fill center with potato salad; sprinkle with parsley. Yield: 8-10 servings.

CREME DE MENTHE FRUIT MOLD

1 1/2 c. boiling water
1 3-oz. package lemon gelatin
3 tbsp. creme de menthe
1 1/2 c. green seedless grapes
2 c. diced canned pineapple
2 c. grapefruit sections

Add water to gelatin; stir until dissolved. Add creme de menthe; chill until slightly congealed. Mix in remaining ingredients; pour into lightly oiled 6 1/2-cup ring mold. Chill until set. Unmold on salad greens; garnish as desired. Yield: 8 servings.

Mrs. Kelly George
Xi Beta Lambda X3583, Charleston, West Virginia

COMEBACK SALAD AND DRESSING

Chopped lettuce
2 cucumbers, chopped
2 radishes, chopped
2 tomatoes, cut up
2 stalks celery, chopped
1 onion, sliced
1 green pepper, chopped
1/4 lb. sliced ham
1/4 lb. slivered salami
1/4 lb. Swiss cheese, slivered
1/4 lb. American cheese, slivered
1 c. mayonnaise
1/2 c. salad oil
1 grated onion
3 grated garlic cloves
1/4 c. chili sauce
1/4 c. catsup
1 tsp. pepper
1 tsp. salt
1 tsp. mustard
1 tsp. paprika
Dash of hot sauce
1 tsp. Worcestershire sauce
3 tbsp. water

Toss all vegetables together in large salad bowl; place meats and cheese on top. Place remaining ingredients in blender; blend for about 3 minutes on high. Pour over salad and serve. Yield: 10-12 servings.

Arvilla Frankenberg
Beta Phi No. 7207, Ledyard, Connecticut

RASPBERRY-APPLESAUCE SALAD

1 c. applesauce
1 3-oz. package raspberry gelatin
1 10-oz. package frozen raspberries
1/2 c. mayonnaise
1/4 c. whipping cream, whipped

Bring applesauce just to boiling point. Add gelatin; mix until dissolved. Thaw raspberries; stir into gelatin mixture. Pour into 9-inch ring mold or individual molds. Chill until set. Unmold salad. Combine mayonnaise and cream; serve with salad. Sour cream may be used instead of mayonnaise mixture. Yield: 6 servings.

Mrs. Judy Hunt
Xi Alpha Lambda X1345, Jackson, Michigan

ROAST BEEF AU VIN

1 3-lb. sirloin tip roast
Salt and pepper to taste
Strip of suet
3/4 c. blackberry wine
4 tbsp. flour

Season roast with salt and pepper. Place roast on aluminum foil; place suet on top of roast. Fold aluminum foil over roast; seal top and 1 end of aluminum foil. Pour wine in open end; seal. Place on baking sheet. Bake at 325 degrees to desired doneness. Drain roast dripping from foil package. Mix 1/2 cup water, 4 tablespoons flour and 2 cups roast drippings in large skillet. Cook over low heat until thickened, stirring well. Pour remaining drippings into thickened mixture gradually, stirring constantly. Cook over low heat to desired gravy consistency. Serve gravy with roast.

Jean Ellis
Gamma Omega No. 6215, Bristol, Virginia

ROAST DUCK WITH SWEDISH RAISIN STUFFING

1/2 c. dark or golden raisins
2 c. cold cooked rice
1/8 tsp. ground cardamom
1 tsp. grated orange peel
2 1/4 tsp. salt
1 tbsp. instant minced onion
2 tbsp. melted butter
1 c. grated apple
1 4-lb. duck
1/3 c. sifted flour

Combine raisins with rice, cardamom, orange peel, 3/4 teaspoon salt, onion, butter and apple. Mix lightly. Stuff mixture loosely into body cavity of duck; close opening with lacing pins and string. Place in shallow roasting pan. Bake at 325 degrees for about 2 hours and 30 minutes. Transfer duck to hot platter. Skim all fat from drippings, reserving 1/2 cup fat. Blend reserved fat with flour in saucepan. Add 2 cups water and pan drippings. Cook, stirring constantly, until thickened. Season with remaining salt. Cut duck into quarters, using kitchen scissors. Pile hot stuffing on platter. Arrange duck pieces over top. Drizzle small amount gravy over duck; serve remaining gravy in gravy boat.

BROILED SCALLOPS WITH PEACHES

1 lb. scallops
2 tbsp. melted butter
2 tbsp. lemon juice
1/2 tsp. salt
Dash of pepper
12 canned peach halves
1/4 tsp. cinnamon
1/4 tsp. cloves
1/4 tsp. mace
3 slices bacon

Remove any shell particles from scallops; wash. Cut scallops into 1/2-inch pieces; saute in butter until golden brown. Combine lemon juice, 1/4 teaspoon salt, pepper and scallops; place peach halves in 11 x 7 x 1-inch baking pan. Combine cinnamon, cloves, mace and remaining salt. Sprinkle over peaches. Place about 2 tablespoons scallop mixture in center of each peach. Cut bacon into fourths, crosswise. Place a slice on each peach. Broil about 4 inches from heat for 8 to 10 minutes or until bacon is crisp. Yield: 6 servings.

Mrs. Betty H. Gregory
Alpha Mu No. 2900, Fredericksburg, Virginia

ROASTED SQUAB

4 squabs
Salt
Pepper
Butter
2 c. dry bread cubes
1 1/2 tbsp. chopped onion
1/8 tsp. poultry seasoning
Sage to taste
Hot broth

Clean squabs. Rub insides with salt and pepper to taste. Brown giblets in butter, combine with bread crumbs, onion, 1/2 teaspoon salt, 1/8 teaspoon pepper, poultry seasoning, sage, 2 1/2 tablespoons melted butter and enough hot broth to moisten. Stuff squabs with mixture. Rub outsides with butter. Place squabs, breast sides up, on rack in shallow pan. Bake at 350 degrees for 45 minutes to 1 hour or until tender. Yield: 4 servings.

Agnes Nilsen
Phi Delta Psi, San Jose, California

DILL POT ROAST WITH CARROT GRAVY

6 tbsp. flour
3 tsp. salt
1/4 tsp. pepper
3 tbsp. oil
1 4-lb. chuck roast
1 med. onion, sliced
1 tsp. dillseed
2 tbsp. vinegar
1 c. grated carrots

Combine 4 tablespoons flour, salt and pepper; dredge roast in mixture. Heat in Dutch oven; brown roast. Drain off excess oil. Add onion, dillseed, vinegar and 1/2 cup water; simmer for 2 hours and 30 minutes. Add carrots; simmer for 1 hour longer. Remove roast. Mix remaining flour with 1/2 cup water; add to pan juices. Cook over low heat, stirring until thickened. Serve gravy with roast. Yield: 6-8 servings.

Mrs. Ireta Green
Carson City Coun., Carson City, Nevada

ROAST LAMB WITH PICKLE MARINADE

1 leg of lamb
1 1-pt. jar sweet mixed pickles
10 peppercorns
3 cloves of garlic, crushed
3 bay leaves
3 whole cloves
1/2 tsp. leaf thyme
2 tbsp. flour
1 onion bouillon cube
Dash of turmeric

Place lamb, pickles, peppercorns, garlic, bay leaves, cloves and thyme in large bowl; cover. Marinate for several hours or overnight. Reserve marinade. Place lamb on rack in shallow roasting pan. Bake in 325-degree oven for 2 hours or until meat thermometer registers 175 degrees for medium doneness. Strain reserved marinade into measuring cup; add enough water to measure 3 cups. Reserve pickles. Stir about 1/4 cup marinade mixture into flour gradually in saucepan to form smooth paste. Add remaining marinade, stirring constantly. Add bouillon cube, turmeric and reserved pickles. Bring to a boil; boil for 1 minute, stirring constantly. Serve with lamb. Yield: 6-8 servings.

Photograph for this recipe on page 23.

BAKED PORK CHOPS WITH APPLE RINGS

8 pork chops
1/2 tsp. sage
1/2 tsp. salt
4 tart apples
1/4 c. brown sugar
2 tbsp. flour
1 c. hot water
1 tbsp. vinegar
1/2 c. seedless raisins

Brown chops in hot fat; sprinkle with sage and salt. Place in baking dish. Core apples; cut into rings. Place apple rings over chops; sprinkle with sugar. Add flour to fat in skillet; cook, stirring until smooth. Add water and vinegar gradually, stirring constantly, until smooth and thickened. Add raisins; pour sauce over chops. Bake, uncovered, at 350 degrees for 1 hour. Yield: 8 servings.

Mrs. Norman T. Hastings
Xi Beta Theta, Neodesha, Kansas

FESTIVE PORK ROAST

1 pkg. dry onion soup mix
1 4-lb. pork roast
1 tsp. garlic powder
1/2 c. milk
1/4 c. diced mushrooms
1 tsp. butter
2 tbsp. flour
Dash of salt
Pepper to taste

Line roasting pan with heavy-duty foil leaving enough foil to cover top of roast. Sprinkle onion soup mix on bottom of pan; place roast over soup mix. Sprinkle top of roast with garlic powder. Combine milk, mushrooms and butter in saucepan. Cook over low heat until butter is melted. Add small amount hot mixture to flour; return to saucepan, stirring constantly, until thickened. Season. Pour over roast; cover with foil. Bake at 350 degrees for about 2 hours or until done. Yield: 6 servings.

Jane Dieter
Delta Iota, Alexandria, Virginia

BEEF WITH MUSHROOM ONION SAUCE

4 tbsp. butter
1 c. chopped onion
1/2 lb. small mushrooms, sliced
1 beef bouillon cube
1/4 tsp. dry mustard
1/4 tsp. paprika
1/2 c. boiling water
1 8-oz. carton sour cream
2 c. cooked roast beef or steak
Freshly ground pepper to taste

Melt 2 tablespoons butter in 10-inch skillet. Add onion; cover. Cook gently, stirring occasionally, until golden brown. Add remaining butter and mushrooms. Cook rapidly until mushrooms wilt. Dissolve bouillon cube, mustard and paprika in water. Add bouillon mixture and sour cream to mushroom mixture. Cook over low heat; stir to blend. Cut beef into strips; add to sauce. Season with pepper. Heat gently without boiling. Yield: 4 servings.

Mrs. Helena Gollogly
Xi Gamma Alpha, Milford, Michigan

FILLET DE SOLE CAPRICE

1 1 1/2-lb. fish fillet
Juice of 1/2 lemon
1/4 c. white wine
1/4 c. water
1 tbsp. whole peppercorns
1 slice onion
1 clove of garlic
Butter or margarine
2 med. carrots, finely shredded
1 tsp. salt
1/4 tsp. pepper
1/4 c. sherry
1 1/2 tbsp. flour
1/4 c. milk
1/4 c. cream

Skin, wash and dry fillet. Place on well-buttered ovenproof dish. Add lemon juice, wine, water, peppercorns, onion and garlic. Bake in 325-degree oven for 15 to 20 minutes. Strain and reserve liquid. Melt 1/2 cup butter in saucepan; add carrots, salt, pepper and sherry. Reduce heat; cook for 10 to 20 minutes or until carrots are soft. Do not brown. Remove from heat; add flour. Stir until smooth. Add reserved liquid from fillet; cook until thickened. Add milk; stir until sauce comes to a boil. Add cream and 2 tablespoons butter. Lower heat; keep warm. Serve sauce over fish and rice. Yield: 4 servings.

Connie Steinke
Xi Alpha Nu, Kansas City, Missouri

JAMBALAYA

2 tsp. salt, divided
1 tsp. hot sauce
1 bay leaf
1 stalk celery with leaves
1 lb. shrimp
1/4 c. butter or margarine
1/2 c. chopped onion
1/2 c. chopped green pepper
1 garlic clove, minced
1 c. rice
1 1-lb. can tomatoes
3/4 c. bouillon
1 1/2 c. diced cooked ham

Place 3 cups water, 1 teaspoon salt and 1/2 teaspoon hot sauce in saucepan. Add bay leaf and celery. Bring to a boil; add shrimp. Return to a boil; cook for 5 minutes. Drain shrimp; cool quickly. Shell and clean. Melt butter in large skillet; add onion, green pepper and garlic. Cook until onion is tender, but not brown. Stir in rice, tomatoes, bouillon, remaining salt and hot sauce. Bring quickly to a boil. Reduce heat; cover skillet. Simmer for 20 minutes. Add ham; cover and cook for 10 minutes longer or until liquid is absorbed. Yield: 4-6 servings.

BAKED RED SNAPPER WITH CHEESE STUFFING

1 2-lb. red snapper
1 tsp. salt
Dash of pepper
1 c. chopped onion
1/4 c. melted fat or oil
2 c. dry bread cubes
2 tbsp. chopped parsley
2 tsp. dry mustard
1 c. grated Cheddar cheese
Paprika

Cut red snapper in half; sprinkle with salt and pepper. Place half, skin side down, in a well-greased baking dish. Cook onion in fat until tender. Combine bread cubes, parsley, mustard and cheese; add onion, mixing thoroughly. Place stuffing on red snapper and cover with remaining half. Brush with fat and sprinkle with paprika. Bake at 350 degrees for 30 to 35 minutes or until red snapper flakes easily when tested with a fork. A whole fish may be used. Clean and cut almost through lengthwise; stuff and bake. Yield: 8 servings.

Pat Koop
Gamma Epsilon, Miami, Florida

SWORDFISH STEAK SUPREME

1/2 c. salad oil
1/2 c. sauterne
1 tsp. parsley flakes
1/4 tsp. dried thyme
1 bay leaf, broken up
6 to 8 peppercorns
1/2 onion, diced
1 lb. swordfish steaks
1/4 dried bread crumbs
1/3 c. Parmesan cheese
Dash of oregano
1/4 tsp. salt

Combine salad oil, sauterne, parsley, thyme, bay leaf, peppercorns and onion in shallow pan; place swordfish steaks in marinade. Refrigerate; turn steaks after 1 hour. Marinate for 2 hours or longer. Combine bread crumbs, cheese, oregano and salt. Place steaks in shallow casserole; cover with crumb mixture. Cover casserole. Bake at 350 degrees for 20 minutes. Uncover; bake for 15 minutes longer. Yield: 4 servings.

Beatrice C. Donoghue
Omicron, Watertown, New York

BAKED STUFFED LOBSTER

12 crackers, crushed
1 can minced clams
2 tbsp. Worcestershire sauce
1/2 tsp. celery salt
1/4 tsp. pepper
1/4 c. melted butter
1 clam can milk
Fresh lobsters
Grated cheese
Paprika
Butter

Mix crumbs, clams, seasoning, melted butter and milk. Add 1/4 to 1/2 can more milk if mixture is dry. Place live lobster on back on a board; hold firmly with left hand between claws and tail. Cut body from head to tip of tail so lobster may be split open. Remove the intestinal vein. Fill lobsters with clam mixture; place in broiler pan. Sprinkle with cheese and paprika. Dot with small cubes of butter. Place about 1/4 cup water in pan. Bake at 425 degrees with rack near top of oven for 20 minutes. Remove from oven if lobster tails curl up; pull down. Claws will turn white.

Mrs. Shirley Ann Fielder
Xi Beta Pi Exemplar, Rome, New York

NEPTUNE CASSEROLE

2 cans asparagus spears
2 cans mushroom soup
1/2 lb. grated sharp cheese
1 5-oz. can lobster meat
1 4 1/2-oz. can deveined shrimp
1 7 1/2-oz. can crab meat
3/4 c. fine bread crumbs
Paprika

Preheat oven to 350 degrees. Place asparagus in large buttered casserole. Cover with 1 can mushroom soup; sprinkle with 1/3 of the cheese. Drain and combine lobster, shrimp and crab meat. Add lobster mixture to casserole. Sprinkle with 1/3 of the cheese. Cover with remaining mushroom soup. Top with bread curmbs and remaining cheese. Sprinkle with paprika. Cover tightly. Bake for 30 minutes. Remove cover; brown before serving. Yield: 8 servings.

Mrs. William R. Petty
Epsilon, Rock Hill, South Carolina

TOMATO PUDDING CASSEROLE

2 c. bread cubes
1 stick butter, melted
3/4 c. boiling water
1/2 tsp. salt
1 10-oz. can tomato puree
1/2 c. brown sugar

Place bread cubes in casserole. Pour butter over top. Combine water, salt, tomato puree and brown sugar; boil for 5 minutes. Pour tomato mixture over bread mixture. Bake in 350-degree oven for 30 to 45 minutes or until brown. Yield: 4-6 servings.

Mrs. Walter W. Ross, III
Beta Sigma Phi Intl., Kansas City, Missouri

FANCY ASPARAGUS CASSEROLE

1 tbsp. (heaping) butter
1 tbsp. (heaping) flour
1 No. 303 can asparagus spears
1/2 c. milk
1 tsp. salt
1/2 tsp. pepper
1/2 tsp. celery salt
1 tbsp. lemon juice
1 tsp. catsup
1 tsp. Worcestershire sauce
1/2 tsp. prepared mustard
1/4 lb. sharp cheese, diced
2 hard-boiled eggs, chopped
1/2 c. broken pecans
8 buttery crackers, crushed

Melt butter in 1 1/2-quart saucepan; add flour, stirring until flour is golden brown. Drain asparagus; reserve liquid. Add milk and reserved asparagus liquid, stirring until smooth. Mix salt, pepper, celery salt, lemon juice, catsup, Worcestershire sauce and prepared mustard together; add to sauce, stirring well. Add cheese, stirring until sauce is smooth. Add asparagus, eggs and pecans; mix well. Pour into 1-quart casserole; cover top with cracker crumbs. Bake in 350-degree oven until mixture bubbles and crackers are brown. May be made up several hours before baking. Yield: 6 servings.

Mildred Hargrove
Preceptor Gamma XP-190, Northport, Alabama

FRENCH BEAN AND MUSHROOM CASSEROLE

1 lge. onion, chopped
1/4 lb. butter
2 cans French string beans
1 can Parmesan cheese
2 cans mushroom soup
1 5-oz. can mushrooms
1/4 c. sherry
Salt and pepper to taste
1 can French-fried onion rings

Saute onion in butter until onion is tender and golden. Heat string beans; drain. Add half the cheese to beans while hot; mix together. Mix soup, mushrooms and liquid, sherry and onion in separate bowl. Add to beans. Season with salt and pepper; mix well. Pour into greased casserole; arrange onion rings on top. Sprinkle remaining cheese over onion rings. Bake at 350 degrees for 35 to 40 minutes until top is bubbling and onions are brown. Yield: 10-12 servings.

Doris P. Hesson
Xi Alpha Kappa No. 1710, Lynchburg, Virginia

CAULIFLOWER-CHEESE CASSEROLE

1 pkg. frozen cauliflower
1 can cheese soup
Italian bread crumbs

Cook cauliflower according to package directions; drain well. Layer in casserole with soup and crumbs. Bake in 350-degree oven until thoroughly heated. Yield: 6 servings.

Mary Lee Ashley
Delta Pi No. 7137, Vidalia, Louisiana

ONIONS GOURMET

36 sm. peeled onions
1 tsp. salt
1 1/2 c. water
4 tbsp. butter
1 tbsp. cornstarch
1/3 c. brown sugar
1/3 c. sherry
1/3 c. buttered bread crumbs

Cook onions slowly in salted water for about 20 minutes or until soft. Melt butter; add cornstarch. Mix to a paste. Add brown sugar; cook slowly until brown sugar is melted. Add sherry; cook until thickened. Drain onions, reserving 1/2 cup liquid. Add reserved liquid to butter mixture; stir well. Place onions in buttered 2-quart casserole; pour syrup over onions. Cover with buttered crumbs. Bake in 350-degree oven for 15 minutes. Yield: 8 servings.

Irene M. Grainger
Xi Lambda X-624, Toronto, Ontario, Canada

POTATOES ROMANOFF

6 c. cubed boiled potatoes
2 c. large curd cottage cheese
1 c. sour cream
1 clove of garlic, minced
1 tsp. salt
2 tbsp. chopped chives
1 c. grated Cheddar cheese
Paprika

Combine potatoes with cottage cheese, sour cream, garlic, salt and chives; place in buttered casserole. Top with cheese; sprinkle with paprika. Bake in 350-degree oven for 25 to 30 minutes. Yield: 8-10 servings.

Madelyn Kennedy
Lambda Xi No. 3733, Gladewater, Texas

BLACK-EYED PEA CASSEROLE

6 strips bacon
1 c. chopped celery
1 c. chopped green peppers
1 c. chopped onions
1 No. 303 can black-eyed peas
1 No. 303 can tomatoes
Salt and pepper to taste

Fry bacon until crisp; remove from pan. Drain and crumble. Simmer celery, green peppers and onions in drippings until done. Add peas, tomatoes and bacon; season with salt and pepper. Simmer for about 20 minutes. Yield: 6 servings.

Joy Keener
Xi Eta Beta No. 912 182, Old Ocean, Texas

COWBOY BLACK-EYED PEAS

1 No. 303 can black-eyed peas
1 med. sweet onion, sliced
1/2 tsp. Worcestershire sauce
2 tbsp. butter

Drain half the liquid from peas; add remaining ingredients to peas. Heat thoroughly; serve hot. Yield: 5 servings.

Colleen Stevenson
Neroosa, Wisconsin

HOT VEGETABLES WITH HERBED WALNUTS

1 tbsp. butter
1 c. walnut halves and pieces
1/4 tsp. dried dill, rosemary or oregano
2 c. hot cooked carrots
2 c. hot cooked wax or green beans
2 c. hot cooked cauliflowerets
Small crisp lettuce leaves
1 tsp. seasoned salt
French or Italian dressing

Melt butter in skillet. Add walnuts; sprinkle with dill. Stir over moderate heat for about 5 minutes or until walnuts are lightly toasted. Arrange hot cooked vegetables and herbed walnuts on crisp lettuce on serving platter. Sprinkle with seasoned salt. Heat dressing; serve separately with salad. Yield: 6 servings.

CINNAMON BREAD

2 pkg. yeast
1/2 c. lukewarm water
1 1/4 c. sugar
2 tsp. salt
2/3 c. instant dry milk
2 eggs
1/2 c. soft shortening
7 2/3 c. flour
2 tbsp. cinnamon
Melted butter

Dissolve yeast in lukewarm water. Combine 1/2 cup sugar, salt, dry milk, eggs, shortening and 1 1/2 cups water; beat with mixer. Add yeast. Beat in part of flour with mixer; beat in remaining flour as needed with spoon. Knead flour in until smooth and elastic; let rise until doubled in bulk. Punch down; let rise again. Roll into three 15 x 9-inch rectangles. Brush each piece with 1 teaspoon water. Mix remaining sugar with cinnamon. Sprinkle each piece with 1/3 of the cinnamon mixture, reserving 2 tablespoons for top. Roll dough up; place in loaf pans. Let rise until doubled in bulk. Brush with butter; sprinkle with reserved cinnamon mixture. Bake at 350 degrees for 35 to 40 minutes. Yield: 3 loaves.

Marilyn Parkes
Xi Beta Beta X-1793, Tampa, Florida

NEW YEAR'S PRUNE BREAD

1 c. sugar
1 1/2 c. flour
1 tsp. soda
1/2 tsp. salt
1 egg
2 tbsp. cooking oil
1/2 c. milk
1/2 c. chopped walnuts
1 jar junior baby food prunes

Combine all ingredients; mix well. Pour into loaf pan. Bake at 350 degrees for 1 hour.

Sandra Kay Speaks
Gamma Epsilon No. 7007, Henderson, Kentucky

HOLIDAY FRENCH BREAD

1 pkg. yeast
1/3 c. sugar
3 c. warm water
1/3 c. oil
1 tsp. salt
Flour

Mix yeast, sugar and water together; let stand for 10 minutes. Add oil and salt; mix well. Add flour until thick enough to stir with spoon. Knead on board until dough springs back at touch, adding flour as needed. Place in greased bowl. Let rise until doubled in bulk. Separate into 3 parts. Roll on pastry board into triangular shape. Pull and roll into round loaves, starting with wide end. Place on greased cookie sheet. Let rise until doubled in bulk. Bake at 200 degrees for 1 hour or until golden brown.

Kathy E. Harris
Gamma Upsilon No. 6780, Fort Smith, Arkansas

CHEESE ROLLS

2 pkg. yeast
1/2 c. warm water
1/2 c. shortening
1/2 tsp. salt
4 tbsp. sugar
1 8-oz. bottle cheese dressing
1 c. boiling water
2 eggs
5 1/2 c. flour

Dissolve yeast in warm water. Combine shortening, salt, sugar and cheese dressing in separate bowl. Pour small amount of boiling water in dressing bottle to clean; add all the boiling water to shortening mixture. Beat in eggs; add yeast. Stir in flour; knead for 1 minute. Chill for at least 2 hours. Form into rolls, muffins or bread. Let rolls rise for 30 minutes, bread for 45 minutes. Bake at 375 degrees for 22 minutes. Yield: 2 loaves or 4 dozen rolls.

Charlotte C. Cooper
Alpha Psi No. 2918, Fort Pierce, Florida

DILLSEED BREAD

1 pkg. yeast
1/4 c. warm water
1 c. creamed cottage cheese
2 tbsp. sugar
1 tbsp. instant minced onions
1 tbsp. butter or margarine
2 tbsp. dillseed
1 tsp. salt
1/4 tsp. soda
1 egg
2 1/4 to 2 1/2 c. flour

Soften yeast in water in large mixing bowl. Combine all ingredients except flour. Add flour gradually to form stiff dough. Beat well after each addition. Cover dough with waxed paper; cover paper with damp dish towel. Let rise for 50 to 60 minutes in warm place until dough is doubled in bulk. Stir down dough with wooden spoon. Turn into well-greased 8-inch round 1 1/2 to 2-quart casserole. Let rise for 30 to 40 minutes in warm place. Bake at 350 degrees for 40 to 50 minutes until golden brown. Brush with additional butter; sprinkle with additional salt. Rising in high altitude will take 20 to 30 minutes longer. Small or large curd cottage cheese may be used; small curd produces finer textured bread. Yield: 8-10 servings.

Geraldine R. Sand
Beta Xi 793, El Paso, Texas

COCONUT FRUITCAKE

1 c. butter or margarine
2 c. light brown sugar
4 eggs
3 c. sifted flour
1 tsp. baking powder
1/2 tsp. salt
1 1/2 c. chopped candied cherries
1 c. raisins
1 1/2 c. chopped candied pineapple
3/4 c. chopped citron
1 1/2 c. blanched almonds, chopped
3 c. shredded coconut
1 c. orange juice

Preheat oven to 275 degrees. Line greased 10-inch tube pan or two 9 x 5 x 2 1/2-inch loaf pans with heavy brown or waxed paper; grease again. Cream butter and sugar until light and fluffy; add eggs, one at a time, beating well after each addition. Sift flour, baking powder and salt together. Combine fruits, almonds and coconut in large mixing bowl; sift flour mixture over fruit mixture, mixing until all fruit is coated with flour. Blend fruit mixture into creamed mixture alternately with orange juice beginning and ending with fruit mixture; pour into pans. Bake for 3 hours and 30 minutes to 4 hours in tube pan or 3 hours to 3 hours and 30 minutes in loaf pans. Remove from oven; cool. Wrap in foil or plastic wrap to store.

Janet Dunn
Eta Omicron No. 5293, Detroit, Michigan

BOURBON-NUT CAKE

1/2 lb. butter
2 c. sugar
6 eggs
4 c. flour
1 tsp. baking powder
1 c. bourbon
1 lb. walnuts, chopped
1 lb. seedless raisins

Preheat oven to 350 degrees. Cream butter and sugar together; add eggs, one at a time, beating in well. Reserve 1 cup flour; sift remaining flour with baking powder. Add to creamed mixture; add bourbon, stirring to mix well. Toss reserved flour with walnuts and raisins. Sprinkle walnut mixture over flour mixture; fold in carefully. Pour mixture over 2 greased and floured 9 x 5 x 3-inch loaf pans. Bake for 1 hour and 30 minutes to 2 hours or until cake tests done. Loaf will not be brown. Remove from oven; cool. Chill in refrigerator; slice in 1/4-inch slices. Store in refrigerator in bourbon-soaked cheesecloth.

Mary Rose Rich
Epsilon Alpha No. 2572, Philadelphia, Pennsylvania

BLUEBERRY HOLIDAY RING

4 c. biscuit mix
1 1/3 c. milk
1 can blueberries
1 stick butter
3/4 c. dry bread crumbs
1/2 c. coarsely chopped walnuts
1/4 c. sugar
1/2 tsp. cinnamon
1 tsp. grated orange rind
Dash of Angostura aromatic bitters
1 c. confectioners' sugar
2 tbsp. orange juice

Combine biscuit mix with milk; prepare dough according to package directions for rolled biscuits. Knead several times on lightly floured board; roll out to 10 x 14 inches. Drain blueberries well, reserving small amount for garnish. Melt butter in small saucepan; stir in bread crumbs, walnuts, sugar, cinnamon, orange rind and bitters. Saute until lightly browned. Gently stir in blueberries. Spread blueberry filling evenly over dough. Roll up like jelly roll, starting at wide end. Shape into ring, joining ends. Place dough in well-buttered 6-quart ring mold. Bake at 375 degrees for 30 to 35 minutes or until golden brown. Turn out of pan onto serving plate while hot. Combine confectioners' sugar and orange juice, stirring until smooth. Spread over top of warm ring to glaze. Garnish with maraschino cherry stars and reserved blueberries. Serve warm. Yield: 8-10 servings.

NO-BAKE FRUITCAKE

48 marshmallows, quartered
3/4 c. evaporated milk
1/3 c. unsweetened pineapple juice
4 3/4 c. crushed chocolate wafers
2 1/2 c. crumbled macaroons
1 c. broken walnuts
1 c. light seedless raisins
1/2 c. chopped candied lemon peel
1/2 c. chopped candied orange peel
1 c. halved candied cherries

Combine marshmallows, milk and pineapple juice; let stand for 3 hours, stirring occasionally. Combine crushed chocolate wafers, macaroons, walnuts, raisins, lemon peel, orange peel and cherries in large bowl; add marshmallow mixture. Mix well. Pack into a foil-lined 9 x 5 x 3-inch pan or 2-quart mold. Cover top with foil. Refrigerate for several days before slicing. Garnish with confectioners' sugar glaze and maraschino cherries if desired.

Photograph for this recipe on page 23.

PEPPERMINT FLUFF

32 lge. marshmallows
1 c. milk
1 pt. whipping cream, whipped
1/2 tsp. peppermint extract
Green or red food coloring
1 lb. chocolate cream cookies

Combine marshmallows and milk in saucepan; heat until marshmallows are melted. Cool; add whipped cream, peppermint extract and food coloring. Crush cookies; pat 1/2 of the crumbs into pan. Pour in marshmallow mixture. Add remaining crumbs. Chill for 24 hours. Yield: 12 servings.

Jo Anne Loennig
Xi Nu X-842, Portland, Oregon

SHERRIED ROCKY ROAD PUDDING

1 4 1/2-oz. package chocolate pudding and pie filling mix
1 1/2 c. milk
1/4 c. sherry
1 c. miniature marshmallows
1/2 c. chopped walnuts
1/2 c. heavy cream, whipped

Combine pudding and pie filling mix with milk and sherry; cook according to package directions. Cool, stirring occasionally. Stir in marshmallow pieces, walnuts and whipped cream. Spoon into sherbet glasses; chill. Garnish with additional whipped cream. Yield: 6 servings.

Loretta M. Spencer
Alpha 290, North East, Pennsylvania

WALNUT-COFFEE PIE

1/2 c. brown sugar
1/2 c. soft butter
1 c. sugar
3 eggs
1/4 tsp. salt
1/4 c. heavy cream
1/2 c. strong coffee
1 1/2 c. chopped walnuts
1 tsp. vanilla
1 unbaked 9-in. pie shell

Cream brown sugar and butter. Add sugar and mix well. Add eggs, one at a time, beating well after each addition. Add salt, cream and coffee. Cook over boiling water, stirring for 5 minutes. Remove from heat; stir in 1 cup walnuts and vanilla. Pour into pie shell. Bake at 350 degrees for 1 hour. Sprinkle remaining walnuts on top. Bake for 5 minutes longer.

Mrs. Phyllis Umstead
Xi Beta Psi X-1994, Harrisburg, Pennsylvania

CREME DE MENTHE PIE

4 egg yolks
3/4 c. sugar
1 tbsp. unflavored gelatin
1/4 c. water
1 1/2 c. whipping cream
1/4 c. creme de menthe
10 drops of green food coloring
22 chocolate wafers, crushed
1/4 to 1/2 c. melted butter

Beat egg yolks and sugar until thick. Dissolve gelatin in water over hot water. Whip cream; fold in creme de menthe, egg mixture, gelatin and food coloring. Combine crumbs and butter; form crust in pie pan. Chill. Add filling. Garnish top with shaved chocolate. Yield: 6 servings.

Betty T. Shoup
Xi Gamma Rho X-1255, Malibu, California

ANGEL PARADISE

1 8 3/4-oz. can crushed pineapple
Sugar
2 tbsp. unflavored gelatin
4 tbsp. cold water
1 c. fresh orange juice
Juice of 1 lemon
Dash of salt
2 1-lb. angel food cakes
1 4-oz. bottle maraschino cherries
3 c. whipped cream
Vanilla to taste

Drain pineapple; reserve juice. Combine pineapple juice and 1 cup water in saucepan; bring to a boil. Pour over 1 cup sugar. Soften gelatin in cold water; add to sugar mixture. Stir until dissolved. Stir in orange and lemon juices; add salt. Pour in pan; chill until partially thickened. Remove brown crusts from cakes; break cake into small pieces. Add cherries and pineapple to gelatin mixture. Whip 2 cups cream; fold into gelatin mixture. Line large mixing bowl with waxed paper; fill with layers of cake and gelatin mixture, beginning and ending with cake. Refrigerate, covered, for 24 hours. Unmold. Whip remaining cream with 1/4 cup sugar and vanilla; spread over dessert. Yield: 12-14 servings.

Rae Fencel
Mu Nu, Edwardsville, Illinois

Lincoln's Birthday is indeed a happy holiday to be celebrating. In a very real sense, on Lincoln's Birthday we celebrate the spirit of man — as exemplified by Lincoln — and the joys of the simpler days in which he lived.

Abraham Lincoln is one of America's most beloved presidents and heroes. Born in poverty to a family which moved west during his childhood, Lincoln exemplified the great American virtues: hard work, a love of education, and a dream that went beyond his frontier background. His dream came true and provided inspiration for millions of young men and women.

For your Lincoln's Birthday celebration, bring the simpler days back to your family and guests by featuring dishes everyone enjoyed a hundred years ago. They're easy to prepare, too, thanks to today's modern

Lincoln's Birthday

convenience foods. Here is a deliciously old-fashioned menu which serves six people. It starts with that pioneer favorite, Roast Venison. This meat is prized by meat-lovers everywhere for its fine texture and rich flavor. Even in Lincoln's day, venison was an extra-special treat to be savored and lingered over. Your family's reaction will be the same. Add Harvest Vegetable Pie — an herb-filled blend of Brussels sprouts, onions, mushrooms, carrots, and potatoes — and Family-style White Bread. Your family and guests will think they are back in the 1800's! For dessert, try the traditional American favorite, Apple Dumplings. They're as popular now as they were a hundred years ago.

Venison is surprisingly easy to find. Maybe you're one of the lucky ones who

doesn't have to look far, whose husband and sons are proficient hunters. If not, try your local specialty food shops. Even if they don't carry it, they probably can tell you who does. Your search will be well worthwhile — your family will praise this delicious roast for weeks to come!

To prepare a 4-pound rolled Roast Venison, rub it with a mixture of 2 teaspoons salt and 1/2 teaspoon freshly-ground black pepper. Place two slices of salt pork over the top. Stick a clove in each of two small onions and place these on the roast. Bake in a 400-degree oven for 20 minutes, then remove. Mix 1 cup apple juice, 1 cup orange juice, 2 tablespoons grated orange rind, and 1/2 teaspoon thyme. Pour over roast. Reduce oven temperature to 350 degrees and bake for an hour and 30 minutes, basting frequently. Remove from oven and take off the salt pork. Combine 3 tablespoons butter and 1 tablespoon Worcestershire sauce. Brush mixture over meat. Place roast on a heated serving platter, let stand 15 minutes, then carve.

Harvest Vegetable Pie is a real pie, complete with a flaky and delicious crust. Sift together 2 1/4 cups sifted all-purpose flour and 1 1/2 teaspoons salt. Add 1 teaspoon celery seed and 1/4 teaspoon summer savory. Blend well. Mix together 1/3 cup ice water and 1/2 cup salad oil.

Return to Hearty Frontier Foods

Add to flour and herb mixture. Stir with fork until mixture leaves side of bowl. Roll out between sheets of waxed paper to form a 14-inch circle. Line one 10-inch pie plate with this pastry, trimming and fluting edges. Prick pastry with fork. Chill. Bake in 450-degree oven for 20 minutes. Cool.

The filling for this pie is just as good as the crust. To prepare it, cook two 10-ounce packages of frozen Brussels sprouts according to package directions. If necessary, drain after cooking. In a saucepan blend together 1/3 cup all-purpose flour, 1/2 teaspoon paprika, and 1/4 teaspoon rosemary. Stir in 2 cups vegetable stock or bouillon, and 2 crushed cloves of garlic. Cook over low heat, stirring constantly, until thickened. Then add 2 medium sliced onions, 1 cup sliced mushrooms, 1 3/4 cups cooked carrots, and 1 3/4 cups diced cooked potatoes. Cook for five minutes or until onions are tender. Stir occasionally. Stir in Brussels sprouts after five minutes. Turn mixture into pastry shell.

With the richness of venison and the herbed goodness of Harvest Vegetable Pie, the only other dish you'll need is old-fashioned Family-style White Bread. To prepare, heat 1/2 cup evaporated milk and 1/2 cup warm water just to boiling point. Stir in 3 tablespoons sugar, 2 teaspoons salt, and 1/3 cup butter or margarine. Cool mixture to lukewarm. Place 1 cup warm water in a three-quart bowl. Add one cake or package yeast and stir until yeast is dissolved. Add milk mixture and 3 cups flour. Beat until smooth. Add enough flour to make a soft dough; turn out onto lightly floured board. (EDITORS NOTE: The total amount of flour used will be about 6 to 6 1/4 cups.) Knead dough until smooth and elastic, about 10 minutes. Place in greased bowl. Brush top of dough with melted butter and cover. Let rise in a warm place until doubled, about an hour and 15 minutes. Punch down, turn out onto lightly floured board. Divide dough in half. Form each half into a bali. Place in greased 9 x 5 x 3-inch pan; cover. Let both loaves rise in warm place until doubled in bulk, about an hour. Bake at 400 degrees for about 50 minutes.

For the pioneer family, apple dumplings were a very special treat. It's funny how little some things have changed — apple dumplings are a special treat for today's family, too! To prepare these delicious dumplings, mix 2 cups flour and 2 teaspoons baking powder. Add 1 1/2 tablespoons lard or shortening and 1 1/2 tablespoons butter. Blend well. Add 1 1/2 tablespoons sugar and 1/2 teaspoon salt. Mix until well blended. Add enough milk to make a stiff dough. Roll out on a floured board to 1/4-inch thickness. Cut the rolled dough into four to six squares. Pare and slice cooking apples. Place a few slices on each square and sprinkle with a small amount of sugar. Fold the corners over each other and press edges together tightly. Place dumplings in a baking pan, folded side down, leaving space between for expansion in baking. Cover dumplings with 2 cups sugar, dot with 2 tablespoons butter, and sprinkle with cinnamon. Pour 2 cups boiling water over the dumplings. Cover and bake at 375 degrees for 45 minutes. Remove cover and bake 15 minutes more. Serve hot or cold with ice cream, cream, or milk.

You can carry the rustic pioneer theme of this Lincoln's Birthday meal into your party decorations and invitations. Write the invitations on brown paper (a paper bag will do) or, if you are very talented, on burlap. Serve your dinner on a bare wooden table with heavy burlap placemats to echo your theme. If you are fortunate enough to have pewter mugs or serving pieces, this is the occasion to use them. And if you can get an old-fashioned kerosene lamp, it would be the perfect centerpiece with clusters of fruit around the base. You can think of many more things that are appropriate to the pioneer days. In fact, with today's fashions harkening back to these simpler times, the magazines and newspaper advertisements are a sure source of inspiration. Whatever you do, be comfortable with it. After all, this is your party. It should reflect you as well as recapturing the peace and simplicity of those earlier, Lincoln days.

QUINTE SALAD

2 c. diced cooked chicken
3/4 c. diced cooked ham
3/4 c. Swiss cheese, diced
2 hard-cooked eggs, chopped
1 c. finely diced celery
3 tbsp. sliced green onion
1 tbsp. chopped green pepper
1 tbsp. chopped pimento
2/3 c. mayonnaise
1/4 tsp. poultry seasoning
1/4 tsp. dry mustard
1 tbsp. lemon juice or vinegar
Salt and pepper to taste
3 c. shredded lettuce

Combine first 8 ingredients in large bowl. Combine mayonnaise, poultry seasoning, mustard and lemon juice for dressing. Pour over chicken mixture. Toss gently; season to taste. Refrigerate until needed. Toss with shredded lettuce to serve, adding mayonnaise if needed. Serve in lettuce-lined bowl; garnish with tomato wedges and radish roses. Yield: 4-6 servings.

Mrs. Dorothy M. Small
Xi Alpha Omicron X1966
Guelph, Ontario, Canada

HOT BAKED HAM SALAD

3 c. diced cooked ham
1 c. diced celery
1/2 c. chopped stuffed olives
2 hard-cooked eggs, chopped
2 tsp. minced onion
2 tbsp. lemon juice
2 tsp. mustard
Dash of pepper
3/4 c. mayonnaise
1 c. crushed potato chips

Combine all ingredients except potato chips; turn into 8 x 8-inch baking dish. Sprinkle with potato chips. Bake in 400-degree oven for 20 to 25 minutes.

Mrs. Arlene Klatt
Preceptor Lambda XP0739, Cedar Rapids, Iowa

SHRIMP-MACARONI SALAD

3/4 lb. cooked shrimp
2 c. cooked shell macaroni
1 c. chopped cauliflower
1 c. sliced celery
1/4 c. chopped parsley
1/4 c. chopped sweet pickles
1/2 c. mayonnaise
3 tbsp. garlic French dressing
1 tbsp. lemon juice
1 tsp. grated onion
1 tsp. celery seed
1 tsp. salt
1/4 tsp. pepper
Salad greens
1 hard-cooked egg, sliced

Cut any large shrimp in half. Combine macaroni, cauliflower, celery, parsley, pickles and shrimp. Mix mayonnaise, French dressing, lemon juice, onion and seasonings; add to shrimp mixture. Toss lightly; chill. Serve on salad greens; garnish with sliced egg. Three 4 1/2 or 5-ounce cans shrimp may be used instead of fresh shrimp. Yield: 6 servings.

Glendel Warren
Epsilon Theta No. 1981, Joliet, Illinois

SHEPHERD'S PIE

1 sm. onion, chopped
2 tbsp. butter
1 1/2 c. diced cooked meat
1/2 c. diced cooked carrots
1 c. leftover roast gravy
1/4 tsp. salt
Dash of pepper
1 c. hot mashed potatoes
Grated cheese to taste

Saute onion in butter until brown. Add meat, carrots, gravy and seasonings. Mix together; pour into greased baking dish. Cover with mashed potatoes. Top with grated cheese. Bake at 400 degrees for 15 to 20 minutes or until golden brown. Yield: 6 servings.

Pat Dyer
Iota Xi, Alice, Texas

ANGOSTURA PEPPERPOT

2 eggs
Salt
1 1/2 c. (about) all-purpose flour
1 1/2 lb. beef chuck, cubed
1 green pepper, chopped
1 onion, chopped
2 peeled potatoes, diced
1 tbsp. Angostura aromatic bitters
2 10 1/2-oz. cans beef broth
Pepper to taste

Beat eggs with 1/2 teaspoon salt until blended. Stir in enough flour to make soft paste. Knead dough on heavily floured board until smooth and elastic. Roll out paper thin; cut into 1 1/2-inch squares with sharp knife. Place noodles on cloth; let dry for several hours. Cover beef with water; simmer, covered, for about 2 hours or until almost tender. Add remaining ingredients with noodles and 2 cups water. Cover; simmer for 15 minutes or until noodles and potatoes are tender. Season with salt and pepper. Yield: 4 servings.

COUNTRY-STYLE CASSOULET

2 lb. dried navy beans
1/4 lb. salt pork, diced
1 c. chopped onion
1 10 1/2-oz. can tomato puree
2 carrots, sliced
4 cloves of garlic
1 sm. jar pimento-stuffed olives
2 lb. smoked pork butt, sliced
1 1/2 lb. Spanish-style sausage
1/2 tsp. pepper
1 5-lb. duckling and giblets
1 tsp. salt
1 c. boiling water

Cover beans with water. Soak overnight; drain. Place beans in large pot; cover with salted water. Bring to a boil. Boil for 2 minutes; let stand for 30 minutes. Fry salt pork; add onion, tomato puree, carrots and garlic. Simmer for about 15 minutes or until onion is tender. Add to beans. Drain and slice olives. Add pork slices, sausage, olives and

pepper to bean mixture. Cover; cook for 2 hours and 30 minutes to 3 hours, stirring occasionally. Add giblets and salt to boiling water. Cover and simmer until tender. Cool. Chop giblets; add with giblet liquid to beans. Rinse duckling with cold water and prick with fork. Place on rack in pan. Bake in 350-degree oven for 2 hours or until done. Remove from oven; slice. Alternate layers of bean mixture and duckling in casserole. Bake in 350-degree oven for 1 to 2 hours, stirring occasionally. Yield: 8-10 servings.

Mrs. Mary Jane Blount
Montgomery, Alabama

QUICK CHICKEN PIE

1 recipe pastry for 2-crust pie
1 8-oz. can peas and carrots
3 cans boned chicken
1 can cream of celery soup
1/4 c. chopped onion

Line 8 x 12-inch baking dish with pastry. Drain peas and carrots. Combine chicken, peas and carrots, soup and onion. Pour over pastry; top with remaining pastry. Bake at 350 degrees until pastry is done. Yield: 4-6 servings

Mrs. Leta Warr
Delta Lambda, Poteau, Oklahoma

CORNISH PASTIES

4 c. flour
1 c. lard
Salt and pepper
8 or 9 tbsp. water
1 1/2 lb. chopped beef
1/2 lb. chopped pork
8 med. potatoes, diced
1 c. diced rutabagas
2 med. onions, chopped

Mix flour, lard and 1 1/2 teaspoons salt together with pastry blender; add enough water to make a soft dough. Divide dough into 6 portions; roll into 10-inch circles. Combine beef, pork, potatoes, rutabagas and onions; season to taste. Place 1/6 of the beef mixture on half of each circle. Fold dough over and crimp edges. Make a slot in each pastry. Place on cookie sheet. Bake for 1 hour in 350-degree oven. Yield: 6 servings.

Mrs. Al Argall
Xi Alpha Tau, Coldwater, Michigan

VENISON SWISS STEAK

1 2 to 3-lb. venison steak
1/4 c. flour
1/2 tsp. salt
Dash of pepper
Dash of cayenne
Dash of cloves
Dash of thyme
Dash of nutmeg
2 tbsp. butter
3 lge. onions
2 c. canned tomatoes
1 1/2 c. Burgundy
1 1/2 tbsp. Worcestershire
1/2 garlic clove
1 sm. can sliced mushrooms

Preheat oven to 350 degrees. Pound steak on both sides. Add flour and seasonings to steak a small amount at a time. Melt butter in large skillet. Add steak; brown on both sides. Slice onions; add to steak. Cook until brown. Add tomatoes, Burgundy, Worcestershire and garlic; cover. Bake for 2 hours and 30 minutes or until steak is tender. Remove from oven; add mushrooms. Return to oven; bake for 5 minutes longer. Yield: 6 servings.

Mrs. Katherine Evans
Gamma Nu, Leadville, Colorado

ENGLISH HARVEST PIE

2 10-oz. packages frozen Brussels sprouts
1/3 c. all-purpose flour
1/2 tsp. paprika
1/4 tsp. rosemary
2 c. vegetable stock or bouillon
2 cloves of garlic, crushed
2 med. onions, sliced
1 c. sliced mushrooms
1 3/4 c. cooked carrot pieces
1 3/4 c. diced cooked potatoes
English-Herbed Pastry Shell

Cook Brussels sprouts according to package directions; drain. Blend flour, paprika and rosemary together. Stir in vegetable stock and garlic gradually. Cook, over low heat, stirring constantly, until thickened. Add onions, mushrooms, carrot pieces and potatoes. Cook for 5 minutes or until onions are tender, stirring occasionally. Stir in Brussels sprouts. Turn into pastry shell.

English-Herbed Pastry Shell

2 1/4 c. sifted all-purpose flour
1 1/2 tsp. salt
1 tsp. celery seed
1/4 tsp. summer savory
1/3 c. ice water
1/2 c. salad oil

Sift flour and salt together. Add celery seed and savory; blend well. Combine water and oil. Add to flour mixture. Stir with fork until mixture leaves side of bowl. Roll out between sheets of waxed paper to form 14-inch circle. Line 10-inch pie plate with pastry. Trim and flute edges. Prick pastry with fork. Chill. Bake at 450 degrees for 20 minutes. Cool.

Photograph for this recipe on page 43.

BRUSSELS SPROUTS VINAIGRETTE

4 c. Brussels sprouts
1 c. cherry tomato halves
1 c. vegetable oil
1/3 c. wine vinegar
1 1/2 tsp. sugar
1 tsp. salt
1/2 tsp. garlic salt
2 tbsp. minced green onion
2 tbsp. minced green pepper
2 tbsp. minced parsley
4 drops of red pepper seasoning

Cut each Brussels sprout in half lengthwise. Cook, covered, in boiling water for 15 minutes; drain. Place in medium bowl; place tomatoes in small bowl. Combine remaining ingredients in jar; cover tightly. Shake well. Pour over Brussels sprouts and tomatoes; cover. Chill for at least 1 hour to season, stirring several times. Spoon Brussels sprouts into serving bowl; mound tomatoes in center. Garnish with romaine leaves around edges. Fresh or frozen Brussels sprouts may be used. Yield: 8 servings.

Frances Dillman
Preceptor Rho X P-262, Whittier, California

GOLDEN HOLIDAY CORN

1 2/3 c. canned corn
2 c. cooked rice
2 1/2 c. grated carrots
1 1/4 c. grated cheese
2 well-beaten eggs
1/4 c. milk
1 tbsp. instant minced onion
1 tbsp. melted butter
1 tsp. salt
1/8 tsp. pepper

Combine all ingredients; mix well. Place in greased baking dish; cover. Bake at 325 degrees for 45 minutes. Yield: 6 servings.

Mary C. Jones
Xi Zeta X625, Charlottesville, Virginia

CREOLE PEAS CASSEROLE

8 slices bacon
1 med. onion, minced
1 green pepper, minced
5 stalks celery, chopped
1 can tomato sauce
Salt and pepper to taste
1 No. 2 can peas, drained
1 can cream of mushroom soup
1 1/2 c. medium white sauce
2 hard-cooked eggs, sliced
Bread crumbs
Grated cheese
Butter

Fry bacon till crisp; drain and crumble. Saute onion, pepper and celery in small amount of bacon drippings until tender. Add tomato sauce, 1 sauce can of water, seasonings and peas. Mix soup and white sauce together. Pour half the pea mixture in well-greased casserole. Cover with half the bacon, 1 egg and half the sauce mixture. Repeat layers of remaining peas, bacon, egg and sauce. Cover with bread crumbs; sprinkle cheese over top. Dot with butter. Bake at 325 degrees for about 45 minutes or until red sauce rises through bread crumbs. Yield: 12 servings.

Mrs. Willanne Ingram
Xi Psi, X1230, Crestview, Florida

BAKED SPINACH WITH CHIVES

2 pkg. frozen chopped spinach
2 3-oz. packages cream cheese with chives
1 tbsp. Worcestershire sauce
1 4-oz. can sliced mushrooms
Juice of 1 lemon
Cracker crumbs

Cook spinach according to package directions; drain well. Add cream cheese; stir until dissolved. Add Worcestershire sauce, mushrooms and lemon juice. Pour into buttered 2-quart casserole; top with cracker crumbs. Bake at 325 degrees for 30 minutes or until bubbly and crumbs are brown. Yield: 6 servings.

Mary Katherine Turnage
Phi No. 1247, Memphis, Tennessee

BARLEY CASSEROLE

3/4 lb. fresh mushrooms
1 stick butter, melted
2 med. onions, chopped
1 1/2 c. barley
1 4-oz. jar pimento strips
1/4 tsp. salt
1/8 tsp. pepper
3 c. beef bouillon

Trim mushrooms; slice. Combine butter, onions and mushrooms in skillet; cook until onions are golden and mushrooms are tender. Add barley; cook until lightly browned. Place in 1 1/2-quart casserole. Chop pimento strips. Add pimento, salt, pepper and 2 cups bouillon; cover. Bake in 350-degree oven for 45 minutes. Add remaining bouillon. Bake for 30 minutes longer. Yield: 6-8 servings.

Mrs. Alan R. Wilson
Pi, No. 7175, Dover, New Hampshire

BAKED WALNUT BROWN BREAD

1 1/4 c. sifted all-purpose flour
2 tsp. baking powder
3/4 tsp. soda
1 1/4 tsp. salt
1 1/4 c. graham flour
1 c. chopped walnuts
1 egg
1/3 c. (packed) brown sugar
1/2 c. light molasses
3/4 c. buttermilk
3 tbsp. melted shortening

Resift flour with baking powder, soda and salt. Stir in graham flour and walnuts. Beat egg lightly; beat in brown sugar, molasses, buttermilk and shortening. Stir into dry mixture just until all of flour is moistened. Spoon into 3 greased 1-pound cans. Bake at 350 degrees for 45 minutes or until bread tests done. Let stand for 10 minutes; turn out onto wire rack. Serve warm or cold.

GRITS AND CHEESE

1 1/2 c. grits
6 c. water
1 lb. Velveeta cheese, diced
1 1/2 sticks margarine
Dash of hot sauce
2 tsp. savory salt

2 tsp. salt
3 eggs, well beaten

Boil grits in water in saucepan for 15 minutes; add remaining ingredients. Mix well; pour into large, well greased casserole. Bake for 1 hour at 350 degrees. Yield: 16 servings.

Effie L. Baker
Xi Alpha Alpha, Dalhart, Texas

BREAD PUDDING

2 c. dry bread crumbs
4 c. hot milk
1/2 c. sugar
3 eggs, beaten
4 tbsp. melted margarine
1/2 tsp. salt
1 tsp. vanilla
3/4 c. raisins
1/4 tsp. nutmeg
1/4 tsp. cinnamon

Add bread crumbs to hot milk; set aside to cool. Add remaining ingredients; pour into buttered pan. Place pudding in pan of hot water. Bake for 1 hour at 350 degrees.

Lorraine Moore
Iota Iota, Willows, California

RHUBARB CRUMBLE

3 c. diced rhubarb
2 tbsp. orange juice
3/4 c. sugar
1/4 tsp. cinnamon
Soft butter
1/3 c. brown sugar
2/3 c. flour
1/8 tsp. salt
1/4 tsp. soda
2/3 c. quick-cooking oats

Spread rhubarb in buttered 8 x 8 x 2-inch pan. Sprinkle with orange juice, sugar and cinnamon. Dot with 1 tablespoon butter. Combine 1/4 cup butter with remaining ingredients; mix until crumbly. Spread over rhubarb. Bake at 375 degrees for 40 minutes.

Carolyn Patrick
Alpha Pi, Tacoma, Washington

BROWN SUGAR-NUT ROLL

2 c. sugar
1 c. brown sugar
1 c. evaporated milk
1/4 c. corn syrup
Dash of salt
1 c. chopped pecans

Butter sides of heavy 2-quart saucepan. Combine sugars, milk, corn syrup and salt. Stir over medium heat until sugar dissolves and mixture boils. Cook to soft-ball stage or to 236 degrees on candy thermometer, stirring frequently. Remove from heat immediately. Cool to lukewarm. Do not stir. Beat until fudge begins to hold shape. Pour onto buttered surface. Knead until of shaping consistency, keeping hands well buttered. Shape into two 7-inch rolls. Roll immediately in chopped pecans; press to coat. Wrap in foil, plastic wrap or waxed paper. Chill. Cut into 1/2-inch slices. Mixture will curdle while cooking, but becomes smooth when beaten. Yield: 28 pieces.

Beverly A. Conklin
Xi Gamma Nu, Plainfield, Iowa

WALNUT-APPLE CAKE

2 eggs
4 c. diced apples
2 c. sugar
1 c. chopped walnuts
2 tsp. cinnamon
1 tsp. vanilla
1/2 c. cooking oil
2 c. flour
2 tsp. soda
3/4 tsp. salt

Break eggs over apples; stir with fork. Add sugar, walnuts, cinnamon, vanilla and oil; mix well. Add dry ingredients. Mixture will be thick. Pour into greased and floured 9 x 13-inch pan. Bake at 350 degrees for 45 to 55 minutes. Serve warm with whipped cream or ice cream. Yield: 20-24 servings.

Mrs. John N. Eggers
Oregon Alpha Pi, Grants Pass, Oregon

In Victorian days, when a young man was courting a girl, the flowers he sent her on St. Valentine's Day had a language of their own. Every girl held her breath, hoping for white roses, which meant "I love you." Today, the language of flowers has all but disappeared. Our lives are too fast-paced for the leisurely niceties of by-gone times. But St. Valentine's Day is still the time for telling the people we love how special they are. Whether the man in your life is a favorite beau or your husband of many years, he still looks forward to St. Valentine's Day. This year, why not make this romantic day a real occasion with a Just-for-two Candlelight Dinner?

There's something wonderfully romantic about a small table set for two, surrounded by the glow of candlelight. Romantic music in the background — "your" music. The songs you haven't heard for a long time. A dinner just for two is the perfect time to relax together, to talk about everything and

St. Valentine's Day

nothing, and to celebrate this holiday for those in love.

The center of this dinner for two is, of course, the menu. And St. Valentine's Day is a day for the best of everything. Start with invigorating Chilled Shrimp Remoulade and sure-to-please Hearts of Palm Salad with tart Lime Dressing. As an entree, Broiled Lobster-Tails are almost impossible to beat. Succulent, rich, and everyone's special occasion favorite, they are almost a meal in themselves. All you'll need to complete your gourmet meal is an Asparagus Casserole and the sweet-and-sour contrast of Beets With Pineapple. This delicious blend of flavors will be a sure hit with your Valentine's Day hero. And for a dessert as romantic as the occasion, try Strawberry Cream in Meringue Hearts.

Chilled Shrimp Remoulade is a tangy and delicious blend of mayonnaise, herbs, and shrimp. To prepare it, combine 1 cup mayonnaise, 1 teaspoon chopped tarragon, 1 minced garlic clove, 1 teaspoon dry mustard, 1 teaspoon capers, 1 teaspoon minced parsley, and 2 small chopped sour pickles. Boil two or three 8-ounce packages of frozen shrimp, drain, and add to the above mixture. Refrigerate and allow flavors to blend for several hours or overnight. Served icy cold, this makes a perfect appetizer.

Hearts of Palm Salad with Lime Dressing is another palate-pleasing dish. Place the contents of one can hearts of palm on a bed of Boston lettuce. Cut a 1 1/3-ounce can pimento into strips, place two strips crosswise over hearts of palm. To prepare the Lime Dressing, combine 1/4 cup wine vinegar, 1 tablespoon Worcestershire sauce, 2/3 cup oil, 1 teaspoon soy sauce, juice of one lime, and 1 crushed garlic bud. Mix well and serve over salad.

As an entree, Broiled Lobster-Tails are perfect — they are not only delicious, but easy to prepare. This recipe allows two tails per person, but you may want to vary it according to your own preferences. Place four lobster-tails in boiling salted water. Boil for 10 minutes or until red color appears on the shell. Do not *overcook*. Remove from water, cut

Prepare a Gourmet Feast for Valentine's Day

around edge of underside with scissors and remove any tissue which might be there. Cut the meat away from the shell with a paring knife. Return meat to the shell. Place shell in broiler pan and broil for 10 minutes or until meat has browned. Brush with melted butter before and after broiling.

Beets With Pineapple provide contrast in color, flavor, and texture for this special dinner. To prepare, in a saucepan combine 2 tablespoons brown sugar, 1 tablespoon cornstarch, 1/4 teaspoon salt. Stir in one undrained 9-ounce can of pineapple tidbits. Cook, stirring constantly, until mixture thickens and bubbles. Then add 1 tablespoon butter, 1 tablespoon lemon juice, and a 1-pound can of sliced beets, drained. Heat the mixture thoroughly and serve.

Asparagus Casserole provides another taste treat and a welcome note of color. Spread a drained No. 2 can of asparagus in a casserole dish. Heat 1 cup milk; add 1 cup corn flakes and 2 beaten eggs. Pour over asparagus and bake at 375 degrees for 20 to 30 minutes. Heat 1/2 cup milk, and add 1/4 pound grated cheese. Stir until cheese is melted. Pour over casserole and return casserole to oven for several minutes to brown.

The perfect final note for your very special St. Valentine's Day dinner party comes with the sparkling pink, delightfully delicious Strawberry Cream in Meringue Hearts. To prepare, let six egg whites reach room temperature. Add 1 1/4 teaspoons salt and 1 1/2 teaspoons cream of tartar. Beat until almost stiff. Gradually add 3/4 cup sugar. Beat until sugar is dissolved. Line a baking sheet with heavy brown paper. *Do not grease.* Shape the meringue into hearts on the paper. Bake at 250 degrees for one hour. Turn off heat and cool meringues in oven. Serve filled with crushed strawberries and sweetened whipped cream.

Your very special guest will love this menu because of the many delicious foods it contains. And you're sure to appreciate the make-ahead aspect. Almost everything on this menu can be prepared ahead of your dinner — even the night before — leaving you lots of time to dress just the way he likes you, to choose music, flowers, and decorations that are certain to illustrate your romantic theme. This is the dinner to feature your best table linen, silver, china, and crystal. Be sure to keep your decorations to scale — this is a very small party, remember?

Above all, be romantic. This is the one day of the year just for the romance in your heart. It is the day for frilly dresses, romantic music, and conversation which reflects your pleasure in being with the one you love.

It is St. Valentine's Day, and you have a wonderful dinner planned for someone very special. This could be the most memorable party you've had for a long time. After all, this is the day when the most unexpected and marvelous things always happen!

ARTICHOKE-OLIVE SALAD WITH HERB DRESSING

2 pkg. frozen artichoke hearts
3 tsp. salt
1 tsp. lemon juice
1/2 c. tarragon vinegar
1 c. olive or salad oil
1/4 c. parsley
2 tbsp. finely chopped onion
1/8 tsp. pepper
1/2 tsp. tarragon leaves
1/2 tsp. basil leaves
1 tsp. sugar
4 tomatoes, cut into eighths
1 c. pitted black olives
1 or 2 heads Bibb lettuce

Cook artichokes with 2 teaspoons salt and lemon juice according to package directions; drain. Combine vinegar, oil, parsley, onion, pepper, tarragon leaves, basil leaves, sugar and remaining salt in jar; cover. Shake well. Spoon 2/3 of the dressing over warm artichokes; cover. Refrigerate for at least 4 hours, turning artichokes occasionally. Cover remaining dressing; refrigerate. Place tomatoes in medium bowl; add olives and chilled dressing. Toss to mix. Arrange lettuce on serving dish; pile tomato mixture in center of lettuce. Arrange artichokes around edge. Yield: 6-8 servings.

Martha True
Mu Tau No. 6316, Carol Stream, Illinois

SNOWY CAULIFLOWER HEAD SALAD

1 pkg. garlic salad dressing mix
1/2 c. sour cream
1/4 c. chopped scallions
1/2 c. crumbled blue cheese
1 lge. head cauliflower
2 slices crumbled cooked bacon
1/4 c. chopped toasted almonds

Prepare dressing mix according to package directions. Add sour cream gradually, stirring constantly. Add scallions and blue cheese; mix well. Chill. Remove outer leaves and stalks of cauliflower; cut off any blemishes. Wash well; trim off stem so cauliflower will stand level. Place in large saucepan; add 1 inch salted water. Cover; cook for 20 to 30 minutes or until just tender. Drain and chill. Place on serving dish; cover with dressing. Sprinkle with bacon and almonds. Garnish base with parsley.

Sondra Ferguson
Xi Iota X-942, Milwaukee, Wisconsin

GRAPEFRUIT-AVOCADO SALAD WITH GRENADINE DRESSING

3/4 c. grenadine
1/4 c. lemon juice
1 tsp. whole celery seed
1 tsp. dry mustard
1 tsp. salt
White pepper to taste
1/2 tsp. grated onion
3/4 c. salad oil
Avocado slices
Grapefruit sections
Thinly sliced sweet onion

Combine first 7 ingredients; beat with a rotary beater until thoroughly mixed. Add oil gradually, beating constantly until dressing is slightly thickened. Chill; stir or shake before using. Dip avocado slices in additional lemon juice. Place avocado, grapefruit sections and onion slices on chilled serving plate lined with lettuce. Pour dressing over top.

Kathleen F. Skiver
Xi Alpha Rho X1425, Meridian, Idaho

CUPID'S RIPE OLIVE MOUSSE

2 env. unflavored gelatin
1/2 c. cold water
2 8-oz. cans tomato sauce with tomato bits
2 tbsp. lemon juice
2 tsp. white wine vinegar
1/2 tsp. Worcestershire sauce
1 2/3 c. pitted ripe olives
1/4 c. mayonnaise
1 tbsp. chopped green onion
1 c. whipping cream, whipped

Sprinkle gelatin on water to soften. Place over low heat, stirring until gelatin dissolves. Remove from heat; blend in tomato sauce, lemon juice, vinegar and Worcestershire sauce. Cool until slightly thickened. Cut olives in wedges; add mayonnaise and onion. Blend mayonnaise mixture into gelatin mixture. Fold in stiffly beaten cream. Turn into 6-cup heart-shaped mold. Chill until firm. Unmold. Garnish as desired. Yield: 8 servings.

ACAPULCO BEEF SALAD

3 c. cooked beef strips
3/4 c. salad oil
1/2 c. red wine vinegar
1 1/2 tsp. salt
1/4 tsp. pepper
1/8 tsp. cayenne pepper
2 tbsp. chili powder
Salad greens
Avocado slices
Red onion rings
Green pepper rings
Tomato wedges
Ripe olives

Place beef strips in shallow dish. Combine oil, vinegar, salt, pepper, cayenne and chili powder in jar; cover tightly. Shake well to blend; pour marinade over beef strips. Cover; marinate overnight. Remove beef from marinade; reserve marinade. Arrange beef over greens. Dip avocado slices in reserved marinade. Garnish with avocado and remaining ingredients; serve remaining marinade as dressing. Serve with corn chips. Yield: 4 servings.

Eunice Langreder
Delta Alpha Delta No. 6616, Bridgeport, California

HEARTS OF PALM SALAD

Torn lettuce
Sliced hearts of palm
Pineapple chunks
Chopped dates to taste
3 c. mayonnaise
1 c. soft vanilla ice cream
1/2 c. crunchy peanut butter
Green food coloring

Combine lettuce, hearts of palm, pineapple and dates in large salad bowl. Combine mayonnaise, ice cream, peanut butter and food coloring; mix well. Add dressing to salad mixture; toss to mix well. Sprinkle small amount of ginger over top.

Anna L. McCormick
Beta XP 117, Marshall, Missouri

CAPON BELLAIR

1 capon, disjointed
Garlic salt to taste
Salt and pepper to taste
Paprika to taste
Butter
1 can mushrooms, drained
1 can cream of mushroom soup
1 med. onion, chopped
Chopped parsley to taste
1/2 tbsp. Worcestershire sauce
1/2 c. sherry

Sprinkle capon generously with garlic salt, salt, pepper and paprika; brown in butter in skillet. Arrange capon in broiler pan; top with mushrooms. Stir soup, onion, parsley, Worcestershire sauce and sherry into skillet drippings; pour over chicken. Bake for 3 hours in 250-degree oven. Sauteed fresh mushrooms may be used if desired. Yield: 4 servings.

Mrs. Frank M. MacGraw, Jr.
Ashland, Oregon

SWEETHEART CHICKEN WITH PINEAPPLE

6 tbsp. flour
1/2 tsp. salt
1/4 tsp. pepper
2 c. uncooked chicken cubes
Cooking oil
3 tsp. soy sauce
2 pineapple slices, quartered
8 pieces green pepper
2 carrots, sliced thin slantwise
1/2 c. vinegar
3 tbsp. brown sugar
1 tbsp. molasses
2 tbsp. cornstarch
1/4 c. pineapple juice

Mix flour, salt, pepper and 6 tablespoons water to a smooth paste; mix with chicken until well coated. Place chicken, a piece at a time, in deep hot oil; fry till lightly browned. Mix soy sauce, pineapple, green pepper, carrots, 1 1/2 cups water, vinegar, brown sugar and molasses in large saucepan; cook slowly, stirring frequently, until vegetables are tender. Mix cornstarch and pineapple juice. Stir into mixture; cook till thickened. Add chicken; mix and serve. Yield: 4 servings.

Billye Johnson
Xi Alpha Iota, Okmulgee, Oklahoma

CHICKEN ROUENNAISE

1 stick butter
1 3 1/2-lb. chicken, disjointed
Salt and pepper to taste
1/2 lb. mushrooms, thinly sliced
1/2 c. cognac, heated
1/2 pt. heavy cream

Melt butter in ovenproof frypan; brown chicken well. Add salt and pepper; cover tightly. Bake at 350 degrees for 30 minutes. Add mushrooms; bake until chicken is tender. Remove from oven; pour in cognac and ignite. Remove chicken from pan when flame goes out. Stir in cream; simmer for 2 minutes, stirring constantly. Arrange chicken on serving dish; pour sauce over chicken. Yield: 4 servings.

Mrs. Irene Hill
Sigma Gamma, Palm Springs, California

ROCK CORNISH HENS

1/4 c. vegetable shortening
2 tsp. Kitchen Bouquet
2 Rock Cornish hens, split
1/4 c. butter
1/4 c. minced onion
1 6-oz. can sliced mushrooms
1 5-oz. can water chestnuts
1/2 c. white wine
3 tbsp. cornstarch
1 bouillon cube
1/2 lb. margarine
1/2 c. sliced celery
1 c. drained mandarin oranges
2 c. cooked rice

Combine shortening and Kitchen Bouquet; brush over hens. Place on broiling rack. Broil for 10 minutes on each side. Melt butter in saucepan; add onion. Simmer for about 3 minutes or until tender. Drain mushrooms and chestnuts, reserving liquid; slice chestnuts. Add wine and enough water to reserved liquid to make 1 pint. Pour into saucepan; bring to a boil. Blend cornstarch in 1/4 cup water. Stir in bouillon cube and cornstarch mixture. Cook until sauce is transparent. Add chestnuts and mushrooms. Place broiled hens in skillet or large electric skillet; pour sauce over hens. Simmer for about 30 minutes or until thoroughly hot. Melt margarine in skillet; add celery and saute. Add oranges. Combine with rice. Serve rice with hens. Yield: 4 servings.

Dorthea Nibali
Xi Eta, Joppa, Maryland

GOURMET CHICKEN ROMANO

1 frying chicken, quartered
Seasoned flour
1/2 c. salad oil
2 tbsp. butter or margarine
1 tbsp. rosemary
1/2 clove of garlic, diced
1 1/2 tsp. salt
Pepper to taste
1/2 c. dry white wine
1 tsp. white vinegar
1/2 c. giblet broth

Dredge chicken with seasoned flour; cook slowly in oil and butter in ovenproof skillet until lightly browned. Add rosemary, garlic, salt and pepper; cook until brown. Add wine, vinegar and broth. Cover. Bake at 350 degrees for about 30 minutes or until tender. Yield: 4 servings.

Veronica M. Cross
Xi Omicron, Kansas City, Missouri

VEAL IN WINE SAUCE

2 eggs
1/8 tsp. salt
1/8 tsp. pepper
1/2 tsp. parsley flakes
1 tsp. monosodium glutamate
1/8 tsp. onion powder
1/8 tsp. garlic powder
6 thinly sliced veal cutlets
Cooking oil or fat
6 slices prosciutto
6 slices American cheese
1 c. water
1/2 c. white wine

Combine eggs, salt, pepper, parsley flakes, monosodium glutamate, onion and garlic powder in large mixing bowl; beat well. Place veal cutlets in egg mixture, covering each cutlet well. Cover bowl; place in refrigerator for 1 hour. Heat enough oil in large frypan to cover bottom. Place cutlets on waxed paper; place 1 slice of prosciutto and 1 slice of American cheese on each cutlet. Roll cutlet tightly; secure with toothpick. Brown on all sides. Drain off excess oil if needed. Lower heat; add water and white wine. Cover; simmer for 20 minutes or until cutlets are tender. Yield: 6 servings.

Mrs. Geraldine Aldi
Beta Nu No. 6478, Waterbury, Connecticut

SHRIMP THERMIDOR

1/4 c. chopped onions
2 tbsp. chopped green pepper
2 tbsp. butter
1 can frozen potato soup
3/4 c. light cream
1/2 c. grated sharp cheese
2 tsp. lemon juice
1 1/2 c. cooked shrimp

Saute onions and green pepper in butter; add soup and cream. Heat slowly, stirring constantly, until blended. Bring just to boiling point; add cheese. Stir to melt. Add lemon juice and shrimp; heat. Serve in pastry shells on toast points or over rice. Yield: 4 servings.

Lanell Buchanan
Lambda Rho No. 3746, Dallas, Texas

TROUT BARNEE

1 c. wild rice
6 boned rainbow trout
Salt to taste
White pepper to taste
Paprika to taste
6 lge. slices tomato
6 lge. mushroom caps
12 sm. strips King crab meat
Melted butter
1 c. macadamia nuts

Cook rice according to package directions; drain. Arrange trout in shallow well-buttered pan. Season lightly with salt, pepper and paprika. Spoon rice into opening of each trout; top each with tomato slice and 1 mushroom cap. Arrange 2 thin strips of crab meat on each. Brush lightly with melted butter. Bake at 350 degrees for about 20 minutes or until trout meat is white and juicy, basting occasionally with butter. Brown macadamia nuts in 1/4 cup melted butter. Serve trout on shredded lettuce with macadamia nut sauce. Yield: 6 servings.

Mrs. Gary Post
Omega, Buhl, Idaho

MOUSSELINES

1 1/2 c. finely ground fresh fish
3/4 tsp. salt
Pinch of nutmeg
1 egg white
6 to 8 tbsp. heavy cream
6 tbsp. butter or margarine

Combine fish, seasonings and egg white; beat vigorously for several minutes until stiff enough to hold shape. Add cream, 2 teaspoons at a time; beat vigorously 1 minute after each addition. Form mixture into 6 to 8 cakes on a floured board. Melt butter in heavy skillet; place cakes in butter. Cover. Cook over low heat for 6 minutes on each side. Yield: 6-8 servings.

Eleanor Smart
Xi Beta Zeta, Scioto Mills, Illinois

ENGLISH PEA AND CHESTNUT CASSEROLE

1 stick butter
1 sm. onion, minced
2 tbsp. chopped green pepper
1 c. diced celery
2 cans English peas, drained
1 can water chestnuts, sliced
1 can mushroom soup
2 pimentos, diced
Buttered cracker crumbs

Melt butter in heavy skillet. Add onion, green pepper and celery. Saute over moderate heat, stirring frequently until soft. Remove from heat; add peas, water chestnuts, soup and pimentos. Place in casserole. Sprinkle with crumbs. Bake at 350 degrees until bubbly hot. Yield: 12 servings.

Mavis Williams
Xi Delta Pi, X-3376, Bragg City, Missouri

WILD RICE CASSEROLE

2 qt. water
Salt
1 c. wild rice
1/4 tsp. pepper
2 c. shredded carrots
6 slices bacon
2 onions, chopped
1 egg yolk, beaten
1/2 c. rich milk
3 tbsp. butter

Bring water and 1 teaspoon salt to a boil; add rice slowly, stirring constantly. Cook for 30 minutes; drain. Add 1/4 teaspoon salt, pepper and carrots. Fry bacon until crisp; drain on paper toweling. Crumble. Fry onions in bacon drippings until golden. Combine egg and milk, beating well. Combine all ingredients except butter in greased casserole; dot with butter. Bake at 350 degrees for 45 minutes. Yield: 6 servings.

Iris Coumbs
Xi Alpha Psi X2187
Kirkland Lake, Ontario, Canada

CURRIED PECAN AND GREEN PEA SHORTCAKES

2 c. prepared biscuit mix
Soft butter or margarine
Milk
2 tbsp. finely chopped onion
1 10-oz. package frozen green peas
1 tsp. salt
1 c. pecan halves
2 tbsp. flour
1/2 tsp. paprika
1/2 to 1 tsp. curry powder
1/2 c. half and half

Combine biscuit mix, 1/3 cup butter and 2/3 cup milk in mixing bowl according to biscuit mix package directions. Roll 1/4 inch thick on lightly floured surface. Cut with 3-inch biscuit cutter. Cut centers from half the rounds with 1 1/2-inch cutter or knife. Stack biscuits with center holes on top whole rounds. Place on baking sheet. Bake according to biscuit mix package directions. Place onion, 3 tablespoons water and 4 teaspoons butter in saucepan; add partially thawed peas and 1/2 teaspoon salt. Cover; cook over low heat until peas are tender. Cut pecan halves in half crosswise; stir into peas. Melt 2 tablespoons butter; stir in flour, paprika, curry powder and remaining salt. Add half and half and 3/4 cup milk. Cook, stirring constantly, until smooth and thickened.

Place biscuits on serving platter; fill holes with pea mixture. Top with sauce. Yield: 4 servings.

CANDLELIGHT BROCCOLI AND ONIONS

2 pkg. frozen broccoli
1 16-oz. can sm. onions
1/4 c. butter or margarine
1/3 c. flour
1/4 tsp. salt
1/8 tsp. pepper
1 c. beef consomme
1/3 c. slivered almonds
1/2 c. grated cheese

Thaw broccoli; drain onions. Place broccoli in baking dish; arrange onions over broccoli. Melt butter in pan; add flour, salt and pepper. Stir until smooth. Add consomme gradually, stirring constantly until sauce thickens. Pour over onions. Sprinkle top with almonds and cheese. Bake in 350-degree oven for 45 minutes to 1 hour. Yield: 6-8 servings.

Mrs. Eleanor Frondorf
Iota No. 1361, Lexington, Kentucky

CHOCOLATE ANGEL FOOD CAKE

1 c. cake flour
1/2 c. cocoa
2 c. sugar
1 1/2 c. egg whites
1 tsp. cold water
1/4 tsp. salt
1 tsp. cream of tartar
1 tsp. vanilla

Preheat oven to 400 degrees. Sift flour one time before measuring. Sift flour, cocoa and 1 cup sugar together several times. Beat egg whites, cold water and salt until frothy. Add cream of tartar; beat until stiff. Beat in remaining sugar and vanilla; fold in sifted flour mixture. Pour into tube pan; reduce oven temperature to 375 degrees. Bake for 35 to 40 minutes. Frost as desired. Yield: 14 servings.

Beth Kupfer
Iota Tau No. 4503, Macomb, Illinois

PINEAPPLE CAKE WITH STRAWBERRY CREAM ICING

1 9-oz. can crushed pineapple
3 eggs, separated
1 1/2 tsp. lemon juice
2/3 c. sugar
3/4 c. sifted cake flour
1/2 tsp. baking powder
Dash of salt
1 qt. strawberry ice cream, softened

Drain pineapple; reserve juice. Beat egg yolks until thick; add lemon juice and 1/4 cup reserved pineapple juice gradually. Beat until very thick. Beat in 1/3 cup sugar; fold in dry ingredients. Beat egg whites until soft peaks form; add remaining sugar gradually. Beat until stiff peaks form. Fold egg whites into egg yolk mixture; fold in pineapple. Pour in ungreased 13 x 9 x 2-inch pan. Bake at 325 degrees for 25 minutes. Invert pan; let cool. Spread softened ice cream over cake in pan; freeze. Remove from freezer several minutes before serving; cut in squares. Yield: 15 servings.

Diana Mahany
Upsilon Chi, Roseville, California

STRAWBERRY-RASPBERRY PARFAIT

1 10-oz. package frozen raspberries
1/4 c. sugar
2 tbsp. cornstarch
2 c. sliced strawberries
2 tsp. lemon juice
1 qt. vanilla ice cream
1 c. sour cream

Thaw raspberries. Drain and reserve syrup; add enough water to reserved syrup to make 1 cup liquid. Combine sugar and cornstarch in small saucepan; stir in raspberry syrup. Add strawberries. Cook and stir over medium high heat till mixture thickens and boils. Remove from heat; stir in raspberries and lemon juice. Chill. Arrange a layer of ice cream, raspberry sauce and sour cream in parfait glasses. Add another layer of raspberry sauce. Repeat; top with scoop of ice cream. Yield: 6-8 servings.

Jean Poulson
Xi Iota Lambda X2369, San Diego, California

HOLIDAY LEMON TORTE

1 sm. package yellow cake mix
1 tbsp. (heaping) cornstarch
Milk
Juice and rind of 1 lemon
1 3/4 c. sugar
1 egg
1 tsp. butter
3 egg whites
1 tsp. cinnamon
Chopped nuts

Bake cake according to package directions; let cool. Dissolve cornstarch in small amount of milk. Combine lemon juice and rind, 1 cup sugar, egg, cornstarch mixture and butter in saucepan; cook until clear and thick. Cool. Spread over cake. Beat egg whites until peaks form; add remaining sugar and cinnamon. Beat until stiff. Spread on top of filling; sprinkle with nuts. Place under broiler until lightly browned.

Mrs. Berverly Banning
Xi Kappa, Nome, Alaska

STRAWBERRY TORTE

2 c. frozen strawberries
1 c. crushed pineapple
1/2 c. butter
1 1/4 c. sugar
4 eggs, separated
5/8 c. sifted cake flour
1/4 c. milk
1/4 tsp. salt
1 tsp. baking powder
3/4 c. chopped nuts
1/2 pt. cream, whipped
1 tsp. vanilla
1 1/2 tsp. powdered sugar

Thaw strawberries. Drain strawberries and pineapple. Cream butter and 1/2 cup sugar together; add egg yolks. Add flour and milk alternately; mix well. Sift salt and baking powder together; add to batter. Pour into 2 layer pans. Beat egg whites until stiff; add remaining sugar, beating constantly. Spread over batter; sprinkle with nuts. Bake at 325 degrees to 350 degrees for 25 minutes; cool. Combine remaining ingredients for filling. Place 1 cake layer meringue side down on plate; spread with filling. Top with remaining layer. Cut in wedges to serve.

Pamela Russo
Phi Alpha Kappa, Jamestown, New York

CREAM CAKE

3 c. sifted cake flour
1 1/2 c. sugar
4 1/2 tsp. baking powder
3/4 tsp. salt
1 1/2 c. cold heavy cream
1 1/2 tsp. vanilla
3 eggs

Grease 3 heart-shaped 8-inch layer cake pans lightly; line bottom with waxed paper. Grease waxed paper lightly. Sift flour, sugar, baking powder and salt together twice. Pour cream and vanilla into deep 1-quart bowl; beat with electric mixer or rotary beater for about 1 minute and 30 seconds or until just stiff. Add eggs; beat until just blended. Add flour mixture; beat at low speed until batter is blended. Turn into prepared pans. Bake in 350-degree oven for about 25 to 30 minutes or until center springs back when lightly touched with finger. Cool cakes in pans on rack for 10 minutes. Remove cakes from pans; peel off waxed paper. Turn cakes right side up on cake rack; finish cooling.

Lemon-Butter Frosting

1/3 c. butter
2 1/4 tsp. grated lemon peel
5 1/4 c. sifted confectioners' sugar
1 c. sweetened condensed milk
2 to 4 tbsp. lemon juice

Beat butter with lemon peel in medium mixing bowl until light and fluffy. Stir sugar in gradually and alternately with sweetened condensed milk, beating after each addition. Stir in lemon juice, a small amount at a time, until of desired tartness. Spread between layers and on cake.

Photograph for this recipe on page 53.

CHERRY SNOW

1 8-oz. jar red maraschino cherries
1 env. unflavored gelatin
1/8 tsp. salt
1 c. milk
1/2 tsp. grated lemon rind
2 tbsp. lemon juice
Red food coloring (opt.)
3 egg whites
1/4 c. sugar

Drain cherries, reserving 1/3 cup syrup. Chop enough cherries to equal 1/4 cup; reserve remaining whole cherries for garnish. Mix gelatin, salt and reserved cherry syrup together in saucepan; stir over low heat until gelatin dissolves. Remove from heat; stir in milk. Chill until mixture mounds from spoon. Stir in lemon rind, lemon juice, chopped cherries and several drops of red food coloring. Beat egg whites until soft peaks form; add sugar gradually, beating until stiff. Fold in cherry mixture; turn into 5-cup heart-shaped mold. Chill for 4 hours or overnight. Unmold onto serving plate; garnish with whole cherries. Pipe with whipped cream if desired. Yield: 6 servings.

Washington's Birthday is a day to commemorate the man who devoted his life to forming a new nation from thirteen colonies — the nation we know as the United States. In a very real sense, when we celebrate Washington's birthday, we are celebrating the spirit which brought our nation into being and made it what it is today.

Celebrating Washington's Birthday is a wonderful perker-upper. Coming in the middle of winter doldrums, this holiday inspires delicious food and gay, eye-pleasing red-white-and-blue decorations. In most places Washington's Birthday is a holiday — and just the day to have your friends in for a Martha Washington lunch.

George's wife was quite a person in her own right — she developed her culinary skills

Washington's Birthday

to such a high point that her recipes are cherished today by homemakers all over the country. Here's a menu to serve four that Martha would have been proud of. Drawing its theme from the story about Washington and the cherry tree, it features cherries in three of its dishes. Begin with coolly elegant Cucumber Soup — a sure-to-please blend of onions, potatoes, and cucumbers. Cherry Chicken, the unusually-flavored and utterly delicious entree, will bring compliments from all your guests. A Broccoli Casserole is the perfect vegetable dish for this elegant luncheon. Add Bing Cherry Salad and Cheese Biscuits, and you'll have a meal as delicious as any served at Mount Vernon. For your dessert, what could be more appropriate than Cherry Tarts with Almond-Flavored Whipped

Cream — rich, melt-in-the-mouth goodness that makes a perfect ending to a perfect luncheon.

Cucumber Soup can be prepared well in advance of your luncheon and served directly from the refrigerator. Mix 1/2 cup sliced onions, 1/2 cup cubed potatoes, 2 cups sliced cucumbers, 1/4 teaspoon dry mustard, salt and pepper to taste, 2 cups chicken broth, and parsley to taste. Cook for 10 minutes. Pour into a blender container and add 1 cup milk. Blend until smooth, and chill. Serve icy cold.

After the cool good taste of this soup, your guests will welcome piping-hot Cherry Chicken. To prepare, coat a 2 1/2 to 3-pound cut up frying chicken with seasoned salt. Brown in fat. Drain fat from pan. In a bowl, blend one 12-ounce jar cherry preserves, 2 tablespoons lemon juice, 4 whole cloves, 1/4 teaspoon salt, 1/4 teaspoon allspice, and 1/4 teaspoon mace. Add to browned chicken. Cover pan and simmer for an hour. Serve hot and listen to the praise of your guests.

Broccoli Casserole is the perfect accompaniment to this delicious chicken dish. Cook two packages frozen broccoli in a small amount of water. Drain and place in a greased 8 x 12-inch casserole dish. Make a cream sauce of 3 tablespoons butter, 3 tablespoons flour, and 2 cups milk. Season to taste with salt and red pepper. Add 1 cup grated cheese.

Celebrate Washington's Birthday with Cherry Favorites

Spread broccoli with 1/4 cup almonds and six slices of cooked bacon, crumbled. Top with cheese sauce, sprinkle with 1/2 cup buttered bread crumbs. Bake at 350 degrees for 20 minutes.

Bing Cherry Salad echoes your Washington's Birthday theme. Drain one No. 2 can pitted Bing cherries and reserve the juice. Drain a small can crushed pineapple, reserving juice. Combine reserved juices and add enough water to make 2 cups liquid. Bring liquid to boiling point in saucepan. Empty two 3-ounce packages of cherry gelatin in a bowl. Pour liquid over gelatin, stirring until completely dissolved. Cool. Add two small bottles of cola beverage. Stir and chill until partially set. Add drained cherries, drained pineapple, and 1 cup chopped pecans. Pour into a large mold which has been rinsed in cold water. Chill until set. Whip softened cream cheese with a small amount of milk until fluffy. Unmold salad onto salad greens. Serve with cream cheese for topping.

Cheese Biscuits bring new flavor to your luncheon with their hot Cheddar-y goodness. To prepare, run 1/2 pound butter or margarine and 1/2 pound New York State sharp cheese through a food chopper. Add 2 1/4 cups flour and cayenne pepper to taste. Mix well. Roll out thin and

cut with small biscuit cutter. Place on cookie sheet. Bake at 425 degrees until golden brown.

Cherry Tarts again remind your guests of the holiday they are celebrating. You will need to have on hand as many tart shells as you have guests. In a saucepan, mix 3/4 cup sugar, 2 tablespoons cornstarch, 1/2 teaspoon salt, 3 tablespoons orange juice, 1 tablespoon lemon juice, and 1 cup unsweetened cherry juice. Cook over direct heat for five minutes or until the mixture is thick and clear. Remove from heat. Add 2 tablespoons butter, 1 teaspoon grated orange rind, and 4 cups red tart unsweetened cherries. Cool. Place in tart shells. Serve with sweetened whipped cream which has been flavored with almond extract to taste.

Red, white, and blue is a very appropriate color scheme for your table and party decorations. Small flag pins would be welcome mementoes for your guests — most jewelry departments carry them. And small paper flags stuck into a log and surrounded with seasonal greens makes an attractive — and appropriate — centerpiece. You might want to continue this patriotic color scheme with red placemats, deep blue napkins, and white china. The possibilities are almost endless.

Nothing will brighten up the inside and outside of your home like brightly-colored flags. If you are among the millions of Americans who have rediscovered the joys of flying our flag, Washington's Birthday is certainly an occasion to commemorate in this manner. And with our present 50-star flag outside, you may want to show one or several of the earlier flags indoors. Particularly appropriate would be the 13-star flag originally made for George Washington in Philadelphia by Betsy Ross.

Let your own imagination guide you in decorating for this wonderful luncheon. Make it a bright occasion that lights up a dull winter day. With your Martha Washington Luncheon menu . . . your own imagination planning a decorating scheme . . . and the delicious party foods described in this section, you can be sure you'll have a party you and your guests will remember for a long time to come.

CHERRY DRESSING FOR COLESLAW

1 8-oz. jar red maraschino cherries
1 egg, well beaten
1/4 c. orange juice
1/2 c. honey
3 tbsp. light cream
Dash of salt
1 qt. shredded cabbage

Drain cherries well. Combine egg, orange juice and honey in top of double boiler; cook over hot water until thickened, stirring occasionally. Cool. Add cream, salt and cherries; blend well. Chill thoroughly. Toss with shredded cabbage at serving time.

ALMOND-BLACK CHERRY SALAD

1 No. 2 can black cherries
1 pkg. cherry gelatin
1 c. chopped blanched almonds
8 stuffed olives, chopped

Drain cherries; reserve juice. Add enough water to reserved juice to make 2 cups liquid; bring to a boil. Remove from heat; add gelatin. Stir until gelatin is dissolved. Chill until thickened. Add remaining ingredients. Pour into mold; chill until firm. Unmold; serve on lettuce. Top with salad dressing if desired.

Norma J. Hardebeck
Zeta Lambda No. 4500, Elwood, Indiana

DOUBLE-DECK CHERRY SALAD

1 No. 2 can sliced pineapple
1 pkg. cherry gelatin
1 3-oz. package cream cheese
2 to 3 tbsp. light cream
1 No. 2 can Bing cherries
1/3 c. lemon juice
1 pkg. orange gelatin
1/2 c. sliced stuffed olives

Drain pineapple; reserve juice. Chop pineapple. Add enough water to reserved juice to make 1 3/4 cups liquid; bring to a boil. Add cherry gelatin; stir until dissolved. Chill until partially set. Add pineapple; pour into oiled 8-inch square pan. Chill until firm. Soften cream cheese with cream; spread over gelatin. Chill until firm. Drain cherries; add enough water to lemon juice and reserved cherry juice to make 1 3/4 cups liquid. Bring to a boil; add orange gelatin. Stir until dissolved; chill until partially set. Add cherries and olives. Spread over cheese; chill until firm. Cut in squares to serve.

Mrs. Tamar B. Burch
Xi Lambda X-129, Jacksonville, Illinois

SHERRY SPECIAL

1 8-oz. can pitted dark sweet cherries
Pecan halves
1 3-oz. package cherry gelatin
1 c. cream sherry

Drain cherries; reserve juice. Insert pecan half in each cherry. Arrange in large greased mold or 6 to 8 individual molds. Add enough water to reserved cherry juice to make 1 cup liquid. Bring liquid to a boil; add gelatin. Stir until gelatin is dissolved. Cool; add sherry. Pour enough cool gelatin into mold to partially cover cherries. Chill until set. Add remaining cooled gelatin; chill until set. Remove from mold. Garnish with lettuce and salad dressing. Yield: 6-8 servings.

Frances A. Broom-Smith
Xi Beta X302, Barrington, Rhode Island

CHERRY-CHICKEN SALAD

2 c. cubed cooked chicken
1/2 c. diced celery
1/2 c. pineapple tidbits
1/4 c. sliced almonds
Salad greens
1 c. fresh sweet cherry halves

Mix chicken, celery, pineapple and almonds together. Line salad bowl with greens. Place chicken mixture on greens; circle top with cherries.

Piquant Dressing

1 c. mayonnaise
1/2 c. sour cream
1/4 tsp. horseradish
1/2 tsp. salt

Combine all ingredients; mix well. Serve over salad.

Karen Marie DeWolf
Eta Mu No. 6595, Muscatine, Iowa

CHERRY-CROWNED HAM LOAF

1 1/2 c. rye bread crumbs
1/2 c. milk
1 lb. ground ham
1 lb. ground pork shoulder
2 tbsp. chopped onion
1/3 c. snipped parsley
1 tsp. mustard
2 eggs, beaten
1 16-oz. can pitted sour red cherries
4 tsp. cornstarch
2 tbsp. sugar
1/4 tsp. salt
1/8 tsp. cinnamon
1/8 tsp. nutmeg
1/4 tsp. red food coloring

Combine bread crumbs and milk in large bowl; add ham, pork, onion, parsley, mustard and eggs. Mix well; pack into 1 1/2-quart round baking dish. Bake for 1 hour at 325 to 350 degrees. Drain cherries, reserving syrup; add enough water to syrup to measure 1 cup liquid. Place liquid in saucepan; stir in cornstarch, sugar, salt, cinnamon and nutmeg. Cook over medium heat, stirring constantly, till thickened and clear; add cherries and food coloring. Cook till heated through. Pour drippings from baking dish. Unmold ham loaf on platter. Top with small amount of cherry sauce. Serve remaining sauce. Yield: 8 servings.

Mrs. Kay Lentz
Murray, Kentucky

BAKED CHOPS WITH SOUR CHERRIES

4 thick pork loin chops
Salt and pepper to taste
1 c. rice
1 No. 2 can sour red cherries
1 tbsp. sugar
Grated rind of 1/2 lemon
Dash of cinnamon

Season chops with salt and pepper; brown on both sides. Place rice in casserole; pour cherries and juice over rice. Sprinkle sugar, lemon peel and cinnamon over cherries. Arrange chops on top; cover. Bake for 1 hour and 15 minutes at 350 degrees. Yield: 4 servings.

Mrs. John B. Lett
Gardena, California

VEAL JUBILEE

1 jar Queen Anne cherries
2 lb. veal scallops
3 eggs, beaten
1 can Italian bread crumbs
Butter
1 1/3 c. light cream
1 c. beef stock or bouillon

Drain cherries; reserve 2/3 cup cherry juice. Dry veal; dip in eggs. Coat with crumbs; refrigerate for 1 hour so crumbs will adhere. Brown quickly in butter. Place in baking dish. Combine cream, reserved cherry juice, cherries and stock in saucepan. Bring to a boil, stirring constantly. Pour over veal. Bake for 1 hour at 325 degrees. Yield: 6 servings.

Mrs. Stuart Konspore
Stamford, Connecticut

CHEERY CHERRY CHICKEN

8 boned chicken breasts
Flour
Hot cooking oil
1 stick butter
6 c. cooked rice
Salt and pepper to taste
1 can pitted Bing cherries
1/4 c. dry sherry

Dust chicken with flour; fry in oil in skillet until browned. Remove from pan. Melt 1/2 of the butter in casserole; add rice. Place chicken over rice. Add seasonings. Pour cherries with juice over chicken and rice. Pour sherry over all; dot with remaining butter. Bake in 325-degree oven for 1 hour. Yield: 8 servings.

Mrs. James R. McDaniel
Greenwich, Connecticut

ELEGANT CHICKEN

6 to 8 chicken breasts
1 tsp. salt
1/4 tsp. pepper
1/4 c. melted margarine
1 1-lb. can sliced peaches
1 1/2 c. dark sweet cherries
1 8-oz. bottle sweet and sour dressing

Place chicken in single layer in baking pan. Sprinkle with salt and pepper; pour margarine over chicken. Broil until brown. Drain peaches and cherries. Combine peaches and cherries with dressing; spoon over chicken. Bake at 325 degrees for 1 hour or until chicken is tender. Yield: 6-8 servings.

Mrs. Barber B. Conable, Jr.
Washington, D. C.

GLAZED CHICKEN WINGS

2 lb. chicken wings
Salt and pepper
Flour
1/2 c. butter or margarine
1 10 1/2-oz. can beef broth
1 12-oz. jar cherry preserves
1/3 c. prepared mustard
1/4 c. (packed) brown sugar

Season chicken with salt and pepper; coat with flour. Brown in butter. Add broth; cover. Cook until tender. Combine preserves, mustard, brown sugar, 1/2 teaspoon salt and 1/4 teaspoon pepper. Stir over low heat until well blended and hot. Place chicken on foil-lined cookie sheet; brush with glaze. Broil until bubbly and well browned; turn chicken. Brush again with glaze; broil until brown.

Barbara Lloyd
Pi Psi, Bryan, Texas

LONG ISLAND DUCKLING WITH BLACK CHERRY SAUCE

1 Long Island duckling
1 1/2 tsp. salt
1 tsp. pepper
2 tsp. poultry seasoning
2 tsp. paprika

Cut duckling in quarters; rub with seasonings. Place in dry skillet, skin side down; cover tightly. Cook at 350 degrees in electric skillet or over medium heat for 1 hour, turning at 20-minute intervals. Do not pour off fat during cooking.

Sauce

1/2 c. port
1 whole clove
Pinch of nutmeg
Pinch of thyme
Pinch of allspice
1/4 tsp. grated orange peel
1/2 c. bottled brown sauce
1/2 c. currant jelly
1/2 c. canned pitted black cherries
Juice of 1/2 orange
1 tbsp. butter

Combine port, spices and grated orange peel; cook over moderate heat until volume is reduced to 1/2. Heat brown sauce; add and blend well. Add jelly, stirring till dissolved. Add cherries, orange juice and butter. Serve hot sauce over duckling. Yield: 4 servings.

Mrs. Nelson Rockefeller
Albany, New York

CHERRY BOUGH CAKE

1 15-oz. package angel food cake mix
1/4 c. chopped drained maraschino cherries
White Snow Frosting
1 1/3 c. flaked coconut
Red food coloring

Prepare angel food cake mix according to package directions. Fold in cherries. Place in 10-inch tube pan. Bake as directed on package. Invert and cool. Turn out cake; spread with White Snow Frosting. Tint coconut a pale pink with food coloring; sprinkle thickly over side of cake. Garnish with stemmed whole maraschino cherries.

White Snow Frosting

2 egg whites
1 1/2 c. sugar
Dash of salt
1/3 c. water
2 tsp. light corn syrup

Combine all ingredients in top of double boiler; beat well. Place over boiling water and continue to beat for 7 minutes or until frosting holds soft peaks. Remove from boiling water; continue to beat until frosting holds stiff peaks.

Photograph for this recipe on page 1.

STRAWBERRY-MARSHMALLOW WHIP

1 13 1/2-oz. can crushed pineapple
1 3-oz. package strawberry gelatin
1 c. boiling water
1 c. cold water
2 c. prepared whipped topping
1 1/2 c. miniature marshmallows

Drain pineapple. Dissolve gelatin in boiling water; add cold water. Chill until slightly thickened. Set bowl of gelatin firmly in bowl of ice. Whip until light and fluffy. Blend into whipped topping. Fold in marshmallows and pineapple. Pour into 8-cup mold; chill until firm. Unmold to serve. Garnish with fresh strawberries if desired. Yield: 8-10 servings.

COCONUT-RASPBERRY BAVARIAN

1 10-oz. package frozen raspberries
1 3-oz. package raspberry gelatin
1 c. boiling water
1 c. cold water
1/4 tsp. almond extract
1 4-oz. can flaked coconut
1 c. heavy cream, whipped
2 tsp. cornstarch

Thaw raspberries; drain and reserve syrup. Dissolve gelatin in boiling water. Stir in cold water and almond extract. Chill until slightly thickened. Set aside 1 tablespoon coconut. Fold remaining coconut and whipped cream into gelatin. Pour into 4-cup mold. Chill until firm. Blend reserved syrup into cornstarch in saucepan; cook, stirring, until thickened. Remove from heat; add raspberries. Chill. Unmold gelatin. Serve with raspberry sauce and additional whipped cream sprinkled with reserved coconut. Yield: 6 servings.

EMPEROR CHERRY TORTE

Confectioners' sugar
1/4 tsp. salt
4 c. ground hazelnuts
1/4 c. cornstarch
16 egg whites, stiffly beaten
1 c. sugar
1 c. cold strong coffee
12 egg yolks, well beaten
2 tsp. vanilla
2 1/2 c. softened butter
2 c. finely chopped red maraschino cherries
3 tbsp. milk

Blend 4 cups sifted confectioners' sugar, salt, hazelnuts and cornstarch together. Fold gently into egg whites. Turn batter into 4 well-greased and floured 8-inch layer pans. Bake at 275 degrees for 1 hour and 30 minutes to 1 hour and 45 minutes or until layers begin to shrink from sides of pans. Cool for about 10 minutes; remove from pans. Cool completely. Mix sugar with 2/3 cup coffee. Cook over medium heat to thread stage or 234 degrees on candy thermometer. Pour slowly over egg yolks, beating constantly until mixture is foamy and cold. Beat in remaining coffee, vanilla and 2 cups butter slowly, beating only until mixture is smooth. Spread a thin layer of mocha butter cream on 1 meringue layer to serve as top layer of torte. Remove 1 1/4 cups mocha cream; mix in chopped cherries. Spread cherry mixture thickly on remaining layers; stack layers. Spread sides of torte with remaining mocha cream; chill. Beat remaining butter until smooth and fluffy. Add 1 pound confectioners' sugar gradually and alternately with milk, beating constantly until smooth and fluffy. Force through pastry tube to decorate top and sides of torte. Garnish with whole maraschino cherries.

Photograph for this recipe on page 65.

CHOCOLATE-CHERRY CAKE

2 1/8 c. all-purpose flour
1 1/2 c. sugar
1 1/2 tsp. soda
3/4 tsp. baking powder
3/4 tsp. salt
1/2 c. shortening
1 1/4 c. buttermilk or sour milk
2 eggs
1/4 c. maraschino cherry juice
2 sq. baking chocolate, melted
1/3 c. chopped maraschino cherries

Spoon flour into dry measuring cup; level and pour measured flour into bowl. Add sugar, soda, baking powder and salt; stir to blend. Add shortening and buttermilk to dry ingredients; beat for 2 minutes with electric mixer. Add eggs, cherry juice and melted chocolate; beat for 2 minutes longer. Stir in cherries. Pour into 2 greased, waxed paper-lined 9-inch layer pans. Bake at 375 degrees for 30 to 35 minutes. Cool cake for 15 minutes before removing from pans. Frost with favorite frosting. Yield: 10-12 servings.

Mrs. Phyllis Skapura
Theta Rho No. 5962, Indiana, Pennsylvania

WASHINGTON'S CHERRY-DATE BALLS

1 1/2 c. chopped dates
1 c. sugar
1/4 c. butter
1 egg, well beaten
1 3/4 c. oven-toasted rice cereal
1/2 c. chopped nuts
1 c. chopped cherries
Coconut

Combine first 4 ingredients; cook over low heat for 10 to 15 minutes. Add rice cereal, nuts and cherries; cool until mixture can be easily handled. Butter hands; roll mixture into small balls. Roll in coconut; place on cookie sheet. Refrigerate. Yield: 30 pieces.

Mrs. Elaine R. Bennett
Xi Pi X2292, Portland, Maine

CHERRY-COCONUT BARS

1 1/2 c. flour
3/4 c. confectioners' sugar

3/4 c. margarine
3/4 c. sugar
1/2 tsp. baking powder
1/4 tsp. salt
2 eggs, slightly beaten
3/4 c. diced maraschino cherries
1/2 c. coconut
3/4 c. chopped nuts

Sift 1 1/4 cups flour and confectioners' sugar together; cut in margarine until mixture resembles coarse crumbs. Reserve 1/4 of the crumbs; press remaining crumbs in jelly roll pan. Bake at 350 degrees for 10 minutes. Sift remaining flour, sugar, baking powder and salt together; add eggs. Stir in cherries, coconut and nuts. Spread over partially baked crust; sprinkle with reserved crumbs. Bake at 350 degrees for 30 minutes. Cool and cut into bars.

Rebecca Weiss
Xi Delta Alpha, Bethlehem, Pennsylvania

CHERRY PIE

1 c. cherry juice
2/3 c. sugar
1/8 tsp. salt
2 tbsp. cornstarch
2 c. pie cherries
1 tbsp. butter
1/4 tsp. almond extract
1 3-oz. package cream cheese
1/2 c. powdered sugar
1 tsp. vanilla
1 c. whipping cream
1 baked 10-inch pie shell

Combine cherry juice, sugar and salt; bring to a boil. Blend cornstarch with small amount of water; add to sugar mixture. Cook, stirring constantly, until thickened. Add cherries, butter and almond extract. Refrigerate until cool. Mix cream cheese, powdered sugar and vanilla until creamy. Whip cream; fold into cream cheese mixture. Pour creamed mixture into pie shell; top with cherry mixture. Refrigerate.

Kathleen Dunbar
Xi Iota, Roy, Utah

ALMOND CRUST-CHERRY CREAM PIE

1/2 c. chopped slivered almonds
Pastry for 1 9-in. pie shell
1 1/2 c. sweetened condensed milk
1/3 c. lemon juice
1 tsp. vanilla
1/2 tsp. almond extract
1/2 c. whipping cream, whipped
2/3 c. cherry juice
1/4 c. sugar
1 tbsp. cornstarch
3 drops of red food coloring
2 c. drained pitted sour cherries

Add chopped almonds to pastry. Roll out on floured surface to fit 9-inch pie pan. Place in pan; prick sides of pie crust. Bake at 425 degrees for 10 to 12 minutes; cool. Combine milk, lemon juice, vanilla and almond extract; mix until thickened. Fold in whipped cream; spoon into cooled shell. Blend cherry juice, sugar and cornstarch in saucepan; cook over low heat, stirring constantly, until thickened and clear. Add red food coloring and cherries; spread over cream filling. Chill for 2 to 3 hours. Yield: 6 servings.

Barbara Connerley
Delta Beta Omicron No. 7040
Arroyo Grande, California

CHERRY-PRETZEL DELIGHT

1 c. pretzel crumbs
1/2 c. sugar
1/4 c. soft butter
1 pkg. dessert topping mix
1 3-oz. package cream cheese
1/4 c. confectioners' sugar
1 No. 303 can cherry pie filling

Mix pretzel crumbs, sugar and butter well. Pat into 9-inch square dish. Prepare topping mix according to package directions; add cream cheese and confectioners' sugar. Whip until well blended. Spread over pretzel mixture. Spread cherry pie filling on top. Refrigerate overnight. Yield: 9 servings.

Caroly Ragan
Beta Sigma Phi, Lancaster, California

St. Patrick's Day

The world, an old adage says, is made up of two kinds of people: those who are Irish and those who wish they were. But whether you're Irish or wish you were, St. Patrick's Day belongs to all of us. And, the lighthearted joy which characterizes this day's festivities is the unmistakable cue for a party.

St. Patrick's Day parades are traditional in many American cities. New York City even paints some of its streets' center stripes green in honor of its marching Irish. Whether you go to the big parade or just catch the highlights on television, you're sure to get a happy glow. After all the excitement, what could be more fun than settling down to a typically Irish party — our After-the-Parade St. Patrick's Day Supper.

With so much joy and good cheer in the air, your party is assured of success. And here is a party supper menu that's as Irish as the Auld Sod. It starts with Corned Beef and Cabbage, an Irish dish successfully transplanted across the ocean and now a national American favorite. Potatoes O'Brien are a delicious complement to this main dish with their cheese goodness. Shamrock Salad — as green as the little plant that gave the salad its name — is a very light, slightly sweet salad sure to please everyone. And what else would you serve with this meal but Irish Oatmeal Bread — typically Irish in its delicious nut-like flavor. Caramel Custards add a welcome sweet note. All in all, this is a meal capturing the joy and gusto which are so much a part of being Irish.

To prepare Corned Beef and Cabbage, wash a 4-pound piece of corned beef in cold water and soak for 30 minutes if it is very salty. Place beef and 1/2 pound salt pork in a pot with three quarts boiling water. Add 1/2

O'Murċaḋa
FORTIS ET HOSPITALIS
Murphy

cup sugar, 3 bay leaves, and a clove of garlic. Simmer for three and a half hours or until the meat is tender. Peel three yellow turnips and slice thickly. Add to meat with three scraped, cut-up carrots, eight white onions, peeled, and six scraped parsnips. Core one small head of cabbage and cut into six wedges. Place in separate cooking pot. From the corned beef pot, dip out two cups cooking liquor. Combine with enough boiling water to just cover the cabbage. Cook cabbage until tender. Serve on heated platter with corned beef and vegetables.

The perfect potatoes for this Irish meal are Potatoes O'Brien. Cook five or six medium potatoes in their jackets. Cool, peel, and dice. In a saucepan combine 1 1/2 cups milk and 2 tablespoons butter. Cook until slightly thickened. Add 1 cup diced cheese, 1 small finely diced onion, 1/2 diced medium green pepper, 1 small jar diced pimento, and 1/2 teaspoon salt. Cook until thoroughly combined. Pour sauce over diced potatoes; pour mixture into baking dish. Cover with fine cracker crumbs and bake at 350 degrees for 40 minutes.

For a Shamrock Salad that is as green as the Emerald Isle, dissolve one 3-ounce package lime gelatin in 1 cup hot water and cool. Add one undrained can crushed pineapple. Pour mixture into a large mold. Chill until set. Dissolve one 3-ounce package lemon gelatin in 1 cup hot water.

Accent St. Patrick's Day with Irish Green

Whip 1 cup cream with one small package softened cream cheese. Add to lemon gelatin mixture. Pour the mixture on top of the set lime gelatin. Chill until set. Mix 1 cup whipping cream with one small package of softened cream cheese and 10 marshmallows, cut into pieces. Refrigerate overnight. Whip just before serving and serve with salad.

Irish Oatmeal Bread is a traditional favorite in Irish-American households from coast to coast. To prepare, preheat oven to 350 degrees. Mix 3 cups sifted all-purpose flour, 1 1/4 cups quick-cooking rolled oats, 1 1/2 tablespoons baking powder, and 1 tablespoon salt. In another bowl, add 1/2 cup honey, 1 1/2 cups milk, and 1 tablespoon melted butter to 1 beaten egg. Pour egg mixture into oat mixture, stirring with a wooden spoon just until dry ingredients are moistened. Mixture will be lumpy. Spread batter in two loaf pans. Bake for one hour or until crusty and tester inserted in center comes out clean. Turn out of pans onto wire rack. Brush with melted butter while warm.

After such a meal, your guests will appreciate the light, sweet taste of Caramel Custard. To prepare, spread 1/2 to 1 cup brown sugar over the bottom of a baking dish or mold. In a bowl, beat three eggs until light.

Add 1/4 cup sugar and 1/8 teaspoon salt. Stir in 2 cups scalded milk. Add 1/2 teaspoon vanilla. Pour over brown sugar. Place baking dish in pan of hot water and bake at 350 degrees until firm. Invert on platter before serving.

The gaiety of St. Patrick's Day and this Irish supper menu will give you a great beginning for a truly memorable party. Add lots and lots of typically Irish decorations to echo your party's theme. You might want to cluster small pipes in seasonal greens. Or if you have a small square or circular mirror, try making a "leprechaun" scene. It's easy with little dolls from the dime store, some small ceramic mushrooms, and a few sprigs of greenery. Placecards could be small shamrock-shaped pieces of white cardboard with your guests' names written in green.

If children are among your guests, occupy them with miniature pipes and bubble mixture. And for the older guests, what could be more fun than an old-fashioned Irish songfest.

There's no end to the fun you can have on this festive holiday. Let the jovial spirit of the Irish capture you on this most Irish of all holidays. Relax with your guests and enjoy your delicious supper and laughter-filled evening which is sure to follow.

SPLIT PEA SOUP

1 lb. split peas
1 lge. hambone
3 qt. water
1 white onion, chopped
1/2 carrot, diced
Salt to taste
Red and white pepper to taste

Place split peas and hambone in cold water; bring to a rapid bowl. Reduce heat to low; add onion, carrots and seasonings. Cook slowly for 2 hours and 30 minutes. Remove ham; strain soup. Remove bits of ham off bone; return to soup. Discard bone and fat. Garnish each serving with crumbled bacon and chopped egg. Yield: 6 servings.

Mrs. Sherry Copp
Phi Alpha Gamma, Shreveport, Louisiana

EMERALD SALAD

1 pkg. lime gelatin
1 c. small curd cottage cheese
1 c. salad dressing
3/4 c. chopped cucumber
1 tbsp. minced onion
1/3 c. chopped nuts

Dissolve gelatin in 1 1/2 cups hot water. Mix cottage cheese and salad dressing well; add to gelatin. Add remaining ingredients; place in 8 x 8 x 2-inch pan. Chill until firm. Yield: 9 servings.

Joyce Johnson
Xi Beta Eta No. 1905, Davenport, Iowa

LEPRECHAUN SALAD

1/4 lb. marshmallows
1 c. milk
1 pkg. lime gelatin
1 8-oz. package cream cheese
1 pkg. dessert topping mix
2/3 c. mayonnaise
1 No. 2 can crushed pineapple

Melt marshmallows in milk in top of double boiler. Pour over gelatin; stir until dissolved. Beat in cream cheese; cool. Prepare dessert topping according to package directions. Blend into gelatin mixture. Add mayonnaise and pineapple. Pour into mold or glass dish; chill until firm. Yield: 8 servings.

Nancy Yingst
Beta No. 295, Harrisburg, Pennsylvania

PADDIE'S AVOCADO MOLD

1 6-oz. package lime gelatin
1 tbsp. instant minced onion
1 tsp. curry powder
1 tsp. garlic salt
1 1/2 c. boiling water
1 c. cold water
2 tbsp. vinegar
2 avocados
1/2 c. mayonnaise
1/2 c. chopped green pepper
1/3 c. sliced stuffed olives

Combine gelatin, onion and seasonings. Add boiling water; stir until gelatin is dissolved. Stir in cold water and vinegar. Chill until mixture mounds on spoon. Cut avocados lengthwise into halves; remove seeds and skin. Sieve avocado; blend with mayonnaise, green pepper, olives and gelatin mixture. Pour into 5-cup mold. Chill until set. Unmold and garnish with avocado slices. Yield: 6-8 servings.

SEAFOAM SALAD WITH PEARS

1 No. 2 1/2 can pears
1 pkg. lime gelatin
1 8-oz. package cream cheese
2 tbsp. cream
1 c. whipping cream, whipped

Drain pears; reserve 1 cup syrup. Mash pears. Heat reserved pear syrup; dissolve gelatin in hot syrup. Blend cream cheese with cream; add to hot gelatin, stirring until cheese is dissolved. Cool until thickened. Fold in pears and whipped cream; pour into glass dish. Refrigerate for at least 12 hours. Cut into squares. Serve on salad greens; garnish with strawberries. Yield: 12 servings.

Cathy Dornbusch
Epsilon Pi No. 2545, Dayton, Ohio

GLAZED CORNED BEEF

1 5 to 7-lb. corned beef
6 peppercorns
1 onion, sliced
4 whole cloves
1 stalk celery, cut up
1/3 c. brown sugar, packed
1 tbsp. prepared mustard
1 tsp. bottled horseradish
1/3 c. catsup
3 tbsp. vinegar
2 tbsp. butter or margarine

Place beef in Dutch oven; cover beef with water. Add peppercorns, onion, cloves and celery. Simmer for 4 hours and 30 minutes to 5 hours or until almost tender. Remove from water; place in baking pan. Combine brown sugar, mustard, horseradish, catsup, vinegar and butter in saucepan. Stir over medium heat until blended and bubbly. Spoon part of sauce over beef. Bake in 350-degree oven for 30 minutes or until tender, basting frequently with remaining sauce. Yield: 8 servings.

Mrs. Jewel St. George
Alpha Alpha Psi No. 6205, China Lake, California

SAINT PATRICK'S IRISH STEW

1 1/2 lb. boneless lamb shoulder
1/4 c. flour
2 tsp. salt
1/2 tsp. pepper
1/2 tsp. paprika
2 tbsp. salad oil
1 c. sliced fresh onions
4 c. thinly sliced pared potatoes
1 1/2 c. beef bouillon

Cut lamb into 1-inch cubes. Combine flour, salt, pepper and paprika in paper bag; add lamb. Shake to coat well. Reserve remaining flour mixture. Brown lamb well in oil in Dutch oven. Remove lamb. Add onions to drippings in pan; brown lightly. Arrange browned lamb and onions in center of 1 1/2-quart shallow casserole. Arrange 1/3 of the potatoes around lamb; sprinkle with 1 teaspoon reserved flour mixture. Repeat layers twice. Pour bouillon into casserole; cover. Bake in 375-degree oven for about 1 hour or until potatoes are tender. Remove cover; bake for 15 minutes longer or until potatoes are lightly browned. Yield: About 4 servings.

PARSLEY STEAK ROLLS

1 can mushroom pieces
1 diced onion
3 tbsp. Parmesan cheese
Salt and pepper to taste
Dry parsley flakes
1 lge. round steak
1 tbsp. cornstarch
1 can beef broth

Place mushrooms, onion, cheese, salt, pepper and parsley over steak. Roll into large roll; secure with string or heavy thread. Brown in fat on all sides in ovenproof frypan. Drain off excess fat. Stir cornstarch in small amount of broth; add to remaining broth. Pour over steak. Cover. Bake at 350 degrees for 1 hour. Yield: 6-8 servings.

Mrs. Elizabeth Patterson
Xi Beta Theta, Broken Arrow, Oklahoma

IRISH STEW

1 1/2 lb. lean lamb
Salt and pepper to taste
2 tbsp. flour
2 onions, sliced
2 tbsp. fat
4 potatoes, diced
4 carrots, diced
2 turnips, diced
1 tbsp. chopped parsley

Cut lamb into 1-inch cubes; sprinkle with salt, pepper and flour. Brown with onions in fat. Add water to cover; simmer for 1 hour and 30 minutes or until tender. Add vegetables; cook until tender. Season with salt, pepper and parsley. Yield: 4 servings.

Mrs. Lawrence J. Hogan
Washington, D. C.

FISH CHOWDER

1/4 c. finely cut bacon
1/4 c. minced onion
1/4 c. finely cut celery
1/4 c. finely cut green pepper
2 1-lb. cans tomatoes
2 tbsp. vegetable flakes
1 tsp. salt
1/8 tsp. pepper
Dash of hot sauce
Dash of Worcestershire sauce
1 1/2 lb. red snapper or haddock

Saute bacon, onion, celery and green pepper together in Dutch oven. Add tomatoes, 3/4 cup water, vegetable flakes, salt, pepper, hot sauce and Worcestershire sauce. Cut red snapper in large strips; add to tomato mixture. Cook over low heat for 1 hour. Serve over rice. Yield: 5 servings.

Bonnie Rent
Gamma Iota, Medfield, Massachusetts

SHRIMP AND CRAB AU GRATIN

1 lb. shrimp, deveined
1 pkg. frozen artichoke hearts
Butter
1/2 lb. fresh sliced mushrooms
1 clove of garlic, crushed
2 tbsp. finely chopped scallions
1/4 c. flour
1/2 tsp. pepper
1 tbsp. snipped fresh dill
3/4 c. milk
1/2 lb. grated sharp Cheddar cheese
2/3 c. dry white wine
2 7 1/2-oz. cans King crab
2 tbsp. seasoned corn flake crumbs

Preheat oven to 375 degrees. Cook shrimp in boiling salted water for 3 minutes or until pink; drain. Cook artichoke hearts according to package directions; drain. Melt 2 tablespoons butter in skillet; saute mushrooms for 5 minutes. Remove from skillet. Add 2 tablespoons butter to skillet; saute garlic and scallions for 5 minutes. Remove from heat. Stir in flour, pepper and dill; stir in milk. Bring to a boil, stirring constantly; cook until thick. Remove from heat. Add half the cheese; stir till melted. Stir in wine. Drain crab; remove cartilage and flake. Combine sauce, crab, shrimp, artichoke hearts, mushrooms and remaining cheese in 2-quart casse-

role. Mix lightly. Sprinkle with corn flake crumbs; dot with 1/2 tablespoon butter. Bake for 30 minutes or until bubbly and corn flake crumbs are browned. Yield: 6 servings.

Joanne Ryno
Iota Iota, Willows, California

SALMON-POTATO SOUP

4 med. potatoes, diced
1 qt. milk
1 pt. half and half cream
1 No. 2 can salmon
1 stick butter
1 sm. onion, finely chopped
Salt and pepper to taste

Cook potatoes in large saucepan in enough salted water to cover until almost done. Add milk, cream, salmon, butter and onion. Season with salt and pepper. Simmer for 20 to 30 minutes. Yield: 4-6 servings.

Barbara Kerwin
Beta Zeta, Perry, Iowa

CELERY AND CHEESE CASSEROLE

1 stalk fresh celery
3 tbsp. butter or margarine
1/4 c. water
1/2 tsp. tarragon leaves, crumbled
2 tbsp. flour
1/2 c. milk
1 can cream of chicken soup
1/2 c. grated Cheddar cheese
1/4 tsp. paprika

Preheat oven to 350 degrees. Trim leaves from celery. Cut ribs into 1/2-inch diagonal pieces to make about 6 cups. Combine celery with 1 tablespoon butter, water and tarragon in medium saucepan; bring to a boil. Cover. Reduce heat; simmer for 10 minutes. Turn into a 2-quart casserole; set aside. Heat remaining butter in same saucepan. Stir in flour; brown lightly. Add milk gradually, stirring until smooth. Add soup; heat thoroughly. Stir in cheese. Pour over celery; mix lightly. Sprinkle with paprika. Bake, uncovered, for 15 minutes or until mixture is bubbly. Serve hot. Yield: 6-8 servings.

HOLIDAY GREEN BEANS

1 lb. fresh green beans
4 med. white onions, chopped
2 med. green peppers, chopped
Salt
Paprika
Butter
Dry bread crumbs

Cut beans in 1-inch lengths. Place alternate layers of vegetables in buttered baking dish, beginning and ending with layer of beans. Sprinkle each layer with salt and paprika. Dot each layer with butter; add 1 cup to 1 1/2 cups water. Cover. Bake at 350 degrees for about 1 hour and 15 minutes or until beans are tender. Place bread crumbs over beans; dot with butter. Place casserole under broiler, 5 inches from heat; broil until crust is brown. Yield: 6 servings.

Polly Manuel
Preceptor Zeta XP0550, Winchester, Virginia

SWEET AND SOUR BRUSSELS SPROUTS

1 lb. fresh Brussels sprouts
1 tbsp. butter or margarine
1/4 c. brown sugar
1/4 c. white vinegar
1 tsp. cornstarch
1 tsp. grated onion
Dash of dry mustard

Cook Brussels sprouts until just tender; drain well. Melt butter; blend in remaining ingredients. Cook, stirring until thickened; pour over Brussels sprouts. Yield: 5 servings.

Freda F. Bennett
Elgin, Nebraska

ZUCCHINI AND OLIVE CASSEROLE

1 1/2 lb. zucchini, sliced
2 eggs, well beaten
1 tsp. salt
1/2 c. milk
2 tbsp. grated onion
1 c. dry bread crumbs
1 c. grated American cheese
1/2 c. diced ripe olives

Cook zucchini in small amount of water until tender; drain. Combine remaining ingredients; add to zucchini. Pour into buttered casserole. Sprinkle with additional bread crumbs if desired. Bake at 350 degrees for 35 minutes. Yield: 6 servings.

Mrs. Polly M. Page
Yerington, Nevada

SHAMROCK GREEN RICE

1 10-oz. package frozen spinach
3/4 c. packaged precooked rice
1/4 c. finely chopped onion
2 lightly beaten eggs
2 c. milk
1 c. shredded sharp Cheddar cheese
1/8 tsp. garlic salt
1 tbsp. cornstarch

Cook spinach according to package directions; drain and chop. Combine all ingredients in mixing bowl. Turn into greased casserole. Bake in 325-degree oven for 35 minutes or until done. Yield: 6-8 servingss.

Kathy Leavene
Kappa Delta No. 7067, Columbia, Missouri

POTATOES O'BRIEN

5 or 6 med. potatoes
2 tbsp. butter
1 tbsp. flour
1 1/2 c. milk
1 c. diced cheese
1 sm. onion, finely diced
1/2 med. green pepper, diced
1 sm. jar pimento, diced
1/2 tsp. salt
Fine cracker crumbs

Cook potatoes in jackets; peel and dice. Place potatoes in baking dish. Melt butter in saucepan; stir in flour. Add milk; cook, stirring constantly, until slightly thickened. Add all remaining ingredients except crumbs. Pour sauce over potatoes; cover with cracker crumbs. Bake at 375 degrees for 40 minutes. Yield: 5-6 servings.

Mrs. Virginia Golden
Big Stone Gap, Virginia

SCALLOPED CABBAGE CASSEROLE

1 lge. head cabbage
2 tbsp. melted butter
2 tbsp. flour
1/2 tsp. salt
1 c. grated American cheese
1/2 c. grated sharp cheese
1 c. crushed potato chips

Cut cabbage into 10 or 12 wedges; place carefully in large pan. Cover with water. Parboil till almost tender. Lift wedges out of water carefully; arrange in oblong casserole, reserving cabbage juice. Blend butter, flour and salt; add 1 cup reserved juice gradually, stirring constantly. Cook and stir until thick and creamy; add cheeses. Pour over cabbage wedges; sprinkle with potato chips. Bake at 350 degrees for 30 minutes or until tender.

Mrs. Sylvia Brush
Missouri Xi Delta Gamma, Raytown, Missouri

COUNTY CORK SODA BREAD

4 c. sifted flour
3 tsp. baking powder
1 tsp. salt
1/2 tsp. soda
1 c. seedless raisins
1 tbsp. caraway seeds
1 3/4 c. buttermilk
1/4 c. cooking oil

Sift flour with baking powder, salt and soda. Add raisins, caraway seeds, buttermilk and cooking oil. Mix just until moistened. Shape dough into 2 mounds on greased baking sheet. Cut deep cross in top each loaf with sharp knife. Bake at 350 degrees for 50 minutes.

Photograph for this recipe on page 75.

ELEGANT GOLDEN ANGEL CAKE

1 1-lb. can cling peach slices
1 c. plum jam
1 10-in. angel cake
1/2 c. roasted diced almonds
1 pt. whipping cream
Sugar to taste

Drain peaches; reserve 10 slices for topping. Chop remaining slices into bite-sized pieces. Combine with plum jam. Cut angel cake crosswise into 3 layers. Spread 1/2 of the peach mixture over first layer; sprinkle with half the almonds. Repeat for second layer. Top with third cake layer. Whip cream until stiff peaks form, adding sugar gradually. Frost side and top of cake with whipped cream. Arrange reserved peach slices on top. Refrigerate for at least 2 hours before serving. Yield: 10-12 servings.

EMERALD MELON PIE

1 3-oz. package lime gelatin
1 c. boiling water
8 to 12 lge. ice cubes
1/2 tsp. almond extract
2 c. honeydew melon balls
Coconut Pie Shell

Dissolve gelatin in boiling water; add ice cubes. Stir constantly for 2 or 3 minutes or until gelatin begins to thicken. Remove ice. Add almond extract; let stand for 2 to 3 minutes. Add melon balls; stir. Pour into Coconut Pie Shell. Chill for about 3 hours or until set. Garnish with whipped cream or prepared topping mix.

Coconut Pie Shell

1/3 c. melted butter
2 pkg. grated coconut

Mix butter and coconut; press evenly into pie pan. Bake at 300 degrees for about 30 minutes.

Dolores Feist
Xi Gamma X-676, Cheyenne, Wyoming

LIME CHIFFON PIE

4 eggs, separated
1 c. sugar
1/2 c. lime juice
1/2 tsp. salt
Food coloring
1 tbsp. unflavored gelatin
1/4 c. cold water
1 tbsp. grated lemon peel
1 c. heavy cream, whipped
1 10-in. baked pastry shell

Combine beaten egg yolks, 1/2 cup sugar, lime juice and salt; cook in double boiler until thick, stirring constantly. Add food coloring to obtain deep lime green color. Soften gelatin in cold water; add to hot mixture. Stir until gelatin dissolves. Add lemon peel. Cool until partially set. Beat remaining sugar into stiffly beaten egg whites; combine with whipped cream and fold into cooled mixture. Pour into pastry shell; chill in refrigerator for several hours until firm. Serve with whipped cream topping if desired. Yield: 7-8 servings.

Vickie S. Brock
Alpha Zeta No. 3944, Burley, Idaho

LEMON-LIME CAKE

1 box lemon cake mix
1 box lime gelatin
4 eggs
3/4 c. salad oil
3/4 c. water
Grated rind of 2 lemons
1/3 c. lemon juice
2 c. powdered sugar, sifted

Place first 5 ingredients in mixing bowl; beat for 4 minutes. Place in 9 x 13-inch pan. Bake at 350 degrees for 40 minutes. Mix grated lemon rind and lemon juice with powdered sugar. Remove cake from oven; prick with fork about 1-inch apart. Pour glaze over top. Serve plain or with whipped cream. Yield: 6-8 servings.

Ethel L. Staton
Xi Zeta X1349, Sitka, Alaska

BROWN SUGAR PUDDING

2 c. brown sugar
2 tbsp. butter
1 c. flour
1/2 c. sugar
3 tsp. baking powder

Combine brown sugar, 1 cup water and butter in saucepan; bring to a boil. Cook, stirring until brown sugar is dissolved. Pour into 8-inch square pan. Mix flour, sugar, baking powder and 1/2 cup water; pour into syrup. Do not stir. Bake for 15 to 20 minutes in 350-degree oven. Serve slightly warm; top with whipped cream if desired.

Patricia Guenther
Alpha Iota 4268, Asotin, Wisconsin

HOLIDAY JAM TARTS

1 3-oz. package cream cheese
2 sticks pie crust mix
1 tbsp. milk
Raspberry jam

Soften cream cheese. Blend pie crust mix, cream cheese and milk together. Divide dough in half; roll each half into 10-inch square. Cut with pastry wheel into sixteen 2 1/2-inch squares. Place 1/2 teaspoon jam in center of each square; pinch 2 opposite corners into middle. Place on greased baking sheet. Bake for 10 to 12 minutes at 350 degrees. Yield: 32 servings.

Ann Pietro
Iota Beta No. 6252, Ishpeming, Michigan

LUCK OF THE IRISH COFFEE

1 oz. or jigger Irish whiskey
1 tsp. sugar or to taste
Strong hot coffee
Whipped cream

Pour whiskey into 7-ounce stemmed glass. Add sugar. Fill glass to within 1/2 inch of brim with black coffee; stir well. Top with whipped cream. Do not stir after adding cream. The flavor is obtained by sipping hot beverage through cool cream. Yield: 1 serving.

Mrs. Norval K. Heath
Syracuse, New York

AVOCADO SLUSH

2 soft avocados
1/4 c. lime juice
1/2 c. honey
1 c. whipping cream, whipped
Ginger ale

Peel, pit and mash avocados; add lime juice and honey. Mix with electric mixer or in blender. Fold into whipped cream. Spoon into freezer tray. Freeze for at least 4 hours or until firm. Blend with small amount ginger ale until slushy. Serve in shamrock cups.

GINGER-LIME PUNCH

2 6-oz. cans frozen limeade
1 6-oz. can frozen lemonade
1 tbsp. chopped candied ginger
4 c. cold water
1 lge. bottle ginger ale, chilled

Thaw limeade and lemonade; pour into bowl. Add ginger. Chill for at least 2 hours to blend flavors. Pour into punch bowl; add water and ice. Pour ginger ale down side of bowl. Fluted lemon slices, small lime slices and mint sprigs may be floated in punch. Yield: 20 servings.

Virginia J. Bickford
Phi Alpha Psi P730, Muncie, Indiana

It's Easter — at last. The long, cold, dark days of winter are officially over. Easter is not only one of the holiest days in the Christian faith: Coming as it does between late March and late April, it is also the signal that spring, the time of rebirth, is here once again. Both for its religious significance and as a herald of springtime, Easter is one of the most cherished holidays in the calendar.

And it's one of the most exciting, too. Remember the thrill when you were a child? The whole family got up early. You eagerly searched for your Easter basket filled with brightly colored eggs. You sometimes attended Easter sunrise service. Then there was the walk through the park or along the streets, seeing friends you hadn't seen for months, with everyone in new finery. Even today, we retain the charming custom of the Easter Parade.

Easter is a time when families get together. For many families, it's the first time

Easter

together since the Christmas holidays. With family gatherings and the thrill of springtime in the air, Easter Sunday Dinner is a gala occasion . . . an occasion which demands the very best of springtime food. If this is your year to entertain the family at Easter Sunday Dinner, what better way to begin than Baked Ham With Apple Juice — a delicious blending of tart flavors. Bring the spring fruits — cherries, pineapple, and oranges — to your table with Easter Salad. Holiday Oven Rice is easy to prepare and is a welcome change from potatoes. Take advantage of the spring vegetables: Peas and Onions Amandine are sure to please every guest at your table, and Crunchy Broccoli Casserole combines the best of spring broccoli with the taste-tempting goodness of mushrooms and cheese. Add light

and rich Butter Dips, and your guests will praise your culinary skill. Top off this elegant springtime menu with Baked Alaska, the all-time favorite melt-in-your mouth dessert.

Baked Ham is easy to prepare when you begin with a five-pound canned ham. Mix together 3 tablespoons brown sugar and 1 tablespoon dry mustard. Rub into ham. Score the ham and insert whole cloves in the middle of each diamond. Pour one pint apple juice around the ham. Bake at 350 degrees for an hour and 45 minutes to two hours, basting frequently with pan glaze. If you choose a smoked ham instead of a canned one, increase the amount of brown sugar and dry mustard according to the increase in weight.

Easter Salad is an appropriate accompaniment to this delicious baked ham. To prepare, mix one large can Queen Anne cherries (drained), one large drained can pineapple, one drained can mandarin oranges and 1/2 pound colored marshmallows which have been quartered. Chill. In a saucepan, combine 2 egg yolks, 1 teaspoon sugar, a pinch of salt, 1/2 cup milk and the juice of one lemon. Cook, stirring constantly, until mixture is thickened. Cool and fold in 1/2 pint whipped cream. Stir into chilled fruit mixture. Refrigerate overnight before serving. This delicious salad may be garnished with whipped cream if desired.

Fill Your Easter Table with Springtime

Try Holiday Oven Rice. It's easy to prepare. Just combine 1 stick melted butter, 1 minced onion, 1 cup converted rice, 1 can sliced mushrooms, 1 can condensed bouillon, and 1 can condensed consomme. Pour into a casserole dish and bake at 350 degrees for 40 minutes.

There are many delicious springtime vegetables, but perhaps the favorite is green peas. Peas and Onions Amandine combine the delicious flavors of peas, onions, and almonds into a dish that's sure to please everyone. Cook 1 cup diagonally-cut celery in boiling salted water until tender but still crisp. Drain. Lightly brown 1/2 cup slivered blanched almonds in 1/2 cup melted butter. Add 1 small can whole onions. Cook one 10-ounce package frozen English peas. Add peas and celery to almond mixture. Season with salt and pepper to taste. Serve piping hot.

Another favorite spring vegetable is broccoli. Serve it in delicious Crunchy Broccoli Casserole. To prepare, cook two packages frozen broccoli in a small amount of water until tender. Drain, reserving 1/2 cup liquid. Arrange broccoli in a casserole dish. Mix 1 can cream of mushroom soup, 1 teaspoon cream, reserved liquid, and salt and pepper to taste. Pour over broccoli. Sprinkle with 1 cup grated Cheddar cheese.

Melt 4 tablespoons butter. Stir in 1 cup Italian-style bread crumbs. Sprinkle over cheese. Top with 1/2 cup slivered almonds. Bake for 30 to 35 minutes in a 300-degree oven. For your convenience, this dish may be prepared ahead of time and refrigerated until you are ready to bake it.

No Easter Sunday Dinner would be complete without home-baked bread, and Butter Dips are an unusual variation of the standard biscuit recipe. Preheat oven to 450 degrees. Melt 1/3 cup butter in oven in a 13 x 9 1/2 x 2-inch pan. Into a bowl sift 2 1/4 cups flour, 1 tablespoon sugar, 3 1/2 teaspoons baking powder, and 1 1/2 teaspoons salt. Add 1 cup milk. Stir slowly with fork until dough barely clings together — about 30 strokes. Turn onto well-floured board and roll over to coat with flour. Knead lightly ten times. Roll out 1/2 inch thick into 12 x 8-inch rectangle. Cut dough in half lengthwise with floured knife. Cut crosswise into 16 strips. Dip each strip in the melted butter on both sides. Lay close together in two rows in pan used to melt butter. Bake for 15 to 20 minutes or until golden brown. Serve hot.

An elaborate, elegant dessert should highlight your Easter Dinner. Perhaps the most elegant of all desserts — and a family favorite is Baked Alaska. To really highlight this holiday, you might decide to prepare it in the shape of an egg! Line an eight-cup mold or mixing bowl with foil, leaving a one-inch overhang. Spread two pints slightly-softened coffee ice cream over the bottom and up the side to the top, leaving the center hollow. Fill this hollow with one pint softened strawberry ice cream. Freeze until slightly firm, smooth flat with a table knife, and freeze until very firm.

To prepare the cake base for your Baked Alaska, cream 1/2 cup shortening with 1/2 cup brown sugar until fluffy. Beat in four egg yolks, one at a time, beating until mixture is well blended. Sift 1 cup sifted flour, 1/8 teaspoon salt, 2 teaspoons baking powder. Add this mixture, a third at a time, alternately with 1/3 cup milk. Stir in 1/2 teaspoon vanilla and 1 cup chopped nuts. Pour batter into a greased and floured 9-inch pan. Bake at 350 degrees for 30 minutes or until top springs back when touched. Cool for five minutes and turn out on a rack to cool completely.

Place a double thick strip of tin foil on a cookie sheet. Put cake on top of foil. Loosen molded ice cream by lifting up overhanging tabs of foil. Invert onto center of cake. Peel off foil and trim cake to within one-fourth inch of ice cream mold. Return to freezer until ready to frost with meringue.

To prepare the meringue, beat four egg whites with 1/2 teaspoon cream of tartar until foamy and doubled in volume. Gradually add 1/2 cup sugar, 1 tablespoon at a time, beating until sugar dissolves and meringue stands in firm peaks. Spread over ice cream-cake mold, swirling in peaks to cover completely. Bake at 475 degrees for three to four minutes.

Delicious food, glorious springtime weather, and the joy of the Easter season are the main ingredients you need for an unforgettable Easter Sunday Dinner. And to highlight the festivities, echo springtime with your decorations in pastel colors — the pale greens, pinks, blues, and yellows reminiscent of spring.

For your centerpiece, perhaps you'll choose all yellow flowers. Lucky you if you can pick them straight from your garden! Or you may mass colored eggs and violets in a bright Easter basket. A child's toy rabbit or lamb in a ring of leaves with a few spring flowers is another appropriate centerpiece.

Perhaps this year, it's someone else's turn to host the Easter Sunday Dinner. If that's the case, why not invite everyone to your home for an Easter Egg Hunt Dessert Party.

An Easter Egg Hunt Party is fun for everyone — and easy on the hostess. Hide Easter eggs around the house or in the yard. Use the traditional colored hard-boiled eggs, jelly beans, chocolate eggs, marshmallow eggs, even cardboard cutout eggs. As your young guests arrive, give each one a basket. When everyone is there, let the hunt begin. It should be limited to about an hour — more than that and younger children may tire. The child who gets the most eggs wins a prize. An elaborately decorated, hollowed-out egg with a gay scene inside would be appropriate. All the children get to take home their baskets of eggs.

Use the Easter Egg theme in your invitations. How thrilled children will be to get an invitation shaped like an egg! Use pastel-colored construction paper in pale greens, pinks, and yellows. The same colors would be appropriate for your party decorations. To make things easy on you, use paper whenever possible. For your refreshment table, perhaps a yellow paper tablecloth with green paper napkins and pink paper plates. Even the cups could be pastel-colored paper.

What's for dessert? The foods everyone loves . . . Ice Cream Cups . . . Gala Party Punch . . . Candy Easter Eggs . . . and the delightful Spring Bonnet Cake pictured on page 87. This cake is so lovely it would make a perfect centerpiece. To prepare, combine 1 package yellow cake mix, 1 cup water, 1/3 cup orange juice, 1 tablespoon grated orange rind, and two eggs in a large bowl. Blend until moistened. Beat according to package directions. Turn half the batter into a greased and floured eight-inch round cake pan. Turn the rest into a greased and floured 1 1/2-quart ovenproof bowl. Bake both in 350-degree oven — the eight-inch layer cake for 30 to 35 minutes and the bowl cake 40 to 45 minutes. Cool for ten minutes; remove cakes from pan and bowl. Cool on rack.

To prepare the frosting for your Spring Bonnet Cake, combine 2 egg whites, 1 1/2 cups sugar, dash of salt, 1/2 teaspoon cream of tartar and 1/2 cup orange juice in the top of a double boiler. Beat until thoroughly mixed. Place over boiling water and beat constantly with electric mixer at high speed for seven minutes, until frosting stands in stiff peaks. Stir frosting up from bottom and sides occasionally while cooking. Remove from heat. Add 1 teaspoon vanilla and 1/8 teaspoon yellow food coloring. Beat for one minute longer.

It's the decorating that turns this cake into something really special. Invert the eight-inch layer on a serving plate and frost sides and top. Cut a thin slice from flat side of bowl cake to make level. Invert the bowl cake on top of the frosted layer. Place in center so that there is an even rim around it. Frost generously, rounding frosting to give the cake a typical hat shape. Slice small green gum drops and place around the base of the bowl cake to make a "hat band." Cut large colored gum drops into four sections with scissors, being careful not to cut all the way through. Cut small colored gum drops into three sections. Separate sections by pinching until cut gum drops resemble flower petals. Cut green gum drops into small pieces to make "flower stems." Place about 1 cup orange sections around the base of the cake.

To prepare Ice Cream Cups, melt 1 package semisweet chocolate bits with 2 tablespoons butter. Brush a thick coat of the chocolate mixture on the bottom and sides of eight small fluted paper baking cups, using spatula. Freeze. Peel off paper and allow the chocolate cups to thaw for about 15 minutes. Fill with scoops of ice cream or any of the yummy sherbets.

Easter Eggs — the rich, candy kind — are sweet and oh-so-good. Combine 1 cup sugar and 1/2 cup water. Cook until mixture spins a thread. Add 2 stiffly beaten egg whites. Beat until well mixed. In another pan, combine 2 cups sugar, 1/2 cup water and 1 cup white corn syrup. Cook until brittle when tested in cold water. Combine egg white mixture with syrup mixture. Beat until thick. Add 1 teaspoon vanilla, coconut and nuts to taste. Form mixture into the shape of eggs and let stand until cold. Melt two small bags butterscotch chips and one large bag chocolate chips together. Coat eggs with mixture. Let set until firm.

Your young guests are sure to raise a big thirst hunting for Easter eggs. Quench that thirst with Gala Party Punch. Combine one 12-ounce can frozen orange juice, one 12-ounce can frozen lemonade, one 1-pound 14-ounce can chilled pineapple juice, and 2 cups ice water. Mix well. Add two quarts chilled ginger ale and one quart chilled soda water. Add 1/2 gallon lime sherbet just before serving. Not only does this punch combine the delicious tartness of citrus fruit juices, but its color is the perfect complement to your springtime table decorations!

ISLAND GRAPEFRUIT APPETIZER

2 grapefruit
1/2 c. rum
2 tsp. sugar
2 tsp. chopped mint
Orange segments
Cherries

Halve grapefruit, cutting in scallop pattern. Section grapefruit, cleaning and reserving shells. Place half the grapefruit sections, rum, sugar and mint in blender container. Blend at high speed until liquefied. Arrange remaining grapefruit sections and orange segments in reserved grapefruit shells; pour blended mixture over top. Garnish with cherries. Chill and serve. Yield: 4 servings.

Mrs. Jane P. Valk
Gamma Zeta No. 6438, Westboro, Massachusetts

SHRIMP COCKTAIL

2 lb. boiled shrimp, deveined
1/2 c. chili sauce
1/3 c. catsup
1/3 c. horseradish
1 1/2 tsp. Worcestershire sauce
1/4 tsp. salt
2 tbsp. strained lemon juice
Dash of pepper
1/4 c. finely diced celery

Chill shrimp. Combine remaining ingredients in order listed; add shrimp. Place in glass container. Cover; refrigerate until ready to serve.

Ginny Benson
Eta Beta No. 6161, Indianola, Iowa

CRAB MEAT COCKTAIL

1 tsp. unflavored gelatin
2 tbsp. cold water
1/4 c. catsup
1 tbsp. lemon juice
1 tsp. Worcestershire sauce
4 tsp. French dressing
Salt to taste
Paprika to taste
1 lb. crab meat

Soften gelatin in cold water; dissolve over hot water. Add catsup, lemon juice, Worcestershire sauce, French dressing, salt, paprika and crab meat. Place mixture in serving dishes. Chill for several hours before serving.

Dorothy Hughes
Hubbardton, Vermont

OYSTER COCKTAIL

1 c. shredded lettuce
1/2 pt. oysters
1/2 c. catsup
1/2 to 1 tsp. horseradish
1/4 tsp. salt

Place lettuce in 4 cocktail glasses; add oysters. Chill. Mix catsup, horseradish and salt; pour over oysters. Serve cold.

Mrs. Ardelle C. Dunn
Fairfax, Vermont

DEVILED EGG MOLD

1 env. unflavored gelatin
1 c. cold water
1 tsp. salt
2 tbsp. lemon juice
1/4 tsp. Worcestershire sauce
1/8 tsp. cayenne pepper
3/4 c. mayonnaise
1/2 c. finely diced celery
1/2 c. finely diced green pepper
1/4 c. sweet pickle relish
1/4 c. chopped pimento
4 hard-boiled eggs, chopped

Soften gelatin in cold water; dissolve over boiling water. Add salt, lemon juice, Worcestershire sauce and cayenne pepper; cool. Stir in mayonnaise; blend well. Fold in remaining ingredients; pour into mold. Chill until firm. Unmold to serve.

Paula Johnson
Xi Upsilon X2771, Kingsville, Maryland

GREEN AND GOLD SALAD

1 ripe papaya
1 c. salad oil
1/3 c. tarragon vinegar
1/4 c. sugar
1 tbsp. lime juice
1/4 tsp. paprika
1/2 tsp. salt
1/2 tsp. dry mustard
1/2 tsp. instant minced onion
4 c. mixed salad greens

Submerge papaya in boiling water for 1 minute; drop into ice water. Pull away peel with tip of paring knife; cube papaya, reserving 1 1/2 tablespoons seeds. Place salad oil, vinegar, sugar, lime juice, paprika, salt, mustard and onion in blender container. Cover; blend thoroughly. Add reserved papaya seeds to blender contents; blend till seeds are size of coarsely ground pepper. Chill. Combine papaya and greens; toss lightly with desired amount of dressing. Yield: 6 servings.

Charlotte H. Palmer
Xi Zeta Delta X-3340, Port Charlotte, Florida

GOLDEN CREAM WALDORF

1 6-oz. package lemon gelatin
1/4 tsp. salt
3 golden apples
Lemon juice
1/2 c. mayonnaise
1 c. heavy cream, whipped
1 c. finely chopped celery
1/2 c. finely chopped walnuts

Dissolve gelatin in 1 1/2 cups hot water. Add 2 ice cubes; stir until melted. Stir in salt until dissolved. Chill until slightly thickened. Partially peel 2 apples, leaving small amount of peel for color; core and dice. Sprinkle with lemon juice. Cut third apple into thin slices; arrange slices, peel side down, around bottom of 8-cup mold. Sprinkle with lemon juice. Place in refrigerator to retain crispness. Blend mayonnaise with gelatin; fold in whipped cream. Stir in diced apples, celery and walnuts carefully. Spoon over apple slices; chill until set. Unmold on salad greens; garnish with ripe olives. Yield: 8-10 servings.

CLASSIC WALDORF SALAD

2 c. diced apples
1 tbsp. sugar
1/2 tsp. lemon juice
Dash of salt
1 c. 1-in. julienne celery sticks
1/2 c. chopped walnuts
1/4 c. mayonnaise
1/2 c. whipping cream, whipped

Sprinkle apples with sugar, lemon juice and salt. Add celery and walnuts. Fold mayonnaise into whipped cream. Fold gently into apple mixture. Chill. Serve in lettuce-lined bowl. Yield: 6 servings.

APPLE-CARROT AND RAISIN SALAD

1/2 c. raisins
2 red apples
1 lge. carrot, grated
Mayonnaise
Lettuce leaves

Cover raisins with water in saucepan; cover. Bring to a boil. Simmer until raisins are plump. Cool and drain. Chill in refrigerator. Core and dice apples. Combine apples, carrot and raisins. Moisten with about 2 tablespoons mayonnaise. Toss until all particles are covered with mayonnaise. Serve chilled on crisp lettuce leaves. Yield: 2-4 servings.

Susan M. Klunk
Theta Chi No. 8205, Hanover, Pennsylvania

GOLDEN EGG SALAD

9 hard-boiled eggs, chopped
1/4 c. chopped green pepper
2 tbsp. chopped pimento
1/4 c. chopped celery
1 tbsp. chopped parsley
2 tbsp. chopped onion
1 1/2 tsp. salt
1/4 tsp. pepper
1 3-oz. package cream cheese
1/4 c. mayonnaise
1 tbsp. chili sauce or catsup

Combine first 8 ingredients; mix well. Blend cream cheese, mayonnaise and chili sauce together. Add to egg mixture; mix well. Pack into individual molds or circular mold; chill for 4 hours. Unmold onto lettuce to serve.

Doris Beavers
Xi Gamma Sigma No. 1432, Lubbock, Texas

LEMON-ORANGE SALAD WITH ORANGE DRESSING

1 11-oz. can mandarin oranges
1 6-oz. package orange gelatin
1 c. boiling water
1 1/4 c. fresh orange juice
1 pt. lemon sherbet
6 oz. cream cheese
1 tbsp. sugar
1 tbsp. grated orange rind

Drain oranges. Dissolve gelatin in boiling water in mixer bowl. Add 1 cup orange juice and sherbet, beating with mixer at low speed until sherbet is melted. Chill gelatin mixture until thickened; fold in oranges. Pour into greased 1 1/2-quart mold; chill until firm. Beat cream cheese and remaining orange juice together until creamy; stir in sugar and orange rind. Unmold salad; serve dressing over salad.

Janice Myers
Xi Alpha Beta X901, Council Bluffs, Iowa

PINEAPPLE PORK CHOPS

1 med. onion
1 med. green pepper
1 can sliced pineapple
3/4 c. sherry
1 10 1/2-oz. can beef broth
2 tbsp. lemon juice
6 1-in. thick pork chops
1 tsp. salt
1 tsp. thyme
1/2 c. red currant jelly
1 tbsp. cornstarch
2 tbsp. water

Chop onion and green pepper fine. Drain pineapple, reserving syrup. Mix pineapple syrup, sherry, broth, lemon juice, onion and green pepper. Arrange pork chops in 13 x 9-inch baking dish; sprinkle with salt and thyme. Pourl liquid mixture around pork chops. Bake, uncovered, at 425 degrees for 50 minutes. Stir jelly with fork; stir into pan liquid. Turn pork chops; bake for 10 minutes. Blend cornstarch and water; stir into pan liquid. Place 1 slice pineapple on each pork chop; arrange any remaining pineapple around pork chops. Bake for 10 minutes longer or until pork chops are tender and liquid is thickened. Yield: 6 servings.

Marge Ruppent
Phi Alpha Eta No. 524, South Bend, Indiana

CROWN OF LAMB ROAST WITH APPLE-MARJORAM STUFFING

1 crown of lamb roast
Salt
Pepper
2 tsp. instant minced onion
1 c. chopped celery
3 c. dry bread crumbs
3 c. chopped apples
6 tbsp. butter
1/2 c. pignolia nuts
1/2 tsp. ground ginger
1 tsp. ground marjoram
Bacon or pork

Preheat oven to 350 degrees. Rub roast with salt and pepper to taste. Saute onion, celery, bread crumbs and apples in butter; add nuts, 1/2 teaspoon salt, 1/8 teaspoon pepper, ginger and marjoram. Mix lightly but thoroughly. Fill roast with bread dressing; place in roasting pan. Wrap bacon around rib ends to prevent charring. Roast for 30 to 35 minutes per pound. Remove bacon; replace with paper frills.

Mrs. Merle M. Blackburn
Montgomery, Alabama

PORK ROAST MARASCHINO

1 tbsp. salad oil
2 cloves of garlic
1 29 1/2-oz. can pineapple chunks
1 c. undrained sweet mixed pickles
1 16-oz. jar maraschino cherries
5 tsp. cornstarch
2 tbsp. cold water
1 tbsp. soy sauce
2 tsp. salt
1 4 to 5-lb. pork loin roast

Heat oil in saucepan; add garlic. Saute for several minutes. Remove garlic. Drain pineapple, pickles and cherries, reserving about 2 cups combined liquid. Blend cornstarch with cold water; add reserved liquid, soy sauce and salt. Add to oil in saucepan; cook, stirring until thickened. Set glaze aside. Place roast on rack in shallow roasting pan. Bake in 325-degree oven for 35 to 45 minutes per pound or until meat thermometer registers 170 degrees, basting with part of glaze during last 1 hour and 30 minutes of baking. Add fruits and pickles to remaining glaze; heat. Pour over and around roast on serving platter. Yield: 6-8 servings.

EASTER DAY PORK TENDERLOIN

1 tbsp. sherry
2 tbsp. brown sugar
2 tbsp. soy sauce
1/2 tsp. salt
1 pork tenderloin roast
1/2 tsp. cinnamon

Combine sherry, brown sugar, soy sauce and salt for marinade. Rub or sprinkle roast with cinnamon; marinate overnight. Place roast in roasting pan. Bake at 250 to 300 degrees until tender.

Mrs. Aline S. Conway
Holloman, New Mexico

LAMB RACK WITH ORANGE-FILLED AVOCADO HALVES

1 7-bone loin or rack of lamb
Salt and pepper to taste
2 oranges
2 avocados

Season lamb with salt and pepper. Place lamb, fat side up, in shallow roasting pan. Bake at 325 to 350 degrees to desired degree of doneness. Peel and section oranges. Cut avocados in half; remove seeds. Fill centers with orange sections. Place around lamb on serving platter. Serve with vinaigrette sauce.

CROWN ROAST OF LAMB WITH RICE STUFFING

1 1/2 lb. ground lamb
1 c. chopped onions
3 c. cooked brown rice
1/2 c. chopped parsley
1 tsp. salt
1 tsp. coarsely ground pepper
1/2 lb. mushrooms, sliced
1 7-lb. crown roast of lamb

Saute lamb and onions until onions are just tender; stir in rice, parsley, salt, pepper and mushrooms. Fill roast with stuffing; place on ovenproof platter. Bake at 325 degrees for 2 hours and 30 minutes. Garnish with watercress. Wrap each rib end with paper frill.

Mrs. H. B. Harper
Phoenix, Arizona

ROAST LEG OF LAMB

1 clove of garlic
1 6 to 8-lb. leg of lamb
Salt and pepper to taste
Grated rind of 1 lemon
1/2 tsp. dried rosemary
1 tbsp. melted butter
1/4 c. olive oil
1 c. water or lemon juice

Cut garlic in 6 slivers. Rub lamb with salt, pepper and lemon rind. Cut 6 slits in lamb; insert garlic and rosemary in slits. Mix butter, olive oil and water. Place lamb, fat side up, on rack in shallow roasting pan. Bake in 325-degree oven for 3 to 4 hours, brushing frequently with butter mixture. Remove lamb to hot platter. Pour fat from roasting pan; stir any remaining butter mixture into browned bits in pan. Season with salt and pepper; serve over lamb. Yield: 8 servings.

Mrs. Maybell G. Mandell
Cassville, Missouri

BAKED HAM SLICE

1 1 1/2-in. thick slice smoked ham
Whole cloves
2 tbsp. brown sugar

2 tbsp. fine dry bread crumbs
2 tbsp. raisins
1/2 tsp. dry mustard
1 1/2 c. orange juice
1 tsp. cornstarch

Place ham in baking pan. Insert cloves in ham at 1-inch intervals. Mix brown sugar, bread crumbs, raisins and mustard; sprinkle mixture evenly over ham. Pour 1 cup orange juice carefully over ham. Bake at 350 degrees for 45 minutes, basting occasionally with liquid in baking pan. Blend remaining orange juice with cornstarch; pour over ham. Bake for 20 minutes longer or until liquid is thickened and clear. Remove cloves before serving. Yield: 1 serving.

Connie Moore
Kappa 707, Hot Springs, Arkansas

EASTER BEEF IN AN EGG SHELL

1 4 to 5-lb. eye-of-round beef roast
1 tbsp. prepared mustard
1 tbsp. soy sauce
Salt
6 tbsp. butter
Flour
3 eggs
Pepper to taste

Place beef on large sheet of aluminum foil. Mix mustard and soy sauce; spread over beef. Fold sides of foil over beef, making double fold; fold ends upward and double back. Place in shallow pan. Bake at 300 degrees for 3 hours. Chill. Combine 3/4 cup water, 1/4 teaspoon salt and butter in saucepan. Bring to a boil; add 3/4 cup flour all at once. Stir over moderate heat until mixture forms ball and follows spoon. Remove paste from heat; cool slightly. Beat in eggs, one at a time. Cool. Remove beef from foil; reserve 2 tablespoons fat and beef drippings. Pat beef dry with paper towel; place on baking sheet. Spread paste over top, sides and ends of beef, sealing well. Place on low shelf of oven. Bake at 425 degrees for about 30 minutes or until browned. Melt reserved fat; blend in 2 tablespoons flour. Add enough water to reserved beef drippings to make 1 cup liquid; stir into flour mixture. Simmer until thickened, stirring constantly. Season with salt and pepper. Serve with beef. Yield: 8 servings.

CHICKEN ROCOCO

10 oz. sharp Cheddar cheese
4 chicken breasts
2 eggs, beaten
3/4 c. dry bread crumbs
1/3 c. margarine
1/2 c. chopped onion
1/2 c. chopped green pepper
1 tsp. salt
1/4 tsp. pepper
1 c. chicken broth
2 cans mushroom soup
2 c. cooked white rice
1 c. cooked wild rice

Cut cheese into eight equal sticks. Skin chicken breasts; cut in half. Debone chicken breasts; roll flat with rolling pin. Roll each piece around a stick of cheese. Dip in egg, then in bread crumbs, shaping into rectangular shape with hands. Brown in small amount of margarine until tender; add seasonings, chicken broth and soup. Cook until blended; stir in white rice and wild rice. Pour into shallow casserole; top with chicken and cheese rolls. Bake at 400 degrees for 20 minutes. One chicken bouillon cube dissolved in 1 cup water may be substituted for chicken broth. Yield: 8 servings.

Barbara Fields
Delta Alpha No. 6273, Fairfax, Virginia

CHICKEN ROSE

1/4 c. rose wine
1/4 c. soy sauce
1/4 c. salad or olive oil
2 tbsp. water
1 clove of garlic, sliced
1 tsp. ginger
1/4 tsp. oregano
1 tbsp. brown sugar
3 chicken breasts, split

Combine wine, soy sauce, oil, water, garlic, ginger, oregano and brown sugar. Arrange chicken in baking dish; pour wine mixture over top. Cover. Bake at 375 degrees for 1 hour and 30 minutes or until chicken is tender. Serve over wild rice. Yield: 3 servings.

Ellie Disante
Alpha Iota No. 6813, Minot AFB, North Dakota

CORNISH HENS WITH WILD RICE DRESSING

1/2 c. wild rice
1 1/2 c. boiling water
1 4-oz. can sliced mushrooms
1 sm. onion, chopped
1/2 c. diced celery
1/2 c. butter
2 tbsp. chopped pimento
4 1-lb. Cornish hens
2 tsp. salt

Add rice to boiling water; cover. Cook for 40 minutes or until rice is tender. Cook mushrooms, onion and celery in 1/4 cup butter until tender but not brown. Add mushroom mixture and pimento to rice; toss lightly to mix. Rub cavities of hens with salt; fill lightly with dressing. Close cavity openings with skewers; fold wings in place. Place hens, breast side up, on rack in roasting pan. Brush with remaining butter. Bake at 350 degrees for 1 hour and 30 minutes, basting frequently with pan drippings. Yield: 4 servings.

Mrs. Darlene Harms Hicks
Midland, Texas

ROAST CHICKEN DELUXE

1 lemon, peeled
1 orange, peeled
7 whole cloves
1 4-lb. chicken
1 oz. brandy
Salt to taste
1 med. onion, peeled
2 tbsp. butter

Stud lemon and orange with cloves. Wash and dry chicken; rinse cavity with brandy. Sprinkle cavity with salt; insert lemon, orange and onion. Truss cavity opening with skewers. Rub outside of chicken with butter;

wrap in foil. Bake at 450 degrees for 1 hour and 30 minutes to 1 hour and 45 minutes. Unwrap foil during last few minutes to brown chicken. Yield: 4 servings.

Mrs. Harold L. Dix
Pueblo, Colorado

ASPARAGUS AMANDINE

1/4 c. slivered blanched almonds
1/4 c. butter
1/4 tsp. salt
2 tsp. lemon juice
2 c. cooked asparagus, drained

Saute almonds in butter until golden, stirring occasionally; remove from heat. Add salt and lemon juice, pour over hot asparagus. Let stand for several minutes before serving. Yield: 4 servings.

Katherine W. Rebbe
Wakefield, Nebraska

GREEN BEANS WITH MIXED HERB BUTTER

1 lb. green beans
Salt
1/4 c. butter or margarine
3/4 c. minced onion
1 clove of garlic, minced
1/4 c. minced celery
2 tbsp. sesame seed
1/4 tsp. rosemary
1/4 tsp. dried basil
1/4 c. snipped parsley

Wash and trim beans; cut in thin diagonal slices. Cook beans, covered, in 1/2 inch boiling salted water for 15 minutes or until tender; drain. Melt butter in saucepan; add onion, garlic, celery and sesame seed. Saute for 5 minutes. Add remaining ingredients and 3/4 teaspoon salt; cover. Simmer for 10 minutes; toss well with beans. Yield: 4 servings.

Jo Anna Littrel
Columbus Junction, Iowa

EGGPLANT PARMESAN

1 lge. eggplant
3 eggs, beaten
1 c. bread crumbs
1/2 c. olive oil
1/2 c. grated Parmesan cheese
2 tsp. oregano
1/2 lb. mozzarella cheese, shredded
3 c. tomato sauce

Preheat oven to 350 degrees. Pare eggplant; cut into 1/2 or 1/4-inch slices. Dip each slice into eggs, then into crumbs. Saute on both sides in hot oil until golden brown. Arrange layer of eggplant in 2-quart casserole; sprinkle with part of the Parmesan cheese, oregano and mozzarella cheese. Cover well with tomato sauce. Repeat layers until eggplant is used; top last layer of tomato sauce with mozzarella cheese. Bake until heated through. Yield: 10 servings.

Mrs. Lois Jean Licciardello
Alpha Epsilon No. 2276, Yardley, Pennsylvania

SWEET POTATO AND APPLE CASSEROLE

6 boiled sweet potatoes
1/2 c. brown sugar
1 tsp. cinnamon
1 tsp. salt
1/4 c. butter
4 apples, pared and sliced
1/2 c. water

Remove potato skins; cut potatoes in slices. Mix brown sugar, cinnamon and salt. Arrange layer of potatoes in buttered casserole; sprinkle with brown sugar mixture and dot with butter. Add layer of apples; sprinkle with brown sugar mixture and dot with butter. Repeat layers, ending with potatoes; pour water over top. Cover casserole. Bake at 400 degrees for 30 minutes or until apples are tender. Uncover; bake until browned. Yield: 6 servings.

Betty Boney
Alpha Omega No. 1132, Gladstone, Missouri

ARTICHOKES WITH CURRIED EGGS

6 med. artichokes
3 1/2 tsp. salt
2 tbsp. finely chopped shallots
1/4 c. butter or margarine
1/4 c. flour
4 tsp. curry powder
1 qt. milk
12 hard-cooked eggs
1/4 tsp. pepper
1/2 tsp. grated lemon peel

Wash artichokes; cut off stems at base. Remove small bottom leaves. Trim tips of leaves; cut off about 1 inch from artichoke top. Stand artichokes upright in deep saucepan large enough to hold snugly. Add 1 1/2 teaspoons salt and 2 to 3 inches boiling water. Cover. Boil gently for 35 to 45 minutes or until base can be pierced easily with fork. Remove artichokes; turn upside down to drain. Spread leaves gently and remove choke from center with spoon. Saute shallots in butter in saucepan; stir in flour and curry powder quickly. Stir in milk gradually; cook, stirring constantly, until sauce boils for 1 minute. Quarter eggs. Add eggs, pepper, lemon peel and remaining salt. Heat thoroughly. Spoon into artichokes; serve immediately. Yield: 6 servings.

EGGS IN GREEN AND WHITE

3 boxes frozen chopped spinach
1/3 lb. ham, chopped
1 sm. onion, chopped
1/4 c. butter
2 lb. potatoes, cooked
1 bouillon cube
7 oz. heavy cream
6 eggs
Salt to taste
1/4 c. grated Parmesan cheese

Cook spinach according to package directions; drain. Saute ham and onion in butter. Mash potatoes with bouillon cube and cream; add ham mixture and spinach. Place in greased 10 x 10-inch pan; make 6 wells in top. Break one egg in each well; sprinkle with salt. Top with cheese. Bake at 350 degrees for 20 minutes. Yield: 6 servings.

Mrs. Giovanina Otten
Epsilon, Mayaguez, Puerto Rico

KING CRAB AND MUSHROOM CASSEROLE

1 can cream of chicken soup
1 can cream of mushroom soup
1 6-oz. can button mushrooms
1/4 tsp. dried basil
1/4 tsp. grated lemon peel
2 tbsp. chopped parsley
2 tbsp. lemon juice
1/2 tsp. paprika
1/2 tsp. curry powder
1/2 tsp. dry mustard
3 c. King crab meat
Buttered crumbs

Combine all ingredients except crab meat and crumbs in saucepan; heat to boiling point. Remove from heat; stir in crab meat. Pour into 1 1/2-quart casserole; top with crumbs. Bake at 350 degrees for 20 minutes or until bubbling and heated through. Yield: 8 servings.

Rosella Smith
Preceptor Delta XP 371, Springfield, Virginia

SEAFOOD CASSEROLE

2 sticks butter
1 1/2 c. long grain rice
1/2 c. raisins
3 c. chicken broth
2 1/2 tsp. salt
3/8 tsp. pepper
1 1/2 c. sliced mushrooms
2 tsp. curry powder
1/2 tsp. ginger
2 6-oz. cans crab, drained
1 5-oz. can lobster, drained
1/4 c. sherry
1/4 c. flour
1/4 tsp. dry mustard
3 c. light cream
1 c. grated Swiss cheese

Heat 1/4 cup butter in large skillet. Add rice; cook gently until rice is golden. Add raisins and chicken broth; bring to a boil. Reduce heat; cover. Simmer for 20 minutes or until rice is tender and liquid is absorbed. Add 1 1/2 teaspoons salt and 1/4 teaspoon pepper; stir together lightly with fork. Spread rice mixture in buttered 13 x 9 1/2 x 2-inch baking dish. Melt 6 tablespoons butter in large skillet. Add mushrooms, curry powder and ginger; cook gently for 3 minutes, stirring. Remove from heat. Add crab, lobster, 1/2 teaspoon salt and sherry; blend lightly. Spoon over rice. Melt remaining butter in saucepan. Sprinkle in flour, remaining salt, remaining pepper and mustard; cook until mixture bubbles up. Remove from heat; add cream all at once, blending well. Return to heat; cook, stirring, until thickened and smooth. Pour mixture evenly over seafood. Sprinkle with cheese. Bake in 400-degree oven for 25 minutes or until heated through. Yield: 6 to 8 servings.

Teresa White
Phi Zeta P1834
Victoria, British Columbia, Canada

MACARONI SURPRISE CASSEROLE CASSEROLE

1 1-lb. box elbow macaroni
Salt to taste
Butter or margarine
4 slices American cheese
1/2 can carrots
1/2 can small green peas
1/8 tsp. pepper
2 strips crisp bacon
Sliced olives

Cook macaroni in large amount of salted water until tender; drain well and stir in 2 tablespoons butter. Chop 2 slices cheese; stir into macaroni until melted. Combine carrots, peas, salt and pepper in saucepan; heat through. Drain well; stir in 1 teaspoon butter. Add carrot mixture to macaroni; mix lightly. Spoon into baking dish. Cut remaining cheese in strips; arrange over macaroni mixture. Garnish with bacon and olives. Bake at 375 degrees until cheese is melted. Yield: 6 servings.

Mrs. Rae Pittman
Gamma Tau No. 5901, Smithfield, Virginia

SHRIMP FRICASSEE

2 5-oz. cans shrimp
1 tbsp. lemon juice
4 tbsp. butter
1/2 c. chopped celery
2 tbsp. chopped onion
2 tbsp. flour
1/8 tsp. pepper
2 c. evaporated milk
1 can cream of mushroom soup
2 c. cooked rice
1/4 c. toasted slivered almonds
Potato chips or buttered crumbs

Rinse shrimp in cold water; drain. Sprinkle with lemon juice. Melt butter in top of double boiler over direct heat. Add celery and onion; cook until tender. Blend in flour and pepper; stir in milk and soup. Cook over boiling water, stirring constantly, until thick. Fold in rice, almonds and shrimp. Pour into greased 3-quart casserole or 8 individual casseroles. Cover with potato chips. Bake at 350 degrees for 30 to 40 minutes. Yield: 8 servings.

Lilian Jean Dawson
Beta Beta No. 6706
Campbell River, British Columbia, Canada

PERFECT WHITE BREAD

1 pkg. yeast
1/2 c. warm water
1 3/4 c. scalded milk
2 tbsp. sugar
2 tsp. salt
2 tbsp. cooking oil
5 to 6 c. flour

Dissolve yeast in warm water. Combine milk, sugar, salt and oil; cool to lukewarm. Stir in yeast, mixing well. Add flour gradually; knead. Cover; let rise till doubled in bulk. Punch dough down; let rise again. Shape in 2 loaves; place in greased loaf pans. Let rise till doubled in bulk. Bake for 25 to 30 minutes at 350 degrees. Yield: 2 loaves.

Lois Lanz
Beta Kappa No. 2989, Lake Worth, Florida

HOME-BAKED BREAD

1 pkg. dry yeast
2 c. lukewarm water
2 tbsp. cooking oil
1/2 c. molasses
6 c. flour
1 c. rye flour
1 1/2 tsp. salt
1 tsp. anise seed
1 tsp. light fennel seed
Margarine

Stir yeast into water in large mixing bowl; let stand for 5 minutes. Stir in oil and molasses. Beat in 1 cup white flour; let stand until bubbly. Add remaining flour, rye flour, salt, anise seed and fennel seed. Knead dough for 10 minutes in bowl. Shape dough into a ball; grease dough. Let rise until doubled in bulk. Punch dough down; knead for about 1 minute until firm. Flour lightly; divide into 3 parts. Flour sticky edges of each loaf; flatten and beat air pockets with fists. Start rolling from one edge, stretching dough and folding ends in to make roll tight. Pinch flap to roll to keep air out. Place in greased loaf pans; cover. Let rise until doubled. Bake for 45 minutes at 375 degrees. Remove from pans immediately; turn onto racks. Rub with margarine before cooling. Bread may be covered while cooling for softer crust.

Sharon Boothman
Alpha Gamma Upsilon No. 7148, DeSota, Texas

BRAN ICEBOX ROLLS

2 cakes yeast
1 c. lukewarm water
1 c. whole bran cereal
2/3 c. sugar
1 c. lard
1 tsp. salt
1 c. boiling water
2 eggs, beaten
7 to 8 c. flour

Dissolve yeast in lukewarm water. Place cereal, sugar, lard and salt in bowl; stir in boiling water. Cool; add yeast and eggs. Beat in enough flour, one cup at a time, to make stiff batter; mix well. Cover; refrigerate until cool. Roll out on floured board; cut into rolls. Place in well-greased pan; let rise for 1 hour or until light. Bake at 400 degrees for about 15 minutes. Batter keeps well in refrigerator.

Virginia L. Harris
Xi Beta Rho X2114, Columbia, Missouri

EASY HOT CROSS BUNS

1 pkg. hot roll mix
2 tbsp. butter, melted
2 tbsp. raisins
2 tbsp. chopped candied fruits
1/3 c. sugar
1 tsp. cinnamon
Light cream
2 c. confectioners' sugar
1 tsp. vanilla
Dash of salt

Prepare roll mix according to package directions, adding butter, raisins, fruits, sugar and cinnamon. Mix well; cover with damp cloth. Let rise in warm place for 1 hour or until doubled in bulk. Turn onto lightly floured board; knead until smooth. Shape in 12 buns; place on lightly greased cookie sheet. Cover; let rise for 45 minutes. Make shallow cross in bun tops with knife or scissors. Bake at 375 degrees for 15 minutes or until done. Cool slightly. Beat enough cream into confectioners' sugar to make of spreading consistency; stir in vanilla and salt. Ice buns and serve. Yield: 1 dozen buns.

Barbara P. Thomas
Alpha No. 6040, Naha, Okinawa

BUTTER-RICH COFFEE CAKE

3 c. sifted all-purpose flour
4 tsp. baking powder
1/2 tsp. salt
2 tsp. grated lemon rind
3/4 c. butter
1 c. sugar
1 tsp. vanilla
3 eggs
1/2 c. milk
1/2 c. apricot preserves
1 c. flaked coconut
3/4 c. chopped nuts
1 1/2 c. sifted confectioners' sugar

Sift flour, baking powder and salt together. Stir in lemon rind; set aside. Cream butter; add sugar gradually, beating well. Add vanilla and eggs, one at a time, beating well after each addition. Combine milk and 1/4 cup apricot preserves; add alternately with dry ingredients to creamed mixture, blending well after each addition. Spread 1/3 of the batter over bottom of buttered and floured 10-inch tube pan. Reserve 1/3 cup coconut for topping. Spoon 1/2 of the remaining coconut and nuts over batter not quite to edge of pan. Top with half the remaining batter. Spoon remaining coconut and nuts over batter; cover with remaining batter. Bake at 350 degrees for 40 to 45 minutes. Cool in pan for 10 minutes; remove from pan. Heat remaining preserves and 1 tablespoon water in small saucepan. Remove from heat; stir in confectioners' sugar. Spread over top of slightly warm cake allowing glaze to drip down sides. Sprinkle reserved coconut over top.

CINNAMON ROLLS

1/2 c. shortening
2 c. scalded milk
2 eggs, beaten
1 tsp. salt
Sugar
1 c. mashed potatoes
2 cakes yeast
1/4 c. lukewarm water
7 c. flour
1 c. raisins
1 c. chopped nuts
Butter
Cinnamon

Dissolve shortening in hot milk; cool. Stir in eggs, salt, 1 cup sugar and potatoes. Dissolve yeast in lukewarm water; add to potato mixture. Stir in flour, raisins and nuts; mix thoroughly. Let rise until doubled in bulk. Roll out 1/2-inch thick; spread with soft butter. Sprinkle with sugar and cinnamon. Roll and cut; place in well-greased baking pan. Let rise until light. Bake at 350 degrees until golden. Yield: 5 dozen rolls.

Sandra Askias
Chi No. 3437, Yerington, Nevada

EASTER LAMB CAKE

1/2 c. shortening
1 1/2 c. sugar
3 eggs, separated
2 1/2 c. flour
1/2 tsp. salt
4 tsp. baking powder
1 tsp. vanilla
1 c. milk
Boiled icing
Raisins

Cream shortening, adding sugar gradually. Beat in egg yolks. Sift flour, salt and baking powder together. Stir vanilla into milk. Add flour mixture to creamed mixture alternately with milk mixture. Fold in stiffly beaten egg whites. Spread batter in well-greased lamb mold; lay toothpicks in each ear on top of batter. Arrange skewer in neck for reinforcement; close mold. Bake at 350 degrees for 25 minutes. Turn mold; bake for 20 minutes longer. Cool cake; remove from mold. Spread cake with frosting. Arrange raisins for lamb's eyes; tie ribbon around neck. Serve on platter of green-tinted coconut, if desired. Yield: 8 servings.

Mrs. Roy W. Liebau
Pittsburgh, Pennsylvania

PINEAPPLE-COCONUT CAKE

1 1/2 c. flour
1 tsp. soda
1 tsp. salt
1/2 c. butter
1 c. sugar
1 egg
1 tsp. vanilla
1 c. crushed pineapple
1/2 c. brown sugar
1/2 c. coconut

Sift flour, soda and salt together. Cream butter, sugar, egg and vanilla. Add creamed mixture to dry mixture; fold in pineapple. Pour batter into greased and floured 9-inch square pan. Combine brown sugar and coconut; sprinkle over batter. Bake at 375 degrees for 45 minutes or until done. Serve with whipped cream or ice cream. Yield: 6 servings.

Sharon Knack
Delta Lambda No. 2394, Battle Creek, Michigan

PRALINE ICE CREAM CAKE

1/2 c. butter
1 pt. vanilla ice cream, softened
2 eggs
1 1/2 c. flour
2/3 c. sugar
1 tbsp. baking powder
1/2 tsp. salt
1 c. graham cracker crumbs
1/2 c. sour cream
1 c. caramel ice cream topping
1/2 c. chopped pecans

Melt butter in 3-quart saucepan; remove from heat. Add ice cream, eggs, flour, sugar, baking powder, salt and graham cracker crumbs; mix until smooth. Pour into greased 13 x 9-inch pan. Bake at 350 degrees for 30 to 35 minutes. Combine sour cream and ice cream topping; pour over warm cake. Top with pecans. Cool; cut into squares. May be served with ice cream or sweetened whipped cream.

Thelma D. Nicholson
Xi Epsilon Pi No. 1634, Sacramento, California

STRAWBERRY CAKE

1 10-oz. package frozen strawberries
1 pkg. white cake mix
1 3-oz. box strawberry gelatin
3 tbsp. flour
1/2 c. water
3/4 c. salad oil
4 eggs
2 c. powdered sugar
1/4 c. melted butter

Thaw strawberries. Blend cake mix, gelatin and flour in mixing bowl; beat in water, oil and eggs. Stir in 3/4 of the strawberries; spread batter in greased and floured 13 x 9-inch pan or layer pans. Bake at 375 degrees for 30 to 35 minutes. Cool cake. Combine remaining ingredients; mix well. Ice cake.

Ruth T. Belding
Preceptor Gamma XP111, Boulder City, Nevada

PETITE POCKETBOOKS

1 c. soft margarine
1/2 lb. cream cheese
1/4 tsp. salt
3 tbsp. sugar
2 c. sifted flour
Blackberry, raspberry or strawberry jam
Powdered sugar

Cream margarine, cream cheese, salt and sugar together until blended. Add flour gradually, working in last part with fingertips. Chill dough for several hours or overnight. Divide dough into 3 parts. Roll each part on floured board to 1/8-inch thick rectangle. Cut into 3-inch squares. Place 1/2 teaspoon jam in center of each square; fold 1 corner over jam 2/3 of the way to opposite corner. Fold 2 side corners into center to just overlap; press together. Fold fourth corner down, enclosing jam. Place on greased cookie sheet. Bake in 350-degree oven for 16 to 18 minutes. Sprinkle with powdered sugar. Yield: 4 1/2 dozen pocketbooks.

Virginia Adent
Omicron Zeta, Bourbonnais, Illinois

ICE CREAM PARFAIT MOLD

2 1-lb. packages frozen strawberries
Milk
2 3-oz. packages strawberry gelatin
2 pt. vanilla ice cream
1 c. whipping cream, whipped
Green coconut (opt.)

Defrost strawberries; drain and reserve syrup. Add enough milk to reserved syrup to make 1 3/4 cups liquid; bring to a boil. Add gelatin; stir until dissolved. Cut each pint of ice cream into 8 pieces; add to gelatin mixture. Stir until ice cream is melted and blended. Chill until partially set; fold in strawberries. Pour into oiled melon mold. Chill until firm. Unmold; decorate Easter-egg fashion with whipped cream and green coconut. Cut parfait into slices to serve. Yield: 8-10 servings.

BANANA CREAM PIE

3 tbsp. flour
1 tbsp. cornstarch
1/2 c. sugar
1/4 tsp. salt
1 c. milk
1 c. cream
2 egg yolks, beaten
1 tsp. vanilla
1 baked 8 or 9-in. pie shell
Sliced bananas

Mix dry ingredients in saucepan. Stir milk into cream; stir in egg yolks. Add to dry ingredients. Cook until thick; add vanilla. Cool. Pour into pie shell. Add bananas. Coconut may be substituted for bananas. Add 1/4 cup coconut to filling; sprinkle 1/2 cup coconut on top. Yield: 5 servings.

Geraldine Kauffman
Xi Eta Lambda X-3333, Lena, Illinois

RASPBERRY VELVET PIE

1 10-oz. package frozen raspberries
1 pkg. raspberry gelatin
1 c. boiling water
1/4 lb. marshmallows
1 c. heavy cream, whipped
Vanilla wafers

Thaw and drain raspberries, reserving syrup; add water to syrup to equal 1 cup liquid. Dissolve gelatin in boiling water; stir in marshmallows until partially melted. Add raspberry liquid. Chill until partially congealed. Beat until fluffy; fold in raspberries and whipped cream. Line 9-inch pie plate with vanilla wafers; fill with raspberry mixture. Chill until set. Serve with additional whipped cream. Yield: 6 servings.

Mrs. Audrey L. Maclean
Xi Alpha X487
Moncton, New Brunswick, Canada

LEMON CHARLOTTE RUSSE

1 env. unflavored gelatin
1/2 c. fresh lemon juice
4 eggs, separated
1 1/2 c. sugar
1/8 tsp. salt
3 tbsp. butter
1 1/2 tsp. grated lemon peel
1 tsp. vanilla
Ladyfingers
Whipped cream

Soften gelatin in lemon juice. Beat egg yolks, 1 cup sugar and salt together until thick. Combine egg yolk mixture, gelatin mixture and butter in top of double boiler. Cook over hot, not boiling, water stirring constantly with wooden spoon for 10 minutes or until thickened. Stir in lemon peel and vanilla. Cool until mixture begins to thicken. Line bottom and sides of 9-inch springform pan with ladyfingers. Beat egg whites until soft peaks form. Add remaining sugar gradually, beating until stiff. Fold egg whites and 1 cup whipped cream into lemon mixture. Turn into prepared pan. Refrigerate until firm; unmold onto serving platter. Garnish with whipped cream. Yield: 10 servings.

Ruth Wade
Xi Alpha Upsilon, Jacksonville, Illinois

PEACH PARFAIT PIE

3 1/2 c. sliced fresh peaches
Sugar to taste
1 pkg. lemon gelatin
1 pt. vanilla ice cream
1 9-in. baked pastry shell
1/2 c. heavy cream, whipped

Place peaches in bowl; stir in sugar. Let stand for 15 minutes. Drain peaches, reserving syrup. Add water to syrup to equal 1 cup liquid. Heat liquid to a boil; stir in gelatin until dissolved. Chop ice cream; stir ice cream and 1/2 cup cold water into gelatin mixture. Chill until partially congealed; fold in peaches. Spoon into pastry shell; chill until firm. Garnish with whipped cream and additional peaches. Yield: 6-8 servings.

Mrs. Lila Foster
Xi Kappa X-893, East Brunswick, New Jersey

BANANA CRUSH PUNCH

1 c. sugar
5 med. ripe bananas
1 6-oz. can frozen orange juice
1 6-oz. can frozen pineapple juice
Juice of 2 lemons
2 lge. bottles sparkling water

Mix sugar and 4 cups water; bring to a boil. Boil for 3 minutes, stirring to prevent scorching. Cool. Whip bananas in blender until smooth; pour into large bowl. Add sugar mixture, orange juice, pineapple juice, lemon juice and 4 juice cans water. Pour into plastic container; freeze. Place frozen block in punch bowl 30 minutes before serving. Pour sparkling water over top. Stir to break frozen block into ice cube-sized pieces. Yield: 20 servings.

Mary Ruth Cole
Gamma Delta No. 6001, McGuire AFB, New Jersey

EGG-HUNT FRUIT PUNCH

1 6-oz. can frozen orange juice
2 6-oz. cans frozen limeade
1 6-oz. can frozen lemonade
1 46-oz. can pineapple juice
1 pt. cranberry juice cocktail
2 to 4 c. cold water
2 qt. ginger ale
1 qt. club soda, chilled

Mix first 6 ingredients; add ginger ale and club soda just before serving. Float ice ring containing cherries and orange slices on top. Yield: 40 servings.

June Mason
Psi Psi No. 5751, Canoga Park, California

MIXED FRUIT PUNCH

1 pkg. cherry powdered drink mix
Sugar to taste
2 qt. water
1 No. 3 can mixed fruit punch
1 No. 3 can pineapple juice
1 qt. ginger ale, chilled

Dissolve drink mix and sugar in water; stir in fruit punch and pineapple juice. Chill. Add ginger ale just before serving. Yield: 35-40 servings.

Mrs. R. P. Hughes, Jr.
Washington, D. C.

SPRING PUNCH

2 cans frozen mixed fruit punch
2 cans frozen pineapple juice
1 can frozen lemonade
3 qt. dry ginger ale

Place frozen punch, pineapple juice and lemonade in punch bowl. Add ginger ale; stir well. Float ice ring in punch bowl. Yield: 24 servings.

Sue Croll
Xi Beta Zeta X-2061, Dearborn Heights, Michigan

PEACHY CHAMPAGNE PUNCH

1 pkg. frozen peaches
1 bottle peach brandy
4 bottles champagne
4 qt. club soda
Ice cubes
Maraschino cherries, chopped

Place frozen peaches in large punch bowl. Pour in brandy, champagne and soda water; mix lightly. Add ice cubes and cherries. Yield: 50 servings.

Mrs. Ernest D. Ficco
Norfolk, Virginia

PINK LEMONADE PUNCH

3 cans pink lemonade
1/2 c. sugar
1/2 c. sliced frozen strawberries
1 qt. ginger ale

Reconstitute lemonade according to label directions; stir in sugar. Pour into punch bowl; stir in strawberries. Chill ginger ale; add to punch just before serving.

Verna Lee Sheffler
Xi Zeta Beta No. 2805, Tampico, Illinois

Memorial Day was originally created to honor Americans who died in the Civil War. Now, more than one hundred years after Appomatox, the Civil War belongs to our very distant past, and other wars have given rise to other memorial days. Today, for most of us, Memorial Day marks the opening of the summer holiday and vacation season, when Americans everywhere take to the road, searching for their favorite outdoor places.

Some of us open summer cabins. Others head for the beach and — especially in the Northern states — the first swim of the season. Recent national legislation making Memorial Day a permanent three-day weekend has added impetus to the restless American inpulse to be on the move on this holiday. Contributing to the movement of families is the rediscovery of a thrifty but fun-filled activity: camping.

The glorious sunshine and warm weather so characteristic of Memorial Day weekend

Memorial Day

makes this a perfect time for camping. Three whole days of outdoor living . . . simple activities like hunting, fishing, and hiking . . . enjoying meals cooked over an open campfire. Meal planning is a very important part of camping out. Meals have to be simple, tasty and nourishing. Here's a menu for four that meets all the requirements . . . and it's especially scrumptious!

Start with Panfried Fish — freshly caught by your proud fishermen in an icy cold stream or lake near your campsite. With this dish, Hush Puppies — traditional camp fare. In fact, their name is supposed to go back to early pioneer times when a man and his dog would camp together for weeks at a time. When the pioneer made these delicious cornmeal and onion tidbits, he would throw

them to his dog with the admonition to "hush, puppy." Add the hearty he-man flavors of Bundled Potatoes and an Asparagus and Cheese Casserole, and you'll have a meal that's sure to fill up even the hungriest campers. Caramelized Peaches, flavorful and crunchy, make the perfect ending for this camping-out meal.

Nothing ever tastes quite as good as freshly-caught fish cooked over an open campfire. If you line your skillet or frying pan with aluminum foil before you begin, food you cook later will not pick up a "fishy" taste from the pan. To prepare Panfried Fish, combine 1 beaten egg, 1 tablespoon milk, 1 teaspoon salt, and pepper to taste. In another bowl, combine bread or cracker crumbs with about 1/2 cup flour. Clean, wash, and dry about two pounds of fresh fish. Dip each piece into the egg mixture; then roll it in the flour and cracker mixture. Fry in hot fat over moderate heat until brown on both sides. Then cook for 8 to 12 minutes. Drain on absorbent paper and serve.

To prepare Hush Puppies, mix 1 3/4 cups cornmeal, 4 tablespoons flour, 1 1/2 teaspoons salt, 3 teaspoons baking powder, and 1/4 teaspoon pepper. Add 1 3/4 cups milk and 2 slightly beaten eggs. Chop one large onion and add to mixture. (You may need to add slightly more water or

Take Your Kitchen to the Great Outdoors

milk to get this mixture to the proper consistency for frying.) Drop spoonfuls of batter into hot fat. Fry until lightly browned on one side. Turn and brown on other side. Drain on absorbent paper and serve.

Bundled Potatoes are a sharply-flavored and delicious accompaniment to this meal. Cut six medium potatoes into strips. Place strips on a large piece of doubled aluminum foil. Top with one large onion, sliced. Dot with 3/4 stick butter. Sprinkle salt and pepper to taste. If desired, sprinkle lightly with caraway seeds. Wrap loosely to allow plenty of room for air to expand. Seal all edges tightly. Grill for 20 minutes about five inches from coals. Turn and grill for another 20 minutes. If you turn foil-wrapped food with barbecue tongs, there will be little danger of puncturing the cooking bag and losing the juices which make this dish the delicious treat that it is.

Asparagus and Cheese Casserole is an eye-pleasing taste treat — and it's easy to prepare. Just drain one can asparagus and place spears on a double sheet of aluminum foil. Cut American or mozzarella cheese into thin strips. Place on foil, well-mixed among the asparagus spears. Dot with butter and season with salt and pepper to taste. Fold foil over, leaving a pocket for air. Seal edges tightly. Place on grill away from the direct center of the heat. Heat through until cheese is melted.

For a delicious but easy-to-fix finale to this outdoor meal, try Caramelized Peaches. To prepare, combine 1/2 cup crushed corn flakes, 1/2 cup chopped pecans, 2 tablespoons brown sugar, and 2 tablespoons melted margarine. Fill the centers of peach halves with this mixture. Place peach halves on center of a piece of foil. Wrap tightly and grill for 10 to 15 minutes. Then serve in their own foil dishes and listen to the praises from your appreciative family.

Yes, there's no doubt about it. Camp cooking is a whole new world, one full of delicious, easy-to-prepare foods. And, like any other new world, camp cooking has its secrets and shortcuts. It's best to stick to fundamentals in your equipment. All you really need is a nesting set of three saucepans (the lid of the nest can be used as a frying pan), a heavy skillet, a coffeepot, and perhaps a Dutch oven. Add an aluminum plate and cup for each camper, and tableware. This equipment, a measuring cup and spoons, and perhaps a storage box that can be converted into a kitchen cabinet once you arrive at your campsite are all you'll need to transform a wilderness into a kitchen which produces delicious meals for that hungrier-than-usual family of yours.

Add to your list two plastic washpans. One can be used to wash dishes, the other to rinse them. But it's easy to cut way down on this unwelcome chore and free yourself for fun with your family. Try lining the aluminum plates with paper ones. After you eat, just put the dirty paper plate in the campfire and wipe the aluminum plate with a damp cloth. You may want to use paper cups instead of the aluminum ones. Just be sure not to take the foam-plastic ones. These cups burn down into a gooey mass of plastic which may be harmful to plant and animal life in the forest.

When you're planning your meals, be sure to take advantage of all the wonderful prepared foods. With just water you can whip up delicious rice dishes, fabulous potatoes, even delectable sauces. Soups, main dishes . . . everything now is prepared. And if you do choose a canned vegetable, here's a cooking shortcut. Remove the label, open the can almost all the way, set it on your grill, and presto! You've got hot vegetables without a dirty saucepan.

As you and your family explore our great country by camping, you are sure to discover many more shortcuts which will reduce your work to almost nothing, leaving you free to enjoy the great outdoors . . . beginning on this Memorial Day camping weekend!

HOT POTATO SALAD

6 slices bacon, finely cut
6 med. potatoes
1 1/2 tsp. salt
1/8 tsp. pepper
1/2 tsp. celery seed
1 tbsp. flour
2 tbsp. chopped onion
1/4 c. vinegar
1/4 c. water
2 tbsp. parsley
Several sliced radishes

Saute bacon in skillet until crisp; remove from skillet. Reserve 1/4 cup bacon drippings. Peel potatoes and dice. Place potatoes in center of 24 x 18-inch rectangle of heavy duty foil. Combine salt, pepper, celery seed, sugar, flour and onion; sprinkle over potatoes. Pour vinegar, water and reserved bacon drippings over potatoes; sprinkle bacon over top. Bring sides of foil together; seal securely by folding over twice. Fold ends to seal. Grill for 20 minutes. Turn package over; grill for about 20 minutes longer. Bake at 425 degrees for 1 hour if desired. Garnish with parsley and radishes to serve. Yield: 6 servings.

Mrs. Paul Pfahler
Eta Nu, Boyne City, Michigan

MARINATED BEAN SALAD

1/2 green pepper
1 can kidney beans
1 can whole green beans
1 can yellow wax beans
1 sm. onion, cut in rings
1/2 c. vinegar
1/4 c. salad oil
2/3 c. sugar
1 tsp. salt
1/4 tsp. pepper
1/4 tsp. garlic salt

Cut green pepper in strips. Drain beans. Mix all ingredients together; refrigerate overnight.

Jeanne C. Primm
Lambda Gamma No. 5114, Evanston, Illinois

CARROT AND RAISIN SALAD

1/2 c. raisins
1/2 c. mayonnaise
1 tbsp. orange juice
1 tsp. lemon juice
1 tsp. grated orange peel
3 c. grated carrots

Cover raisins with warm water; soak until plump. Drain. Mix mayonnaise with raisins, juices and orange peel. Add to carrots; toss lightly with fork. Serve on salad greens. Yield: 6 servings.

Mrs. John W. Bogan
Milden Hall, England

FAMILY COLESLAW

1 c. vinegar
1 c. sugar
1/2 c. water
1 tsp. prepared mustard
1 qt. shredded cabbage
1/2 c. chopped green pepper
1/2 c. grated carrot
1 tbsp. salt
1 c. chopped celery

Combine vinegar, sugar, water and mustard in saucepan; bring to a boil. Cool. Combine cabbage, green pepper, carrot and salt in large bowl; cover with ice water. Soak until vegetables are chilled; drain. Add celery to cabbage mixture. Cover with cooled dressing; refrigerate. May be stored in refrigerator for several days.

Lenora Humphries
Zeta Alpha No. 2540, Rock Island, Illinois

CAMPER'S SHISH KABOBS

1 4-lb. round steak
Salt and pepper to taste
Meat tenderizer
1/4 c. cooking oil
1 8-oz. bottle Italian dressing
3 lge. green peppers
3 lge. tomatoes

1 lge. Bermuda onion
3 1-lb. cans sm. white potatoes

Cut steak into 1-inch cubes. Sprinkle with salt, pepper and meat tenderizer. Let set for 30 minutes. Place oil in large frypan; add steak cubes. Brown well on all sides over medium heat. Add water to cover steak; cover with lid or foil. Cook for 1 hour. Remove from heat; let cool until just warm. Place in large container with tight lid. Add dressing; place lid on container and refrigerate. Wash peppers and tomatoes; cut into 1-inch pieces. Place in container; cover with tight lid. Chill peppers and tomatoes. Prepare fire 45 minutes before meal. Cut onion into 2-inch pieces; drain potatoes. Drain steak; reserve marinade. Thread 8 shish kabob skewers, alternately with steak cubes, pepper, tomato and potatoes. Cook over fire until heated through, basting with reserved steak marinade. Fruit pieces may be skewered and heated for dessert. Yield: 8 servings.

Jeanne Kamholtz
Zeta Psi, Salamanca, New York

BARBECUED SHORT RIBS OF BEEF

3 lb. short ribs
1 tsp. monosodium glutamate
1 bay leaf
1/4 tsp. pepper
1/2 tsp. salt
1/2 c. vinegar

Cut ribs in serving pieces. Combine ribs, monosodium glutamate, bay leaf, pepper, salt and vinegar in large kettle; cover ribs with water. Bring to a boil. Reduce heat; simmer for 1 hour or until ribs are almost tender. Drain.

Basting Sauce

1/4 c. salad oil
2 tbsp. vinegar
2 tbsp. brown sugar
1 env. onion soup mix
1/4 tsp. hot sauce

Combine all ingredients with 1/3 cup water in small saucepan; bring to a boil, stirring. Remove short rib meat from bones; thread meat chunks on skewers. Place foil pan under meat to catch drippings. Grill 5 inches from prepared coals for 10 minutes on each side. Baste frequently with sauce. Cook to desired doneness. Yield: 4-6 servings.

Mrs. Janet Baker
Zeta Eta No. 6221, Hooker, Oklahoma

BROILED HONEY-SWEET RIBLETS

5 to 5 1/2 lb. lamb riblets
2 tsp. salt
1 c. chili sauce
1/2 c. chopped onion
1/4 c. orange juice
2 tbsp. honey
1 tsp. prepared horseradish

Place riblets in large Dutch oven or kettle; sprinkle with salt. Add water to cover. Simmer, covered, for 1 hour; drain. Mix remaining ingredients together. Broil riblets 4 to 5 inches from heat for 8 to 10 minutes; brush with half the chili mixture. Turn riblets; brush with remaining sauce. Broil for 5 to 8 minutes longer or until browned.

PATRIOTIC BEEFBURGERS

3/4 c. chopped onion
1 tbsp. cooking oil
1/2 10-oz. package frozen chopped spinach
1 egg
1 3/4 tsp. salt
1/8 tsp. pepper
1/2 tsp. oregano
1 1/2 lb. ground beef chuck
6 buttered toasted French rolls

Cook onion slowly in oil until transparent but not browned. Add spinach; heat until thawed and liquid evaporates. Cool. Beat egg with salt, pepper and oregano. Mix in beef and spinach mixture with fork. Shape into 6 patties about 4 inches in diameter. Grill over hot coals or broil to desired degree of doneness, turning once. Serve on toasted rolls. Yield: 6 servings.

ALUMINUM FOIL STEW

15 potatoes
5 carrots
3 onions
1 1/2 lb. hamburger
Salt and pepper to taste

Peel potatoes, carrots and onions; slice into large pan. Cover with water. Grease squares of aluminum foil. Shape hamburger into patties; place one on each square of foil. Place vegetables on top of hamburger; season with salt and pepper. Fold aluminum foil to seal. Place on prepared outdoor fire. Cook for 30 minutes; turn foil package over. Cook until hamburger and vegetables are tender.

Mrs. Jim Houseworth
Delta No. 2603, Carrollton, Missouri

COFFEE CAN CASSEROLE

1 1/2 lb. ground beef
2 med. onions, sliced
3 med. potatoes, sliced thin
4 carrots, sliced thin
Butter
Salt to taste
Pepper to taste

Cover bottom of large coffee can with ground beef; place layer of onions on ground beef. Place layer of potatoes over onion layer. Add layer of carrots. Repeat until all vegetables are used; dot top with butter. Season with salt and pepper; cover. Place on rack over hot coals; cook until ground beef and vegetables are tender. Yield: 6-8 servings.

Sue B. Odell
Beta Alpha No. 2791, Gainesville, Georgia

CAMPFIRE CHICKEN WITH RAISIN DUMPLINGS

2 2 1/2-lb. broiler-fryers
1/2 c. flour
2 tsp. salt
1/8 tsp. pepper
Cooking oil
1 onion, sliced
1 stalk celery, sliced
2 carrots, sliced
1 c. seedless raisins
2 c. biscuit mix
3/4 c. milk

Cut fryers in serving pieces. Combine flour, salt and pepper in paper bag. Add chicken, 1 piece at a time; shake until well coated. Shake off excess flour; place on flat surface without overlapping until ready to cook. Heat 1/4 cup oil in Dutch oven. Add chicken, a few pieces at a time; cook over high heat until well browned on all sides. Add oil if needed. Return all pieces of browned chicken to Dutch oven. Add onion, celery, carrots and 2 cups water. Cover; simmer gently for 30 to 45 minutes or until largest pieces of chicken are tender. Mix raisins and biscuit mix together. Add milk; stir with fork until well mixed. Drop by spoonfuls onto hot chicken. Cook, uncovered, over low heat for 10 minutes. Cover; cook for 10 minutes longer. Yield: 8 servings.

HONEY CHICKEN

2 lge. fryers
Salt to taste
1 can peach nectar
1 tbsp. Worcestershire sauce
2 to 3 tbsp. honey
1 stick oleo or butter

Cut fryers in half; rub with salt. Combine remaining ingredients in saucepan; bring to a slow boil. Cook chicken over a hot charcoal fire; brush with peach sauce. Turn and baste frequently for 45 minutes to 1 hour or until done. Yield: 4-6 servings.

Reva Wagner
Alpha Alpha Mu, Dyona, Texas

FISH FRIED IN BEER BATTER

Fresh fish fillets
1 c. beer
1 c. biscuit mix

Dry fish fillets. Combine beer and biscuit mix; dip fillets in batter. Fry in oil deep enough to cover fish. Turn after 1 minute or when brown. Fry other side. Yield: 4-6 servings.

Mrs. Doy Hampton
Alpha Chi, Chanute, Kansas

SCRAMBLED ROE AND EGGS

1/2 lb. whitefish roe
1/4 c. butter
6 eggs
Salt to taste

Break membrane of roe. Melt butter in skillet over medium heat; add roe. Cook, stirring until almost done. Add eggs; season with salt. Cook, stirring constantly, until eggs are done. Yield: 4 servings.

Mrs. Lynda Sullivan
Eta Upsilon, Port St. Joe, Florida

LIMA BEANS WITH SOUR CREAM

1 lb. large dried lima beans
2 tsp. salt
1/3 c. margarine
1 c. dark corn syrup
1 tsp. salt
1 med. onion, chopped
1 tsp. dry mustard
1 c. sour cream

Soak beans overnight in at least 2 1/2 quarts water with 1 teaspoon salt. Drain and rinse with hot water; drain well. Melt margarine in large saucepan; stir in corn syrup and remaining salt. Add beans. Cover; boil gently for 50 to 60 minutes or until beans are tender. Stir in onion, mustard and sour cream. Turn into 2 1/2-quart casserole; cover. Bake in 350-degree oven for 1 hour. Yield: 6 servings.

Photograph for this recipe on page 109.

BAKED POTATOES IN ROCK SALT

Rock salt
4 potatoes

Place rock salt 1 inch deep in 3-pound coffee can. Place potatoes in salt without touching can or each other. Pour rock salt around potatoes. Place metal cover on can; place on bed of white coals. Place hot coals on top of can. Bake for 25 minutes or until fork tender. Yield: 4 servings.

Mrs. John H. Rogers
West Allis, Wisconsin

HASHED BROWN OMELET

4 slices bacon
2 c. hashed brown potatoes
1/4 c. chopped onion
1/4 c. chopped green pepper
4 eggs
1/4 c. milk
1/2 tsp. salt
Dash of pepper
1 c. shredded cheese

Cook bacon until crisp in skillet. Remove bacon leaving drippings; crumble. Mix potatoes, onion and green pepper; pat into skillet. Cook over low heat until underside is crisp and brown. Blend eggs, milk, salt and pepper; pour over potatoes. Top with cheese and bacon; cover. Cook over low heat for about 20 minutes or until done. Cool until cheese is set. Cut into wedges; serve. Yield: 4 servings.

Mary Beth Barton
Gamma Beta No. 1083, Odessa, Texas

FRIED CORN BREAD CAKES

1 c. white cornmeal
1/2 c. self-rising flour
1 tsp. salt
Vegetable oil

Sift cornmeal, flour and salt together into saucepan. Stir in enough boiling water to make mixture consistency of dough. Scoop out lump about size of golfball while dough is still hot; roll and flatten in wet palm. Cake should be biscuit-shaped. Repeat procedure for remaining dough. Fry corn bread cakes to a golden brown on medium-high heat in enough vegetable oil to cover bottom of frying pan. Yield: 4 servings.

Mrs. Kenneth B. Swain, Jr.
Xi Alpha Iota, Raleigh, North Carolina

SOUTHERN HUSH PUPPIES

1 c. yellow cornmeal
1/2 c. flour
1 tsp. salt
1/2 tsp. garlic salt
1 1/2 tsp. baking powder
2 beaten eggs
1 sm. chopped onion

Combine all ingredients; add several drops of boiling water. Batter should be stiff. Drop by teaspoonfuls into hot grease. Fry till brown; drain. Yield: 4 servings.

Barbara Myers
Alpha Beta Chi No. 6907, Lufkin, Texas

APPLE-SESAME CRISSCROSS PIE

6 to 8 lge. tart apples
1 c. sugar
1 tbsp. flour
1/2 tsp. cinnamon
1/4 tsp. nutmeg
2 tbsp. toasted sesame seeds
Pastry for 2-crust pie
2 tbsp. butter or margarine
1 slightly beaten egg yolk (opt.)

Core and pare apples; slice thin. Combine sugar, flour and spices; add to apples. Mix well. Add 1 tablespoon sesame seeds to half the pastry. Roll; fit into 9-inch pie pan. Fill with apple mixture. Dot with butter. Sprinkle with remaining sesame seeds. Roll out remaining pastry; cut into 1/2-inch strips. Arrange lattice-fashion on apple mixture. Trim edges. Flute. Brush strips with slightly beaten egg yolk mixed with small amount of water. Bake at 425 degrees for 10 minutes. Reduce oven temperature to 350 degrees; bake for about 30 minutes longer.

Jane Pownall
Delta, Decatur, Illinois

FRENCH CHOCOLATE ICE CREAM

1/4 c. sugar
1/3 c. water
1 6-oz. package semisweet chocolate pieces
3 egg yolks
1 1/2 c. heavy cream, whipped

Combine sugar and water in small saucepan. Bring to a boil and boil rapidly for 3 minutes. Place chocolate in electric blender container; add hot syrup. Cover; blend on high speed for 20 seconds or until chocolate sauce is smooth. Add egg yolks; stir to combine. Cover; blend on high speed for 10 seconds. Fold chocolate mixture into whipped cream. Spoon into refrigerator tray or 1-quart container. Cover with waxed paper; freeze. This needs no stirring; will not form ice crystals. Yield: 1 quart.

June Hackett
Delta Sigma No. 2429, Sunbury, Pennsylvania

ORANGE SLICE CAKE

1 lb. candy orange slices
1 8-oz. package chopped dates
1 c. chopped nuts
3 1/2 c. sifted flour
1 c. margarine
2 c. sugar
4 eggs
1/2 c. buttermilk
1 tsp. soda
1 can shredded coconut

Cut candy slices into small pieces. Coat dates, candy and nuts in 1/2 cup flour; set aside. Cream margarine with sugar; add eggs, one at a time, blending well. Add buttermilk. Sift remaining flour with soda; add to buttermilk mixture. Fold in candy mixture, stirring well; add coconut. Place in greased and floured 9-inch tube pan. Bake for 3 hours at 250 degrees. Leave cake in pan.

Glaze

2 c. confectioners' sugar
1 c. orange juice

Mix sugar and juice well; pour on hot cake. Leave cake in tube pan until well cooled.

Mary Bayley
Beta Nu, Carmi, Illinois

HOMEMADE ICE CREAM

2 c. sugar
2 tbsp. flour
7 c. milk
4 beaten egg whites
1 tsp. salt
5 c. cream
1 tbsp. vanilla

Combine sugar, flour and 2 cups milk in saucepan; cook until mixture begins to thicken. Cool. Pour over egg whites; fold in well. Add all remaining ingredients. Pour into ice cream freezer; freeze according to freezer directions. Yield: 1 gallon.

Barbara Kelley
Delta Rho No. 3012, Corydon, Iowa

Summertime . . . hot, lazy days with high temperatures and even higher humidity. Days which seem literally to melt into each other, forming a blue-green blur in our memories.

Yet even in the midst of that blur, there are some days that stand out sharply. The Fourth of July is one. What a marvelous holiday this is! The most American of all holidays celebrated in a purely American way — firecrackers lighting up the sky, flags unfurling in the breeze, and the inevitable cookout or picnic. Over the years, many American families have added a special touch of their own to this holiday — it is their time for family reunions. July Fourth is a nationally-recognized three-day weekend. Chances are that many families will take advantage of this tailor-made chance to get together.

Remember the family reunions when we were growing up? The ever-building excitement . . . wondering who would

Fourth of July

come . . . who had new babies . . . seeing which of the cousins had grown the most. And the marvelous old ice cream freezer! Cranking it was never work . . . it was a delightful privilege to be fought over.

Shouldn't your children have the opportunity to experience all the wonderment of a family reunion at least once during their lifetimes? And wouldn't it be marvelous to recapture the spirit of family togetherness once again! This year could be your time to renew this great American custom.

If you're organizing the reunion, be sure to plan well in advance. Are you counting on the farmer whose property you're using for the reunion to provide firewood? Don't. It's best to bring your own. If you plan to buy

corn or watermelon once you get near the picnic area, be sure to check with the owners of your picnic spot well in advance. Let them know what your needs are. Then, if they can't meet your needs, you'll have plenty of time to shop. Do bring blankets, flashlights, a good first aid kit, and mosquito repellent. These items might not be needed, but it's best to be prepared just in case.

To reduce your preparation and clean-up time, try using paper supplies — not just napkins, but brightly colored tablecloths, cups, and cutlery. Damp facecloths wrapped in foil are a must to clean sticky faces and hands.

What about food? Most picnic areas will have a stove that can be used to heat casseroles, rolls, and meats that are to be served hot. Cold food should be wrapped in waxed paper or foil — never in a damp towel — and refrigerated immediately after preparation. Chill the food thoroughly; overnight chilling is preferable. Pack these foods last and try to eat them first. This care will reduce the possibility of salads or meats turning bad in the heat.

Let each family group bring food enough for itself. Then put all the dishes out and let each person choose for himself what he would like. Sure, you'll probably get five bowls of potato salad. But each salad will

Reunite the Family for Picnic Fun

be subtly different from the other — and what a wonderful taste treat for everyone!

Here's a menu of cook-ahead dishes which are sure-fire family eating favorites. Marinated Potato Salad . . . 24-Hour Fruit Salad . . . both salads will bring compliments from everyone. For main dishes, what else but the all-American favorite, Fried Chicken. Mushrooms and Beef makes an unusual and delicious main dish. Vegetables are a must, of course. Surprise Baked Beans . . . Tote Along Macaroni . . . Deviled Peas . . . and Festive Green Beans. You'll want to prepare some extra-special breads for this happy occasion. Date-Nut Bread is everyone's favorite any time of the year. Garlic French Bread — warmed at the picnic grounds and served dripping with butter — will please all who enjoy tangy food. Be traditional when it comes to desserts. Try Fresh Peach Pie (this holiday is at the peak of the peach season!) and delicious German Chocolate Cake. Compliments are sure to be yours!

Marinated Potato Salad can be prepared the night before the great reunion. Cook and dice six large potatoes. Place potatoes, two diced hard-boiled eggs, and 1 tablespoon chopped green pepper in a mixing bowl. Add salt and pepper to taste. In a small bowl, mix 3 tablespoons vinegar, 2 tablespoons salad oil, 1/2 teaspoon sugar, 2 teaspoons prepared mustard, and 1 tablespoon grated onion. Pour over potato mixture. Chill for two or three hours or overnight. Just before serving, add enough mayonnaise to moisten. This salad is especially eye-pleasing served in cups of crisp lettuce leaves.

No summertime reunion would be complete without a scrumptious fruit salad. In this case, we suggest 24-Hour Fruit Salad. Mix 3 egg yolks, 2 tablespoons sugar, a dash of salt, 2 tablespoons butter or margarine in a double boiler or heavy saucepan. Cook until thick, stirring constantly. Cool. In a bowl, combine 2 cups drained pineapple tidbits, 5 peeled and diced oranges, 3/4 pound white seedless grapes, 1 bottle of maraschino cherries (chopped), and 2 cups quartered marshmallows. Mix well and chill for 24 hours. If desired, before serving decorate with orange sections, pineapple slices, and long-stemmed maraschino cherries.

Fried Chicken on the Fourth of July is a great American tradition. To prepare, cut one 2 1/2 to 3-pound frying chicken into serving pieces. Coat pieces with 1/2 cup flour. In a bowl, combine one beaten egg with 3 teaspoons water. Dip chicken pieces into this mixture. Combine 3/4 cup cracker meal with 1 tablespoon onion salt, 2 teaspoons salt, 2 teaspoons paprika, 1/4 teaspoon pepper, 1/4 teaspoon thyme. Roll the chicken pieces in this mixture and let dry on a rack for 30 to 45 minutes. For crispy crust, remove cover for the last ten minutes of cooking time.

Maybe you can start a new July Fourth tradition with another delicious meat dish — Mushrooms and Beef. This casserole is sure to be a favorite with the beef-and-gravy loving men at your family reunion. Cut two pounds round steak or chuck roast into cubes. Fry cubes lightly in 4 tablespoons butter. Place browned cubes in a small roaster. To the skillet drippings, add 4 tablespoons flour. Brown lightly. Add 1 small can mushrooms, 1 can cream of mushroom soup, 1 tablespoon horseradish, and 1 tablespoon lemon juice. Season with salt and pepper to taste. Stir mixture into beef cubes. Mix well; add milk just to cover. Bake in 350-degree oven for two or three hours or until beef is tender.

Don't forget the vegetables. In addition to their well-known nutritional value, vegetables can bring a welcome note of color and texture to your picnic table. Surprise Baked Beans combine some new flavor notes with an old favorite. Mix two 1-pound cans baked beans and tomato sauce, 1/2 cup chopped onion, 10 dried apricot halves (quartered), 6 sliced weiners, 2 tablespoons brown sugar and 1 teaspoon dry mustard. Turn into a greased 1 1/2-quart casserole dish. Bake at 350 degrees for one hour.

Tote-Along Macaroni is just perfect for a picnic. To prepare, add 1 tablespoon salt to 3 quarts rapidly boiling water. Gradually add 2 cups or

8 ounces elbow macaroni as water continues to boil. Cook, uncovered, stirring occasionally until tender. Drain in colander. Saute 1/2 pound sliced mushrooms and 2 tablespoons chopped onion in 2 tablespoons salad oil until tender-crisp. Add one pound lean ground beef, and brown lightly. Stir in 1 teaspoon salt, 1/4 teaspoon pepper, 1/4 teaspoon tarragon leaves, 1/8 teaspoon garlic powder, and two 8-ounce cans tomato sauce. Simmer, uncovered, for 10 minutes. Combine with macaroni. Turn into a 1 1/2-quart casserole dish. Sprinkle with 1/2 cup grated sharp Cheddar cheese. Bake in 400-degree oven for 15 minutes or until bubbling hot and cheese is lightly browned.

Deviled Peas are devilishly delicious. Combine 1 can English peas (drained), 1 cup chopped celery, 1 chopped bell pepper, 1 cup grated cheese and 1 can tomato soup. Arrange alternate layers of this vegetable mixture, 6 sliced hard-boiled eggs, and 1 1/2 cups white sauce in a casserole dish. Bake for 30 minutes at 300 degrees.

Green beans are everyone's favorite, and here's a new way to prepare them — Festive Green Beans. Cook two packages frozen green beans in a small amount of water until tender. Drain and place beans in a buttered casserole dish. Top with 1 can water chestnuts (sliced), 1 teaspoon monosodium glutamate, and slivered almonds. In a saucepan, melt 4 tablespoons butter. Add one minced onion. Cook until onion is transparent. Remove from heat. Stir in 2 tablespoons flour and mix to a smooth paste. Add 2 cups milk gradually and return to heat. Cook, stirring constantly, until mixture is thickened. Add 1/2 pound shredded sharp Cheddar cheese. Stir until cheese is melted. Add one pound sliced fresh mushrooms. Pour sauce over beans. Top with contents of one can French-fried onions. Bake at 350 degrees for 30 minutes.

Part of the fun of family reunion picnics is the wide variety of foods sure to be served. Everyone likes to choose from lots of different breads. Here are two recipes which are very different from each other but very delicious. First, Date-nut Bread. Mix 3/4 cup chopped nuts, 1 cup cut-up dates, 1 1/2 teaspoons soda, and 1/2 teaspoon salt with a fork. Add 3 tablespoons shortening and 3/4 cup boiling water. Let stand for 20 minutes. In a mixing bowl, beat two eggs with a fork. Still stirring with a fork, add 1 teaspoon vanilla, 1 cup sugar, and 1 1/2 cups flour. Add date mixture, mixing just to blend. Pour into greased 9 x 5 x 3-inch loaf pan. Bake at 350 degrees for 1 hour and 5 minutes or until done.

The other bread on this menu is Garlic French Bread — very different from the gentle blend of flavors that you find in Date-nut Bread but just as good. To prepare, preheat oven to 350 degrees. In a loaf of French bread, make diagonal cuts at one-inch intervals, leaving base intact. Combine 1/2 cup soft butter or margarine, one crushed garlic clove, 3 tablespoons grated Parmesan cheese, 1 teaspoon dried marjoram leaves, 1/4 teaspoon pepper, and a dash of cayenne. Mix until well blended. Spread mixture between bread slices. Place bread on an ungreased cookie sheet. Sprinkle top with a few drops of water. Bake for 10 minutes or until butter is melted and bread is hot. Serve immediately. If desired, this could be prepared at home and baked over a grill at the picnic area.

Everyone — young and old — looks forward to dessert time with the greatest of anticipation. Reward their hearty appetites with two favorite desserts — Fresh Peach Pie and German Chocolate Cake. Fresh peaches are in season now, and this pie is both delicious and economical to prepare. Fill a nine-inch baked pastry shell with 2 cups sliced fresh peaches. In a saucepan, boil 1 cup mashed peaches, 1/2 cup orange juice, 1 cup sugar, and 2 1/2 tablespoons cornstarch until mixture is clear and slightly thickened. Pour heated mixture over peaches in pie shell. Cool thoroughly before serving.

German Chocolate Cake is lovely to look at and richly delicious to eat. To prepare, dissolve 1 package sweet cooking chocolate in 1/2 cup boiling water. In a mixing bowl, cream 2 cups sugar and 1 cup shortening. Add four egg yolks, one at a time. Sift 2 1/2 cups flour, 1 teaspoon soda, and 1/2 teaspoon salt together. Add to creamed mixture alternately with 1 cup buttermilk. Add chocolate and 1 teaspoon vanilla. Fold in four stiffly beaten egg whites. Place in a 12 x 8-inch pan. Bake at 350 degrees for 35 minutes or until cake tests done. For the rich icing which is so much a part of this favorite dessert, combine 1 stick butter, 1/2 cup evaporated milk, 3 beaten egg yolks, 1 cup sugar, and 1/2 teaspoon salt in a pan. Cook, stirring constantly, until the mixture thickens. Add 1 cup coconut, 1 cup pecans, and 1 teaspoon vanilla. Cool and spread on cake.

After such a feast, some activity is necessary. Croquet and pitching horseshoes are old-fashioned activities as enjoyable today as they were years ago. And everyone enjoys softball! If you're near a beach, try the water version of softball, played with a beachball and a paddle. It's almost as much fun for onlookers as it is for the players. Remember the games you played as a child? Potato sack races . . . treasure hunts . . . hide-and-seek . . . hare and hounds. Your children will delight in these time-honored favorites just as you did.

By the end of this memorable Fourth of July, you'll be heading home, sunburned . . . full of delicious home-cooked food . . . and with warm memories of family love and togetherness that are sure to last until next year's Fourth of July family reunion.

OLD-FASHIONED EGG SALAD

1 head lettuce
6 hard-cooked eggs, sliced
1 lge. onion, thinly sliced
1 1/2 tsp. salt
1/4 tsp. pepper
Dash of paprika
1/4 c. salad oil
2 tbsp. vinegar
1 tsp. Worcestershire sauce
1 tbsp. minced parsley
1/4 c. grated sharp cheese

Break lettuce in bite-sized pieces. Place lettuce in salad bowl; arrange eggs and onion in alternate layers over lettuce. Combine remaining ingredients; pour over top. Toss lightly. Yield: 6 servings.

Laura Frye
Theta Psi No. 6325, Tyrone, Pennsylvania

PICNIC MACARONI SALAD

1 c. macaroni
1/2 c. sweet pepper corn relish
1/4 c. chopped pimentos, drained
1/4 c. diced green peppers
1 tsp. chopped onion
1 tsp. chopped parsley
2/3 c. mayonnaise
1/2 c. sour cream
1/4 c. milk
1 tsp. salt

Cook macaroni according to package directions. Drain and rinse with cold water. Add corn relish, pimentos, green peppers, onion and parsley; mix well. Combine mayonnaise, sour cream, milk and salt in small bowl. Pour over macaroni mixture; toss lightly until well combined. Refrigerate, covered, until chilled. Garnish with pepper rings, pimentos and hard-boiled eggs, if desired. Salad dressing may be substituted for mayonnaise. Yield: 4-6 servings.

Judi Kennedy
Beta Alpha No. 7154, Rockford, Illinois

SAVORY SPINACH SALAD

1 sm. package lemon or lime gelatin
1/2 tsp. salt
1 c. boiling water
1/2 c. cold water
3 tbsp. vinegar
1 1/2 c. chopped cooked spinach
2 tsp. grated onion

Dissolve gelatin and salt in boiling water. Add cold water and vinegar. Chill until thick. Fold in spinach and onion; pour into 1-quart mold or individual molds. Chill until firm. Unmold onto crisp lettuce. Garnish with mayonnaise and sliced hard-cooked egg, if desired. Yield: 6 servings.

Rosalie Hawthorne
Xi Gamma Mu No. 2513, Indianapolis, Indiana

OVERNIGHT FRUIT SALAD WITH LEMON DRESSING

2 oranges
2 cans mandarin oranges
1 No. 2 can pineapple chunks
2 eggs
1/2 c. sugar
1/3 c. lemon juice
Grated rind of 1 lemon
1/2 tsp. salt
1 c. whipped cream
3 c. quartered marshmallows
1 c. halved green grapes
1 c. halved Bing cherries
2 bananas, diced

Peel and dice oranges; drain well. Drain mandarin oranges and pineapple chunks. Beat eggs lightly in top of double boiler; stir in sugar, lemon juice, lemon rind and salt. Cook, stirring, until thickened. Cool completely; fold in whipped cream, marshmallows, diced oranges, mandarin oranges, pineapple chunks, grapes and cherries. Fold together gently. Spoon into salad bowl; cover. Refrigerate overnight. Fold in bananas just before serving. Garnish with fresh fruits, if desired. Yield: 12 servings.

Eleanor M. Oimoen
Xi Beta X-235, Madison, Wisconsin

BEET AND CELERY SALAD

1 tsp. sugar
1/3 c. French dressing
2 c. diced cooked beets
1/2 c. diced celery
1/2 c. diced unpeeled cucumber
2 tbsp. minced pickle
2 tbsp. chopped onion
Salt and pepper to taste

Mix sugar and French dressing. Add remaining ingredients; chill for about 30 minutes. Serve on lettuce leaves; garnish with additional cucumber.

Marilyn MacKay
Xi Beta Gamma X2346
Woodstock, Ontario, Canada

SWEET AND SOUR BEAN SALAD

1 can cut green beans
1 can cut yellow beans
1 can red kidney beans
1 can lima beans
1 can chick peas
2 sm. onions
3 stalks celery
1 green pepper
1 tsp. salt
1/4 tsp. pepper
Dash of garlic salt
3/4 c. sugar
1/3 c. vegetable oil
3/4 c. vinegar

Drain beans and peas. Cut onions in thin slices. Chop celery and green pepper fine. Combine beans, peas, onions, celery and green pepper in large container. Mix remaining ingredients well; pour over vegetable mixture. Cover container tightly. Refrigerate for several hours, turning container occasionally. Salad keeps well in refrigerator.

Georgina Woodin
Delta Upsilon No. 6145, Capreol, Ontario, Canada

TOSSED HOLIDAY SALAD

Romaine lettuce
1/2 head lettuce
1/2 head curly endive
2 c. torn spinach
3 tbsp. chopped chives
3 tbsp. chopped parsley
1/3 c. sliced radishes
1/3 c. French dressing
Radish rose
Sliced cherry tomatoes

Line salad bowl with romaine lettuce leaves. Tear head lettuce, curly endive and spinach into bite-sized pieces; place in bowl. Add chives, parsley and sliced radishes; pour French dressing over salad. Garnish with radish rose and cherry tomatoes.

French Dressing

1 c. salad or olive oil
3 tbsp. fresh lemon juice
3 tbsp. red wine vinegar
2 tbsp. finely chopped green pepper
3 tbsp. finely chopped chives
1 tsp. basil leaves
1 tsp. tarragon leaves
1 1/2 tsp. salt
1 clove of garlic, quartered
1/4 tsp. pepper

Combine all ingredients; mix well.

PICNIC SALAD BOWL

1/2 10-oz. package frozen peas
1/4 c. canned sliced mushrooms
1/4 c. Italian dressing
1/2 c. instant rice
2 tbsp. minced green onions
1/4 c. chopped cucumber
2 tbsp. sliced stuffed olives
1/3 c. mayonnaise
Lettuce leaves
1 tomato, cut in wedges.

Cook peas according to package directions; drain and cool. Drain mushrooms. Combine 1/4 cup cold water and Italian dressing in saucepan; bring to boiling point. Remove from heat; add rice. Let stand, covered, for 5 minutes. Fluff rice with fork; turn into medium bowl. Add peas, mixing with fork; chill. Add onions, mushrooms, cucumber, olives and mayonnaise; mix well with fork. Refrigerate, covered. Pack in insulated carryall. Wrap lettuce and tomato separately; place in carryall. Toss salad again before serving. Garnish with lettuce leaves and tomato wedges. Cooked salad dressing may be substituted for mayonnaise. Yield: 4 servings.

Alice D. Hickok
Psi No. 7132, Indianapolis, Indiana

TANGERINE-WALNUT TOSS

1 head lettuce, shredded
2 c. tangerine sections
1/2 onion, sliced
1/3 c. Italian dressing
1 tbsp. butter, melted
1/4 tsp. salt
1/2 c. walnuts

Combine lettuce, tangerine sections, onion and dressing; toss lightly. Combine butter, salt and walnuts in skillet over low heat. Stir until walnuts are crisp. Top salad with walnuts. Canned mandarin orange segments may be substituted for tangerine sections. Yield: 6-8 servings.

Mary Jo Bell
Xi Alpha Eta X1055, Charlevoix, Michigan

MOLDED POTATO-TOMATO SALAD

1 env. unflavored gelatin
1/4 c. cold water
1 1/2 c. hot chicken broth
1/4 tsp. pepper
1 tsp. salt
1 hard-cooked egg, sliced
1 c. sliced tomatoes
1 c. diced cooked potatoes
1 c. diced celery
1 tsp. minced onion
1 c. cottage cheese
Radishes

Soften gelatin in water; stir into chicken broth. Add pepper and salt, stirring until gelatin is dissolved. Pour 1/8 of the mixture into loaf pan; chill until firm. Arrange egg and tomatoes in pattern over congealed layer. Combine potatoes, celery, onion, cottage cheese and remaining gelatin mixture; pour over egg and tomatoes. Chill until set. Garnish with radishes and additional tomatoes. Yield: 12 servings.

Rae Morton
Preceptor Zeta X270, Highland Park, Michigan

CONEYS

2 lb. hamburger
1 onion, chopped
1/2 bottle catsup
1/2 tsp. salt
2 tbsp. garlic salt
1/2 tsp. pepper
1 tbsp. chili powder
Buns

Combine hamburger and 1/2 cup water in saucepan; cook, stirring frequently, for 30 minutes. Drain hamburger; add onion. Cook, stirring frequently, for 15 minutes. Stir in 1 cup water, catusp and seasonings; simmer for 1 hour, stirring occasionally. Serve mixture on buns. Yield: 8 servings.

Patricia Cotton
Zeta Lambda No. 2771, Lawrenceville, Illinois

OPEN-FACED ENGLISH HAMBURGERS

1/2 c. garlic dressing
2 lb. hamburger
6 English muffins, split
Seasoning salt to taste

Mix garlic dressing and hamburger; form 12 patties. Broil in oven 4 to 6 inches from heat until browned on one side. Place patties on muffin halves, browned-side down; sprinkle with seasoning salt. Broil until muffins and hamburger patties are browned. Serve immediately. Sprinkle patties with Parmesan cheese while broiling or allow sliced Swiss or Cheddar cheese to melt on patties just before serving, if desired. May be served as an appetizer by cutting each muffin into several wedges before serving. Yield: 6 servings.

Wanda Mills
Xi Lambda Iota, Lompoc, California

STROGANOFF BURGERS

2 lb. ground beef
1/3 c. chopped onion
1/3 c. catsup
3 tbsp. prepared mustard
1 tsp. salt
1 12-oz. carton sour cream
Buns

Brown ground beef. Add onion and brown slightly. Add catsup, mustard, salt and sour cream; mix well. Cover and simmer for 20 minutes. Serve on heated buns. Yield: 12 servings.

Susan Beck
Xi Omicron No. 1962, Sioux Falls, South Dakota

SPEGWICHES

1 can luncheon meat
Butter
6 slices American cheese
6 slices buttered bread
6 eggs

Cut luncheon meat in 6 slices; brown lightly on one side in butter. Turn; top with cheese. Cook until cheese begins to melt. Arrange meat and cheese on bread. Fry eggs; place eggs over meat and cheese. Serve as open-faced sandwiches. Bread may be toasted, if desired. Yield: 6 servings.

Virginia L. Fuller
Preceptor Sigma Exemplar XP-266
Los Gatos, California

HAM AND CHEESE BUNS

12 hamburger buns
1/2 lb. ham, finely diced
1/4 lb. Velveeta cheese, diced
1/4 lb. Cheddar cheese, diced
1 tbsp. chopped onion
2 hard-cooked eggs, chopped
1/4 c. pickle relish
3 tbsp. mayonnaise
1/4 tsp. mustard
1 tbsp. catsup or barbecue sauce

Hollow out centers of bun halves. Mix remaining ingredients well; fill centers of bun halves. Wrap individually in foil. Bake at 400 degrees for 15 minutes. Yield: 12 servings.

Mrs. Verna J. Erickson
Marion, Ohio

CLUB SANDWICHES

8 slices toast
Salad dressing
8 slices cooked turkey
4 lge. slices tomato
16 slices fried bacon
8 lettuce leaves

Spread toast with salad dressing. Place 2 slices turkey, 1 slice tomato, 2 slices bacon and 2 lettuce leaves on each of 4 slices toast. Cover with remaining toast. Cut diagonally into fourths. Yeild: 4 servings.

Mrs. Virginia Kendrick
Pawhuska, Oklahoma

COUNTRY MEAT LOAF

4 slices bread, trimmed
2 med. onions, minced
2 tbsp. butter or margarine
1 1/2 lb. ground lean chuck
1/2 tsp. salt
1/4 tsp. pepper
1 egg, beaten
2 tbsp. mustard
1 c. cubed Cheddar cheese
1 can tomato soup

Soften bread in small amount of water. Cook onions lightly in butter. Combine chuck, bread, onions, salt, pepper, egg and mustard; mix well. Shape half the chuck mixture into flat loaf; top with cheese. Shape remaining chuck mixture in flat loaf; place over cheese. Mold and seal loaf with fingers. Place in baking dish; pour soup over loaf. Cover dish. Bake at 350 degrees for 1 hour. Uncover; bake for 15 to 20 minutes longer to brown loaf. Yield: 6 servings.

Barbara Bukata
Kappa Epsilon No. 6826, Deerfield Beach, Florida

MISSOURI BAKED HAM

1 10 to 12-lb. ham
Cinnamon to taste
Whole cloves
1/2 lb. brown sugar
1 tbsp. prepared mustard
1 1/2 c. vinegar

Place ham in large container; add water to cover. Bring to a boil. Reduce heat and simmer for 1 hour. Drain ham, reserving 1 1/2 cups broth. Remove skin and trim fat. Place ham in baking pan, fat side up; score fat. Sprinkle ham with cinnamon; stud thickly with cloves. Pat brown sugar evenly over fat. Place reserved broth in saucepan; stir in mustard and vinegar. Bring to a boil; pour into baking pan. Cover pan tightly. Bake at 300 to 350 degrees for 1 hour.

Jane Parnell
Fort Sumner, New Mexico

PO-BOY STEAK

1/2 c. chopped celery
1 lge. onion, chopped
1 med. green pepper, chopped
1 lb. ground beef
1 sm. can English peas
1/2 c. cooked rice
1/2 tsp. garlic salt
1 env. chili mix
1 can mushroom soup
1 can tomatoes or tomato soup
1 c. grated cheese
1 sm. can onion rings

Cook celery, onion and green pepper lightly in small amount of water; drain. Brown beef in skillet; stir in onion mixture, peas, rice, garlic salt, chili mix, soup and tomatoes. Turn into baking dish. Bake at 350 degrees until bubbly. Top with cheese and onion rings; bake until cheese is melted and onion rings are browned. Yield: 6 servings.

Mrs. Charles A. Cates
Xi Xi, Tifton, Georgia

LIME RIBS

3 to 4 lb. spareribs
3/4 c. lime juice
1/3 c. salad oil
3 tbsp. brown sugar
1/2 tsp. coriander
1/2 tsp. ginger
1 1/2 tsp. salt

Have spareribs sawed across rib bones. Combine lime juice, salad oil, brown sugar, coriander, ginger and salt. Place spareribs in shallow dish; pour lime marinade over spareribs. Cover; refrigerate for 6 to 8 hours. Place spareribs on rack in roasting pan; reserve marinade. Cover spareribs tightly. Bake at 350 degrees for 1 hour. Uncover; turn spareribs. Brush with marinade; bake for 1 hour to 1 hour and 30 minutes longer, brushing with marinade every 30 minutes. Remove spareribs to heated platter. Garnish with lime wedges. Yield: 3-4 servings.

Mrs. Nancy Barrow
St. Louis, Missouri

OVEN-FRIED CHICKEN

1/2 c. fine dry bread crumbs
2 tsp. salt
1 tsp. paprika
1/4 tsp. pepper
1 broiler-fryer chicken
1/4 c. corn oil

Combine bread crumbs, salt, paprika and pepper. Cut chicken into 8 pieces; brush each piece of chicken with corn oil. Roll in bread crumb mixture. Place chicken pieces, skin side up, in shallow baking pan. Bake in 425-degree oven for 25 to 30 minutes or until chicken is tender.

Photograph for this recipe on page 119.

GOLDEN CHICKEN NUGGETS

4 sm. whole chicken breasts
1/2 c. fine dry bread crumbs
1/4 c. grated Parmesan cheese
2 tsp. monosodium glutamate
1 tsp. salt
1 tsp. dried leaf thyme
1 tsp. dried leaf basil
1/2 c. butter or margarine, melted

Bone chicken breasts; remove skin. Cut each breast half into 6 or 8 nuggets. Combine bread crumbs, cheese, monosodium glutamate, salt and herbs. Dip chicken nuggets into butter, then in crumb mixture. Place nuggets in single layer on foil-lined baking sheet. Bake in 400-degree oven for 10 minutes. Yield: 4 to 5 dozen nuggets.

Betty D. Frye
Alpha, Billings, Montana

PARMESAN-FRIED CHICKEN

2 3-lb. fryers, cut up
Salt to taste
2 c. cracker crumbs
1 c. grated Parmesan cheese
2 tsp. paprika
Dash of pepper
1 1/3 c. evaporated milk
1 c. margarine

Wash chicken; pat dry. Sprinkle with salt. Mix cracker crumbs, cheese, paprika and pepper in paper bag. Dip chicken pieces in milk; drop in crumb mixture. Shake until chicken is coated. Melt margarine in two 9 x 13-inch pans. Place chicken, skin side down, in pans. Bake in 350-degree oven for 30 minutes. Turn chicken; bake for 30 to 40 minutes longer. Yield: 8-10 servings.

Mrs. Sharon Born
Xi Alpha Sigma, New Castle, Indiana

FRIED CHICKEN WITH PICKLE SAUCE

1/2 c. flour
2 tsp. salt
1/4 tsp. pepper
2 3-lb. chickens, disjointed
Olive or salad oil
2/3 c. French dressing
2/3 c. chili sauce
2/3 c. drained sweet pickle relish

Combine flour, salt and pepper. Coat chicken with flour mixture. Heat 1/2 inch oil in skillet. Add chicken; cook over medium heat for about 15 to 20 minutes or until browned on both sides. Cover; cook over low heat for 20 minutes or until tender. Drain on absorbent paper. Combine remaining ingredients; mix well. Serve chicken with pickle sauce. Yield: 8 servings.

BROCCOLI-GARLIC CASSEROLE

1 med. onion, chopped
3 tbsp. margarine
2 pkg. chopped broccoli
1 can cream of mushroom soup
1 roll garlic cheese, chopped
3/4 tsp. monosodium glutamate
1 4-oz. can mushrooms
1/3 c. chopped blanched almonds
1/2 c. bread crumbs

Cook onion lightly in margarine in saucepan. Add broccoli; cover. Cook over low heat until broccoli is tender. Add soup, cheese, monosodium glutamate, mushrooms and about 3/4 of the almonds; mix well. Pour into casserole; sprinkle remaining almonds and bread crumbs over top. Bake at 300 degrees until heated through and bubbly. Recipe is easily doubled. Yield: 6-8 servings.

Barbara Brewer
Theta Epsilon No. 5536, Caruthersville, Missouri

OLD-FASHIONED BAKED BEANS

2 lb. pea beans or great northern beans
3 qt. water
1 med. onion, peeled
1 1/2 to 2 c. unsulphured molasses
1 1/2 tsp. salt
2 tsp. dry mustard
2 tbsp. instant minced onion
2 c. light brown sugar
4 to 5 slices bacon

Place beans in large kettle; add water. Bring to a boil; boil for 5 minutes. Cover; let stand for 1 hour. Return to a boil; cover. Reduce heat; simmer for 2 hours and 30 minutes or until beans are tender. Drain beans, reserving 1 cup liquid. Place whole onion in bean pot. Mix beans, molasses, salt, mustard and minced onion; spoon half the bean mixture into pot. Pour in half the reserved liquid; sprinkle with half the brown sugar. Add half the bacon; repeat layers. Bake for about 6 hours at 275 degrees. Yield: 20 servings.

Darlene Ford
Gamma Gamma No. 6847, Murray, Kentucky

PACIFIC COAST BEANS

3 c. brown beans
2 tsp. soda
1 lb. hamburger
Salt and pepper
Brown sugar to taste
Chopped onions
Canned tomatoes, undrained

Soak beans overnight in water with soda added. Drain beans; cover with fresh water. Add salt to taste. Bring to a boil; reduce heat. Cover and simmer for 2 hours or until beans are tender. Brown hamburger lightly, breaking in small pieces; season to taste with salt and pepper. Layer beans, hamburger, sugar, onions and tomatoes in large casserole until beans are used, ending with tomatoes. Bake at 300 degrees for about 4 hours, adding water or tomato juice as needed. Yield: 10 servings.

Virginia Thompson
Xi Beta Lambda, Dallas, Oregon

HOLIDAY BROWN BREAD

1 1/2 c. raisins
1/2 c. boiling water
1/4 c. shortening
1 c. sugar
1 tbsp. molasses
3 c. flour
1/2 tsp. salt
1 tsp. soda
2 tsp. baking powder
1/2 tsp. cinnamon
1 1/2 c. chopped nuts

Preheat oven to 350 degrees. Place raisins in boiling water; cool. Drain raisins, reserving water. Cream shortening, sugar and molasses. Sift flour, salt, soda, baking powder and cinnamon together. Add flour mixture to creamed mixture alternately with reserved raisin water, mixing well. Fold in raisins and nuts. Spoon batter into 6 greased and floured gold-lined soup cans. Bake for 30 minutes or until bread tests done.

Carol B. Rhodes
Xi Alpha Delta X-3327, Mobile, Alabama

BLACKBERRY CAKE

2/3 c. butter
1 1/2 c. sugar
2 eggs
2 c. flour
1 tsp. soda
1/2 c. milk or cream
1 tsp. cinnamon
1 tsp. nutmeg
2 tsp. cocoa
3 c. blackberries

Cream butter, sugar and eggs. Add flour and soda alternately with milk. Add spices and cocoa; fold in blackberries. Batter will be thick. Spoon batter into loaf pan. Bake in 350-degree oven for 40 to 45 minutes. Yield: 12 servings.

Esther Watts
Xi Eta Alpha, Litchfield, Illinois

STATE FAIR CRANBERRY-APPLE-NUT PIE

1 pkg. pie crust mix
1 1-lb. can whole-berry cranberry sauce
1/2 c. chopped nuts
3 med. apples, finely chopped
1/2 c. seedless raisins
1/2 c. sugar
3 tbsp. flour
1 tsp. cinnamon
1/2 tsp. nutmeg
2 tbsp. melted butter or margarine

Prepare pie crust according to package directions. Shape 2/3 of the pastry into flat round. Roll out to form circle large enough to line ungreased 9-inch pie pan, allowing pie crust to hang over edge about 1 inch. Combine remaining ingredients; pour into pastry-lined pan. Roll out remaining pastry; cut into 1/2-inch strips. Attach strips to rim of shell; twist and press strips across filling. Fold excess pastry over strips; flute edge. Bake at 425 degrees for 40 to 50 minutes or until filling bubbles and crust is browned. Serve warm.

CHOCOLATE CREAM PIE

2 sq. unsweetened chocolate
1 1/2 c. sugar
3 tbsp. cornstarch
1/2 tsp. salt
3 c. milk
3 egg yolks, lightly beaten
1 tbsp. butter
1 1/2 tsp. vanilla
1 9-in. baked pie shell

Shave chocolate into strips. Mix sugar, cornstarch, chocolate and salt in saucepan; stir in milk gradually. Cook over medium heat; stirring constantly, until mixture thickens and boils. Boil for 1 minute. Remove from heat. Stir half the hot mixture into egg yolks; blend egg yolk mixture into hot mixture remaining in saucepan. Boil for 1 minute, stirring constantly. Remove from heat. Blend in butter and vanilla; pour immediately into pie shell. Chill pie for 2 hours. Garnish with whipped cream. One-half cup cocoa may be substituted for chocolate.

Sharon Longanecker
Phi Alpha Rho P2241, Sterling, Illinois

TOASTED ALMOND PARFAIT

3/4 c. light corn syrup
1/4 c. sugar
3 egg whites
1 c. heavy cream
1/2 tsp. vanilla
1/2 c. toasted almonds, chopped

Combine corn syrup and sugar in saucepan. Cook over medium heat, stirring occasionally, until sugar is dissolved and mixture comes to a boil. Beat egg whites until slightly mounded when beater is raised. Add syrup mixture gradually, beating constantly until soft peaks form. Cool to room temperature. Whip cream and vanilla in cold bowl with cold beaters. Fold whipped cream and almonds into egg white mixture. Place in parfait glasses. Freeze.

SWEET CHOCOLATE CAKE

1 pkg. sweet cooking chocolate
1/2 c. boiling water
1 c. butter or margarine
2 c. sugar
4 eggs, separated
1 tsp. vanilla
1/2 tsp. salt
1 tsp. soda
2 1/2 c. sifted cake flour
1 c. buttermilk

Melt chocolate in boiling water; cool. Cream butter and sugar until fluffy; beat in egg yolks, one at a time. Add chocolate and vanilla; mix well. Sift salt, soda and flour together; add flour mixture to chocolate mixture alternately with buttermilk, beating until smooth. Fold in stiffly beaten egg whites; pour into three 8-inch waxed-paper lined cake pans. Bake in 350-degree oven for 30 to 40 minutes. Cool layers; spread with Coconut-Pecan Frosting. Stack layers; do not frost sides.

Coconut-Pecan Frosting

1 c. evaporated milk
1 c. sugar
3 egg yolks, beaten
2 tbsp. margarine
1 tsp. vanilla
1 1/3 c. flaked coconut
1 c. chopped pecans

Mix milk, sugar, egg yolks, margarine and vanilla in saucepan. Cook, stirring, over medium heat for 12 minutes or until thickened. Add coconut and pecans; beat until thick enough to spread. Yield: 15 servings.

Louise S. Basile
Puerto Rico Beta No. 5774
Guaynabo, Puerto Rico

SOUR CREAM POUND CAKE

3 c. flour
1/4 tsp. soda
1/8 tsp. salt
2 sticks butter
3 c. sugar
6 eggs, separated
1 tsp. vanilla flavoring

1 tsp. lemon or almond flavoring
1 c. sour cream
3/4 c. powdered sugar
Juice of 1 lemon

Sift flour, soda and salt together. Cream butter and sugar; beat in egg yolks, one at a time. Stir in flavorings; beat in flour mixture alternately with sour cream. Fold in beaten egg whites. Place batter in greased tube pan. Bake at 300 degrees for 1 hour and 30 minutes or at 350 degrees for 1 hour and 15 minutes. Cool cake in pan for 10 minutes; turn onto rack. Blend powdered sugar and lemon juice; drizzle over hot cake.

Sylvia Walls
Xi Gamma Gamma X-2045, Reading, Pennsylvania

GRANDMA'S PEACH ICE CREAM

1 1/2 c. milk
1 c. sugar
2 tbsp. flour
Few grains of salt
2 eggs
1 1/2 tsp. vanilla extract
1 1/2 c. heavy cream
1 1/2 c. fresh peach puree
Almond extract to taste

Scald milk in top of double boiler. Mix 3/4 cup sugar, flour and salt; stir in enough milk to make smooth paste. Stir paste into remaining milk. Cook, stirring, until thickened. Cover; cook for 10 minutes. Beat eggs lightly; stir cooked mixture into eggs, a small amount at a time. Return to double boiler; cook for 1 minute longer. Cool; stir in remaining ingredients. Pour mixture into 2-quart ice cream freezer container. Pack with ice and salt; turn freezer handle until ice cream is frozen.

Mrs. J. K. Pirkle
Augusta, Georgia

MINT TEA

1 c. mint leaves (firmly packed)
1 bag orange pekoe tea
3 c. sugar
1 stick cinnamon
Juice of 8 lge. lemons

Place mint leaves, tea bag, sugar and cinnamon in 1-gallon container; pour in 2 quarts boiling water. Cover and let stand for 1 hour. Strain and return to container. Stir in lemon juice and enough water to fill container. Serve hot or cold. Yield: 16 servings.

Mrs. Thomas J. Boyd
Amarillo, Texas

INDEPENDENCE PARTY PUNCH

1 pkg. raspberry drink powder
1 pkg. strawberry drink powder
2 c. sugar
1 to 2 qt. water
2 1-qt. 14-oz. cans red mixed fruit punch
1 6-oz. can frozen lemonade
1 lge. bottle ginger ale

Dissolve drink powder and sugar in water; stir in fruit punch and lemonade. Add ginger ale; mix thoroughly. Chill until ready to serve. Yield: 48 servings.

Kathleen Jensen
Phi Mu, Omaha, Nebraska

TEN GALLON PICNIC PUNCH

2 46-oz. cans pineapple juice
1 46-oz. can grapefruit juice
1 46-oz. can orange juice
2 lge. cans frozen lemon juice
10 lb. sugar
2 oz. citric acid
4 pkg. frozen raspberries
10 lb. dry ice

Mix fruit juices, sugar and citric acid; stir in raspberries and enough cold water to make 10 gallons liquid. Pour over ice in punch bowl. Yield: 50 servings.

Della Sorensen
Xi Rho X1270, Salt Lake City, Utah

Labor Day — the day for honoring all of America's workers — is the time when families traditionally hail the passing of summer holidays. Schools resume just after Labor Day . . . Offices are back on regular working hours . . . and thoughts begin to turn toward the fall and winter holiday preparations. To commemorate the passing of summer, millions of American families take to the road, searching for one more beach . . . a brand-new camping site . . . or a stream that hasn't quite been fished out. Millions of other families stay at home, enjoying leisurely visits with family, friends, and neighbors. The barbecue grill — symbol of the comfortably lazy eating habits of summer — is brought out for one more cookout.

Labor Day is the perfect holiday for a barbecue party. Why not invite the neighbors to bring a dish? Perhaps it's just going to be a casual gathering of good friends in the backyard for a relaxed evening of good food

Labor Day

and good conversation. Whatever the setting, here's a delightful party menu for you to try. It starts with Grilled Cornish Hens — a long-time gourmet favorite sure to be a winner with your family and guests. Add steaming hot Grilled Rice Pilaf, an oh-so-easy and taste-tempting blend of rice, vegetables, and seasonings. Succotash on the Grill combines the flavors of corn and lima beans into a delicious and colorful vegetable casserole. Apricot Salad is tart and tangy — and can be prepared the day before your party. Its icy cold taste is a welcome contrast to the piping-hot foods coming off the barbecue grill. Top off this fabulous party menu with rich and chocolate-y Brownies Deluxe and listen to the compliments from your guests.

Grilled Cornish Hens take on an extra-special flavor when marinated before cooking. To prepare the marinade, blend 1 teaspoon salt, 1/2 teaspoon ginger, 1 crushed garlic clove, 2 tablespoons lemon juice, 4 tablespoons vegetable oil, 1/2 cup frozen orange juice concentrate, 1/2 cup giblet stock, and 2 teaspoons soy sauce. Hens should be marinated for at least an hour. If longer than an hour, they should be marinated in the refrigerator. When ready to cook, drain and reserve marinade. Pull neck skin back and secure wings against body. Tie tail and legs together. Secure hens on spit according to manufacturer's directions. Start motor. Grill for 45 to 60 minutes brushing occasionally with reserved marinade until golden brown and tender. Your guests will agree — these hens are unusual barbecue fare but their tangy flavor makes them a sure-fire favorite!

Complementing these delicious birds is Grilled Rice Pilaf. You can prepare this in advance and let it cook with the hens. In a small saucepan, slowly heat 1/4 cup salad oil. Add 1/2 cup finely chopped onion and 1/2 cup chopped green pepper. Sauté until tender — about five minutes. Add one beef bouillon cube, 2 teaspoons seasoned salt, a dash of cayenne, 1/2 teaspoon dried oregano leaves, and 1 1/2 cups water. Bring to a boil, stirring occasionally. Cut two 18 x 20-inch rectangles of heavy duty foil. Press inside a 1 1/2-quart bowl to make lining. Be sure

End Summer with a Barbecue

foil extends above bowl. In this lined bowl, combine 1/2 cup coarsely chopped ripe olives and one 5-ounce package precooked rice. Add boiling liquid and stir to combine. Fold foil over top to seal securely. Remove foil package from bowl. Place on grill, five inches above prepared coals. Cook 20 minutes. After cooking, turn back foil and fluff up rice with fork. Sprinkle with parsley and serve right in its own foil packet.

Succotash on the Grill is another dish which is cooked in its own foil packet — think of all the cleaning up you are saving! Cut two 18 x 15-inch rectangles of heavy-duty foil. Dot center of each rectangle with 1 tablespoon butter. Place one 10-ounce package frozen whole kernel corn, thawed, on one rectangle. Place one 10-ounce package frozen Fordhook lima beans, thawed, on the other. Dot each vegetable with 1 tablespoon butter, and sprinkle each with 1/2 teaspoon salt and a dash of pepper. Bring long sides of each rectangle together, fold over twice to seal securely. Fold ends over twice to seal. Place on grill five inches from prepared coals. Cook 20 minutes. Turn, cook 20 minutes longer. Turn vegetables into bowl and toss with 1/4 cup hot light cream.

Apricot Salad is another dish which saves on cleaning up after the party — it can be prepared the day before. Drain 1 can peeled apricots and reserve juice. Dissolve one package apricot gelatin in 1/2 cup boiling water. Add enough water to reserved apricot juice to make 1 1/2 cups liquid. Add to gelatin. Chop apricots, add to gelatin. Add one 3-ounce package cream cheese, cut into small cubes, and 1/4 cup chopped nuts. Pour into salad mold and chill until set.

Such a superb party menu deserves an equally superb dessert. We suggest Brownies Deluxe as a sure-to-please everyone climax to this meal. To prepare, melt two sticks margarine and four squares unsweetened baking chocolate in the top of a double boiler over simmering water. In a bowl, beat four eggs thoroughly. Gradually add 2 cups sugar. Sift 1 1/2 cups presifted flour and 1 heaping teaspoon baking powder together. Add to egg mixture. Add melted chocolate and mix well. Add 2 teaspoons vanilla and 1 cup broken nutmeats. Spread mixture in a 15 x 10 x 1-inch sheet pan. Bake in 300-degree oven for 30 minutes. The topping is cooked in the same pot used for melting the chocolate and butter; the pot should not be washed. Melt one stick margarine and four squares baking chocolate over simmering water. Add 1 small can evaporated milk and 1 cup sugar. Cook slowly over simmering water while brownies bake. Remove brownies from oven when done; cover top immediately with a large package of miniature marshmallows. To the mixture in the double boiler, add one 1-pound box of confectioners' sugar and 1 tablespoon vanilla. Beat until smooth. Pour over marshmallows while still hot. Let stand in pan overnight. When you and your guests are ready to enjoy these rich tidbits, cut them and serve. Then just listen to your guests praise your cooking and ask for your recipes!

FRESH FRUIT DELIGHT SALAD

Cantaloupe balls
Watermelon balls
Diced peaches
Halved strawberries
Diced pears
Sliced bananas
Diced orange sections
Diced apples
Halved grapes

Combine all ingredients in salad bowl. Refrigerate for several hours before serving.

Mrs. Shirley Moore
Xi Alpha Eta X489, Norwalk, Ohio

COLD BROCCOLI SALAD

1 10-oz. package chopped broccoli
Dash of lemon juice
1 can sm. green peas, drained
3 stalks celery, chopped
1 med. onion, finely chopped
Salt and pepper to taste
Mayonnaise

Thaw broccoli; drain well, pressing out as much moisture as possible. Sprinkle broccoli with lemon juice; add peas, celery, onion, salt and pepper. Mix lightly; moisten to taste with mayonnaise. Spoon into lettuce-lined bowl to serve.

Beverly Yount
Nu Xi No. 6574, Piqua, Ohio

TWENTY-FOUR HOUR CABBAGE SALAD

1 med. head cabbage, shredded
1 sm. onion, grated
1 green pepper, diced
1/2 c. sugar
1 c. vinegar
1 tsp. salt
1 tsp. celery seed
1 tsp. prepared mustard
1/8 tsp. pepper
1/2 c. salad oil

Place vegetables in large bowl; sprinkle with sugar. Mix remaining ingredients in saucepan; bring to a boil. Cook for 3 minutes; pour over vegetables. Cover; refrigerate for 24 hours before serving. Salad keeps well in refrigerator.

Naomi Tyer
Theta Lambda No. 7710, Washington, Iowa

Family Favorite

MARINATED FLANK STEAK

also used Mock Tender chuck steaks

1/4 c. soy sauce
3 tbsp. honey
2 tbsp. vinegar
1 1/2 tsp. garlic powder
1 1/2 tsp. ground ginger
3/4 c. salad oil
1 green onion, finely chopped
1 1 1/2-lb. flank steak

Mix soy sauce, honey and vinegar; blend in garlic powder and ginger. Add oil and green onion. Place steak in shallow pan; cover with marinade. Let stand for at least 4 hours. Cook steak over glowing coals for 5 minutes on each side for medium rare, basting occasionally with marinade. Yield: 4 servings.

Sandra Bernhardt
Delta Alpha No. 6273, Fairfax, Virginia

BARBECUED CHUCK STEAK

2 cloves of garlic
2 1 1/2 to 2-lb. chuck steaks
1/2 c. red wine or wine vinegar

Crush garlic; rub into both sides of steaks. Marinate steaks in wine at room temperature for 4 to 6 hours, turning occasionally. Place on broiler rack 4 inches from heat; broil for 6 to 10 minutes on each side. Cut into thin diagonal slices. Yield: 4-6 servings.

Mrs. V. C. Ives
Antioch, California

BEEF KABOBS

1 1/2 lb. round steak
1 lb. mushrooms
2 green peppers
1/2 c. spicy brown mustard
1/4 c. oil
2 tbsp. soy sauce
2 tsp. lemon juice

Cut steak into 2-inch cubes. Wash mushrooms in warm water; drain. Dry on paper towel. Cut green pepper into square pieces. Place steak cube and green pepper square on skewer; add steak cube and mushroom. Repeat until skewer is filled 1 inch from top. Prepare 2 more skewers. Combine remaining ingredients; mix well. Brush on kabobs. Broil 4 to 5 inches from source of heat until of desired degree of doneness. Brush with sauce 3 minutes before removing from heat. Yield: 3 servings.

Photograph for this recipe on page 135.

CHUCK STEAK COOKOUT

1 chuck roast
Salt
Pepper
Garlic salt
Soy sauce
Salad oil

Sprinkle entire surface of roast with salt, pepper and garlic salt to taste; rub seasonings into roast. Moisten roast with generous coating of soy sauce and salad oil. Broil over charcoal, turning occasionally, until of required doneness. Cut in 1/2-inch diagonal slices. Yield: 4-6 servings.

Mickie Wralstad
Gamma Gamma, Sierra Vista, Arizona

BONELESS PORK LOIN ROAST

1 4 to 6-lb. pork loin roast
Salt and pepper to taste
Italian salad dressing

Have butcher bone, roll and tie roast. Season with salt and pepper. Let charcoal burn until gray ash is formed on coals. Insert rod lengthwise through center of roast; secure rod with prongs inserted in ends of roast. Test for balance by rotating in palm of hand. Insert meat thermometer at slight angle so tip is in center of roast but not resting in fat or on rotisserie rod. Make certain thermometer clears cooking unit and drip pan while meat turns. Roast for 3 hours and 30 minutes to 4 hours and 30 minutes or until thermometer registers 170 degrees. Brush roast with salad dressing 2 or 3 times during last 30 minutes of cooking time.

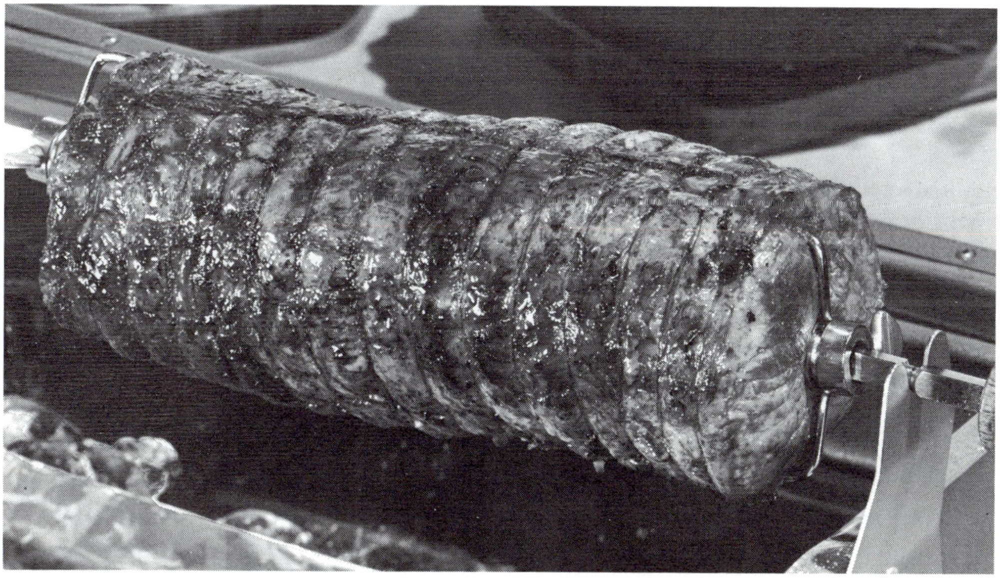

GRILLED BEEF KABOBS

1/4 c. salad oil
2 tbsp. cider vinegar
1 tsp. celery salt
3/4 tsp. garlic salt
1/2 tsp. salt
1/4 tsp. oregano
1/2 tsp. pepper
1 tbsp. prepared mustard
1 sm. bay leaf
1/2 sm. onion, chopped
2 lb. beef, cut in cubes
Green pepper chunks
Mushroom caps

Mix first 10 ingredients for marinade. Place in saucepan; bring to a boil. Cool; add beef. Cover and refrigerate for 6 hours or overnight. Remove beef from marinade, reserving marinade. Thread beef, green pepper chunks and mushroom caps on skewers. Broil over hot coals for 15 to 20 minutes, turning and basting with reserved marinade. Yield: 4-6 servings.

Mrs. Joyce Knudsen
Xi Alpha Beta, Council Bluffs, Iowa

BARBECUED PORK CHOPS

12 to 15 pork chops
1 c. water
1 c. barbecue sauce
1/4 c. lemon juice
4 dashes of charcoal seasoning
Dash of salt
Garlic powder to taste

Cook pork chops on grill over hot coals for 10 minutes on each side or until brown. Mix water and barbecue sauce; add lemon juice, charcoal seasoning, salt and garlic powder. Place pork chops on foil or in pan; pour sauce over pork chops. Cover or close foil; simmer on grill for 30 minutes. Yield: 5 servings.

JoAnn Panuska
Gamma Iota, Newport News, Virginia

SPITTED LAMB ROLL WITH GINGER-PINEAPPLE GLAZE

1 6-lb. leg of lamb
1 clove of garlic, split
1 1/4 tsp. salt
Freshly ground pepper
Dash of rosemary
1/2 c. dark corn syrup
1/2 c. pineapple juice
2 tbsp. lemon juice
1/4 tsp. ground ginger

Have lamb boned and rolled. Rub lamb with garlic; sprinkle with 1 teaspoon salt, pepper and rosemary. Insert spit through lamb, balancing evenly. Shape pan of heavy aluminum foil; place to catch drippings. Set spit in motion; roast lamb about 6 inches from fire for 1 hour. Combine corn syrup, pineapple juice, lemon juice, remaining salt and ginger in saucepan; simmer for 5 minutes. Brush on lamb; broil for 30 minutes longer. Pour drippings from foil pan into saucepan; add any remaining glazing sauce and enough boiling water to make about 1 cup sauce. Heat well; skim off fat. Serve with lamb. Yield: 6 servings.

Mrs. Frank Morgan
Zeta Pi No. 6687, Davis, Oklahoma

GRILLED CORNISH HENS WITH ORANGE MARINADE

1 tsp. salt
1/2 tsp. ginger
1 clove of garlic, crushed
2 tbsp. lemon juice
1/4 c. vegetable oil
1/2 c. orange juice concentrate
1/2 c. giblet stock
2 tsp. soy sauce
3 or 4 Rock Cornish hens

Mix first 8 ingredients for marinade. Pour marinade over hens; let stand for at least 1 hour. Remove hens from marinade, reserving marinade. Secure whole hens on spit or split hens and place on grill. Cook for 1 hour, turning and basting frequently with reserved marinade. Allow 1 hen for each serving.

Mrs. Ardith Day
Alpha Omega, Portland, Oregon

ORANGE-BROILED CHICKEN

Cooking oil
1/2 c. orange marmalade
1/4 c. red wine vinegar
2 tbsp. water
2 tsp. ground ginger
1 env. Italian salad dressing mix
2 broiling chickens, split

Combine 2/3 cup oil, marmalade, vinegar, water, ginger and dressing mix in blender container; cover. Blend well. Place chicken on grill, skin-side down; brush with oil. Broil over low coals for 25 to 30 minutes. Turn; broil for 20 minutes. Brush with orange sauce. Broil for 15 minutes longer or until tender, turning occasionally and brushing with sauce. Yield: 4 servings.

Clodell Taylor
Omega Psi No. 6493, Glen Rose, Texas

PATIO-BROILED CHICKEN

2 2-lb. chickens
1 c. salad oil
1/3 c. lemon juice
3 tbsp. soy sauce
1 clove of garlic, minced
1 tsp. monosodium glutamate
1/2 tsp. salt
1/4 tsp. pepper

Split chickens; break halves at joints. Mix remaining ingredients for marinade; pour over chicken. Cover and refrigerate for 4 hours or overnight, turning chicken occasionally. Lift chicken from marinade, reserving marinade. Arrange chicken on grill, bony side down. Cook for 20 to 30 minutes, brushing with reserved marinade. Turn chicken; cook for 30 minutes longer, brushing occasionally with marinade. Yield: 4 servings.

Gina Balderston
Xi Alpha Gamma, Montrose, Colorado

PICKLE-SPICED CHICKEN

2 2-lb. broiler-fryers
1 c. sweet pickle liquid
Salt and pepper to taste

Combine chickens and pickle liquid. Cover; chill for 2 hours, turning chickens occasionally. Drain and reserve marinade. Sprinkle chickens with salt and pepper. Arrange on spit. Cook in rotisserie or on outdoor grill for about 40 minutes or until chickens are tender. Turn and brush with reserved marinade frequently during cooking period.

BARBECUED CHICKEN

1 pt. vinegar
1 sm. jar mustard
1/2 stick margarine
1 tbsp. pepper
1/2 tbsp. red pepper
1 tbsp. salt
4 chicken halves

Combine first 6 ingredients for basting sauce. Pour into saucepan; simmer for 15 minutes. Place chicken on grill over hot coals. Cook for 45 minutes to 1 hour, turning and basting with sauce. Yield: 4 servings.

Mrs. Harold G. Moore
Xi Rho, Ashland, Kentucky

BARBECUED CARROTS IN WINE

8 med. carrots, whole or sliced
1/2 tsp. garlic salt
1/4 c. minced onion
1/2 c. consomme
1/4 c. sauterne

Place carrots on large sheet of heavy-duty aluminum foil; fold sides up to shape container. Sprinkle carrots with garlic salt and onion. Combine consomme and sauterne; pour over carrots. Seal foil lightly; do not puncture. Place on grill over hot coals. Cook sliced carrots for about 20 minutes; cook whole carrots for 30 minutes or until just tender. Turn once during cooking. Yield: 5 servings.

Mrs. Pat Thomas
Montgomery, Alabama

PEANUT BUTTER-GRILLED CORN

Corn on the cob
Peanut butter
Bacon slices

Husk and clean corn. Spread ears lightly with peanut butter; wrap corn in bacon. Fasten bacon with toothpick. Cook over hot coals for 10 minutes or until done.

Ruth Schmitz
Luxemburg, Wisconsin

CHEESE POTATOES IN FOIL

5 slices bacon
3 lge. potatoes, peeled
Salt and pepper to taste
1 lge. onion, sliced
1/2 lb. cheese, cubed
1 stick butter

Fry bacon until crisp; crumble. Slice potatoes on large piece of foil. Add salt, pepper, bacon, onion and cheese; slice butter over top. Fold foil in drugstore fold; seal ends well. Grill over coals for about 1 hour, turning several times. Serve in foil. Yield: 4 servings.

Mrs. Pat Chaney
DeFuniak Springs, Florida

OLD-FASHIONED BEAN BAKE

1/4 c. unsulphured molasses
1 tbsp. prepared mustard
1 tbsp. vinegar
3 1-lb. cans baked beans in tomato sauce
2 med. onions, sliced
2 tomatoes, sliced

Combine molasses and mustard; add vinegar. Mix well. Turn beans into casserole or baking pan; stir in molasses mixture. Arrange onions and tomato slices over beans. Bake in 375-degree oven for 35 minutes. Yield: 8 servings.

BARBECUED POTATOES

6 lge. baking potatoes
Butter
Salt

Peel and slice potatoes into 1/4-inch slices. Melt 1/2 cup butter in skillet or cake pan. Coat potato slices with butter on both sides; place directly on charcoal grill. Brown on one side; turn and brown on other side. Serve hot and crisp directly from grill. Spread with butter; sprinkle with salt. Yield: 8 servings.

Mrs. Evling Rohm
Decorah, Iowa

GRILLED TOMATOES

6 med. tomatoes
Salt to taste
Worcestershire sauce
Parmesan cheese

Core and halve tomatoes; place on oiled aluminum foil, cut sides up. Salt each half. Sprinkle 2 or 3 drops of Worcestershire sauce onto each half; sprinkle generously with cheese. Fold aluminum foil over; seal. Grill over coals for 15 to 20 minutes. Yield: 6 servings.

Mrs. C. Thomas Bell
Pope AFB, North Carolina

CHARCOALED ONIONS

6 med. onions, peeled
6 bouillon cubes
3 tsp. butter
Salt and pepper to taste

Scoop out small hole in top of each onion; fill with bouillon cube, butter, salt and pepper. Wrap separately and tightly in aluminum foil. Cook on hot coals for about 30 minutes, turning frequently. Unwrap and serve immediately. Yield: 6 servings.

Lois Aaronson
Detroit, Michigan

FRESH PEACH CAKE

1 box white or yellow cake mix
1 tsp. cinnamon
1/2 tsp. nutmeg
1/4 c. butter, melted
2 c. fresh sliced peaches

Divide dry cake mix in half. Prepare 1/2 of the mix according to package directions. Measure 1 cup batter; set aside. Pour remaining batter in greased 9-inch square cake pan. Combine remaining dry cake mix with cinnamon and nutmeg; stir in melted butter to make crumb mixture. Sprinkle half the crumb mixture over batter in pan; arrange peach slices over crumb mixture. Spoon and spread reserved batter evenly over peaches. Sprinkle with remaining crumb mixture. Bake at 350 degrees for 40 minutes. Serve warm with whipped cream or ice cream or serve cold with powdered sugar sprinkled on top. Yield: 8 servings.

Shiela Demartino
Alpha No. 587, Portland, Oregon

CHOCOLATE BAR-ICE CREAM DESSERT

10 almond chocolate bars
1 c. margarine
6 eggs, separated
1 c. powdered sugar
1 c. nutmeats
5 c. crushed vanilla wafers
1/2 gal. ice cream, softened

Melt chocolate bars and margarine in saucepan; combine with beaten egg yolks. Cook over low heat, stirring constantly, for several minutes; add powdered sugar and nuts. Cool; fold in stiffly beaten egg whites. Line 17 x 11 x 2-inch pan with vanilla wafer crumbs to 1/4 to 1/2-inch thickness. Cover with ice cream; pour on chocolate mixture. Cut through several places to mix. Sprinkle top with remaining wafer crumbs. Freeze. Yield: 24 servings.

Mrs. Robert Nissew
Xi Alpha Nu, Webster City, Iowa

HOMEMADE FRUIT SHERBET

1 egg, separated
1/2 c. instant nonfat dry milk
1/3 c. water
1/3 c. sugar
3 tbsp. lemon juice
1 10-oz. package frozen raspberries

Beat egg white, instant milk and water in small bowl until stiff. Add sugar and lemon juice gradually, beating until mixture is stiff. Beat in egg yolk until just mixed. Thaw raspberries; fold into milk mixture. Place in ice tray; freeze for 1 hour before serving. Yield: 6 servings.

Sharon Toutant
Beta Alpha Omicron No. 6360
San Gabriel, California

PATIO COFFEE ICE CREAM

6 tbsp. ground coffee
3 c. milk
2 eggs
1 1/2 c. sugar
2 tbsp. arrowroot
2 c. cream, stiffly whipped

Scald coffee and milk; strain through cheesecloth. Beat eggs, sugar and arrowroot together. Stir in milk; cook in double boiler until mixture thickens. Remove from heat; cool. Add cream. Pour into freezer container; freeze according to freezer directions. Yield: 2 quarts ice cream.

Mrs. Arzo Carson
Huntsville, Tennessee

KIRSCH KABOBS

6 canned peach halves
3 lge. bananas
2 apples, peeled
1 fresh pineapple
2 grapefruit
1 c. grapefruit juice
1/2 c. honey
2 tbsp. kirsch
1 tsp. finely chopped fresh mint

Drain peaches; cut in half. Slice bananas into 3-inch lengths. Cut apples in wedges. Peel and cube pineapple. Peel grapefruit; sever 2 sections at a time, leaving membrane between sections. Combine grapefruit juice, honey, kirsch and mint for marinade. Add fruits; let marinate for at least 1 hour at room temperature. Thread fruits alternately on bamboo skewers. Broil over hot coals for 5 minutes, basting with marinade. Yield: 6 servings.

Mrs. John B. Kohagen
Dayton, Ohio

RASPBERRY-LEMON MOUSSE

1 qt. vanilla ice cream
1 egg white
1/2 c. sugar
1 6-oz. can frozen raspberry-lemon punch
2 tbsp. water
1 c. whipping cream
1 10-oz. package frozen raspberries

Let ice cream soften slightly at room temperature. Spread ice cream evenly in bottom of 9 x 9 x 2-inch pan; freeze until firm. Beat egg white until soft peaks form. Add sugar gradually, beating until stiff peaks form. Thaw punch; combine with water in cup. Fold into meringue slowly until completely blended. Beat cream until stiff. Thaw raspberries; fold into cream. Fold raspberry mixture into meringue mixture; spoon evenly over ice cream in pan. Freeze for 3 hours or until firm. Cut into 9 squares. Yield: 9 servings.

Mildred Hidy
Preceptor Delta No. 152, Tacoma, Washington

CANTALOUPE WITH WINE-BLUEBERRY SAUCE

1/2 c. sugar
1 tbsp. cornstarch
3 thin slices lemon
3/4 c. port
1 1/2 to 2 c. blueberries
Firm vanilla ice cream
Peeled cantaloupe rings or halves

Combine sugar, cornstarch, lemon slices and port in small saucepan; simmer for about 5 minutes or until clear. Remove lemon slices; add blueberries and chill thoroughly. Spoon ice cream into cantaloupe rings; top with chilled blueberry sauce. Yield: 6-8 servings.

Mrs. Nonnie Coombs
Rho Sigma 4912, Woodland, California

LEMON MERINGUE PIE

4 tbsp. vinegar
2 c. water
1 tbsp. pure lemon extract
2 c. sugar
6 tbsp. cornstarch
4 eggs, separated
2 baked pie crusts

Mix vinegar, water and lemon extract in saucepan; bring to a boil. Combine 1 1/2 cups sugar and cornstarch; add to vinegar mixture gradually, stirring until thickened. Pour small amount of hot liquid into beaten egg yolks; return to saucepan. Cook until mixture is clear, stirring constantly. Pour into crusts. Beat egg whites until soft peaks form. Add remaining sugar gradually, beating until stiff peaks form. Spoon over filling. Bake at 425 degrees until meringue is lightly browned.

Margaret Brown
Omicron Zeta, Sanger, California

HOSPITALITY TEA PUNCH

4 qt. water
5 tbsp. tea or 15 tea bags
2 c. lemon juice, strained
4 c. orange juice, strained
1 1/2 qt. grape juice
2 c. sugar
1 qt. ginger ale

Pour 2 quarts water into saucepan; bring to a boil. Remove from heat; add tea. Let steep for 4 minutes. Pour remaining water, juices and sugar into large container; add tea. Stir to mix well. Pour tea mixture into punch bowl over block of ice; stir in ginger ale. Yield: 50 servings.

Donna L. Keller
Alpha Beta No. 7041, Scottsbluff, Nebraska

LEMON ZINGO

1 lge. bottle carbonated water
1 6-oz. can frozen lemonade
1 6-oz. can frozen pineapple juice

Chill carbonated water. Combine frozen juices; pour over ice cubes. Add carbonated water; serve at once in tall glasses. Yield: 4 servings.

Mrs. Judy Douglass
Alpha Beta, Gering, Nebraska

PINK PUNCH

1 pkg. strawberry drink powder mix
1 pkg. raspberry drink powder mix
1 can frozen orange juice
1 can frozen lemonade
1 qt. ginger ale

Dilute drink powder mixes and juice with water according to package directions; chill. Add ginger ale just before serving. Yield: 50 servings.

Nancy Luedke
Xi Gamma, Minot, North Dakota

MELONADE

1 4-lb. watermelon
1/4 c. sugar
3 tbsp. lemon juice
1 qt. carbonated lemon-lime beverage
Lime sherbet
Fresh mint leaves
Maraschino cherries

Remove rind and seeds from watermelon. Puree watermelon in blender or with rotary beater; stir in sugar and lemon juice. Chill thoroughly. Pour about 1/3 cup puree mixture into tall glass; fill with carbonated beverage. Top with scoop of lime sherbet; garnish with mint leaves and cherries. Yield: 12 servings.

Betty Jean Papanek
Alpha Chi No. 743, Downey, California

Witches . . . jack o'lanterns . . . black cats . . . pale clouds scurrying across a high-riding moon — it has to be Halloween! This holiday is beloved by both children and adults — perhaps because all of us enjoy a momentary escape into the wonderful world of make-believe. With its many costumes, fantastic decorations, and scary legends, Halloween does seem to be from another world. It's the perfect holiday for a party where you let your imagination take you where it pleases!

Fun-filled Halloween parties are always popular, especially among the younger set. Children of all ages adore dressing in costumes. When they can dress in their spooky atire *and* go to a party, their joy knows no bounds! If you're giving a children's party, try to have at least three adults on hand for every 25 children. You'll need that many to organize games and to cope with lost overshoes and misplaced coats.

Halloween

Very young children — under six years old — love parties but sometimes may hesitate to join in. To break the ice, have each child lie down on a big piece of paper while an adult traces around him. Children may color their "paper dolls" as they wish, and adults can cut them out. At the end of the party, each child has something to take home. Beanbag games are good with very young children. They love to try to hit wooden bottles, pins, or any designated target.

Party refreshments for very young are best limited to finger foods — apple sections, small popcorn balls, pumpkin cookies, punch, and finger sandwiches. For very special party favors, give each child his own party mask!

Older children — six to about ten — love parties that feature traditional games.

Bobbing for apples will be as popular with this group as it was with you when you were growing up. Remember the excitement of finding the apple that had a dime or a quarter stuck into it? You can capture the same excitement for your children. Just be sure to place a big piece of plastic under the bobbing bucket — water does get spilled in all the hilarity. Try a Halloween version of "Pin the Tail on the Donkey" — "Pin the Head on the Skeleton"! If you have an older child or adult who is willing to play the role, have a fortune telling session. Children love it! By all means, include time for telling ghost stories. A crackling fire adds to the scary atmosphere, but if you don't have a fireplace, try building a centerpiece of leaves and cornstalks and surrounding it with blue and green Christmas lights. These lights make the centerpiece glow eerily and heightens the ghost-filled atmosphere. This age group will love traditional party fare — hot dogs, cake and ice cream.

A Halloween party for teenagers? Let your teenagers do most of the planning themselves — this is the "I'd rather do it myself" age group, remember? You might suggest a "Secret Ambition" party — each guest comes as his secret ambition and everyone tries to guess what that ambition is. Or a "Left Bank" party where everyone dresses as he imagines the Bohemian residents of Montmartre do. Games for this age group

Treat Your Guests to Out-of-This-World Parties

need to be creative . . . like a sculpturing contest. Each boy brings an uncut pumpkin. Boys and girls are paired and each couple is given a sharp knife, a candle and plenty of newspaper to protect the floor. The object is to carve the most imaginative jack o'lantern. Prizes are awarded for the best and worst sculpture. Then candles are placed inside the jack o'lanterns and they are placed around the party room. These glowing, grinning monsters build an atmosphere all their very own.

Dancing is a must at teenagers' parties and so is food. There's just one rule for these parties — whatever the refreshments are to be, be sure to have plenty on hand. Let your youthful host decide what he wants for party foods. You might suggest he capitalize on the teenagers' independence and let them make their own goofy hamburgers — combinations of hamburger meat, sauces, and condiments that are particular favorites of your young guests.

But let's not limit Halloween parties to children and teenagers. After all, adults need to escape into the world of fantasy, too. Try a "Come as You Were" party — guests wear costumes to represent people they might like to have been in times past. Or perhaps a "Come as You Are" party —

invitations are issued by telephone just an hour or so before the party, and guests must come dressed as they were when they received the invitation. If you let the guests guess what each of them was doing, the results can be hilarious!

Party decorations should capitalize on the season, not only the Halloween holiday but the entire autumn spectacle. Brightly colored leaves wired in bunches . . . stalks of Indian corn . . . scarecrows . . . the variety of seasonal decorations is endless. And here again, you can use blue or green Christmas lights to cast an other-world glow over everything.

Since you're in the world of fantasy tonight, why not try some absolutely fantastic games? Perhaps someone in your group can read tarot cards . . . tell fortunes . . . conduct a mock seance . . . or do any one of the hundred and one things associated with the occult. And surely you'll have at least one teller of ghost stories.

Yes, Halloween is your night to escape from the real world into a fantastic other land where strange things happen all the time . . . where anything is possible . . . where people we see every day turn into mysterious creatures with the help of a costume and a mask. With the aid of your own creative imagination, you can make your party the most fabulous, out-of-this-world event ever — just try it and see.

BLENDER TUNA DIP

1 6 1/2-oz. can tuna
2 med. carrots, coarsely chopped
1 stalk celery, coarsely chopped
1/4 sm. onion
Mayonnaise

Place first 4 ingredients in blender container; blend, using enough mayonnaise to make of dip consistency.

Barbara Shaffer
Beta Beta No. 3811, Linwood, New Jersey

HAM-CHIP DIP

1/4 pt. sour cream
1 4-oz. package whipped onion cream cheese
1 2 1/4-oz. can deviled ham

Whip sour cream and cream cheese together until smooth; stir in ham until blended. Serve with crackers or corn chips.

Bonita J. Mitchell
Xi Beta Psi X1994, Harrisburg, Pennsylvania

HOLIDAY DIP

2/3 c. sour cream
2/3 c. mayonnaise
1 tsp. dillweed
1 tbsp. chopped green onion
1 tbsp. Beau Monde seasoning
1 tbsp. parsley

Mix all ingredients together. Serve with carrot sticks, celery sticks, chips or crackers.

B. Collins
Alpha Chi No. 474, Grand Rapids, Michigan

PINEAPPLE DIP

1 8-oz. package cream cheese
1 14-oz. can crushed pineapple

Let cream cheese stand at room temperature until softened; mash with fork. Combine pineapple and juice gradually with cream cheese, blending until fluffy. Yield: 20 servings.

Pat Robik
Alpha Beta No. 1580, Stratford, Connecticut

DEVIL'S DIP

1 1-lb. 13-oz. can pork and beans
1/2 c. grated Cheddar cheese
1/2 tsp. garlic salt
1 tsp. chili powder
1/2 tsp. salt
2 tsp. cider vinegar
2 tsp. Worcestershire sauce
Dash of cayenne pepper
1/2 tsp. smoke-flavored salt
6 slices cooked bacon, crumbled

Combine all ingredients except bacon in blender container; cover. Blend until smooth. Pour into saucepan; cook over low heat until thoroughly heated. Sprinkle with bacon before serving. Serve with potato or corn chips. Yield: About 2 cups.

Ruth Mancl
Gamma Xi No. 6701, Milwaukee, Wisconsin

PIZZA FONDUE DIP

1 onion, chopped
1/2 lb. ground beef
2 tbsp. shortening or margarine
1 tbsp. cornstarch
1 1/2 tsp. fennel seed
1 1/2 tsp. oregano
1/4 tsp. garlic powder
2 10 1/2-oz. cans pizza sauce
10 oz. Cheddar cheese, grated
1 c. grated mozzarella cheese

Brown onion and beef in shortening in fondue pot over high heat; reduce heat to medium. Combine cornstarch, seasonings and pizza sauce; add to beef mixture. Stir well and cook until mixture is thick and bubbly. Add cheeses by thirds, stirring well after each addition. Adjust heat to medium to maintain bubbly consistency. Serve with garlic bread cubes or toasted English muffin cubes for dunking. May be prepared in saucepan on stove.

Manuella Jefferson
Xi Alpha Phi No. 1311, Indianapolis, Indiana

PATIO SHRIMP SALAD

2 env. unflavored gelatin
2 c. milk
1/2 c. sour cream
1/2 c. salad dressing
3 tbsp. vinegar
1 1/2 tsp. seasoned salt
1 tsp. prepared horseradish
1 4 1/2-oz. can shrimp
1/2 c. finely chopped celery
1/3 c. chopped green pepper
2 tbsp. diced pimiento

Soften gelatin in 1/2 cup milk. Dissolve over low heat. Add remaining milk. Chill until partially set. Add sour cream, salad dressing, vinegar, salt and horseradish; mix well. Drain shrimp, dice. Fold shrimp and remaining ingredients into gelatin mixture; pour into lightly oiled individual molds. Chill until firm. Unmold; serve on crisp salad greens. Yield: 6-8 servings.

CHICKEN AND BACON SALAD

1 1/2 c. diced cooked chicken
1/2 c. diced crisp bacon
1/2 c. diced celery
2 hard-cooked eggs, chopped
Salt and pepper
3/4 c. mayonnaise
1/4 c. chili sauce

Combine first 4 ingredients; season to taste with salt and pepper. Chill. Mix mayonnaise and chili sauce; stir into salad mixture. Serve in salad bowl. Yield: 4-6 servings.

Louis L. Dreher
Xi Beta Beta No. 2117, Buffalo, New York

TRICK OR TREAT HAM SALAD

6 hard-cooked eggs
1 1/2 c. diced cooked ham
1/2 c. diced celery
1/2 c. sliced gherkins
1/3 c. mayonnaise or salad dressing
2 tbsp. mustard
1 tbsp. lemon juice
Salt and pepper to taste

Dice eggs coarsely; add ham, celery and gherkins. Blend mayonnaise, mustard and lemon juice; add to ham mixture, tossing lightly. Season with salt and pepper. Chill. Yield: 6 servings.

Beverly Walker
Phi Delta Lambda P2029
Norristown, Pennsylvania

BANANA-CABBAGE SLAW

1/2 med. head cabbage, shredded
1/2 c. mayonnaise
2 tbsp. sugar
1 tbsp. milk
2 to 3 bananas, sliced

Place cabbage in salad bowl. Combine mayonnaise, sugar and milk; mix well. Pour over cabbage. Add bananas; toss lightly. Serve immediately. Yield: 6 servings.

Jan Rae Anderson
Phi Beta Zeta P-907, Elgin, Illinois

SPOOK'S SALAD

2 6 1/2-oz. cans chunk tuna
1 lge. orange
1 unpeeled Golden Delicious apple
1 c. seedless grapes, halved
1/2 c. broken walnuts
1 c. mayonnaise
1 tsp. grated lemon rind
2 tbsp. fresh lemon juice
Salad greens
Paprika

Drain tuna; peel orange and cut into bite-sized pieces. Core apple; dice. Combine tuna, orange, apple, grapes and walnuts in bowl. Blend mayonnaise, lemon rind and lemon juice together. Stir half the blended mayonnaise into tuna mixture lightly. Spoon salad mixture onto crisp salad greens; garnish with remaining mayonnaise mixture. Sprinkle with paprika; serve. Yield: 6 servings.

Mrs. Jean Boyce
Xi Kappa No. 616, Guelph, Ontario, Canada

CABBAGE-MARSHMALLOW SALAD

1 can crushed pineapple
1 sm. head cabbage, finely shredded
1 c. colored miniature marshmallows
1/4 c. shredded coconut
1/2 c. mayonnaise

Drain pineapple, reserving 1/4 cup syrup. Combine pineapple, cabbage, marshmallows and coconut in salad bowl. Blend reserved pineapple syrup and mayonnaise until smooth; pour over salad. Toss lightly and chill for at least 1 hour before serving.

Sharon Scarfone
Phi Alpha Eta P2006
Sault Ste. Marie, Ontario, Canada

CARROT AND RAISIN SALAD

5 med. carrots, grated
1 c. raisins
1 c. mayonnaise

Combine carrots, raisins and mayonnaise; mix well. Chill. Yield: 5 servings.

Barbara L. Foose
Zeta Iota No. 3642, Lancaster, Pennsylvania

PEPPERONI PIZZA

1 pkg. dry yeast
3/4 c. warm water
1/2 tsp. salt
2 tbsp. oil
1/4 c. sugar
3 c. flour

Stir yeast into warm water; let stand for 5 minutes. Mix salt, oil and sugar until dissolved. Add yeast; beat well. Stir in flour gradually until dough is of desired consistency. Knead until smooth. Place in greased bowl; grease top. Cover with waxed paper and tea towel. Allow to rise for 1 hour and 30 minutes. Roll dough out on 2 medium cookie sheets or pizza pans.

Sauce

1 sm. can tomato paste
1 sm. can tomato sauce
1/2 tsp. oregano
2 tsp. oil
1/4 tsp. garlic powder
Pinch of dried red pepper
1/2 tsp. salt

Mix all ingredients for Sauce. Spoon portion of Sauce onto each pizza.

Topping

1 stick pepperoni, sliced
Chopped olives
1 lb. longhorn cheese, grated
1 pkg. mozzarella cheese

Arrange pepperoni and olives on each pizza. Sprinkle longhorn cheese over olives; top with mozzarella cheese. Bake at 450 degrees for 7 to 10 minutes or until dough browns on bottom and cheese becomes bubbly. Dough will keep well for as long as 2 days.

Ann P. Rexrode
Alpha Sigma No. 2809, Elkins, West Virginia

CHILI CON CARNE

2 garlic cloves, minced
1 c. minced onion
1 c. diced green pepper
2 tbsp. salad oil
1 lb. ground beef
2 lge. cans tomato sauce
Chili powder to taste
Salt to taste
2 No. 2 cans kidney beans
1 can mushrooms
Dash of cayenne (opt.)

Saute garlic, onion and green pepper in hot oil for 5 minutes in large heavy kettle; stir occasionally. Add beef; cook slowly until lightly browned, stirring often to break beef apart. Mix in tomato sauce and seasonings; cover tightly. Cook over low heat for 20 minutes. Add kidney beans and mushrooms; stir well. Simmer uncovered for 20 to 25 minutes. Yield: 6-8 servings.

Mrs. Judy Cabreana
Antigo, Wisconsin

ITALIAN SPAGHETTI SAUCE

1 lge. onion, cut up
2 tbsp. salad oil
2 lb. hamburger meat
2 sm. cans tomato paste
2 tomato paste cans water
1 sm. can stewed tomatoes
4 tbsp. oregano
2 tbsp. thyme
1 lge. bay leaf
1 tbsp. salt
1 tbsp. pepper

Saute onion in oil until transparent. Brown meat in large saucepan; drain off excess fat. Add tomato paste, water, tomatoes, oregano, thyme, onion and bay leaf. Sprinkle with salt and pepper. Bring to a boil; simmer until meat is tender and flavors are blended, stirring occasionally. Sauce may be frozen. Yield: 6-8 servings.

Mrs. Ramona Tounsend
Alpha Tau 748, Wichita Falls, Texas

BEEF IN COSTUME FOR HALLOWEEN

1 4-lb. pumpkin
1 lb. lean ground beef
1 c. chopped onion
Cooking oil
1/3 c. chopped red pepper
1/3 c. chopped green pepper
1 minced garlic clove
1 tsp. salt
1/4 tsp. thyme
1/4 tsp. pepper
1 7 1/2-oz. can pitted ripe olives
1 8-oz. can tomato sauce
2 beaten eggs

Cut top from pumpkin; scrape out seeds and fibers. Simmer in salted water to cover for about 20 to 25 minutes or until almost tender. Drain. Brown beef and onion in 1 tablespoon oil. Add red pepper, green pepper and garlic. Cook for 1 minute longer. Remove from heat; stir in remaining ingredients. Spoon into pumpkin; place lid on top. Brush pumpkin with oil. Bake at 350 degrees for about 1 hour. Let stand about 10 minutes; cut into wedges to serve. Yield: About 8 servings.

BARBECUED WIENERS

1 1/2 lb. wieners
1 med. onion, diced
2 tbsp. butter
2 tbsp. vinegar
2 tbsp. brown sugar
4 tbsp. lemon juice
1 c. catsup
1/2 tbsp. dry mustard
1/2 c. water
1/2 c. diced celery

Prick wieners; cook in boiling water for 5 minutes. Combine remaining ingredients in saucepan; simmer for 30 minutes. Place wieners in baking dish; cover with sauce. Bake at 350 degrees for 30 to 40 minutes. Yield: 6 servings.

Mrs. Levonda Andrick
Preceptor Epsilon XP-499
Richwood, West Virginia

FRIENDLY FRANKS

8 to 10 frankfurters
8 to 10 frozen tortillas
2 10-oz. cans chili
1 tbsp. instant minced onion
1 8-oz. can tomato sauce
1 c. shredded Cheddar cheese

Roll each frankfurter up in tortilla; place in greased baking dish. Blend chili, onion and tomato sauce and pour over frankfurters. Bake at 375 degrees for 30 minutes. Remove from oven; sprinkle with cheese. Several drops of hot sauce or chopped fresh onion may be added if desired. Yield: 8 servings.

Mrs. Virginia A. Lowcock
Xi Alpha Theta X-1928, Bartlesville, Oklahoma

STUFFED HAMBURGERS

1 lb. hamburger
1/2 c. evaporated milk
1 sm. onion, chopped
Salt and pepper to taste
1/2 c. whole kernel corn
1/2 c. diced cheese
1/4 c. diced green pepper
2 tbsp. chili sauce
Dash of chili powder

Combine first 4 ingredients; shape into patties. Combine remaining ingredients. Spoon stuffing on half the patties; place remaining patties on top, sealing edges well. Place patties on broiler pan. Bake at 350 degrees for 30 minutes or until done. Yield: 4-6 servings.

Esther Gruling
Xi Pi X-2067, Merrill, Wisconsin

FRANK KABOBS

Frankfurters
American cheese strips
Bacon strips

Cut each frankfurter crosswise into 5 pieces; slit down center. Insert cheese strips. Wrap bacon strip around each frankfurter piece; secure with toothpick. Place frankfurters on baking sheet. Broil for 3 to 5 minutes.

Janet E. Caouette
Beta Epsilon No. 3560, Webster, Massachusetts

PRONTO PUPS

1 egg
1/2 c. milk
1 c. prepared biscuit mix
2 tbsp. yellow cornmeal
1/4 tsp. paprika
1/2 tsp. dry mustard
1/8 tsp. cayenne pepper
1 lb. miniature frankfurters

Heat deep fat to 375 degrees in electric skillet. Blend egg and milk together; stir in dry ingredients. Dip frankfurters into batter; fry until brown. Serve on cocktail picks. Bake in 400-degree oven for about 5 minutes if necessary to reheat.

Karen Cairat
Rho Chi No. 4945, Upland, California

BUMSTEADS

1/4 lb. Cheddar cheese, grated
2 tbsp. chopped green pepper
2 tbsp. chopped olives
2 tbsp. chopped sweet pickle
2 tbsp. chopped onion
1/2 c. mayonnaise
3 hard-cooked eggs, diced
1 can tuna, drained
6 to 8 wiener buns

Combine all ingredients except buns; spread filling in buns. Wrap in aluminum foil or place in paper bag. Place on baking sheet. Bake at 325 degrees for 25 minutes. Yield: 6-8 servings.

Margaret Lauderdale
Waterloo, Wisconsin

BEST-EVER BUNS

4 c. diced turkey or ham
1 c. chopped ripe olives
1 c. grated Cheddar cheese
1 c. chopped celery
1 c. salad dressing
16 hamburger buns

Mix all ingredients except buns together in large mixing bowl. Scoop centers out of buns; fill with turkey mixture. Wrap buns tightly in foil paper; place on baking sheet. Bake in 350-degree oven for 15 minutes. Serve hot. Yield: 16 servings.

Mrs. Virginia Hobbs
Gamma Iota, Beloit, Kansas

SLOPPY JOES

1 onion, diced
1/2 c. diced celery
2 tbsp. butter
2 lb. ground beef
3 tbsp. Worcestershire sauce
Juice of 1/2 lemon
1 bottle catsup
2 tbsp. vinegar
2 tbsp. brown sugar
1/2 tbsp. dry mustard
Buns

Saute onion and celery in butter in skillet until tender. Combine beef, Worcestershire sauce, lemon juice, catsup, vinegar, brown sugar and mustard in large kettle. Add onion mixture and mix well. Bring to a boil, stirring. Reduce heat and simmer for 30 minutes. Serve beef mixture on buns.

Mrs. Shirley Hostens
Xi Beta Alpha, Davenport, Iowa

PEANUT BUTTER SANDWICH

Sliced bread
Butter
Sliced bananas
Peanut butter

Spread several slices bread with butter; cover with bananas. Spread same number of slices bread with peanut butter; invert on bananas.

Mrs. Ray Whittlef
Crown, Minnesota

FILLED BUN SURPRISE

1 lb. ground beef
Cooking oil
1/4 lb. mild cheese, grated
3 hard-boiled eggs, diced
1/2 c. mayonnaise
2 tbsp. chopped green pepper
2 tbsp. chopped onion
2 tbsp. chopped black olives
2 tbsp. chopped sweet pickles
6 hamburger buns

Brown ground beef in small amount of oil; drain well. Combine beef and remaining ingredients except buns; mix lightly. Split buns; fill with mixture. Wrap individually in foil. Bake at 250 degrees for 30 minutes. Yield: 6 servings.

L. Lorraine Vodopich
Xi Alpha Alpha X-2055, Sunnyside, Utah

GOBLIN'S PEANUT BUTTER BREAD

2 c. all-purpose flour
3 tsp. baking powder
1/2 tsp. salt
1/2 c. sugar
1/2 c. peanut butter
2 well-beaten eggs
1 c. milk
1 tsp. grated lemon rind
1/2 c. chopped salted peanuts
Melted butter

Sift dry ingredients together; rub in peanut butter until mixture is crumbly. Combine eggs, milk and lemon rind; add to flour mixture. Pour into greased 9 x 5-inch loaf pan; sprinkle with peanuts. Bake for 50 to 60 minutes at 325 to 350 degrees. Brush hot bread with melted butter. Let set overnight; remove from pan and slice.

Gerda Livingstone
Xi Nu X-3117, Rosetown, Saskatchewan, Canada

POPCORN BALLS

1/2 lb. popcorn
1 c. sugar
1 c. white corn syrup
1 3-oz. package orange gelatin

Prepare popcorn according to package directions; place in large pan. Bring sugar, syrup and gelatin to a boil in saucepan, stirring until sugar and gelatin are dissolved. Pour over popcorn mix until popcorn is completely coated. Form balls quickly with hands; place on waxed paper. Cool. Yield: 18 balls.

Julie Ann Knopp
Xi Lambda 1155, Idaho Falls, Idaho

FIRESIDE FUDGE

1 c. sugar
1 c. (packed) brown sugar
2/3 c. evaporated milk
1/4 c. butter or margarine
1/2 c. peanut butter
1 7-oz. jar marshmallow creme
2 tsp. vanilla

Combine sugars, milk and butter in saucepan. Bring to a boil, stirring frequently. Cook to soft-ball stage, 238 degrees on candy thermometer, stirring occasionally. Add peanut butter, marshmallow creme and vanilla; stir to blend thoroughly. Pour into greased 8-inch square pan; refrigerate until firm. Cut into squares.

Charlotte Cisco
Xi Epsilon Zeta X 1529, Glendora, California

HOBGOBLIN COOKIES

Melted butter
3/4 c. salad oil
1 c. sugar
1 c. brown sugar
2 eggs
1 tsp. vanilla
1 1/4 c. flour
1 tsp. soda
1 tsp. cinnamon
Dash of salt
3 c. oatmeal
1 c. chocolate chips

Add enough butter to oil to make 1 cup liquid. Mix sugars, eggs, vanilla and oil mixture together; beat with electric mixer until well blended. Sift flour, soda, cinnamon and salt together; add to egg mixture. Add oatmeal and chocolate chips. Drop by spoonfuls onto cookie sheet. Bake at 350 degrees for 12 to 14 minutes. Yield: 4 dozen.

Jo Ann Overbey
Theta Psi, San Luis Obispo, California

CARAMEL APPLES

1 14-oz. can sweetened condensed milk
1 c. sugar
1/2 c. light corn syrup
1/8 tsp. salt
1 tsp. vanilla
6 med. apples
6 wooden skewers

Mix milk, sugar, corn syrup and salt in heavy 2-quart saucepan. Cook over low heat, stirring constantly, until mixture comes to a boil and sugar is dissolved. Continue cooking over low heat, stirring constantly, for about 30 to 40 minutes or until temperature reaches 230 degrees on candy thermometer or until mixture spins 2-inch thread when dropped from spoon. Remove from heat; stir in vanilla. Cool for 5 minutes. Insert wooden skewers in apples; dip in caramel until well covered, tilting pan as needed. Cool on lightly greased baking sheet.

HAUNTED HOUSE COOKIES

2 c. sugar
1/2 c. milk
1 c. margarine
1 tsp. vanilla
3 c. quick-cooking oats
1/2 c. peanut butter
1 c. nuts

Combine sugar, milk and margarine in saucepan; bring to a rolling boil. Boil for 1 minute; remove from heat. Add vanilla, oats, peanut butter and nuts; stir until peanut butter melts. Drop on waxed paper by spoonfuls; cool. Serve. Yield: 3 dozen.

Elsie Krohn
Phi 2681, Henderson, Nevada

BROWN-EYED SUSANS

1/2 c. margarine
1/2 c. butter
3 tbsp. sugar
2 c. sifted flour
1/2 tsp. salt
1/2 tsp. almond extract
1 tsp. vanilla
1 c. confectioners' sugar
2 tbsp. cocoa
2 tbsp. hot water
25 blanched almonds, halved

Cream margarine and butter together; add sugar gradually. Add flour, salt, almond extract and 1/2 teaspoon vanilla. Chill dough. Form scant teaspoons of dough into balls. Place on ungreased cookie sheet. Flatten balls slightly by pressing gently with fingers. Bake at 375 degrees for about 12 minutes or until slightly browned. Cool. Combine confectioners' sugar, cocoa, water and remaining vanilla; let stand for several minutes. Ice each cookie with scant 1/2 teaspoon icing. Press almonds into icing. Yield: About 45 cookies.

June Mitchell
Providence Beta, Warwick, Rhode Island

SUGARED YEAST DOUGHNUTS

1 c. milk
1 env. yeast
3 1/2 c. sifted flour
1/4 c. shortening
1 tsp. salt
1/4 c. sugar
1 egg
Shortening

Heat milk slightly; dissolve yeast. Add 1 1/2 cups flour; beat until smooth. Cover; let rise in warm place for about 2 hours, until doubled in bulk. Cream shortening, salt and sugar together; add egg, blending well. Stir into yeast sponge; add remaining flour. Beat well for 5 minutes by hand. Rub top with shortening; let rise again until doubled in bulk. Roll out 1/2-inch thick; cut with floured doughnut cutter. Allow to rise for 45 minutes. Fry for about 3 to 5 minutes in deep 365-degree shortening until brown. Drain; sprinkle with additional sugar. Yield: 2 dozen doughnuts.

Anne T. Stefun
Chi Omicron No. 5480
Rancho Cordova, California

EASY-DO DONUTS

Sugar
1/2 c. milk

1 egg
Melted shortening
1 1/2 c. sifted all-purpose flour
2 tsp. baking powder
1/2 tsp. salt
1/2 c. seedless raisins
1/2 tsp. nutmeg or cinnamon

Blend 1/3 cup sugar, milk, egg and 2 tablespoons melted shortening together. Sift flour, baking powder and salt together; add to liquid mixture. Stir lightly. Mix in raisins. Drop by heaping teaspoonfuls into melted 365-degree shortening. Fry for 2 to 3 minutes or until golden brown. Drain on paper towels. Mix 1/4 cup sugar and nutmeg in bag. Shake warm donuts in bag with sugar. May coat in confectioners' sugar without nutmeg if desired. Yield: 2 1/2 dozen.

BAKED DOUGHNUTS

5 tbsp. butter, creamed
1/2 c. sugar
1 egg
1 1/2 c. flour
2 1/4 tsp. baking powder
1/4 tsp. salt
1/4 tsp. nutmeg
1/2 c. milk

Mix butter, sugar and egg together; add dry ingredients and milk alternately. Blend well; fill buttered muffin tins 1/2 full. Bake at 425 degrees for 20 to 25 minutes. Remove from tins; pour Glaze over muffins.

Glaze

6 tbsp. butter
1/2 c. sugar
1/2 tsp. cinnamon

Melt butter; stir in sugar and cinnamon. Yield: 12 servings.

Lynne Robinson
Gamma Epsilon No. 1573, Flint, Michigan

HOT COCOA

1 1/2 c. cocoa
2 c. sugar

1/2 tsp. salt
2 tsp. vanilla
1 pt. warm water
1 qt. boiling water
8 qt. milk
50 marshmallows

Blend cocoa, sugar, salt and vanilla with warm water; add to boiling water in saucepan. Boil gently for about 5 minutes. Add milk and heat; do not boil. Serve hot with marshmallow floating on each cup of cocoa. Yield: 50 servings.

Mrs. Harold Rushton
Salt Lake, Utah

SPECTER'S SUNDAE

3 tbsp. butter
1 c. brown sugar
1/2 tsp. cinnamon
1/2 c. light cream
4 lge. bananas, sliced
Ice cream
Toasted coconut

Melt butter in saucepan; add brown sugar and cinnamon. Heat gently until sugar melts. Remove from heat; stir in cream. Return to low heat; continue stirring. Drop in bananas gently. Serve hot over ice cream; sprinkle with toasted coconut.

Verna Kidd
Xi Alpha Beta X 557, Nelson, British Columbia

THE GREAT PUMPKIN PUNCH

2 6-oz. cans frozen orange juice
1 1/2 c. white corn syrup
1 pt. orange sherbet
3 trays ice cubes
2 qt. ginger ale

Blend orange juice and corn syrup together in punch bowl; add sherbet and ice cubes. Pour ginger ale into mixture; let frozen ingredients melt partially. Float orange slices and colored ice on top if desired. Yield: 20 servings.

Patti Sorg
Alpha Delta, Baraboo, Wisconsin

DEVIL'S BREW

3 c. pineapple juice
3 c. water
1 tbsp. whole cloves
1 1/2 tsp. whole allspice
3 2-in. cinnamon sticks, broken
1/4 tsp. salt
1/2 c. light brown sugar

Pour pineapple juice and water in 9-cup percolator; place remaining ingredients in percolator basket. Perk for 10 minutes; remove basket. Serve hot. Yield: 8-10 servings.

Eleanor Atwood
Zi Epsilon, Waterville, Maine

DEMON PUNCH

1/4 c. whole cloves
3 c. water
1 c. sugar
1/2 gal. orange juice
1 46-oz. can pineapple juice

Add cloves to water; boil gently in saucepan until spicy and tea-colored. Remove cloves from water; add sugar. Combine juices; add clove mixture. Heat; serve hot. Yield: 20 servings.

Velma Jackson
Beta Lambda, Scotia, New York

WITCHES' BREW

4 c. milk
3 tbsp. sugar
3 tbsp. instant coffee
1/3 c. quick chocolate-flavored drink mix
1/2 tsp. cinnamon

Heat milk in saucepan. Mix sugar, coffee, chocolate-flavored drink mix and cinnamon. Stir into hot milk; heat. Pour into serving cups or mugs. Garnish with whipped cream and cinnamon stick if desired. Yield: 4 servings.

Photograph for this recipe on page 147.

CALYPSO SHAKE

4 c. milk
8 tsp. (heaping) chocolate drink powder
2 ripe bananas, finely mashed
1/2 pt. vanilla or banana ice cream

Combine first 3 ingredients in 1 1/2-quart refrigerator container; spoon in ice cream. Stir to blend; cover. Chill. Shake well before serving. Yield: 4 servings.

Melody Forbes
Phi Eta Mu P-2282, Los Angeles, California

HALLOWEEN DOUGHNUTS

3 1/3 c. pancake mix
1/3 c. sugar
1 tsp. cinnamon
1/2 tsp. mace
1/4 tsp. cardamom
1/3 c. soft shortening
2 eggs, beaten
Milk
1 c. sifted confectioners' sugar
1/2 tsp. vanilla

Combine pancake mix, sugar, cinnamon, mace and cardamom. Cut in shortening until mixture resembles coarse crumbs. Add eggs and 2/3 cup milk; mix thoroughly. Turn out on lightly floured board or canvas; knead gently for several seconds. Roll out to 1/2-inch thickness; cut with floured doughnut cutter. Fry in hot deep fat for 2 to 3 minutes or until golden brown. Drain on absorbent paper. Cool. Beat confectioners' sugar, 4 tablespoons milk and vanilla together until smooth. Drizzle glaze on doughnuts. Decorate with chocolate shot, nonpareils or candy corn. Yield: 12 doughnuts.

MAPLE CANDIED APPLES

2 c. maple-blended syrup
1 c. sugar
1/4 tsp. cream of tartar
9 wooden skewers
9 med. apples
Chopped peanuts

Bring syrup to a boil in top of double boiler. Stir in sugar and cream of tartar, stirring until sugar is dissolved. Cover; boil for 3 minutes. Uncover; cook over medium-high heat to hard-crack stage or 300 degrees on candy thermometer. Remove from heat; place over hot, not boiling, water. Insert wooden skewer into each apple. Dip apple into candy, turning to coat evenly. Let excess drip from bottom of apple. Roll bottom half of apple immediately in peanuts; press lightly with palm of hand to make peanuts adhere to candy. Place on lightly greased aluminum foil to cool. Combine remaining syrup and remaining peanuts; spread on lightly greased aluminum foil. Cool; break into pieces for candy.

MERRY JACK-O'-LANTERNS

6 c. puffed rice
1/4 c. butter or margarine
4 c. miniature marshmallows
1 tsp. orange extract
1/4 tsp. red food coloring
1/4 tsp. yellow food coloring
8 med.-sized green gumdrops
Thick confectioners' sugar frosting
8 med.-sized black gumdrops
8 2-in. pieces black string licorice

Preheat oven to 350 degrees. Place puffed rice in shallow baking pan. Bake for 10 minutes. Pour into large greased bowl. Melt butter and marshmallows in top of double boiler over boiling water, stirring occasionally until smooth. Stir in orange extract and red and yellow food coloring. Pour over puffed rice, stirring until evenly coated. Shape into 8 balls with greased hands. Let stand for several hours or until firm. Fasten green gumdrop on top of each ball with frosting for a stem. Cut each black gumdrop into 3 triangles; arrange triangles on each ball for nose and eyes. Add black string licorice for mouth. Let jack-o'-lanterns stand until frosting is set.

COOKIE OWLS

2/3 c. shortening, soft
1 c. (firmly packed) brown sugar

1 egg
1 tsp. vanilla
1 c. crunchy peanut butter
1 1/3 c. sifted all-purpose flour
1 tsp. baking powder
1/2 tsp. salt
1 c. oatmeal
1 1-oz. envelope no-melt chocolate
Semisweet chocolate pieces
Whole cashews

Combine shortening and sugar; beat until creamy. Add egg, vanilla and peanut butter; blend thoroughly. Sift flour, baking powder and salt together. Add to creamed mixture; blend well. Stir in oatmeal. Divide dough in half. Shape one half to form roll 8 inches long. Add chocolate to remaining dough. Roll out chocolate dough on waxed paper to form an 8-inch square. Place roll on chocolate dough. Wrap chocolate dough around roll; pinch seam together. Wrap in waxed paper; chill for at least 1 hour. Let stand at room temperature for 10 minutes before cutting. Cut into 1/4-inch slices. Pinch chocolate dough to form 2 ears for each owl face. Use 2 chocolate pieces for eyes and 1 cashew for beak. Place on ungreased cookie sheets. Bake in preheated 350-degree oven for 12 to 15 minutes. Yield: About 30 cookies.

SPELL-BREAKER CANDY SQUARES

2 c. semisweet chocolate or butterscotch pieces
2/3 c. sweetened condensed milk
1 tsp. vanilla
1/8 tsp. salt
3/4 c. oatmeal
1/3 c. chopped nutmeats
1/4 c. flaked or shredded coconut

Melt chocolate pieces over hot water. Add remaining ingredients; blend thoroughly. Spread in greased 8-inch square pan. Chill until firm. Cut into squares. Yield: 36 squares.

An old New England hymn begins "We gather together to ask the Lord's blessing . . . and our thanks to make known." Those few words capture the wonderfully warm spirit of Thanksgiving as few others do. Thanksgiving is a time when family members gather to give thanks for their bounty during the year which has passed . . . a bounty which includes not just material prosperity, but the love we all have for one another.

Remember the family Thanksgiving of childhood? The long ride to grandmother's. The excitement of seeing relatives you hadn't seen since last Thanksgiving. The quiet joy of the church service followed by the riotous excitement of a local football game. Yes, these things are all part of our Thanksgiving heritage.

Revive that heritage this year with a family-style Thanksgiving. You might want to prepare the entire dinner yourself. Or you might ask each family group to bring one or two dishes for the dinner. If you have many

Thanksgiving Day

children coming, try a large table — for adults — and a smaller one for the children. You might even cook two turkeys, one for each table!

Above all, build your own traditions. Perhaps you'll want to share your Thanksgiving with someone who would otherwise be alone. This warm and hospitable custom has long been a highlight of American Thanksgivings. Or build a family portrait album. Each year, have someone take a family picture. What a priceless treasure such an album will be! And do try to develop a tradition just for the children. Why not let them make placecards for the guests. You provide paper, scissors, crayons, glue, and old shirts for smocks. They provide the imagination.

Of course, the high point of Thanksgiving is the turkey dinner with all the trimmings. Here's a menu to serve six that combines the very traditional dishes with some brand-new ideas. Center of attraction is the magnificent Roast Turkey. This year, try a new dressing — fabulously-flavored Orange Rice Stuffing. For a complementary flavor note, add Baked Tangerines. November is the peak of the tangerine season, and you're sure to find the fresh fruit needed to prepare this delightful dish. For vegetables, add two all-time favorites — cauliflower and Brussels sprouts. Cauliflower with Almonds is a sure-to-please taste treat. And the unusual flavor of Brussels Sprouts Royal will bring compliments from family and guests. For a tart and mouth-watering side dish, try Orange-Cranberry Relish. It's the perfect flavor note for this meal. For dessert, offer your family and guests their choice of Pumpkin Chiffon Pie or elegant Orange Crepes. As you browse through the recipes, you'll note that many of them have been selected because they can be prepared in advance of the great turkey day — leaving you free to visit with your guests.

Thanksgiving just wouldn't be the same without the turkey — it's been an American tradition ever since the first Thanksgiving at Plymouth Colony. To prepare, wash a 12 to 14-pound turkey in cold running

Serve a Traditional Harvest Feast

water. Pat the inside dry with paper toweling; leave the outside moist. Sprinkle the inside cavities with salt and pepper. In a large saucepan, heat 1 cup butter or margarine. Add 1 cup chopped onion and cook until onion is tender but not brown. Add 4 cups water, 1 cup orange juice, 3 tablespoons grated orange rind, 4 cups chopped celery, 2 tablespoons salt, and 1 teaspoon poultry seasoning. Bring to a boil and stir in 5 1/3 cups packaged precooked rice. Cover and remove from heat. Let stand for 5 minutes. Add 1/2 cup chopped parsley. Fluff with fork. Stuff rice mixture in neck and body cavities of turkey. Fasten neck skin to body with skewer. Push legs under band of skin at tail or tie to tail. Place turkey, breast side up, on rack in shallow open roasting pan. Cover with a loose tent of aluminum foil if desired. Bake at 325 degrees for 4 hours and 30 minutes of cooking time. If you wish, gravy may be prepared from turkey drippings. If you plan your cooking schedule so that the turkey has 15 to 20 minutes to set after being removed from oven, carving will be much easier.

To prepare Baked Tangerines, make eight verticle cuts in the tangerine skin from blossom end to about one inch from the bottom.

Pull peel down; turn pointed ends in. Remove white membrane from fruit. Loosen sections at center; pull apart slightly. Place in baking pan. Fill center of each tangerine with 1 teaspoon sugar and dot with 1 teaspoon butter. Pour 2/3 cup orange juice over tangerines. Bake in 325-degree oven for 30 minutes. Spoon a small amount of Orange-Cranberry Relish in center of each and serve with turkey.

Orange-Cranberry Relish is good, not only with Baked Tangerines, but by itself as a side dish. It can be prepared several weeks before your dinner. Quarter two oranges and remove seeds. Force orange with peel and 4 cups fresh cranberries through food chopper. Add 2 cups sugar and mix well. Chill in refrigerator for several hours before serving. Relish will keep in refrigerator for several weeks.

Brussels Sprouts Royal combines the flavors of water chestnuts and Brussels sprouts into an exciting vegetable dish. Halve the larger sprouts of two 10-ounce packages frozen Brussels sprouts. Drain one 5-ounce can of water chestnuts, reserving liquid. Dice chestnuts. Add enough water to chestnut juice to make 1 cup liquid. Pour liquid into saucepan. Add 2 teaspoons salt, 1 teaspoon sugar, 1/2 teaspoon seasoned salt, and 1/2 cup snipped parsley. Bring to a boil. Add Brussels sprouts. Simmer, covered, for 8 to 10 minutes. Drain off liquid; toss in 1/4 cup butter and diced chestnuts. What an utterly delicious dish!

Another great flavor combination is Cauliflower with Almonds. To prepare, steam one large cauliflower for 20 minutes. Meanwhile, saute 1/2 cup slivered almonds, 1 cup soft bread crumbs, and one minced garlic clove in 4 tablespoons butter until almonds are golden and crumbs crisp. Serve the sauce over cauliflower.

Everyone enjoys a choice of great desserts. With this meal, try offering two tempting favorites. Pumpkin Chiffon Pie is the traditional Thanksgiving favorite with a lighter-than-usual touch. Beat 3 egg yolks and 1/2 cup sugar until thick. Add 1 1/4 cups canned pumpkin, 1/2 cup milk, 1/2 teaspoon salt, 1/2 teaspoon ginger, 1/2 teaspoon cinnamon, and 1/2 teaspoon nutmeg. Cook in double boiler until thick. Then add one envelope unflavored gelatin softened in 1/4 cup cold water. Stir until gelatin dissolves. Beat 3 egg whites with 1/2 cup sugar until stiff. Add to pumpkin mixture. Pour into a 9-inch pie shell. Chill until set. If desired, top with sweetened whipped cream before serving.

Your second dessert is an eye-pleaser as well as a delight to the palate . . . Orange Crepes. Beat three eggs and two egg yolks together. Add 1/2 cup milk, 1/2 cup orange juice, 2 tablespoons salad oil, 1 cup all-purpose flour, 3/4 teaspoon salt, 1 tablespoon sugar, and 1 teaspoon grated orange rind. Beat until smooth. Let stand at room temperature for at least one hour. Then brush a hot 7 or 8-inch skillet lightly with salad oil. Pour 2 tablespoons batter onto skillet. Tip skillet so that mixture covers the bottom evenly. Batter will set immediately into a thin, lacy pancake. Cook for about 15 to 20 seconds until brown. Loosen with spatula and flip over. Brown other side and turn crepe out onto foil or waxed paper. Repeat until all batter is used.

To prepare the orange sauce that gives these crepes their delightful flavor and texture, cream 1/2 cup soft butter with 1/2 cup confectioners' sugar and 1 tablespoon grated orange rind. Gradually blend in 3 tablespoons grenadine. Spread about 1/2 teaspoon of this mixture over each

crepe, spreading it on the last-browned side. Roll up crepes so that the side first browned — the most attractive side — shows. Place the rest of the butter mixture in a large chafing dish. Add 1/3 cup orange juice. Heat in dish until bubbly. Add rolled crepes and heat, spooning sauce over top. Add 1 cup orange sections, and heat for two or three minutes longer.

To highlight this marvelous dinner, you'll want the very best table decorations and settings. Plenty of candles, of course. If you choose to have two tables, one for adults and the other for the younger set, make the small table a replica of the adult one but with a plastic tablecloth and the sturdier china and glassware.

Echo the "plentiful bounty" theme in your decorations. Perhaps a huge basket laid on its side and spilling out great shiny red apples, plump grapes, ripe bananas, and golden oranges and tangerines. To make fruit beautifully elegant, dip each piece into egg white which has been beaten until frothy, then into sugar. Let set on a rack for at least an hour, and arrange in a glass compote or other dish. If you want to use a centerpiece which is not fruit, try filling various sized apothecary jars with unshelled nuts. Cluster the jars on boughs of bittersweet or seasonal greens and shiny berries. The possibilities of appropriate and beautiful centerpieces for this holiday are endless!

It seems far too soon that the big day is ending. Youngsters are being hustled into waiting cars for the long trip home . . . the search for lost gloves is beginning . . . promises are being exchanged of visits "before next Thanksgiving." After the guests have gone . . . after the excitement has burned down to a warm glow . . . what do you feed that once-again-hungry family of yours?

Turkey, of course. But in a new and deliciously different casserole . . . Leftover Turkey Delight. This is the main course of a Thanksgiving Night Supper menu that's especially easy on you. With this turkey dish, serve Chafing Dish Spinach Salad and a richly filling Mincemeat Cake.

Leftover Turkey Delight features the flavors of Italian cooking in a certain-to-please dish. Combine one 1-pound 12-ounce can tomatoes, 2 1/4 cups tomato juice, 1/4 cup cooking oil, 1/4 cup chopped onion, 1/4 cup chopped green pepper, 1 teaspoon salt, and 1 teaspoon garlic salt in a large saucepan. Stir in 1 cup long grain rice. Cover and bring to a boil. Add two 9-ounce packages frozen artichoke hearts — thawed — 3 to 4 cups diced cooked turkey, and 1/2 cup sliced stuffed green olives. Turn into a 3-quart casserole dish or into two small casserole dishes. Cover and bake, stirring occasionally, in a 350-degree oven for 1 hour and 25 minutes or until rice is tender. Garnish with stuffed green olives. (NOTE: This dish may be frozen after baking and served later, if desired.)

Such a marvelous flavor combination deserves an equally delicious salad — Chafing Dish Spinach Salad. Wash one pound fresh spinach and discard stems. Pat dry on paper towels; tear into bite-sized pieces. Place in bowl and add four green onions and tops, sliced. Sprinkle with coarsely ground black pepper and chill. Dice and fry five slices bacon slowly in a deep chafing dish or electric skillet until crisp. Add 2 tablespoons wine vinegar, 1 tablespoon lemon juice, 1 teaspoon sugar, and 1/2 teaspoon salt. Add spinach. Toss just until leaves are coated and slightly wilted. Sprinkle with one coarsely chopped hard-cooked egg.

The wonderful combination of flavors and textures of these two dishes is perfectly matched by Mincemeat Cake. This delicious cake may be prepared weeks in advance, wrapped in foil, and refrigerated. Combine 1 cup mincemeat, 1 cup chopped walnuts or pecans, 1 teaspoon rum flavoring, and 1 teaspoon vanilla. In a separate bowl, blend 1 cup mayonnaise with 1 1/2 cups buttermilk. Into this mixture sift 3 1/4 cups sifted flour, 1 1/2 cups sugar, 1 teaspoon salt, and 3/4 teaspoon soda. Add the grated rind of one orange and mix well. Stir in mincemeat mixture. Pour into tube cake pan lined with heavy brown paper. Bake at 325 degrees for two hours. Cool on wire racks. Frost with your favorite fruit-flavored butter frosting.

With these two menus and the recipes that accompany them, you've got the ingredients for two great Thanksgiving meals. But maybe your family has its own favorite foods we haven't included on these menus. As you browse through the following pages, you're sure to find recipes for every kind of food you can imagine on your holiday table. Taste-tempting appetizers . . . poultry, including home-tested recipes for duck and pheasant . . . great stuffings . . . irresistible vegetables . . . and even casseroles you'll want to prepare for that after-the-big dinner supper. To these delightful foods, add your own imagination in planning table and party decorations, and the delightful traditions you and your family enjoy so much. With such a winning combination, you'll remember Thanksgiving Day with pleasure for a long time to come!

BROCCOLI CHOWDER

2 lb. (about) fresh broccoli
2 12 1/2-oz. cans chicken broth
3 c. milk
1 c. chopped cooked ham
2 tsp. salt
1/4 tsp. pepper
1 c. light cream
1/2 lb. Swiss cheese, grated
1/4 c. butter

Cook broccoli, covered, in 1 can chicken broth in large kettle for about 7 minutes or until just tender. Remove broccoli from broth; cool and chop coarsely. Add remaining chicken broth, milk, ham, salt and pepper to broth in kettle. Bring to a boil over medium heat, stirring occasionally. Stir in remaining ingredients and chopped broccoli; heat just to serving temperature.

ARTICHOKE HEARTS

1 can artichoke hearts
1/2 c. melted butter
Bread crumbs

Drain artichoke hearts and slice lengthwise into 6 pieces. Arrange on baking sheet; pour melted butter on top. Sprinkle with bread crumbs. Cook under broiler for several minutes, until sizzling. Serve with wooden picks. Yield: 15 servings.

Shirley McIntire
Xi Zeta, Dover, New Hampshire

SHRIMP COCKTAIL WITH REMOULADE SAUCE

3 tsp. cooked egg yolk
3 tbsp. hot water
3 tbsp. vinegar
3 tbsp. pepper vinegar
2 tbsp. olive oil
1 tsp. horseradish
1 tsp. salt
1/2 tsp. mustard
Celery seed
4 c. boiled shrimp

Mash egg yolk fine; dissolve in hot water. Add vinegar and pepper vinegar; stir in olive oil. Add horseradish, salt, mustard and celery seed. Marinate shrimp in sauce in refrigerator for 3 hours or longer. Serve on crisp lettuce leaves in cocktail glasses. Yield: 6 servings.

Virginia Young Putzka
Beta Sigma Phi Intl., Kansas City, Missouri

BLUE CHEESE BITES

1 8-oz. package refrigerator biscuits
1/4 c. butter
3 tbsp. crumbled blue cheese

Cut biscuits in quarters; arrange in two 8-inch round baking dishes. Melt butter and cheese together. Pour cheese mixture over biscuit pieces, coating well. Bake at 400 degrees for 10 to 12 minutes or until golden brown. Serve hot. Yield: 40 pieces.

Kathy Ingersoll
Nu, Council Bluffs, Iowa

CRAB MEAT DELIGHT

1 7-oz. can crab meat
1 honeydew melon
Juice of 2 limes
1 tsp. lemon juice
Lettuce

Drain and chill crab meat. Chill melon. Make small balls from melon with melon scoop. Combine melon balls and crab meat in large bowl; sprinkle with lime juice and lemon juice. Arrange lettuce leaves in stemmed serving glasses; add melon balls and crab meat. Garnish with fresh lime slices and serve immediately. Yield: 6-8 servings.

Mrs. Judith Teti
Gamma Theta, No. 6679, Fitchburg, Massachusetts

APRICOT SALAD

1 No. 2 1/2 can apricots
2 sm. packages apricot gelatin
1 1/2 c. boiling water
1 qt. vanilla ice cream
1 sm. can mandarin oranges, drained
1/2 c. chopped walnuts

Drain apricots; reserve 2 cups juice. Quarter apricots. Dissolve gelatin in boiling water; add reserved apricot juice. Add ice cream, apricots, oranges and walnuts. Pour into large cake pan or decorative mold; refrigerate until firm. Yield: 16-18 servings.

Mrs. Joyce D. Benick
Xi Gamma Delta X2091
McKeesport, Pennsylvania

APPLE DREAM SALAD

2 pkg. lemon gelatin
7 tbsp. sugar
Dash of salt
1 No. 2 can crushed pineapple
2 red apples, chopped
2 bananas, chopped
1 egg, beaten
1 tbsp. flour
1 pkg. whipped topping mix
Chopped walnuts

Prepare gelatin according to package directions; add 3 tablespoons sugar and salt. Pour into 9 x 13 or 9 x 15-inch dish; chill until syrupy. Drain pineapple, reserving juice. Add pineapple, apples and bananas to gelatin mixture. Chill until firm. Combine remaining sugar, egg, flour and reserved pineapple juice in saucepan; cook until thick. Cool. Prepare topping mix according to package directions; fold into egg mixture. Spread over gelatin. Top with chopped walnuts. Yield: 12 servings.

Janice Bethel
Xi Gamma X1231, Salem, Ohio

CONGEALED GREEN PEA SALAD

1 pkg. lemon gelatin
1 3/4 c. hot water
1/2 c. nuts
1 c. small English peas, drained
1 c. chopped celery
1 c. sliced olives
2 tbsp. lemon juice or vinegar

Dissolve gelatin in hot water; chill until partially set. Add remaining ingredients; pour into mold. Chill till set. Serve on lettuce with mayonnaise. Yield: 4-6 servings.

Marie H. Davidson
Xi Alpha Pi X-3122, Knoxville, Tennessee

HOLIDAY MINCE MOLD

1 pkg. mincemeat
3 sm. packages apple gelatin
4 1/2 c. boiling water
1/2 c. chopped nuts

Prepare mincemeat according to package directions, using 1/2 cup less water; cool. Dissolve gelatin in water; chill until partially set. Fold in mincemeat and nuts; pour into 9 x 13-inch mold or 18 to 20 individual molds. Chill until set; cut into squares. Arrange on lettuce leaves. Serve with mayonnaise dressing. Yield: 18-20 servings.

Verelda W. Schmitz
Alpha Gamma No. 213, Aurora, Illinois

MOLDED CRANBERRY RELISH

1 3-oz. package raspberry gelatin
1/4 tsp. ground nutmeg
1 c. boiling water
1 c. pineapple juice
1 1/2 c. fresh cranberries, ground
3/4 c. diced celery
1/3 c. slivered almonds

Mix gelatin and nutmeg together; add boiling water. Stir until dissolved. Add pineapple juice. Chill until thickened. Stir in remaining ingredients. Pour into 5-cup mold or small molds. Chill until firm. Unmold to serve. Yield: 8-10 servings.

CRANBERRY MOLD

1 3-oz. package cherry gelatin
1 10-oz. package frozen cranberry relish
1 3-oz. package lemon gelatin
1 c. salad dressing
1 c. heavy cream, whipped

Dissolve cherry gelatin in 1 1/2 cups boiling water; chill until slightly thickened. Thaw cranberry relish; fold into gelatin mixture. Pour into 1 1/2-quart mold. Chill until firm. Dissolve lemon gelatin in 1 cup boiling water; cool. Add to salad dressing gradually; fold in cream. Pour over molded cranberry layer; chill until firm.

Olivia Brand
Phi Gamma Gamma, Chambersburg, Pennsylvania

THANKSGIVING JELLIED SALAD

1 9-oz. can pineapple tidbits
2 pkg. cherry gelatin
2 c. hot water
1 c. cold water
2 tbsp. lemon juice
Dash of salt
3/4 c. sugar
1 1/2 c. coarsely ground cranberries
1/2 c. finely ground orange with peel
1 c. mandarin oranges
3/4 c. sliced celery
1/3 c. coarsely broken walnuts

Drain pineapple and reserve juice. Dissolve gelatin in hot water; add cold water, reserved juice, lemon juice and salt. Chill until partially set. Stir sugar into ground fruits; fold into partially set gelatin. Add pineapple, oranges, celery and walnuts. Pour into 6 1/2-cup ring mold. Chill until firm. Yield: 8-10 servings.

Mrs. Shirley Herring
Delta Theta No. 2439, South Bend, Indiana

ROAST DUCK

1 5-lb. duckling
2 tbsp. soy sauce
1 clove of garlic, minced
1 tsp. sugar
1 tbsp. honey
1 tsp. salt
1/4 tsp. pepper
1 tbsp. ginger

Clean duckling. Combine remaining ingredients for marinade. Marinate duck in roasting pan for 1 hour, turning occasionally. Bake at 350 degrees for 2 hours, turning and basting. Yield: 4 servings.

Mrs. Gene Fowler
Fort Ritchie, Maryland

ROAST GOOSE WITH PICKLE-SPICED STUFFING

1 8-oz. package herb-seasoned stuffing mix
3 c. cooked rice
2 med. oranges, sectioned
1 c. cranberries, chopped
1 c. sweet mixed pickles, chopped
1/4 c. sweet pickle liquid
1/4 c. butter
1/2 tsp. ground sage
1 9-lb. goose
Salt to taste
1 1/2 c. orange juice
2 tbsp. light corn syrup
1/2 c. orange marmalade

Mix stuffing mix, rice, orange sections, cranberries, pickles, pickle liquid, butter and sage together. Stuff neck cavity of goose with stuffing; skewer or sew skin to back of goose. Rub inside of goose with salt; fill with stuffing. Close with skewers or sew. Place on rack in shallow roasting pan. Bake in 325-degree oven for 2 hours; drain off fat. Combine 1 cup orange juice and corn syrup; brush over goose. Bake for 1 hour and 45 minutes longer, brushing occasionally with orange juice mixture. Place goose on platter. Drain off fat. Combine 2 tablespoons drippings, remaining orange juice and marmalade in saucepan. Heat until blended. Serve with goose. Yield: 8 servings.

BAKED TURKEY

2 1/2 to 3 c. water
1 12-lb. turkey
Butter

Preheat oven to 450 degrees. Pour water into roasting pan. Butter turkey well on breast side. Place in roasting pan; cover. Bake for 1 hour and 10 minutes. Turn off oven; do not open oven door. Leave turkey in oven overnight.

Betty Ramey
Xi Pi, Seneca, South Carolina

ROAST TURKEY WITH DRESSING

1 young turkey with giblets
1/2 c. flour
1/4 tsp. pepper
1/4 tsp. poultry seasoning
1 tsp. salt
1 tsp. paprika
Margarine
1/2 c. white wine
1/2 c. minced onions
1/2 c. minced celery
1 tbsp. minced parsley
1 tsp. sage
1/2 lb. mild sausage
3 c. bread cubes
1/2 c. water

Cut turkey in serving pieces. Combine flour, pepper, poultry seasoning, salt and paprika; rub turkey pieces with flour mixture. Melt 1/2 cup margarine in heavy frypan. Fry turkey for 30 minutes, turning each piece until browned. Pour wine over turkey. Simmer turkey giblets in water to cover until giblets are tender. Saute onions and celery in about 3 tablespoons margarine. Combine parsley, sage, sausage, bread cubes and water; mix well. Add giblet broth if additional moisture is needed. Pack in baking dish; place turkey on top of dressing and cover. Bake at 325 degrees for 45 minutes. Uncover; bake for 10 minutes longer. Serve with giblet gravy.

Leah M. Broseke
Xi Delta Lambda 1806, Kenton, Ohio

CREAMED TURKEY

1/4 c. margarine
1/4 c. flour
2 c. milk
1/2 tsp. salt
Dash of pepper
1/4 c. chopped pimento
1/4 c. chopped green pepper
1 tsp. Worcestershire sauce
2 c. diced turkey
1 can mushroom soup
1 tbsp. grated onion

Melt margarine in saucepan; blend in flour. Stir in milk gradually. Cook, stirring constantly, until thick. Add salt, pepper, pimento, green pepper, Worcestershire sauce, diced turkey, mushroom soup and grated onion. Heat thoroughly. Serve on crisp toast. Yield: 6 servings.

Mrs. Sue Jones
St. Stephens Church, Virginia

TURKEY AMANDINE

2 tbsp. butter
1 c. thinly sliced celery
1/4 c. thinly sliced onions
1/2 c. mushrooms
1 tbsp. cornstarch
3 tbsp. soy sauce
1 c. water or mushroom juice
1 6-oz. can water chestnuts
2 c. diced turkey
1 c. toasted almonds
Hot rice or Chinese noodles

Melt butter in large skillet; add celery, onions and mushrooms. Cook until tender, but not brown. Combine cornstarch, soy sauce and water. Stir into vegetables slowly; cook, stirring constantly, until smooth and thickened. Slice water chestnuts; add with turkey to vegetable mixture. Heat thoroughly; stir in almonds. Serve on rice or noodles. Chicken or shrimp may be substituted for turkey. Yield: 6 servings.

Barbara Toups
Pi, Metairie, Louisiana

ROAST TURKEY WITH CRANBERRY-STUFFED ORANGES

1 12-lb. turkey
Salt
Pepper to taste
Melted butter
1 c. chopped onion
1 c. diced celery
1/2 tsp. hot sauce
1/2 tsp. poultry seasoning
8 c. bread cubes
2 tbsp. chopped parsley
Turkey or chicken broth

Rub turkey cavity with salt and pepper to taste; rub turkey skin generously with melted butter. Combine 1/2 cup melted butter, chopped onion, diced celery, hot sauce, poultry seasoning and 1 1/2 teaspoon salt in heavy frypan; cook until the onion is tender and transparent but not brown. Add bread cubes and chopped parsley, stirring until all ingredients are thoroughly blended. Add enough broth to moisten stuffing mixture to desired consistency. Fill turkey cavity loosely with stuffing mixture. Place on large sheet of aluminum foil in large baking dish. Bake at 325 degrees for about 45 minutes per pound, basting occasionally with butter and pan drippings.

Cranberry-Stuffed Oranges

2 c. water
2 c. sugar
1 lb. cranberries
9 oranges

Combine water and sugar in saucepan; stir well until sugar is completely dissolved. Boil for 5 minutes. Pick over and wash cranberries thoroughly. Add cranberries to boiled syrup. Cook, uncovered, very gently without stirring until cranberries are thick and clear. Skim foamy mixture from top. Slice tops off oranges, scoop out about 1/2 of the pulp. Place oranges in the oven with the turkey. Bake for about 1 hour and 30 minutes. Fill oranges with cranberry sauce just before serving. Garnish stuffed oranges with fresh mint, parsley sprigs, pineapple sticks or pecan halves.

Photograph for this recipe on page 167.

STUFFED APPLES

4 apples
1/4 c. red cinnamon candies
3/4 c. sugar
1/2 c. water
1 c. mashed sweet potatoes
1/4 c. brown sugar
1/4 c. chopped pecans
4 marshmallows

Core apples; peel. Combine candies, sugar and water in saucepan large enough to hold apples. Cook over moderate heat for about 15 minutes or until sugar and candies are dissolved and syrup thickened. Place apples in syrup; simmer until apples are coated with syrup and partially cooked. Remove apples; place in baking dish. Reserve syrup. Combine sweet potatoes, pinch of salt, brown sugar and pecans. Stuff apples with potato mixture; pour reserved syrup over top. Bake at 350 degrees for about 25 to 30 minutes or until tender, basting frequently. Place large marshmallow on top of each apple just before removing from oven; continue baking for about 5 minutes or until brown. Serve with pork or fowl.

GUINEA HENS WITH ORANGE SAUCE

2 guineas, cut in serving pieces
Salt and pepper to taste
4 tbsp. butter
2 oranges
1 tbsp. shredded orange rind
1 bouillon cube
1/2 c. hot water
1/2 c. white wine or dry vermouth

Season guineas with salt and pepper; brown in butter in ovenproof skillet. Peel and quarter oranges. Add orange quarters and rind to hot mixture. Dissolve bouillon cube in hot water. Add bouillon and wine to hot mixture; cover. Bake at 300 degrees for 2 hours. Serve with sauce over wild or white rice. Yield: 4-6 servings.

Mrs. Harold J. Moore
Brookfield, Missouri

ROASTED PHEASANT

1 pheasant
Salt to taste
Pepper to taste
1 c. wild rice
1 c. apricot juice

Place pheasant on aluminum foil; place in roaster. Rub interior with salt and pepper; stuff with wild rice. Pour apricot juice over all. Wrap tightly with foil. Bake at 325 degrees for 1 hour or until breast is easily pierced with fork. Other juices may be substituted for apricot. Yield: 4 servings.

Mrs. Floyd King
Malden, Illinois

NECTARINE-GLAZED DUCKLING

1 4 1/2 to 5-lb. duckling
1/2 tsp. salt
1/4 tsp. garlic salt
1/4 tsp. pepper
2 or 3 peeled onions
2 or 3 fresh nectarines
1/2 c. red currant jelly

Rub duckling skin and cavity with salt, garlic salt and pepper. Stuff cavity with onions; truss. Place breast side up on rack in roasting pan. Bake at 325 degrees for 2 hours and 30 minutes to 3 hours or until thick portion of leg is tender. Drain fat from pan twice during baking time. Finely chop enough nectarines to yield 1 cup fruit and juice; combine with jelly in saucepan. Heat until jelly is melted. Spoon nectarine glaze over duckling twice during last 30 minutes of baking time, using 1/4 cup each time. Chop about 1/2 cup nectarines; stir into remaining glaze. Heat; serve as sauce with duckling. Small unpared apples may be used for onions if desired. Yield: 4 servings.

CORN BREAD-SAUSAGE STUFFING

5 1/2 to 6 c. crumbled corn bread
1 1/2 lb. bulk sausage
4 onions, chopped
1 stalk celery, chopped
6 c. soft white bread crumbs
1 tbsp. salt
2 tsp. poultry seasoning
1 tbsp. herb seasonings
1 to 2 tbsp. steak sauce
2 eggs, slightly beaten
1 c. chicken broth or bouillon

Place corn bread in large bowl. Cook sausage in large skillet over low heat, breaking up with fork. Drain sausage on paper towel; add to corn bread. Pour off all but 1/2 cup drippings. Cook onions and celery in drippings for about 5 minutes or until golden. Add onions, celery and remaining ingredients to corn bread mixture; mix well. Cool before using. Yield: Stuffing for 12 to 14-lb. turkey.

Mrs. Francis L. McGuire
Minneapolis, Minnesota

CRANBERRY STUFFING

1 c. chopped fresh cranberries
1/4 c. sugar
1 c. chopped tart apples
1 c. finely chopped celery
1 1/2 c. boiling water
1 tsp. salt
2 tbsp. minced parsley
1/4 c. butter, melted
8 c. stale bread cubes

Combine cranberries, sugar and apples. Cook celery in boiling water until tender. Turn into large bowl; cool. Add salt, parsley, butter and bread cubes; blend well. Stir in cranberry mixture. Use to stuff turkey or game fowl.

Mrs. Juanita King
Sacramento, California

ORANGE STUFFING FOR DUCKLING

1/2 c. hot water
3 c. toasted bread crumbs
2 tsp. grated orange rind
2/3 c. diced orange pulp
2 c. diced celery
1/4 c. melted butter
1 egg, beaten
1/2 tsp. salt
1/8 tsp. pepper
1/4 tsp. savory
1/2 c. raisins

Pour hot water over bread crumbs in large bowl; let stand for 10 minutes. Add remaining ingredients; stir lightly to combine. May be used to stuff duckling. Yield: 6 servings.

Mrs. Brenda Cummings
Seattle, Washington

SAUSAGE STUFFING FOR POULTRY

2 med. onions, chopped
2 c. chopped celery
Butter
1/2 lb. mild sausage
1 lge. loaf stale bread
4 saltine crackers
1 c. chopped fresh parsley
1 1/2 tsp. salt
1/2 tsp. pepper
Monosodium glutamate
1 tbsp. poultry seasoning
2 eggs, lightly beaten
1/2 c. milk

Cook onions and celery lightly in small amount of butter in skillet. Fry sausage lightly, scrambling to separate; drain. Crumble bread and crackers into large bowl. Add onion mixture, sausage, parsley, seasonings, eggs, milk and 1/2 cup melted butter; mix well. Yield: Stuffing for 12-pound turkey or 2 chickens.

Mrs. Charles Baldwin
Virginia Beach, Virginia

PECAN STUFFING

1 c. chopped onions
1 c. chopped celery and leaves
1/2 c. butter
1/2 tsp. pepper sauce
1/2 tsp. poultry seasoning
Salt to taste
8 c. bread cubes
2 tbsp. minced parsley
1/4 c. white cooking wine
1/2 c. sliced mushrooms
1/2 c. chopped pecans

Cook onions and celery lightly in butter; stir in seasonings. Place bread cubes and parsley in large bowl; add onion mixture, wine, mushrooms and pecans. Toss lightly to mix. Yield: Stuffing for 12-pound turkey.

Mrs. Michael P. Reardon
Bedford, Massachusetts

THANKSGIVING OYSTER DRESSING

6 tbsp. margarine
6 tbsp. oil or shortening
1 1/2 c. chopped onions
1 1/2 c. chopped celery
6 to 8 slices bread
3 tbsp. minced parsley
Salt and pepper to taste
3/4 tsp. thyme
3/4 tsp. sage
3/4 tsp. marjoram
3/4 tsp. oregano
1/2 c. chopped oysters
2 eggs, lightly beaten

Melt margarine in skillet; add oil, onions and celery. Cook, covered, until onions are soft but not browned. Crumble bread into large bowl; add just enough water to moisten bread. Stir in onion mixture, parsley, seasonings, oysters and eggs; mix well. Spoon into greased casserole. Bake at 400 degrees until browned.

Mrs. Martha Berthelson
Dallas, Texas

CRAB CASSEROLE

2 6-oz. cans crab meat
1 5-oz. can water chestnuts
2 cans cream of celery soup
1 1/2 c. herb stuffing mix
1/2 tsp. dried dillweed
Salt and pepper to taste
Buttered bread crumbs

Drain crab meat; flake. Drain and thinly slice water chestnuts. Combine all ingredients except bread crumbs. Dilute soup slightly if desired. Turn into buttered casserole; top with crumbs. Bake in 350-degree oven until bubbly and brown. Yield: 8 servings.

Betty Lou Weeks
Xi Beta X-293, Birmingham, Alabama

SHRIMP-ARTICHOKE CASSEROLE

1 No. 2 can artichoke hearts
3/4 lb. shrimp
1/4 lb. fresh mushrooms
Margarine
3 tbsp. all-purpose flour
1/4 tsp. salt
1 1/2 c. milk
1 tbsp. Worcestershire sauce
1/4 c. dry sherry
1/4 c. grated Parmesan cheese
Paprika

Arrange artichoke hearts in greased 1 1/2-quart baking dish. Shell and devein shrimp. Slice mushrooms. Spread shrimp over artichokes. Saute sliced mushrooms in 2 tablespoons margarine for 6 minutes. Add mushrooms to baking dish. Melt 3 tablespoons margarine in saucepan over low heat. Blend in flour and salt. Add milk all at once. Cook quickly, stirring constantly, till mixture thickens and bubbles. Remove from heat. Mix Worcestershire sauce with sherry and white sauce; pour into baking dish. Sprinkle top with Parmesan cheese and paprika. Bake for 20 to 30 minutes in 375-degree oven. Garnish with parsley. Yield: 4 servings.

Carolyn T. Bobola
Nu Zeta No. 4128, Houston, Texas

OYSTER CASSEROLE

1 pkg. saltine crackers
1 pt. oysters
1 stick butter
1 tsp. salt
1/2 tsp. pepper
2 eggs
1 to 2 c. milk

Crumble layer of crackers into 1-quart greased casserole; cover with layer of oysters. Dot with butter and add salt and pepper. Repeat layers until all oysters and crackers are used. Beat eggs with milk; pour over oysters. Bake at 250 degrees for 30 to 35 minutes or until set. Yield: 4 servings.

Ina Bycroft
Xi Phi X2519, Montgomery, Alabama

MARYLAND CRAB IMPERIAL

4 tbsp. butter
4 tbsp. flour
2 c. milk
1 tsp. salt
1/8 tsp. pepper
1/2 tsp. celery salt or seed
Dash of cayenne pepper
1 tsp. minced parsley
1 tsp. minced onion
1 egg yolk, beaten
2 tbsp. sherry
1 c. soft bread crumbs
1 lb. back fin crab meat
1/4 c. buttered bread crumbs
Paprika

Melt butter in skillet; stir in flour until smooth. Add milk gradually, blending well. Cook over low heat, stirring constantly, until smooth and thickened; stir in seasonings. Add small amount of hot cream sauce to egg yolk, blending well; return to cream sauce. Cook for 2 minutes longer, stirring. Add sherry, bread crumbs and crab meat, mixing in gently with fork. Spoon crab meat mixture into greased baking dish; top with bread crumbs. Sprinkle with paprika. Bake at 400 degrees for 20 to 25 minutes. Yield: 6 servings.

Mrs. Lola B. Crawford
Xi Zeta Exemplar X1122, Westminster, Maryland

GERMAN NOODLE CASSEROLE

1 lge. package noodles
1 1-lb. carton cottage cheese
3 c. sour cream
Salt and pepper to taste
Butter
Milk

Cook noodles according to package directions; drain. Arrange layers of noodles, cottage cheese and sour cream in baking dish. Season each layer; dot with butter. Pour enough milk over mixture in baking dish to moisten well. Bake at 350 degrees for 45 minutes or until milk is absorbed. Yield: 6-8 servings.

Mary Ann Cramer
Gamma Phi No. 3753, Sarasota, Florida

GREEN RICE CASSEROLE

3 c. cooked rice
3 eggs, well beaten
1 1/2 c. chopped parsley
1 med. onion, grated
1 sm. clove of garlic, mashed
3 tbsp. butter, melted
3 tbsp. grated Swiss cheese
2/3 c. milk
Salt and pepper to taste
1/2 c. sliced stuffed olives

Combine rice, eggs, parsley, onion, garlic, butter, cheese, milk, salt and pepper; add olives. Pour into greased 1 1/2 to 2-quart casserole. Bake in 350-degree oven for 35 to 40 minutes or until top browns. Yield: 4-6 servings.

Mavourneen Rustell
Beta Sigma Phi Intl., Kansas City, Missouri

SAVORY MASHED YAMS WITH APPLE

4 med. cooked yams, peeled
6 tbsp. butter or margarine
2 tbsp. chopped parsley
3/4 tsp. salt
Dash of onion salt
1/8 tsp. ground thyme
Pepper to taste
1 tbsp. lemon juice
1 med. tart apple

Mash yams with 4 tablespoons butter, parsley, seasonings and lemon juice. Turn into 9-inch pie plate; spread evenly. Cut apple into thin wedges; saute in remaining butter for 1 minute. Arrange apple slices on yams. Pour melted butter on top. Bake in 375-degree oven for 15 minutes. Serve with baked ham.

SWEET POTATO CASSEROLE

3 med. sweet potatoes
3 tbsp. margarine
2 tbsp. brown sugar
1/2 c. orange marmalade
1/4 c. sherry
Marshmallows

Boil sweet potatoes in jackets until done. Peel; mash. Add margarine and brown sugar, mixing well. Add marmalade and sherry; mix thoroughly. Place in baking dish. Bake at 350 degrees for 30 minutes. May be topped with marshmallows. Yield: 6 servings.

Betty Allen
Gamma Pi, No. 1164, Dallas, Texas

LIMA BEAN-OLIVE CASSEROLE

3 cans baby green lima beans
1 c. chopped onions
1 c. chopped green peppers
4 tbsp. olive oil
1 c. chopped ripe olives
1 tbsp. chili powder
1 clove of garlic, grated
1 tsp. salt
1 tbsp. cornstarch
1 c. grated Cheddar cheese

Drain lima beans; reserve 1 1/4 cups liquid. Saute onions and green peppers in oil. Combine olives, chili powder, garlic, salt, cornstarch and bean liquid in saucepan. Cook until slightly thickened. Add onions, green peppers, beans and half the cheese. Place in buttered casserole. Bake in 375-degree oven for 30 minutes. Sprinkle with remaining cheese; bake until cheese melts. Dish is better if prepared at least 1 day before serving. May be frozen. Yield: 18-20 servings.

Mrs. Ivanell S. Harris
Florence, Mississippi

BAKED CORN IN CASSEROLE

1 No. 2 can cream-style corn
1 12-oz. can whole kernel corn
1/2 c. grated onion
1/2 c. chopped green pepper
2 pimentos, chopped
2/3 c. milk
1 egg, well beaten
1 c. rolled cracker crumbs
1 c. grated American cheese
1/4 c. melted butter
2 tbsp. sugar
Black and red pepper to taste
Salt to taste

Combine all ingredients; mix well. Pour into buttered 2-quart casserole. Bake at 350 degrees for 1 hour. Yield: 8 servings.

Melba Taff
Xi Zeta Ro X-2083, Silsbee, Texas

EGGPLANT-ZUCCHINI SUPREME

1/2 sm. eggplant
2 sm. zucchini, unpeeled
Uncooked spaghetti
1/2 c. sliced celery
1/2 c. sliced green pepper
1 clove of garlic, sliced
1 c. grated mozzarella cheese
1 8-oz. can tomato sauce
1/4 c. water
2 tsp. Worcestershire sauce
1/2 tsp. salt
1/2 tsp. oregano

Peel eggplant; cut in 1/4-inch slices. Cut zucchini in 1/4-inch slices. Break spaghetti into 1-inch pieces. Arrange layers of eggplant, zucchini, spaghetti, celery, green pepper and garlic in greased 1 1/2-quart casserole. Cover with cheese. Combine tomato sauce with water, Worcestershire sauce, salt and oregano; pour over spaghetti mixture. Cover. Bake at 350 degrees for 1 hour. Yield: 6-8 servings.

Thelma Pfeiffer
Xi Omega, X1779, Memphis, Tennessee

HOLIDAY ONIONS

20 sm. onions, peeled
Butter or margarine
2 tbsp. sugar
2 tbsp. flour
3/4 c. chicken broth
3/4 c. cream
1 1/2 tsp. seasoned salt
Dash of pepper
3/4 c. bread crumbs

Cook onions in boiling, salted water until almost tender; drain. Heat 3 tablespoons butter in skillet; add sugar. Stir until dissolved. Add several onions at a time; cook until lightly browned, turning to glaze evenly. Remove onions with slotted spoon to shallow baking dish; set aside. Heat 2 tablespoons butter in saucepan; blend in flour. Cook until mixture bubbles. Remove from heat; stir in chicken broth and cream. Bring to a boil rapidly; add salt and pepper. Cook for 1 to 2 minutes longer, stirring constantly until smooth and thickened. Pour sauce over onions. Heat 2 tablespoons butter in skillet; add bread crumbs. Brown lightly. Sprinkle over onions. Bake in 350-degree oven for 30 minutes. Yield: 4-6 servings.

Judith M. Brown
Phi Alpha Psi P-1886, Danville, Virginia

SQUASH CASSEROLE

2 No. 303 cans cooked squash
1/2 pt. sour cream
1 onion, grated
1 can cream of chicken soup
1 sm. jar pimentos, diced
Salt and pepper to taste
1 can chow mein noodles

Preheat oven to 350 degrees. Drain squash; place in deep casserole. Add sour cream, onion, soup and pimentos. Add salt and pepper; stir in 3/4 can noodles. Mix thoroughly; sprinkle remaining noodles on top. Bake for 25 to 30 minutes or until heated thoroughly.

Karen Bradley
Gamma Xi No. 5150, Claxton, Georgia

DILL-SEASONED GREEN BEANS

2 No. 2 cans cut green beans
2 tsp. dillseed
1 tbsp. bacon drippings
Bean stock
Milk
4 tbsp. flour
4 tbsp. melted butter
Salt and pepper to taste
Dash of hot sauce
Soup croutons

Cook beans, dillseed and bacon drippings in bean liquid for 30 to 40 minutes; drain and reserve liquid. Blend reserved bean liquid with enough milk to make 2 cups liquid. Blend flour and small amount of bean liquid until smooth; add to melted butter in saucepan. Add remaining liquid and seasonings. Cook until thickened, stirring constantly. Layer beans, white sauce and croutons in 1 1/2 to 2-quart casserole. Bake at 350 degrees for 15 to 20 minutes. Yield: 8-10 servings.

Mrs. Bernice Bagwell
Waco, Texas

SCALLOPED TURNIPS AND PEAS

2 c. cooked mashed turnips
1 c. cooked peas
4 tbsp. butter
4 tbsp. flour
2 c. milk
1 tsp. salt
1/4 tsp. pepper
1/2 c. bread crumbs
1/2 c. grated cheese

Place turnips and peas in 1-quart casserole. Melt butter in saucepan; add flour, stirring until well blended. Add milk; cook until thickened, stirring constantly. Add salt and pepper. Pour white sauce over vegetable mixture. Sprinkle with crumbs and cheese. Bake at 375 degrees for 25 to 30 minutes. Yield: 6 servings.

Mrs. Joseph Revell
Alpha No. 2023
Sherwood, Prince Edward Island, Canada

BAKED DILL-STUFFED TOMATOES

6 med. tomatoes
Salt and pepper to taste
1 1/2 c. coarse dry bread crumbs
1 tbsp. finely chopped onion
1 tbsp. chopped parsley
1/2 tsp. dillseed
1/4 c. butter, melted

Slice stem end from tomatoes; remove pulp. Sprinkle insides with salt and pepper; invert to drain. Combine remaining ingredients with tomato pulp; stuff tomatoes. Place in shallow baking dish. Bake at 350 degrees for 15 to 20 minutes. Yield: 6 servings.

Mrs. Doris G. Kruger
Bumsville, Minnesota

POTATO BUTTERHORN ROLLS

2 tbsp. sugar
1 tbsp. salt
4 tbsp. melted shortening
2 c. hot mashed potatoes
2 eggs, well beaten
1 pkg. yeast
2 c. milk
6 c. flour

Mix sugar, salt, shortening and potatoes. Cool; add eggs. Soften yeast in milk; add to potato mixture. Add flour, small amount at a time, beating well after each addition. Turn onto lightly floured board; knead until smooth and elastic. Dough should be as soft as possible to handle. Cover with damp cloth; set in warm place. Let rise until doubled in bulk; turn onto lightly floured board. Roll into 1/2-inch thick circle. Cut into pie-shaped sections, having each section about 3 inches wide at outer edge. Begin at outside; roll each section toward center. Form into crescents. Place on oiled baking sheet; cover with warm damp cloth. Let rise until doubled in bulk. Bake at 450 degrees for about 12 minutes. Yield: 32 rolls.

Mary Ann Adams
Xi Alpha Beta No. 910, Kansas City, Missouri

HARVEST BREAD

1 1/2 c. finely chopped dried apples
1/2 c. butter or margarine
2/3 c. sugar
2 eggs
2 c. sifted all-purpose flour
1 tsp. soda
1/2 tsp. salt
3/4 c. shredded Cheddar cheese
1/2 c. chopped walnuts

Cook apples in water to cover for about 20 to 25 minutes; drain. Cream butter and sugar until light and fluffy. Add eggs; beat well. Sift flour, soda and salt together; add to creamed mixture. Stir in apples, cheese and walnuts; turn into greased 9 x 5 x 3-inch loaf pan. Bake at 350 degrees for 50 to 55 minutes. Cool for 10 minutes; remove from pan. Cool on rack. Yield: 16 servings.

Carolyn Sue Burford
Eta Mu No. 2691, Bay City, Texas

PUMPKIN MUFFINS

1 c. sifted flour
Sugar
2 tsp. baking powder
1/2 tsp. cinnamon
1/2 tsp. nutmeg
1/4 tsp. salt
1/4 c. butter
1 egg, beaten
1/2 c. canned pumpkin
1/2 c. evaporated milk
1/2 c. seedless raisins

Sift flour, 1/2 cup sugar, baking powder, cinnamon, nutmeg and salt together into medium-sized mixing bowl. Cut in butter until mixture resembles cornmeal. Combine egg with pumpkin and milk; stir in raisins. Add egg mixture to dry ingredients, stirring just enough to mix lightly. Fill greased muffin pans or paper muffin cups, set in pans, 2/3 full. Sprinkle 1/4 teaspoon sugar over each muffin. Bake in 400-degree oven for 20 to 25 minutes, until done and nicely browned. Yield: 16 muffins.

MINCEMEAT COFFEE RINGS

3/4 c. milk, scalded
1/2 c. sugar
2 tsp. salt
1/2 c. margarine
2 pkg. yeast
1/2 c. warm water
1 egg
4 c. flour
1 lge. jar mincemeat

Mix hot milk, sugar, salt and margarine in mixing bowl; cool to lukewarm. Dissolve yeast in water; add to milk mixture. Add egg and 2 cups flour; beat until smooth. Add remaining flour, blending well; cover tightly. Refrigerate for 2 hours or overnight. Divide into 2 equal parts; roll each part out into rectangle. Spread with mincemeat; roll up as for jelly roll. Place rolls in circle in greased baking pan, pressing ends together. Cut 4 slashes on top; cover. Let rise in warm place until doubled in bulk. Bake at 350 degrees for about 30 minutes; cool. Frost with confectioners' sugar frosting if desired.

Kar Lynn Roberts
Xi Tau X1991, Pine Bluff, Arkansas

ORANGE AND MINCEMEAT BREAD

1 c. warm water
2 pkg. yeast
2/3 c. orange juice
1/2 c. sugar
1/4 c. margarine, softened
1 1/2 tsp. salt
1 tbsp. grated orange peel
5 1/4 c. (about) flour
1/2 c. prepared mincemeat

Pour warm water into large warm bowl; sprinkle yeast over water. Stir until dissolved. Add orange juice, sugar, margarine, salt and orange peel. Stir in 2 cups flour. Beat until smooth. Cover; let rise in warm place, free from draft, for about 30 minutes or until light and bubbly. Stir batter down; add enough flour to make soft dough. Turn out onto lightly floured board. Knead for about 10 minutes or until smooth and elastic. Place in greased bowl, turning to grease top. Cover; let rise in warm place, free from draft, for about 50 minutes or until doubled in bulk. Punch dough down. Turn out onto lightly floured board; divide in half. Roll each half out into 10 x 8-inch rectangle. Spread 1/2 of the mincemeat on each rectangle. Shape each half into loaf. Place loaves in greased 9 x 5 x 3-inch loaf pans. Cover; let rise in warm place, free from draft, for about 1 hour or until doubled in bulk. Bake at 400 degrees for about 35 minutes or until done. Yield: 2 loaves.

PUMPKIN-RAISIN BREAD

3 1/2 c. sifted flour
1/2 tsp. baking powder
2 tsp. soda
1/2 tsp. cloves
1 tsp. cinnamon
1 1/2 tsp. salt
2/3 c. nuts
2/3 c. raisins or dates
2 2/3 c. sugar
2/3 c. salad oil
4 eggs
2 c. canned pumpkin
2/3 c. water

Mix flour, baking powder, soda, spices and salt together; toss nuts and raisins lightly into flour mixture. Beat sugar and oil together with mixer at low speed. Add eggs, one at a time; add pumpkin. Add flour mixture and water; beat until thoroughly mixed. Pour into greased and floured loaf pan. Bake at 350 degrees for 1 hour.

Dorothy Miller
Epsilon Upsilon No. 2314, San Marcos, Texas

HOLIDAY CRANBERRY BREAD

2 c. sifted flour
1 c. sugar
1 1/2 tsp. baking powder
1 tsp. salt
1/2 tsp. soda
Juice of 1 orange
2 tbsp. shortening
1 well-beaten egg
1 c. chopped nuts
1 c. halved cranberries

Sift first 5 ingredients together in large mixing bowl. Combine orange juice with enough boiling water to measure 3/4 cup liquid. Stir in shortening and egg; add to dry ingredients. Mix until dry ingredients are moistened; stir in nuts and cranberries. Turn into greased 9 x 5 x 3-inch pan. Bake at 350 degrees for 55 to 65 minutes.

Barbara Shemela
Xi Alpha Omega X2649, Springfield, Virginia

MINCEMEAT CAKE

3/4 c. shortening
1 3/4 c. sugar
1 pkg. dry mincemeat
2 c. water
3 c. flour
2 tsp. soda
1 tsp. salt
3/4 c. chopped nuts

Combine first 4 ingredients in large saucepan; bring to a boil. Boil for 3 minutes, stirring occasionally. Remove from heat; let cool. Add remaining ingredients to mincemeat mixture; mix well. Turn into greased 10-inch tube pan. Bake at 375 degrees for 55 to 65 minutes. Cool cake for 1 hour before turning out of pan.

Sharon Oliver
Chi Tau No. 5507, Smith River, California

PRUNE CAKE

1 1/2 c. sugar
1 c. vegetable oil
3 eggs
1 tsp. cinnamon
1 tsp. nutmeg
1 tsp. allspice
2 1/4 c. flour
1 tsp. soda
1 c. buttermilk
1 tsp. vanilla
1 c. nuts, chopped
1 c. cooked chopped prunes

Blend sugar and oil; add eggs, one at a time, beating thoroughly after each addition. Mix spices, flour and soda together; add alternately with buttermilk to egg mixture. Add vanilla, nuts and prunes. Pour into greased and floured 9 x 13-inch pan or two 8-inch square pans. Bake at 300 degrees for 50 to 55 minutes. Remove from oven.

Buttermilk Icing

1 c. sugar
1/2 c. buttermilk
1/2 tsp. soda
1 tbsp. white corn syrup
1/4 c. butter
1 tsp. vanilla

Combine first 5 ingredients in saucepan; boil to soft-ball stage. Add vanilla; pour icing over hot cake without beating. Yield: 16 servings.

Ann Kirk
Xi Alpha Rho, Springfield, Illinois

THANKSGIVING CRANBERRY CRUNCH

1 c. oats
1/2 c. flour
1 c. brown sugar
1/2 c. butter
1 can whole cranberries

Mix oats, flour and brown sugar together; cut in butter. Spoon half the flour mixture into greased 9 x 9-inch pan; cover with cranberries. Add remaining flour mixture. Bake for 45 minutes at 350 degrees. Serve with ice cream if desired. Yield: 9 servings.

Mabel Hammons
Xi Epsilon X 232, Claremont, California

FIGS AFLAME

1 lge. can Kadota figs
1 tsp. cornstarch
2 thin lemon slices
6 tbsp. brandy
1/2 pt. heavy cream
Lemon wafers

Drain syrup from figs into chafing dish. Add cornstarch; stir until thickened. Add figs, lemon slices and 2 tablespoons brandy; heat thoroughly. Heat remaining brandy; ignite brandy just before serving. Pour over figs, coating well. Serve at once with cream and lemon wafers. Yield: 4 servings.

Mrs. Raymond M. Harris
Little Creek, Virginia

SPICY WALNUT MERINGUE SHELLS

3 egg whites
1/4 tsp. cream of tartar
1/8 tsp. salt
1 c. sugar
1/2 tsp. cinnamon
1/2 c. finely chopped walnuts
Chiffon Cranberry Filling
Chiffon Pumpkin Filling

Beat egg whites with cream of tartar and salt in a medium-sized deep bowl until soft peaks form. Beat in sugar gradually, about 2 tablespoons at a time, until meringue stands in stiff glossy peaks. Beat in cinnamon with last 1/4 cup sugar. Fold in walnuts gently. Pile meringue in lightly greased 9 or 10-inch pie plate. Spread over bottom and up side to form crust. Bottom of shell should be about 1/4 inch thick, side about 1 inch. Bake at 275 degrees for 50 to 60 minutes, until light tan in color. Turn oven off; leave meringue in oven to cool with door closed. Meringue will crack and fall in center; press center lightly to level before filling. Individual meringue shells may be made by spooning meringue into 8 mounds on lightly greased baking sheet. Shape with spoon into shells, piling up sides. Bake as directed for pie shell allowing 45 minutes for individual shells.

Chiffon Cranberry Filling

1 c. whole cranberry sauce
1 1/2 env. unflavored gelatin
2 tbsp. water
1 c. sugar
2 egg whites
1/4 tsp. cream of tartar
1/8 tsp. salt
1 c. whipping cream

Press cranberry sauce through sieve. Soften gelatin in water. Add 2/3 cup sugar and cranberry sauce. Bring to a boil, stirring constantly. Remove from heat; cool. Chill until mixture begins to thicken. Beat egg whites, cream of tartar and salt together until soft peaks form. Beat in remaining sugar to form meringue. Beat cream until stiff. Fold meringue and whipped cream into cranberry filling. Add several drops of red food coloring. Turn into cooled meringue shell; chill until firm. Garnish with walnut halves and cranberries. Yield: 6-8 servings.

Chiffon Pumpkin Filling

1 env. unflavored gelatin
1/4 c. orange juice
2/3 c. (packed) brown sugar
1/2 tsp. salt
1 tsp. cinnamon
1/2 tsp. nutmeg
1/2 tsp. ginger
3 eggs, separated
3/4 c. milk
1 c. canned pumpkin
1/3 c. sugar
1 c. finely chopped walnuts

Soften gelatin in orange juice. Combine with brown sugar, salt, spices, beaten egg yolks and milk. Cook for 5 to 10 minutes, sitrring constantly until mixture thickens. Remove from heat; add pumpkin. Chill until thickened. Beat egg whites until soft peaks form; beat in sugar. Fold meringue and 2/3 cup walnuts into pumpkin mixture. Spoon into baked meringue shells; sprinkle with remaining walnuts. Chill until firm.

BRANDY PEACHES

4 tbsp. butter
1/2 c. sugar
1/4 c. water
4 fresh peaches, peeled
3 oz. brandy

Melt butter and sugar in double boiler, stirring to blend. Stir in water; add peaches. Cook for 30 to 35 minutes, turning peaches several times. Add brandy and serve. Yield: 4 servings.

Sue Vedral
Camp Hill, Pennsylvania

BLACK CHERRIES JUBILEE

2 c. canned black cherries
1 tbsp. sugar
1 tbsp. cornstarch
1/2 c. brandy
1 1/2 pt. ice cream or orange sherbet

Drain cherries, reserving 1 cup juice. Mix sugar and cornstarch; add reserved juice gradually. Cook gently for 3 minutes, stirring constantly. Add cherries. Warm brandy; pour over cherries. Ignite. Spoon juices in pan over cherries; serve flaming. Serve over vanilla ice cream.

Dawn W. Hendrix
Gamma Alpha Delta No. 6401
Bellflower, California

FRUIT DELIGHT

1 c. mandarin oranges
1 c. pineapple chunks
1 c. white grapes
1 c. miniature marshmallows
1 c. sour cream
6 maraschino cherries, halved

Mix oranges, pineapple chunks, grapes, marshmallows and sour cream together in serving bowl. Garnish with cherries. Chill for 2 hours before serving. Yield: 10 servings.

Helen N. Borden
Xi Delta X 612, Morrisville, Pennsylvania

OLYMPIAN NECTAR

1 c. strawberries
1 c. cooked blueberries
1 1/2 c. diced pineapple
1 c. applesauce
2 c. diced apples
2/3 c. raisins
2 c. grape juice
1 c. shredded coconut
4 bananas, diced
2 c. pineapple juice
1 sm. jar cherries and juice
1 c. chopped pecans

Combine all ingredients; mix well. Refrigerate until ready to serve. Yield: 6 servings.

Mrs. Harry T. Howle
Galivants Ferry, South Carolina

GRASSHOPPER CREAM CORNUCOPIAS

1/4 c. butter
1/2 c. blended maple syrup
1/2 c. flour
1 c. heavy cream
2 tbsp. creme de menthe
1 tbsp. clear creme de cacao

Heat butter and syrup over high heat until blended; boil rapidly about 30 seconds. Remove from heat; add flour, beating until smooth. Grease and warm baking sheet; drop mixture by level tablespoon about 2 inches apart onto sheet. Bake at 300 degrees for 9 to 12 minutes. Cool slightly; remove each wafer. Lap over two edges quickly to form cornucopia shape. Place on wire rack to cool. Return to oven for several seconds if wafers harden before they all are rolled. Beat cream, creme de menthe and creme de cacao together until stiff. Do not overbeat. Spoon mixture lightly into cornucopias without packing; wrap individually for freezing. Place in freezer at once. Serve without defrosting. Cornucopias may be stored in tightly covered container and filled with cream mixture at serving time. Yield: 12 servings.

Mrs. Edwin H. Moore
Roanoke, Virginia

FRESH COCONUT PIE

1 c. sugar
1/2 c. cornstarch
1/4 tsp. salt
3 c. hot milk
3 egg yolks, beaten
1 tsp. vanilla
1/2 tsp. almond extract
2 c. grated fresh coconut
1 9-in. baked pie shell
1 c. heavy cream, whipped

Combine sugar, cornstarch and salt in saucepan; stir in milk gradually until smooth. Bring to a boil; boil for 2 minutes. Remove from heat; stir small amount of hot mixture into egg yolks. Return to hot mixture in saucepan. Cook over low heat, stirring constantly, for 5 minutes, until mixture boils and is thick enough to mound from spoon. Turn into bowl; stir in vanilla, almond extract and half the coconut. Place waxed paper over filling; refrigerate for 1 hour. Turn into pie shell; refrigerate for 3 hours. Spread whipped cream over filling; top with remaining coconut. Yield: 6 servings.

Virginia L. Miller
Xi Alpha Lambda, Dauphin, Pennsylvania

PUMPKIN-MINCE PIE

2 c. mincemeat
1 unbaked 9-in. pie shell
1 c. pumpkin
1/2 c. brown sugar
1/4 tsp. ginger
1/2 tsp. cinnamon
1 tbsp. molasses
1/2 tsp. salt
2 eggs, beaten
3/4 c. evaporated milk

Spread mincemeat evenly in pie shell. Bake at 425 degrees for 15 minutes. Combine remaining ingredients; pour over mincemeat. Reduce oven temperature to 350 degrees. Bake for 30 to 40 minutes or until custard is set. Yield: 6 servings.

Verna Howe
Xi Lambda Tau X-2835, Long Beach, California

GRAPEFRUIT BAKED ALASKA

3 lge. grapefruit
Sugar
1/8 tsp. salt
3 egg whites
1/2 tsp. vanilla
1 pt. vanilla ice cream

Cut grapefruit in halves; remove cores. Cut around each section, loosening fruit from membrane. Sprinkle lightly with sugar; chill. Preheat oven to 500 degrees. Add salt to egg whites; beat until foamy. Add 6 tablespoons sugar, beating until stiff and glossy. Add vanilla. Place 1 heaping spoonful ice cream in center of each grapefruit half; cover with meringue, sealing well around edges. Bake for about 1 minute or until lightly browned; serve at once. Yield: 6 servings.

M. Lee Smith
Xi Eta Psi X2078, San Jose, California

APPLE-CHAMPAGNE COMPOTE

3 yellow apples
1 1/2 c. champagne
2 c. frozen sliced strawberries
1 c. powdered sugar

Peel, core and slice apples into thin circles. Cover with champagne and strawberries. Sprinkle with powdered sugar; chill for 3 hours. Sprinkle with coconut before serving. Yield: 6-8 servings.

Mrs. Edward C. Fritsch, Jr.
Oak Harbor, Washington

MINCEMEAT CHIFFON PIE

1 env. unflavored gelatin
1/2 c. water
1 1/2 c. mincemeat
3 egg whites
1/3 c. sugar
1/8 tsp. salt
1 c. heavy cream, whipped
1 baked pie shell

Sprinkle gelatin on water to soften. Place over low heat, stirring constantly, until gelatin is dissolved. Remove from heat; stir in mincemeat. Chill until mixture mounds when dropped from spoon. Beat egg whites until stiff; beat in sugar and salt. Fold gelatin mixture into egg white mixture; fold in whipped cream. Turn into pie shell; chill until set. Yield: 8 servings.

Roberta Lawson
Gamma Kappa No. 4115, Bremerton, Washington

RAISIN-NUT PIE

3 eggs
2/3 c. brown sugar
1/4 tsp. salt
1/4 c. butter, melted
3/4 c. dark corn syrup
1 tsp. vanilla
1/2 c. raisins
1/2 c. chopped walnuts
1 unbaked 8-in. pie shell
Whipped cream

Preheat oven to 400 degrees. Beat eggs with rotary beater; beat in sugar, salt, butter and syrup. Add vanilla, raisins and walnuts; mix well and pour into pie shell. Bake for 35 minutes or until set. Serve with whipped cream. Yield: 6 servings.

Anne Stoddard
Xi Nu Exemplar, Presque Isle, Maine

RHUBARB-CUSTARD PIE

3 eggs
3 tbsp. milk
2 c. sugar
1/4 c. flour
3/4 tsp. nutmeg
4 c. diced rhubarb
1 unbaked pie shell
Butter

Beat eggs lightly; beat in milk, sugar, flour and nutmeg. Stir in rhubarb. Pour filling into pie shell; dot with butter. Bake at 425 degrees for 1 hour or until custard is set.

Jackie Stahlecke
Xi Tau X 1305, Havre, Montan

PECAN PIE

3 eggs, beaten
1/2 c. sugar
1 c. light corn syrup
1 c. chopped pecans
2 tbsp. melted butter
1/4 tsp. salt
1 tsp. vanilla
1 unbaked pie shell

Mix filling ingredients together. Pour into pie shell. Bake for 30 to 40 minutes in 375-degree oven. Yield: 6 servings.

Mrs. Michael Grant
Sigma, Charleston, Illinois

THANKSGIVING AMBROSIA

2 grapefruit, sectioned
3 oranges, sectioned
2 tangerines, sectioned
1/3 to 1/2 c. sugar
1/2 c. shredded coconut

Place half the fruits in serving dish; sprinkle with half the sugar and coconut. Add remaining fruits, sugar and coconut; chill for at least 1 hour before serving. Yield: 8 servings.

CHOCOLATE RUSSE

2 c. milk
1 pkg. vanilla pudding
1 tsp. unflavored gelatin
1 sq. sweet cooking chocolate
1/2 pt. heavy cream
16 ladyfingers

Bring first 3 ingredients to a boil. Remove from heat; add chocolate, mixing until chocolate is melted. Cool. Whip half the cream; add to cooled mixture. Line loaf pan with waxed paper. Stand split ladyfingers around sides and spread on bottom of pan. Fill with half the chocolate mixture. Add another layer of ladyfingers; add remaining chocolate mixture. Place in refrigerator for at least 2 hours before serving. Whip remaining cream; decorate russe. Yield: 8 servings.

Mrs. Carolyn F. Nemec
Xi Alpha Theta X-2694
Haddon Heights, New Jersey

HOLIDAY PIE

1 1/2 c. Brazil nuts
Sugar
1 env. unflavored gelatin
3 eggs, separated
1/8 tsp. salt
1 1/2 c. milk
1/2 c. thinly sliced glace cherries
2 tbsp. light rum
3/4 c. heavy cream

Grind 1 1/4 cups nuts fine. Pour 1 cup boiling water over remaining nuts and let stand for 30 minutes. Drain nuts and shave thin. Combine ground nuts and 3 tablespoons sugar; mix well. Press mixture against bottom and side of 9-inch pie plate building up rim. Bake at 400 degrees for 8 minutes or until lightly browned. Cool. Soften gelatin in 1/4 cup cold water. Beat egg yolks with salt and 1/4 cup sugar. Scald milk in top of double boiler; add small amount of hot milk to egg yolk mixture. Mix well and return to remaining milk. Cook, stirring, until smooth and thickened. Stir in gelatin until dissolved. Chill until partially congealed; whip until smooth and fold in cherries and rum. Beat egg whites until stiff, adding 1/4 cup sugar gradually; fold into custard mixture. Mound into baked crust and refrigerate overnight. Whip cream and sweeten to taste. Spoon whipped cream around edge of pie; sprinkle with shaved nuts. Keep pie refrigerated until ready to serve. Yield: 6-8 servings.

Mrs. R. E. Sink
San Diego, California

HARVEST PUMPKIN PIE

1 c. brown sugar
1/2 tsp. salt
1/2 tsp. ginger
1 tsp. cinnamon
2 eggs, slightly beaten
1 1/2 c. milk
1/2 c. cream or evaporated milk
1 tbsp. Angostura aromatic bitters
1 1/2 c. cooked pumpkin
1 unbaked pastry shell

Mix brown sugar, salt and spices; add eggs, milk, cream, Angostura and pumpkin. Mix well. Pour into pastry shell. Bake at 425 degrees for 40 to 45 minutes or until knife inserted in center comes out clean.

RIPE OLIVE CHOP-CHOP

3 sm. cans chopped ripe olives
1 1/2 c. finely chopped celery
1 c. chopped dill pickles
1/2 c. finely chopped onion
1 clove of garlic, minced
1 2-oz. can anchovy fillets
1/2 c. salad oil
1/4 c. wine vinegar
1/4 tsp. pepper

Combine olives, celery, dill pickles, onion and garlic in large bowl; toss lightly to mix. Drain oil from anchovies; add oil to olive mixture. Cut anchovies into tiny pieces; stir into olive mixture. Combine salad oil, wine vinegar and pepper; toss with olive mixture. Yield: 5 cups.

Jeannette DeHaven
Xi Alpha No. 100, Danville, Illinois

SPICED HARVEST VEGETABLES

4 thin carrots
4 stalks celery
1 head cauliflower, broken
1/4 lb. mushrooms, stemmed
1 tbsp. salt
4 cloves of garlic
1/2 c. white vinegar
3 c. water
1 tbsp. mixed pickling spices
1 tsp. mustard seed
1 1/2 tsp. dillseed

Scrape carrots, cut into 3-inch strips. Cut celery into thin strips; cut into 3-inch lengths. Combine carrots, celery, cauliflower and mushrooms in bowl. Sprinkle salt over garlic and mash. Add to vegetable mixture. Combine vinegar, water, pickling spices, mustard seed and dillseed in saucepan; bring to a full boil. Pour over vegetable mixture. Cool. Cover; refrigerate for several days before serving. Drain vegetable mixture; arrange on relish plate to serve.

Mrs. Carrie McGill
Xi Zeta X-178, Philadelphia, Pennsylvania

MARINATED MUSHROOMS AND ARTICHOKE HEARTS

2 9-oz. packages frozen artichoke hearts
2 lb. small fresh mushrooms
1 1/2 c. water
1 c. cider vinegar
1/2 c. salad oil
1 clove of garlic, halved
1 1/2 tbsp. salt
1/2 tsp. pepper
1/2 tsp. dried thyme
1/2 tsp. dried oregano
1/2 tsp. dried chervil
1 bay leaf
Chopped parsley

Cook artichoke hearts according to package directions; drain. Slice mushrooms in half through stems. Combine water, vinegar, oil, garlic, salt, pepper and spices; add artichokes and mushrooms. Toss lightly; marinate overnight. Yield: 10-12 servings.

Patricia Anderson
Lambda Delta No. 5125, Palatine, Illinois

SOUTHERN SWEET RELISH

1 gal. green tomatoes
10 med. green peppers
10 med. red peppers
10 med. onions
Salt to taste
1 qt. vinegar
7 1/2 c. sugar
2 tbsp. cornstarch
1 9-oz. jar salad mustard

Grind tomatoes, green peppers, red peppers and onions together. Sprinkle with salt and let stand for 2 hours. Drain well. Combine vinegar and sugar in large kettle; bring to a boil. Add vegetables, cornstarch and mustard; mix well and return to a boil. Reduce heat and simmer, stirring frequently for 20 minutes. Ladle into sterilized 1-pint jars and seal.

Mrs. Pauline G. Brookshier
Xi Rho No. 182, Herrin, Illinois

Christmas Eve

Call it peace . . . call it the end of Christmas shopping . . . call it the spirit of Christmas . . . there is something very special about Christmas Eve. An air of quiet, almost of serenity. You feel it at midnight church services, in the streets, in the sky around you. It is Christmas Eve, and no other time is quite like it.

In the midst of this quiet, many families trim their Christmas trees, enjoying the simple pleasure of being together at this most important of all holiday seasons. No matter how scattered a family may be, it almost always manages to reunite at Christmas time. Close friends may share the joy of the holiday and drop in during the evening . . . sometimes to bring intriguing and beautifully-wrapped packages and other times just to visit with you and the returned members of your family.

If your family enjoys the wonderful American tradition of Christmas Eve tree-trimming, why not plan a small buffet party. In the pages that follow, we've outlined a Christmas Eve buffet menu to serve four to six people. Most of the dishes can be prepared for cooking or actually cooked in advance, leaving you free to share in the wonderful spirit of Christmas Eve.

Start by offering Savory Meatballs — a delicious combination of herb seasonings and ground beef. Stuffed Baked Potatoes are a festive way to serve an old favorite. And few vegetables are more associated with Christmas than butternut squash — here it is presented in a Butternut-Orange Casserole. Highlight the holiday season with Three-layer Christmas Salad. With such a filling menu, you'll want a light dessert — everyone's favorite, Egg Custard Pie.

To prepare Savory Meatballs, combine one beaten egg, 1/2 cup bread or cracker crumbs, 1/2 cup milk, 1/2 teaspoon onion powder, 3/4 teaspoon sweet basil, 1/2 teaspoon marjoram, and salt and pepper to taste. Let mixture rest for 20 to 30 minutes. Then add one pound hamburger and mix thoroughly. Shape into meatballs and brown in a well-greased frying pan. Add more fat if needed as they cook. Remove meatballs from frying pan; drain off fat. Pour one can mushroom soup into pan and add one soup can water. Mix until smooth. Add 1/2 teaspoon sweet basil and mix. Add meatballs and simmer for 20 to 30 minutes. These can be kept at the peak of their hot goodness by serving them in a chafing dish.

Stuffed Baked Potatoes are so easy to prepare, they're sure to become a favorite with you. Bake six medium baking potatoes in a 400-degree oven for 60 minutes or until done. Cut crisscross slits in the top of each potato. Scoop out pulp and mash. Add 3 tablespoons butter, 1/2 cup warm cream, salt and pepper to taste, and 1/4 cup crumbled bacon. Refill potato shells and sprinkle generously with one cup grated cheese. Return to oven until heated through and browned. If desired, these potatoes may be prepared in advance, wrapped in foil, and frozen. When ready to serve, thaw and bake in 350-degree oven for 20 to 30 minutes

Enjoy Christmas Eve Buffet Dishes

before serving. Nothing could be easier . . . or more delicious!

An unusual flavor combination — Butternut-Orange Casserole — will bring compliments from your guests. To prepare, peel and slice one large butternut squash. Boil in salted water until barely tender; drain. Mash with 1/4 cup butter, 1/2 cup orange juice, and 1/4 cup brown sugar. Add 1/2 teaspoon salt, 1/4 teaspoon cinnamon, 1/8 teaspoon ginger, and a pinch of powdered cloves. Spoon into buttered casserole dish. Spread top with orange marmalade. Bake in 350-degree oven for about 30 minutes.

Three-Layer Christmas Salad is another one of those wonderful dishes that can be prepared well in advance of your party. Dissolve one 3-ounce package strawberry gelatin in 1 1/4 cups boiling water. Add one 1-pound can cranberry sauce. Mix well and chill until partially thickened. Pour into an eight-cup ring mold and chill until set. Then dissolve one 3-ounce package lemon gelatin in 1 1/4 cups boiling water. Add an 8-ounce package cream cheese, softened, and beat with mixer until smooth. Add one 9-ounce can crushed pineapple. Chill until partially set

and pour over strawberry-cranberry gelatin. Chill until firm. Then dissolve one 3-ounce package lime gelatin and 2 tablespoons sugar in 1 cup boiling water. Add 2 cups grapefruit sections, with juice. Chill until partially set. Pour over lemon gelatin mixture. Chill until firm. Unmold on lettuce and garnish as desired.

Top your buffet menu with cool and delicious Egg Custard Pie; then listen to the compliments flow! To prepare, combine 3 well-beaten eggs, 1/2 cup sugar, 1/4 teaspoon salt, 1/4 teaspoon nutmeg, and 2 cups evaporated milk. Beat well. Pour into one 8-inch unbaked pie shell. Bake at 425 degrees for 10 minutes. Reduce temperature to 350 degrees and bake for 25 to 30 minutes or until custard is set.

Use your decorating skill to plan table and room decorations that highlight the festivity of this season. Cover your buffet table with a gay red tablecloth with pairs of silver bells sewn along the hem. Or perhaps you'll prefer to use pure white linen and highlight it with bright red or deep green napkins. Candles, of course, but let your taste dictate whether you choose an elegant candelabra, great fat candles massed in bunches along the table, or perhaps pairs of tall tapers.

For the door, focus light on your holiday wreath. If you have candle lights, be sure your windows echo the holiday greetings. Holiday music playing quietly in the background . . . just a lovely relaxed evening with friends and loved ones . . . plenty of good food . . . beautiful decorations . . . everything you need to bring the serenity of Christmas Eve into your home as you share a joyous Trim-the-Tree Buffet.

SWEDISH MEATBALLS

1 lb. ground chuck
1/4 c. fine dry bread crumbs
1 tbsp. instant minced onion
1 tsp. salt
Dash of pepper
1/2 tsp. allspice
1 2/3 c. evaporated milk
3 tbsp. butter
2 tbsp. flour
1 beef bouillon cube
1 c. boiling water
1 tbsp. Worcestershire sauce

Mix ground chuck, crumbs, onion, salt, pepper, allspice and 2/3 cup milk together. Shape into meatballs, using teaspoon as measure for meat mixture. Melt butter in large, heavy skillet over medium heat. Add meatballs; fry, turning frequently, to brown on all sides. Remove skillet from heat. Sprinkle flour evenly over meatballs, stirring to blend well. Dissolve bouillon cube in boiling water; add to meatballs. Stir in remaining milk and Worcestershire sauce to make smooth mixture. Return pan to low heat; cook, stirring frequently, until gravy is thickened. Serve over hot cooked noodles. Yield: 6 servings.

MINESTRONE

1 lb. beef shank
2 1/2 qt. cold water
3 tbsp. salt
1 c. dried white or red beans
1 tbsp. olive or salad oil
2 cloves of garlic, minced
1/2 c. minced onion
1/2 c. minced parsley
1/8 tsp. pepper
1 c. frozen green beans
2 med. potatoes, diced
3/4 c. diced celery
2/3 c. frozen peas
2 c. finely shredded cabbage
1 c. diced carrots
1 c. chopped canned tomatoes
3/4 c. shell macaroni
Grated Parmesan cheese

Place beef in deep cooker; add water, 2 tablespoons salt and beans. Cover; bring to a boil. Skim off fat. Simmer for 4 hours. Heat oil in skillet; brown garlic. Remove garlic from skillet; discard. Add onion and parsley; saute until tender but not brown. Cut beef into bite-sized pieces removing fat and gristle. Set aside. Add all ingredients except macaroni, cheese and beef to broth. Cover; simmer for 30 minutes. Add macaroni and beef, cooking until macaroni is tender. Serve with cheese. Yield: 10 servings.

Mrs. Luana Larson
San Pablo, California

MAINE LOBSTER STEW

3 tbsp. butter or margarine
2 c. cooked lobster meat
1 qt. milk
1 1/2 tsp. salt
1 tsp. paprika
1/8 tsp. pepper
Dash of cayenne pepper

Heat butter in small skillet; saute lobster for about 5 minutes. Scald milk in saucepan; season with salt, paprika, pepper and cayenne pepper. Add lobster; simmer for 5 minutes. Let stand for several minutes before serving.

Anita Brown
Noank, Connecticut

SHRIMP AND CRAB GUMBO

8 slices bacon
1 pkg. frozen okra, sliced
1 lge. onion, chopped
1 green pepper, chopped
1/3 c. chopped parsley
1 c. tomato sauce
1 tsp. salt
1/4 tsp. pepper
6 boiled cleaned crabs
1 lb. boiled shrimp, cleaned
1 tbsp. gumbo file
Boiled or steamed rice

Chop bacon finely; brown in 6-quart kettle over medium heat. Remove bacon from kettle; reserve. Brown okra in bacon drippings; add bacon bits, onion, green pepper, parsley, tomato sauce, salt, pepper and 4 cups water. Simmer for 1 hour. Add crabs and shrimp; simmer for 1 hour longer. Stir file into gumbo. Serve over rice. Additional water may be added for thinner gumbo. Yield: 6 servings.

Mrs. Jo-Ann Ferrell
Zeta No. 567, New Orleans, Louisiana

NEVER-FAIL CLAM CHOWDER

3 qt. milk
2 cans cream-style corn
2 cooked potatoes, cubed
1/2 lb. bacon, cubed
1 med. onion, chopped
1 8-oz. can clams
Salt and pepper to taste
Cornstarch

Combine milk, corn and potatoes in large saucepan. Bring to a slow boil. Fry bacon and onion in skillet; add to milk mixture. Add clams; heat through. Add salt and pepper; thicken with cornstarch just before serving. Yield: 8-10 servings.

Delpha Blohm
Pi, Vancouver, Washington

CRAB MEAT DIP

3 lge. packages cream cheese
2 cans crab meat
2 cloves of garlic, minced
1/2 sm. onion, minced
2 tsp. mustard
1/4 c. white wine
2 tsp. confectioners' sugar
1 tsp. seasoned salt

Combine all ingredients in double boiler; heat gently until cream cheese is melted and dip is well blended. Serve in chafing dish with crackers or melba toast.

Mrs. Robert Weyburne
Delta Delta No. 1966, Meadville, Pennsylvania

CRAB MEAT FONDUE

2 lb. sharp cheese
1/4 c. flour
1 c. dry sherry
1 8-oz. can crab meat
1 loaf French bread, cubed

Melt cheese in greased saucepan over low heat. Blend flour into sherry until smooth; stir into cheese, blending well. Add crab meat; cook gently for about 15 minutes or until heated through and thickened. Pour into fondue pot. Serve with bread cubes for dipping. Yield: 6-8 servings.

Cora A. Neyer
Alpha Iota Chap. No. 567
Mount Pleasant, Michigan

TRIM-THE-TREE CHEESE FONDUE

1 can frozen shrimp soup
1 roll garlic cheese
1 sm. can mushroom pieces
1 tbsp. Worcestershire sauce

Heat soup and cheese in double boiler until melted. Drain mushrooms; add mushrooms and Worcestershire sauce to cheese mixture, blending well. Pour into fondue pot or chafing dish. Serve with crackers or melba toast for dipping.

Norma Reineck
Iota Delta No. 3874, Fremont, Ohio

CRAB VOLTAIRE

2 c. cooked crab claw meat
1/4 c. butter
1 tsp. chopped shallot or onion
1/4 lb. fresh mushrooms, sliced
2 tbsp. brandy
6 tbsp. sherry
2 c. heavy cream
2 tsp. minced chives
2 egg yolks
Salt to taste
Cayenne pepper to taste

Saute crab meat in foaming butter in skillet with shallot and mushrooms for 3 minutes. Add brandy and sherry; bring to a boil. Add 1 3/4 cups cream; boil for 3 minutes. Add chives; boil for 1 minute longer. Beat egg yolks with remaining cream; stir into crab mixture gradually. Remove skillet from heat. Heat gently until thickened; do not boil. Season with salt and cayenne pepper. Serve from chafing dish. Yield: 4 servings.

Mrs. Rachel Larson
Southern California Council, Justin, California

MACARONI-HAM SALAD

1 7-oz. package elbow macaroni
1/2 lb. American cheese
1/2 lb. baked or broiled ham
1 13 1/2-oz. can pineapple tidbits
1/2 c. chopped sweet pickle
1 c. sliced celery
1 tsp. minced onion
1/3 c. diced pimento
1/2 c. mayonnaise
1 tsp. salt
1 tsp. curry powder
Salad greens

Cook macaroni according to package directions; blanch in cold water. Drain and chill. Cut cheese into cubes; cut ham into 2-inch strips. Drain pineapple. Combine all ingredients except salad greens; toss lightly to mix well. Chill. Serve on salad greens in bowl. Yield: 8-10 servings.

Carol Pahs
Phi Beta Sigma P1052, La Porte, Indiana

PINEAPPLE-LAMB SALAD

1 1-lb. 4-oz. can pineapple chunks
2 c. cubed lamb roast
1 lge. cucumber, thinly sliced
1 1/2 tsp. (about) salt
3/4 tsp. pepper
3/4 tsp. dried dillweed
1/4 c. (about) sour cream

Drain pineapple. Toss lamb, pineapple and cucumber together in salad bowl, adding seasonings and just enough sour cream to moisten. Chill for at least 1 hour. Yield: 6 servings.

Nell Streeter
Preceptor Iota, Tampa, Florida

CHICKEN-CRANBERRY SALAD MOLD

2 env. unflavored gelatin
1 can cream of chicken soup
1/4 c. mayonnaise
2 tbsp. lemon juice
2 c. diced chicken
1/4 c. chopped celery
Dash of pepper
3 tbsp. slivered almonds
1 tbsp. minced onion
1 1-lb. can cranberry sauce
1 lge. orange, sectioned
Salad greens

Soften 1 envelope gelatin in 1/2 cup cold water. Stir over boiling water until dissolved. Blend soup, mayonnaise and lemon juice. Stir in dissolved gelatin. Fold in chicken, celery, pepper, almonds and onion. Pour into 1 1/2-quart ring mold; chill until firm. Soften remaining gelatin in 1/2 cup cold water; dissolve over hot water. Crush cranberry sauce with fork; add gelatin. Fold in orange pieces. Pour over congealed chicken layer. Chill until firm. Unmold; serve on salad greens. Garnish with orange wedges. Yield: 8 servings.

Helen Hardy
Xi Epsilon Rho, Center, Texas

FESTIVE MAIN DISH SALAD

2 c. diced cooked chicken
3/4 c. diced cooked ham
3/4 c. diced Swiss cheese
2 hard-cooked eggs, chopped
1 c. finely diced celery
3 tbsp. sliced green onion
1 tbsp. chopped green pepper
1 tbsp. chopped pimento
Mayonnaise
1/4 tsp. poultry seasoning
1/4 tsp. dry mustard
1 tbsp. lemon juice or vinegar
3 c. shredded lettuce

Combine chicken, ham, cheese, eggs, celery, onion, green pepper and pimento in large bowl. Blend 2/3 cup mayonnaise, poultry seasoning, mustard and lemon juice; pour over chicken mixture. Toss gently; cover and refrigerate for several hours. Add lettuce; toss to mix, adding mayonnaise as needed. Serve salad in lettuce-lined bowl; garnish with tomato wedges and radish roses. Yield: 4-6 servings.

Mrs. Dorothy M. Small
Xi Alpha Omicron X1966
Guelph, Ontario, Canada

CHICKEN POINSETTIAS

2 c. diced cooked chicken
1/2 c. diced celery
2 pimentos, diced
1/2 c. salad dressing
1/2 tsp. dry mustard
1/2 tsp. salt
1/4 tsp. red pepper sauce
4 lge. tomatoes
Salad greens
2 sprigs of fresh dill, snipped

Combine chicken, celery and pimentos. Blend salad dressing, mustard, salt and red pepper sauce. Toss 2/3 of the dressing mixture lightly with chicken mixture. Chill. Reserve remaining dressing. Cut tomatoes in sixths, almost through to bottom; spread open slightly to form flowers. Fill centers with chicken salad; place on salad greens. Serve with remaining dressing. Garnish with dill. Yield: 4 servings.

Vera Fulgham
Xi Gamma Lambda X1450, Eastlake, Ohio

WALNUT JEWEL SALAD

1/2 c. crushed pineapple
1 pkg. pineapple gelatin
1 c. hot water
1/2 tsp. salt
1 c. chopped cranberries
1/2 c. diced celery
1/2 c. chopped walnuts

Drain pineapple; reserve juice. Add enough water to reserved juice to make 1 cup liquid. Dissolve gelatin in hot water. Add salt and reserved pineapple juice mixture. Chill until slightly thickened. Fold in remaining ingredients. Turn into 1-quart mold. Chill until firm. Unmold onto bed of crisp lettuce. Garnish with walnut halves.

Honey-Creme Salad Dressing

1 3-oz. package cream cheese
1/4 tsp. salt
2 tbsp. honey
1/4 c. sour cream

Combine all ingredients in small bowl. Whip until smooth. Serve with salad.

CRAB LOUIS

3/4 c. chili sauce
1/2 c. mayonnaise
2 tsp. instant minced onion
1/4 tsp. salt
1/2 tsp. sugar
3 tbsp. lemon juice
2 tbsp. finely chopped parsley (opt.)
1 pkg. frozen King crab, thawed

Mix first 8 ingredients in bowl for sauce; chill for 20 minutes. Remove membrane from crab. Combine with 1/2 cup sauce; toss lightly. Serve on salad greens; garnish with ripe olives, radishes, green onion and hard-boiled eggs. Refrigerate remaining sauce for future use.

Charlene Parkinson
Preceptor Alpha Kappa, Oxford, Ohio

CURRIED SHRIMP SALAD

4 c. hot cooked rice
1/4 c. French dressing
3/4 c. mayonnaise
2 tbsp. minced onion
1/2 tsp. curry powder
1/2 tsp. salt
1/4 tsp. ground white pepper
3 drops of hot sauce
1/2 tsp. dry mustard
1 c. diced celery
1 1/2 c. cooked peas
2 cans shrimp
Crisp salad greens

Combine rice and French dressing; cool to room temperature. Mix mayonnaise and seasonings. Place celery and peas in large mixing bowl; pour mayonnaise mixture over celery and peas. Add rice mixture; toss lightly with fork to coat. Chill salad well. Drain and chill shrimp; add to salad just before serving. Turn salad into lettuce-lined bowl. Garnish with tomato wedges and additional whole shrimp. Yield: 8 servings.

Carolyn L. Lyons
Theta Theta No. 5776, Kalamazoo, Michigan

TANGY CABBAGE SALAD

1 3-oz. package lemon gelatin
1/2 tsp. salt
1 c. boiling water
1 1/2 c. cold water
2 tsp. vinegar
2 tbsp. horseradish
1 1/2 c. shredded cabbage
1 tbsp. chopped pimento (opt.)
1/4 c. chopped dill pickle
3 drops of hot sauce

Dissolve gelatin and salt in boiling water. Add cold water and vinegar. Chill until slightly thickened; add remaining ingredients. Pour into mold. Chill until firm. Yield: 6-8 servings.

Pat Logan
Zeta Xi No. 2849, Godfrey, Illinois

CAESAR SALAD CHATEAUBRIAND

1 clove of garlic, crushed
1 c. oil
2 c. croutons or bread cubes
2 heads romaine
1 head Boston lettuce
1 bunch watercress
3/4 c. grated Parmesan cheese
1/2 tsp. salt
1/4 tsp. dry mustard
1/4 tsp. freshly ground pepper
1/3 c. lemon juice
2 eggs, beaten
Dash of Worcestershire sauce
1 2-oz. can anchovies

Add garlic to oil; let stand for 1 hour. Remove garlic; discard. Saute croutons in 1/4 cup oil. Wash, drain and dry salad greens thoroughly; tear into pieces in salad bowl. Sprinkle cheese, salt, mustard and pepper over greens; pour on remaining oil, lemon juice and eggs. Add Worcestershire sauce, anchovies and croutons; toss gently. Serve immediately. Yield: 6 servings.

Louise H. Silva
Chi No. 2823, Adelphi, Maryland

BEEF FONDUE WITH SAUCES

1 1/2 lb. beef tenderloin
Peanut oil
Red Sauce
Horseradish-Sour Cream Sauce

Cut beef in 1 1/2-inch cubes. Fill fondue pot to within 1 1/2 inches from top with oil. Heat over medium heat to 425 degrees on deep-fat thermometer. Transfer fondue pot to heating unit. Allow each guest to spear beef cubes with fondue fork and cook in oil to desired doneness. Transfer cube to dinner fork. Dip into sauces. Yield: 4 servings.

Red Sauce

1 8-oz. can tomato sauce
1/3 c. steak sauce
2 tbsp. brown sugar
2 tbsp. cooking oil
Seasonings to taste

Combine all ingredients; heat to boiling point. Serve hot. Yield: 1 1/2 cups.

Horseradish-Sour Cream Sauce

1 c. sour cream
3 tbsp. horseradish, drained
1 tsp. vinegar or lemon juice
1/2 tsp. salt
1/4 tsp. pepper
1 sm. onion, grated

Combine all ingredients; chill for at least 2 hours to blend flavors. Yield: 1 1/2 cups.

Mary Anne DeAnna
Mu Beta No. 5766, Parma, Ohio

LAMB FONDUE

1 1/2 lb. boneless leg of lamb
1 tbsp. wine vinegar
2 tsp. chopped onion
1/4 tsp. tarragon leaves
1/2 c. butter
3 egg yolks
1/4 tsp. salt
Dash of cayenne pepper
Salad oil

Trim lamb; cut into 3/4-inch cubes. Refrigerate until about 15 to 20 minutes before serving time. Combine 2 tablespoons water, vinegar, onion and tarragon in saucepan. Simmer until liquid is reduced to 1 tablespoon. Add butter; heat until melted. Blend egg yolks, 2 tablespoons water, salt and cayenne pepper in electric blender until thick. Add hot butter mixture gradually through hole in top of blender, blending on low speed. Pour sauce into heatproof dish; keep warm over hot water, stirring occasionally. Pour oil to depth of 2 to 3 inches in fondue pot. Heat to just below smoking point. Place on table over alcohol burner. Spear lamb cubes on fondue forks; cook in hot oil for 1 to 2 minutes or until of desired doneness. Push lamb from fork onto plate. Dip in sauce. Yield: 4 servings.

CRANBERRY POT ROAST

1 3 to 4-lb. rolled chuck roast
Flour
2 tbsp. shortening
Salt and pepper to taste
2 c. tart cranberry sauce

Dredge roast in flour; brown in hot shortening. Season with salt and pepper. Cover with cranberry sauce. Place roast in Dutch oven; pour 1 cup water into oven. Cover tightly. Bake at 325 degrees for about 3 hours or until tender, adding water as necessary. Remove roast to platter. Blend flour with small amount of water to form smooth paste; stir into pan drippings. Cook over low heat, stirring constantly, until thickened. Serve gravy with roast.Yield: 6-8 servings.

Mrs. Ross Gutierrez
Hurst, Texas

PIQUANT LAMB CHOPS

8 rib lamb chops, 3/4 in. thick
2 c. apple juice
3 tbsp. lemon juice
1 garlic clove, halved
1/2 c. fine cracker crumbs
1/2 tsp. salt
4 tbsp. (about) butter
2 tbsp. cornstarch
2 tbsp. brown sugar
1/4 tsp. mace
1/4 c. dark seedless raisins
1/4 c. toasted slivered almonds

Trim excess fat from chops. Blend apple and lemon juice in shallow dish; add garlic and chops. Turn chops until well coated. Refrigerate for about 2 hours, turning occasionally. Remove garlic; pour off marinade and reserve. Blend cracker crumbs and 1/4 teaspoon salt. Roll chops in crumb mixture until evenly coated. Panfry chops in large skillet in hot butter for about 7 minutes on each side or to desired degree of doneness. Blend cornstarch, brown sugar, mace and remaining salt in medium saucepan. Add reserved marinade and raisins. Bring to a boil; cook for 2 minutes, stirring constantly. Add almonds just before serving. Serve sauce with chops. Yield: 4 servings.

DOWN THE CHIMNEY FLANK STEAK

1/4 c. wine vinegar
1/4 c. oil
3/4 c. water
1 tbsp. instant onion flakes
1/4 tsp. dried dill
1/8 tsp. garlic powder
1/2 tsp. salt
1/8 tsp. pepper
1 1 1/2 to 2-lb. flank steak
1 tbsp. cornstarch
1 1/2 tsp. sugar

Combine vinegar, oil, 1/4 cup water, onion flakes, dill, garlic powder, salt and pepper. Place steak in shallow glass dish. Pour vinegar mixture over steak. Cover; let stand for 2 to 3 hours. Drain steak; remove to broiling pan, reserving marinade. Broil in oven or over grill for about 5 minutes on one side and 4 minutes on other side for rare steak. Remove to heated serving platter. Combine cornstarch, sugar and remaining water with reserved marinade. Add to drippings in broiler pan. Cook, stirring constantly, until mixture boils and is thickened. Cut thin diagonal slices of steak; top each slice with sauce. Yield: 6 servings.

Mrs. Jeanne B. Murray
Zeta Iota No. 5372, Deerfield, Florida

MARINATED BEEF FONDUE

2 1/2 lb. beef tenderloin tips
1/2 c. soy sauce
2 c. peanut oil

Cut beef into 1-inch cubes; cover with soy sauce. Marinate for about 4 hours. Bring peanut oil to a boil; fill fondue pot 3/4 full. Serve beef in separate dish at dinner table. Dip in peanut oil with fondue forks; cook to desired doneness at table. Yield: 4-6 servings.

Mrs. Suzan Pfister
Zeta Nu, Quincy, Illinois

BOEUF BOURGUIGNONNE

1 2-lb. round steak
4 tbsp. butter
1 pkg. dry onion soup mix
1 can mushroom soup
1 c. red wine or 1/2 c. brandy
1 1/4 c. water
6 c. (about) cooked rice

Cut steak into 1/2-inch cubes; saute in butter until well browned. Place steak cubes in 3-quart casserole. Add soups, wine and water; cover. Bake in 350-degree oven for 2 hours. Serve over rice. Yield: 6 servings.

Dixie Rader
X- Alpha Zeta X1855, Stone Mountain, Georgia

HOLIDAY BUFFET

1/2 c. chopped onion
1/4 c. diced green pepper
2 tbsp. butter
1 1/4 lb. ground beef
1 10 1/2-oz. can tomato soup
1/2 c. catsup
Salt and pepper to taste
2 3-oz. packages cream cheese
1/3 c. milk
2 tsp. lemon juice
1/4 tsp. garlic salt
1 tsp. Worcestershire sauce
1 8-oz. package med. noodles
1/2 c. shredded Cheddar cheese

Cook onion and green pepper in butter until transparent. Add beef; stir until brown. Add soup, catsup, salt and pepper; cook, uncovered, over low heat for about 8 minutes, stirring occasionally. Blend cream cheese, milk and lemon juice; add garlic salt and Worcestershire sauce. Cook noodles according to package directions; drain. Add cream cheese mixture to noodles. Spread noodle mixture in 8 x 12 x 2-inch glass baking dish. Pour beef sauce on top; sprinkle with shredded cheese. Bake in 350-degree oven for 30 minutes. Yield: 8 servings.

Vicki L. Harrell
Phi Alpha Delta No. P1797, Montgomery, Alabama

CORNED BEEF CASSEROLE

1 1-lb. can cut Blue Lake green beans
1/3 c. butter or margarine
1/3 c. flour
1 1/2 c. milk
1/2 c. beef broth
1 tbsp. prepared horseradish
1/2 tsp. savory, crumbled
2 c. diced boiled corned beef
1 c. sliced cooked carrots
3 to 4 c. hot mashed potatoes
1 tsp. onion powder
1 egg yolk

Drain beans, reserving 1/2 cup liquid. Melt butter in saucepan, blend in flour until smooth. Stir in reserved bean liquid, milk and broth. Cook, stirring, until mixture is thickened and comes to a boil. Stir in horseradish and savory. Fold in beans, corned beef and carrots; turn into 2 or 2 1/2-quart shallow casserole. Blend mashed potatoes with onion powder and egg yolk; pipe or spoon around edge of casserole. Bake at 425 degrees for 15 to 20 minutes, until lightly browned and bubbling hot. Yield: 6 servings.

BEEF AND MUSHROOM CASSEROLE

1 1/2 lb. round steak, cubed
Seasoned flour
Butter
1 lb. mushrooms, cut up
2 med. onions, chopped
1/2 c. tomato juice
2 beef bouillon cubes
2 c. boiling water
2 tbsp. sour cream
Cooked rice

Shake steak in paper bag with seasoned flour. Brown in butter in skillet; place in 2-quart casserole. Brown mushrooms and onions lightly; place in casserole with steak. Add tomato juice. Dissolve bouillon cubes in boiling water; pour over steak mixture. Cover casserole. Bake at 325 degrees for 1 hour. Uncover; bake for 30 minutes longer. Add sour cream just before serving. Serve over rice. Yield: 4-6 servings.

Mrs. Ralph D. Gale
Xi Theta X3209, Dorval, Quebec, Canada

BAKED DEVILED EGG CASSEROLE

6 hard-boiled eggs
2 tsp. prepared mustard
1 c. sour cream
1/4 tsp. salt
2 tbsp. margarine
1/2 c. chopped green pepper
1/3 c. chopped onion
1/4 c. chopped pimento
1 can cream of mushroom soup
1/2 c. shredded Cheddar cheese

Halve eggs lengthwise; remove yolks. Mash yolks, mustard, 3 tablespoons sour cream and salt together. Fill whites with yolk mixture. Melt margarine in large skillet; saute green pepper and onion until tender. Remove from heat; stir in pimento, soup and remaining sour cream. Place 1/2 of the soup mixture in 1 1/2-quart shallow baking dish; arrange eggs, cut side up, in single layer in dish. Pour remaining soup mixture over top; sprinkle with cheese. Bake at 350 degrees for 20 minutes or until heated through. May be prepared in advance and and refrigerated until baking time.

Genella Eads
Xi Lambda Xi X3325, Clarendon, Texas

DIRTY RICE

2 sticks margarine
2 c. long grain rice
2 lge. onions, chopped
1/2 green pepper, chopped
1 2-oz. can mushrooms, drained
3 cans beef bouillon soup

Melt margarine in skillet. Add rice, onions and green pepper; cook over medium heat until rice is browned and vegetables are transparent. Place in casserole; add mushrooms and soup. Cover. Bake for 1 hour at 350 degrees. Yield: 5-6 servings.

Mrs. Sherry Barnett
Alpha Tau No. 4666, Holly Springs, Mississippi

HOT HOMINY

2 No. 303 cans hominy, drained
1 sm. can chopped green chilies
1 can cream of mushroom soup
1 c. grated Cheddar cheese

Combine all ingredients; mix well. Place in casserole; cover. Bake in 350-degree oven for 1 hour. Yield: 8 servings.

Connie L. Williams
Lambda Alpha, No. 3586, Kermit, Texas

CHEESE CASSEROLE

5 slices buttered white bread
1/2 lb. sharp cheese, grated
4 eggs
2 c. milk
1 tsp. dry mustard

Trim crusts from bread; cut into cubes. Place bread in casserole; cover with cheese. Beat eggs; add milk and mustard. Pour milk mixture over bread and cheese. Refrigerate for at least 12 hours. Place casserole in pan of water. Bake at 325 degrees for 1 hour or until knife inserted in custard comes out clean. Yield: 6 servings.

Virginia McCormick
Xi Alpha Nu X-2617, Atlanta, Georgia

SPAGHETTI AND CHEESE

1 8-oz. wedge mellow cheese
1 8-oz. package spaghetti
1 16-oz. can tomatoes, chopped

Shred cheese. Cook spaghetti according to package directions; drain well. Layer half the spaghetti, half the tomatoes and half the cheese in ungreased 1-quart casserole. Repeat layers. Bake at 350 degrees for 20 minutes. Yield: 6 servings.

Sandra Curtis
Alpha No. 482, Columbia, South Carolina

ASPARAGUS WITH FRIED ONION RINGS

2 sm. cans asparagus tips
1 1/2 c. grated American cheese
1 can mushroom soup
1 sm. can evaporated milk
1 3 1/2-oz. can fried onion rings

Drain asparagus tips; place in greased casserole. Cover with cheese. Mix soup and milk well; pour over asparagus and cheese. Bake 30 minutes at 350 degrees; sprinkle onion rings over top. Bake for 10 minutes longer. Yield: 8-10 servings.

Mrs. S. L. Norrell
Cleburne, Texas

HOT AND TANGY MUSHROOMS

3 lb. mushrooms
2 cloves of garlic, diced
1/4 c. olive oil
1 tbsp. oregano
1 tsp. crushed hot red pepper
3 oz. cooking wine

Boil mushrooms for 5 minutes; drain. Brown garlic in oil with oregano. Add mushrooms, hot pepper and wine. Simmer for 1 hour or until mushrooms are completely cooked. Yield: 6-8 servings.

Rose Lazzaro
Clifton, New Jersey

QUICK NUT BREAD

2 c. sifted flour
3 tsp. baking powder
1/2 tsp. salt
1/2 c. brown sugar
1 c. milk
1 egg, beaten
2 tbsp. melted shortening
1 c. chopped pecans

Sift flour, baking powder, salt and brown sugar together. Combine milk, egg, shortening and pecans; add to dry ingredients, mixing well. Pour into greased loaf pan. Bake in 350-degree oven for 1 hour or until lightly browned. Yield: 1 loaf.

Sally Bernard
Kappa Theta No. 6887, Pensacola, Florida

WALNUT-MINCEMEAT LACE

1 13 3/4-oz. package hot roll mix
1 egg
1/2 c. finely chopped walnuts
1 tsp. cornstarch
1/4 c. orange juice
1 tbsp. brown sugar
1 c. prepared mincemeat
1/3 c. coarsely chopped walnuts
1/4 c. chopped candied cherries
Powdered sugar glaze

Prepare hot roll mix according to package directions, using egg. Mix in finely chopped walnuts with flour mixture. Cover; let rise for 30 to 40 minutes or until doubled in bulk. Combine cornstarch and orange juice in small saucepan; heat, stirring until thickened. Stir in brown sugar, mincemeat, coarsely chopped walnuts and cherries. Roll dough out on lightly floured surface to 14 x 10-inch rectangle. Carefully lift onto greased baking sheet. Spread filling down center third of dough. Cut slits on each side of filling in dough as far in as filling and about 1 inch apart. Fold strips at angle across filling, alternating from side to side. Tuck ends underneath after lacing last 2 strips. Cover; let rise for about 30 minutes. Bake at 350 degrees for 30 minutes. Cool. Frost with powdered sugar glaze. Garnish with walnut halves and candied cherries.

HOMEMADE HOLIDAY BREAD

2 pkg. dry yeast
2 c. warm water
1 tbsp. sugar
1 tbsp. salt
Salad oil
6 1/2 c. flour
Butter

Dissolve yeast in warm water. Add sugar, salt and 2 tablespoons oil; mix well. Add half the flour; mix until blended. Add remaining flour; beat with mixing spoon until dough is elastic. Knead into ball with oiled hands. Cover, let rise until doubled in bulk. Roll out on floured surface; halve dough. Knead each half; place in greased loaf pans. Oil tops lightly; cover with cloth. Let rise until center is higher than pan. Bake at 425 degrees for 30 to 35 minutes. Remove from pan; butter lightly. Let set for several minutes before slicing. Recipe may be halved. Yield: 2 loaves.

Ethel Divinia
Epsilon Lambda No. 2218, Greenville, Texas

FILLED MUSCAT STARS

2 c. seeded muscat raisins
1 tbsp. cornstarch
2/3 c. orange juice
1 tbsp. grated orange peel
1 1/2 c. sugar
2/3 c. chopped nuts
1/2 tsp. ginger
Butter
1 tbsp. grated lemon peel
2 tbsp. lemon juice
4 1/2 c. sifted flour
1/2 tsp. soda
1 1/2 tsp. salt

Chop raisins. Combine raisins, cornstarch, orange juice, orange peel, 1/2 cup sugar, nuts, ginger and 2 tablespoons butter in saucepan. Cook over medium heat for about 10 minutes, stirring frequently, until thickened. Cool. Blend remaining sugar and 2 cups butter; beat until fluffy. Add lemon peel and juice. Sift flour with soda and salt; stir into butter mixture until blended. Cover; chill for 30 minutes. Roll out small amounts of dough on lightly floured board to about 1/4 inch thick. Dough is rich and needs to be handled gently; press together again if dough breaks. Cut into 3-inch rounds. Cut small star shape in center of half the rounds. Spoon raisin filling in center of whole rounds; moisten edges. Top round with star. Press edges together with fork and prick tops. Place on baking sheet. Bake at 375 degrees for 10 to 12 minutes or until lightly browned. Yield: 2 1/2 dozen filled cookies.

Photograph for this recipe on page 193.

PETITE FRUITCAKES

1 15-oz. package golden raisins
1 c. orange juice
1/2 c. butter
1 c. orange marmalade
1/2 c. brandy
1 lge. egg, beaten
1 c. chopped walnuts
2 c. chopped candied fruits
2 c. sifted flour
1 tsp. salt
1/2 tsp. soda
1 tsp. cinnamon
1/2 tsp. nutmeg
1/2 tsp. cardamom

Combine raisins, orange juice and butter in saucepan; cover. Simmer for 10 minutes. Cool; stir in marmalade and brandy. Add egg, walnuts and candied fruits. Sift flour, salt, soda and spices together; blend with raisin mixture. Spoon into paper-lined muffin tins. Bake in 300-degree oven for 50 minutes or until cakes test done. Cool in pan for 10 minutes; remove to wire racks. Let stand until cold. Drizzle with additional brandy or rum. Store for 1 week; drizzle frequently with brandy or rum. Yield: 1 1/2 dozen cakes.

Suzanne Rinella
Xi Beta Delta X-2808, South Holland, Illinois

ANGEL SWEET

1 6-oz. package semisweet chocolate bits
2 tbsp. butter
1 egg
1 c. sifted confectioners' sugar
1 c. chopped almonds
2 c. miniature marshmallows
1/2 c. coconut

Melt chocolate and butter in saucepan over low heat. Remove from heat; cool. Beat in egg. Stir in confectioners' sugar, almonds and marshmallows. Blend well. Shape into 1-inch balls; roll in coconut. Refrigerate until served. Yield: 3 1/2 dozen.

Viola C. Miller
Xi Psi Exemplar, Spokane, Washington

CANDY MINTS FOR SANTA'S SNACK

2 oz. cream cheese
1 2/3 c. powdered sugar
1/4 tsp. peppermint flavoring

Combine all ingredients, mixing well. Shape into ball or squares; refrigerate until serving time.

Mrs. Lee Riddiough
Omega Pi, Lompoc, California

LEMON TARTS

2 c. brown sugar
1 tbsp. butter
3 eggs
Juice and rind of 1 lemon
Unbaked tart shells

Cream sugar and butter; add eggs, one at a time, beating well after each addition. Blend in juice and rind. Place tart shells on baking sheet; spoon filling into shells. Bake at 350 degrees until golden brown.

Edith J. Howell
Xi Alpha Omicron X-611, Los Angeles, California

CHRISTMAS CHEER CANDY

3 c. sugar
1 c. white corn syrup
1 1/2 c. light cream
1 tsp. vanilla
1/2 lb. black walnuts
1/2 lb. almonds
1/2 lb. pecans
1/2 lb. candied pineapple
1/2 lb. candied cherries

Combine sugar, syrup and cream in heavy aluminum boiler; bring to a boil. Boil for 8 minutes, stirring constantly, to soft-ball stage. Remove from heat; add vanilla. Beat until mixture begins to thicken and is light in color. Add nuts and fruits. Pour into buttered 10 x 15-inch pan. Cool; cut into squares. Let stand in tightly covered container for 2 or 3 weeks to mellow. May be frozen.

Mrs. John C. Martin
Clayton, Alabama

SPRINGERLE CHRISTMAS COOKIES

4 eggs
1 lb. confectioners' sugar
3 1/2 c. cake flour
Grated rind of 1 lemon
1 tbsp. melted butter
8 drops of anise oil
1/2 tsp. aniseed
1 tsp. baking powder

Beat eggs until thick and lemon colored; add sugar gradually, beating well. Beat for 15 minutes. Add 1 cup flour, lemon rind and butter. Add remaining flour, anise oil and aniseed. Mix in baking powder. Chill dough. Roll out to 1/4-inch thickness. Press with springerle rolling pin; cut into squares. Chill overnight. Place on greased cookie sheet. Bake at 325 degrees for 20 minutes. Store in tight container for 3 to 4 weeks.

Mrs. Walter L. Clarke, Jr.
Lemoore, California

CHRISTMAS PIE

1 c. sugar
1/4 c. butter, melted
2 eggs, lightly beaten
1 tbsp. flour
1 tsp. vanilla
1/2 c. cooked raisins, drained
1 c. chopped nuts
1 unbaked pie shell

Cream sugar and butter; add eggs, beating well. Add flour, vanilla, raisins and nuts. Pour filling into pie shell. Bake at 350 degrees for 35 to 40 minutes. Garnish with whipped cream and candied cherries.

Irma M. Reed
Delta Beta Phi No. 7157, March AFB, California

CAROLER'S WASSAIL

1 gal. sweet cider
1/2 tsp. ground nutmeg
1 tsp. cloves
3 tsp. allspice
4 sticks cinnamon
2 c. sugar
Juice of 8 oranges
Juice of 4 lemons

Combine all ingredients; bring to a boil. Serve hot.

Joan Payne
Iota Theta, Concord, California

CHOCOLATE MARSHMALLOW PUNCH

3 13-oz. cans evaporated milk
2 c. chocolate syrup
2 c. water
12 lge. marshmallows
1 tbsp. vanilla

Mix milk, chocolate syrup, water and marshmallows in large saucepan. Heat over medium heat, stirring until marshmallows are melted. Stir in vanilla. Pour into cups; garnish with marshmallows and grated chocolate. Yield: About 12 servings.

CHRISTMAS WREATH PUNCH

6 6-oz. cans frozen orange juice
1 1/2 c. light corn syrup
1/4 c. lime juice
5 qt. ginger ale, chilled

Combine all ingredients except ginger ale in punch bowl; mix thoroughly. Add ginger ale just before serving. Float ice ring in punch.

Ice Ring

Orange wedges
Red and green maraschino cherries

Fill 6-cup ring mold 2/3 full with water; freeze. Alternate orange wedges, peel-side down, and cherries, in groups of 3, on top of ice. Add thin layer of water. Freeze for about 30 minutes. Fill ring mold with water slowly; freeze. Run warm water on sides of mold to unmold. Yield: 50 servings.

Patricia Junkins
Alpha Zeta No. 6511, Gorham, Maine

Christmas has always been more than just another holiday. It is a special atmosphere, an altered way of looking at the world, something so rare and unique it can only be called the "Christmas spirit." If you experience it, those are the only words you need. If you don't, no words will explain what you are missing.

For many of us, the Christmas spirit first appears on the long trip home for a holiday with all the family . . . somehow the usually interminable waits in air terminals, bus stations, and on turnpikes are not quite so exasperating . . . we smile at other people and chat about the family we have waiting at the end of the trip. For some people, the Christmas spirit is captured in the host of projects designed to provide joy for those less fortunate than ourselves . . . the refurbishing of toys . . . the gathering of Christmas goodies . . . the preparation of extra-special Christmas stockings. Somehow for each of us, in some

Christmas Day

near-miraculous way, the promise and innocence of the first Christmas seem to rekindle each year at this holiday time.

Perhaps no two things capture the Christmas spirit more than the custom of gift giving and the delicious aroma of holiday foods. As we search for just the right gift, we are thinking very much of others and very little of ourselves. Of all Christmas gifts, nothing is appreciated quite so much as those gifts which we make ourselves. Food gifts such as homemade breads . . . cookies . . . candies . . . and those delightful holiday cookies . . . does any gift mean more?

Here, in this section, we have gathered favorite recipes so special they are just perfect for the Christmas holiday season. You're certain to find just the recipe you have been looking

MERRY
CHRISTMAS
MERRY
CHRISTMAS

for. Did you want to give a loaf of bread to that very good friend? You'll find it in this section. And what makes a nicer gift than a still-fragrant loaf of bread on its own breadboard, with your recipe tucked inside the wrapping paper!

Your table decorations ... your Christmas dinner ... the home-baked gifts you share with those you love will all say "Merry Christmas" in the nicest, most personal way possible. They will reflect you at your very best — the excellent cook, the imaginative homemaker, and, above all, the talented hostess! And isn't that a wonderful image of you! So do browse through these pages to find the many delightful ways to celebrate the holiday season with the foods you love best. From hundreds of women all over the country, here are beloved recipes, gifts from them to you! Use them — as they were given — in the spirit of friendship.

Here, too, are great holiday cookies — pressed cookies decorated with bits of candied fruits ... rolled cookies just waiting to be perked-up with your favorite icing ... and the old-fashioned but still-beloved gingerbread man! Your entire family will delight in decorating these cookies — and what better way for all of you to share the spirit of Christmas! Perhaps this is your family's year for a Victorian Christmas

Crown the Holiday Season with Family Tradition

tree — full of cookies you make yourself and attach to fragrant tree boughs with bits of string ... long, long chains of popcorn and cranberries ... maybe even some marzipan! And don't forget the peppermint canes — they're almost as much of a holiday tradition as the tree!

If this is a "do-it-ourselves" Christmas at your home, be sure to try your hand at wreath-making. There are literally hundreds of ways to try it. Some people vow that a bent coat hanger with lots of pine, holly, and nuts makes the best wreath. Others extoll the virtues of bent chicken wire. And some folks — with the help of a home workshop — make a frame of wood and nail down their wreath! Whatever your preference, make this year's wreath uniquely your own. Does your family love the just-fallen snow effect of flocking? You can get the material you need in cans at your hardware store. Maybe their preference is for the breath-taking beauty of a pure gold wreath. It's easy! Just make your wreath, then spray it with the cans of gold spray paint — also available from your hardware store. The variety is as endless as your imagination!

Once the door is decorated, the rest of the house will almost cry out for attention. If you're lucky enough to have a staircase, swag that

banister with chains of real or artificial greenery. For a bright note, attach an artificial poinsettia at each peak in your swagged chain! You'll want a bowl of holiday greenery just inside your entrance to say "welcome" in the very best Christmas tradition. Around the door frames, try taping up greeting cards — your friends will delight in seeing theirs displayed. If you have a blank wall, try making a "tree" of Christmas cards on a piece of heavy paper and hanging it up as a perfect holiday mural. And if you've got a fireplace, the mantle is sure to be the place for a little holiday scene — Santa and his reindeer or a snowbound village. Of course, the mantle is where you'll hang your Christmas stockings!

On the wonderful day itself, what better way to begin than church services with all the family in attendance. If the weather allows and it's not too far, do walk to church. Something about seeing old friends and calling out greetings in the crisp holiday air captures so well the loving spirit of Christmas.

Christmas is one of the most tradition-steeped holidays of the year and no part of Christmas is quite so traditional as the big dinner. If you and your family are among those who are looking for a change from turkey, perhaps this is your year for an English Christmas Dinner. In place of the perennial bird, our menu for an English Christmas Dinner for six features an elegant Standing Rib Roast with Yorkshire Pudding. What could be more traditional — or more sure to please your family and guests! You'll be delighted to discover how easily this English holiday fare makes the transition to American dining tables. Try two extra-special vegetable dishes with this meal: Creamed Celery Parmesan, combines the flavors of mild celery and crisp almonds with the bite of Parmesan cheese. Match it with Brussels Sprouts and Carrots in an easy-to-prepare but utterly delicious Mushroom Sauce. Christmas wouldn't be complete without eggnog — for this dinner, it's Eggnog Christmas Salad! Red Caviar Ring is an elegant and fabulous-tasting dish for your table. With this holiday meal, offer your guests their choice of desserts. Ambrosia — in Greek mythology, it was the nectar of the gods; nowadays, it's a delightful dessert which combines tart citrus fruit flavors with sweet coconut. And of course, no English Christmas Dinner would be complete without a dessert pudding — English Steamed Pudding. Our recipe, which we share with you, is almost priceless. It was originally brought to this country from London in the 1800's.

The featured meat is one of the most fabulous of all beef cuts, the standing rib roast. It is sure to delight your family. To prepare, place one roast in a baking pan. Sprinkle with salt and pepper to taste; place one sliced onion over the top. Insert meat thermometer according to manufacturer's directions. Bake in a 325-degree oven to desired doneness.

The pan drippings from this roast are the foundation for Yorkshire Pudding. You prepare the pudding batter while the meat is cooking. Mix 1 cup sifted flour and 1/2 teaspoon salt. Add 1 cup milk gradually, beating until smooth. Add two eggs, one at a time, beating until smooth. Cover and place in refrigerator until roast is done. After removing roast from oven, increase oven temperature to 425 degrees. Pour 1/4 cup hot beef drippings from baking pan into a shallow 8 x 10-inch pan. Place pan in oven until drippings are hot. Remove pan and pour in refrigerated pudding mixture. Return to oven and bake for 25 minutes. Do not open oven door while baking. Cut into squares and serve immediately with hot roast beef. Your family and guests will rave over this unusual food combination.

Creamed Celery Parmesan is an elegant vegetable treat. To prepare, melt 2 tablespoons butter in a large skillet until frothy. Add 1 cup slivered almonds and 3 cups diced celery. Cover; saute for 15 to 20 minutes, stirring occasionally. Add 2 more tablespoons butter and let melt. Blend in 2 tablespoons flour and cook, stirring, for one minute. Add 1/2 cup light cream, 1/8 teaspoon pepper, and 1 cup boiling chicken broth. Stir until blended. Cook over moderately high heat, stirring, until the sauce comes to a boil and thickens. Spoon into a one-quart casserole dish and sprinkle with 3 tablespoons grated Parmesan cheese. Broil until the cheese browns.

Match the elegance of Creamed Celery Parmesan with Brussels

Sprouts and Carrots in Mushroom Sauce. Simmer 2 packages frozen Brussels sprouts and 4 large carrots, sliced, in 1/2 cup boiling water to which 1 teaspoon salt has been added. Let cook until tender. Add 1 can cream of mushroom soup and heat thoroughly. Add 1/2 cup grated cheese and stir slightly. Serve immediately.

What a delightful note of holiday color Eggnog Christmas Salad will bring to your table! To prepare, drain one No. 2 can crushed pineapple. Pour the juice into a saucepan and heat to the boiling point. Soften 1 tablespoon unflavored gelatin in 3 tablespoons lemon juice. Dissolve in heated pineapple juice and cool to room temperature. Add 1 1/2 cups eggnog, the drained pineapple, and 3/4 cup chopped celery. Pour into a five-cup mold. Chill until firm. Then dissolve one 3-ounce package raspberry gelatin in 1 3/4 cups boiling water. Add Cranberry-Orange Relish (recipe follows) and cool. Pour over congealed eggnog-gelatin mixture, and chill until firm.

For the Cranberry-Orange Relish which is such an important part of this salad, grind one pound fresh cranberries and two whole oranges, seeded, in a food grinder. Or blend the fruits in an electric blender. Add 1 cup sugar and chill for several hours to blend flavors. Its tangy good taste is just what you need to give Eggnog Christmas Salad a perfect color — and a delightfully unexpected tartness!

Red Caviar Ring also brings a festive holiday note to your Christmas party table — and announces that this is indeed a special occasion. Soften one envelope unflavored gelatin in one 7-ounce bottle lemon-lime carbonated drink. Heat in double boiler, stirring, until completely dissolved. Chill until slightly thickened. Combine 1/2 pint sour cream and 1 tablespoon lemon juice. Fold in 1 cup heavy cream, whipped, and gelatin mixture. Add one 4-ounce jar red caviar and pour into a one-quart ring mold. Chill until firm. Unmold on a serving platter and garnish with salad greens. For the perfect finishing touch, fill the hollow center of the caviar ring with crab meat salad. This delicious dish is sure to bring you compliments from all your guests!

For a light touch with dessert, try Ambrosia. To prepare, cut 12 large peeled oranges into segments and remove the membranes. Reserve any orange juice. Drain 1 cup shredded fresh coconut and reserve the milk. Drain two 1-pound cans pineapple chunks and reserve a small amount of syrup. Layer orange segments, coconut, and pineapple chunks in a glass serving bowl. Mix reserved orange juice, coconut milk, and pineapple syrup and pour over fruits. Chill thoroughly.

In keeping with the English tone of this holiday dinner, you must offer the traditional English Steamed Pudding. Mix 1 cup ground suet, 2 cups bread crumbs, 1 cup sugar, 1 cup flour, 1 cup raisins, and 1 cup currants. Mix in 1 teaspoon cinnamon, 2 teaspoons nutmeg, and 1/4

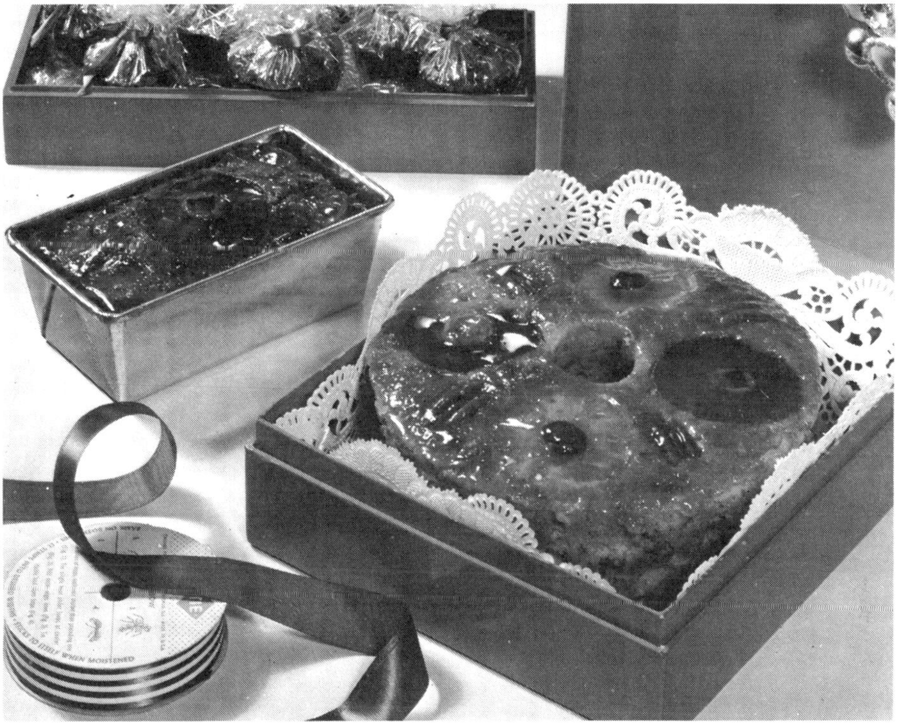

pound chopped nutmeats. Stir in 1 cup sour milk or buttermilk and 1 teaspoon soda. Mix well. Pour into a greased pudding mold (fill more than 2/3 full). Tie a greased paper over the mold. Place mold on rack in a large pan of boiling water. Steam for three hours. What a perfect finish for this English Christmas Dinner!

Such an elegant dinner deserves the very best table decorations. You'll want to use candles to complement your china, silver, and crystal. And for the centerpiece itself, try red carnations and gay green-and-red holly in a white milk glass container! Or perhaps a beautiful Christmas wreath with tall red candles set just inside and the center filled with heaped pine cones. Pure white flowers in a silver dish add a superbly elegant note to any table. If flowers are your choice for a centerpiece, try scattering them in a low bowl among pine boughs and silvered pinecones. And here's a centerpiece the entire family can help make. It's a miniature Yule log — very appropriate for the English Christmas Dinner suggested above! In a 15-inch cut of birch, have someone drill two holes just big enough to hold the candles of your choice. Let your children add their own decorations to the log — small holiday ornaments, pieces of pine, holly, or mistletoe. Add two small pieces of wood to the bottom for legs, and you've got a beautiful centerpiece — even more beautiful because it's something your family made.

SHRIMP CHRISTMAS TREE

3 lb. fresh or frozen shrimp
1/2 c. salt
2 qt. water
4 lge. bunches curly endive
1 2 1/2-ft. high styrofoam cone
1 12 x 12 x 1-in. styrofoam sq.
1 sm. box round toothpicks
Cocktail sauce

Thaw frozen shrimp. Place shrimp in boiling salted water. Cover; simmer for about 5 minutes or until shrimp are pink and tender. Drain. Peel shrimp, leaving last section of shell. Remove sand veins; wash. Chill. Separate and wash endive. Chill. Place cone in center of styrofoam square; draw a circle around base of cone. Cut out circle; insert cone in square. Cover base and cone with overlapping leaves of endive. Fasten endive to styrofoam with toothpick halves. Start at the outside edge of base and work up. Cover fully with greens to resemble Christmas tree. Attach shrimp to tree with toothpicks. Provide Cocktail sauce for dunking.

AVOCADO SOUP WITH GARLIC

4 fully ripe avocados
2 c. chicken broth
2 tsp. lime juice
1/2 tsp. salt
1/8 tsp. garlic powder
2 c. heavy cream

Halve avocados lengthwise, twisting gently to separate; remove seeds. Peel avocado halves; place in electric blender. Add broth, lime juice, salt and garlic powder. Process until smooth. Stir in cream; chill thoroughly. Garnish with sliced lemon or whipped cream.

Mrs. Jeanette Heywood
Biloxi, Mississippi

CREAM OF WATERCRESS SOUP

1 env. cream of leek soup mix
1/8 tsp. nutmeg
4 13 3/4-oz. cans clear chicken broth
2 c. light cream
1 bunch watercress, without stems

Place soup mix and nutmeg in large kettle; stir in chicken broth, small amount at a time. Bring to a boil, stirring frequently. Reduce heat and cover; simmer for 10 minutes. Place 1/2 cup cream and half the watercress in blender container; blend well at high speed. Add 1/2 cup cream and remaining watercress; blend well. Stir watercress mixture and remaining cream into soup; simmer for 5 minutes longer. Serve with heated butter crackers.

Mrs. Wanda Kyles
Cleveland, North Carolina

TOMATO BOUILLON

1 beef knuckle soupbone
2 tsp. salt
1/4 tsp. pepper
1 tsp. monosodium glutamate
1 No. 2 can tomatoes

Place soupbone in large pot; add 1 gallon water and seasonings. Bring to a boil; reduce heat. Simmer for 2 hours. Add tomatoes; simmer for 20 minutes. Strain and cool; Skim off fat. Heat to boiling point to serve. Garnish with thin lemon slices. Yield: 6-8 servings.

Mrs. Ruth Yelvington
Corsicana, Texas

ZIPPY TOMATO DRINK

1 lge. cucumber
2 c. tomato juice
1 tsp. lemon juice
1/2 tsp. salt
1/4 tsp. pepper
Few drops of hot sauce
3/4 c. cracked ice

Peel, seed and grate cucumber. Place all ingredients in blender; blend for 10 to 15 seconds. Serve in frosted glasses. Garnish with thin lemon slices. Yield: 3-4 servings.

Mrs. John R. Erickson
Woods Hole, Massachusetts

DILLED SALMON MOUSSE

3 sprigs of parsley
2 ribs celery, cut in strips
1 carrot, quartered
1 lge. onion, quartered
1 bay leaf
1 2 1/4-lb. piece of fresh salmon
1 c. sour cream
1 c. mayonnaise
2/3 c. finely chopped onion
2 tsp. Worcestershire sauce
2 tsp. salt
1/8 tsp. pepper
1 c. chopped dill pickle, drained
Unflavored gelatin

Place parsley, celery, carrot, quartered onion, bay leaf, salmon and enough water to cover salmon in large saucepan. Poach fish for about 15 minutes or until easily flaked when tested with fork. Remove salmon; cool. Strain and reserve 1 cup stock; discard vegetables. Skin salmon; remove bones and flake. Blend sour cream and mayonnaise in large bowl. Add chopped onion, Worcestershire sauce, salt, pepper, pickle and salmon; mix well. Soften 1 envelope and 1 1/2 teaspoons gelatin in 1/3 cup cold water. Heat reserved fish stock until hot; stir into gelatin mixture gradually. Blend gelatin mixture into salmon mixture; pour into 8-cup ring mold. Smooth surface with spatula. Chill overnight. Unmold onto large plate; garnish with chicory and cherry tomatoes. Two 16-ounce cans and one 7 3/4-ounce can salmon may be used for fresh salmon. Drain, bone and flake salmon; add 1 cup chicken broth or bouillon for fish stock. Reduce salt to 1 teaspoon. Yield: 8-12 servings.

APRICOT SALAD

2 3-oz. packages orange gelatin
Juice of 1 lemon
Juice of 3 oranges
1 12-oz. can apricot pie filling

Dissolve gelatin in 2 cups boiling water. Mix lemon juice and orange juice; add enough cold water to make 2 cups liquid. Stir liquid into gelatin; chill until partially thickened. Stir in pie filling; pour into 13 x 9-inch pan. Chill until firm. Yield: 12 servings.

Diane Wertz
Xi Kappa, Council Bluffs, Iowa

COLESLAW SOUFFLE SALAD

1 pkg. lemon gelatin
1 c. hot water
1/2 c. mayonnaise
1/2 c. cold water
2 tbsp. vinegar
1/4 tsp. salt
1 1/2 c. finely shredded cabbage
1/2 c. sliced radishes
1/2 c. diced celery
3 tbsp. diced green pepper
1 tbsp. diced onion

Dissolve gelatin in hot water. Blend in mayonnaise, cold water, vinegar and salt. Chill until partially congealed; beat until fluffy. Add remaining ingredients. Pour into greased individual molds or 1-quart mold; chill until set. Unmold onto lettuce. Garnish with radish roses. Yield: 6-8 servings.

Pauline S. Grove
Xi Beta Xi X1628, Huntingdon, Pennsylvania

CRAB ASPIC

2 env. unflavored gelatin
1/2 c. cold water
1 can tomato soup
3 3-oz. packages cream cheese
1 c. chopped celery
1 sm. onion, chopped
1/4 c. chopped green pepper
1 c. Thousand Island dressing
1 7 1/2-oz. can crab meat

Soften gelatin in water. Heat soup in top of double boiler; add cream cheese and gelatin. Stir until cream cheese is melted; add celery, onion, green pepper, dressing and crab meat. Place in mold; refrigerate for 3 hours or until set before serving. Yield: 8 servings.

Mrs. A. B. Scott
Oakland, California

DELIGHTFUL CUCUMBER SALAD

1 6-oz. package lemon gelatin
1 c. boiling water
1 tbsp. vinegar
1 med. cucumber, chopped
1 med. onion, chopped
1 carton sm. curd cottage cheese
1 c. salad dressing
1/2 c. chopped walnuts

Dissolve gelatin in boiling water; stir in vinegar. Chill until partially congealed. Add remaining ingredients; mix well. Place in dish or mold; chill until firm. Yield: 6-8 servings.

Mrs. Jean Sayre
Preceptor Alpha Alpha XP758, Durand, Michigan

ENVY SALAD

1 lge. box lemon gelatin
1 1/3 c. hot water
1 lge. package cream cheese
1 sm. can crushed pineapple
2 tbsp. sugar
1 tsp. vanilla
1 10-oz. bottle lemon-lime carbonated beverage
1/2 c. chopped pecans
2 drops of green food coloring

Dissolve gelatin in hot water in electric mixer bowl; add cream cheese. Beat at medium speed until blended. Stir in remaining ingredients by hand. Pour into mold; chill until firm.

Rosalyn Guyton
Xi Gamma Iota X1193, Mt. Vernon, Illinois

NOODLES ALFREDO

1/4 c. salt
8 to 12 qt. boiling water
2 lb. medium egg noodles
1 lb. butter, softened
4 c. freshly grated Parmesan cheese
1 c. heavy cream

Add salt to rapidly boiling water. Add noodles gradually so water continues to boil. Cook, uncovered, stirring occasionally, until tender. Drain in colander. Place butter in hot 4-quart casserole; add noodles and toss gently. Add cheese; toss again. Pour in cream; toss. Sprinkle with freshly ground pepper if desired. Yield: 12-16 servings.

HONEY HAM PIQUANTE

1 10-lb. ham
6 whole cloves
1/2 c. cider vinegar
2 c. pickled peach juice
1 c. honey
1 c. brown sugar
1 c. diced oranges
1 c. diced pineapple
1 c. white grapes, cut and seeded

Wash ham; place, fat side up, in roaster. Insert cloves in ham. Pour vinegar and peach juice over ham; rub with honey, then brown sugar. Bake, uncovered, at 300 degrees for 1 hour. Cover; bake for 2 hours, basting frequently with pan liquid. Add fruits; bake for 1 hour longer or until ham is tender. Serve sliced ham with fruit sauce from roaster.

Mrs. Paul E. Ross
Valdosta, Georgia

STEAK AND STUFFING

1 sm. package chicken livers
1/2 c. butter
1 lge. onion, chopped
16 slices dried bread, cubed
1/4 tsp. sage
Salt and pepper to taste
2 tsp. dried celery flakes
1/2 tsp. dried parsley flakes
1 can onion soup
1 1/2 to 2 lb. round or sirloin steak
Flour
1 can cream of mushroom soup
2 c. cooking sherry or dry wine

Thaw chicken livers. Saute chicken livers in butter. Mix onion, bread, sage, salt, pepper, celery flakes, parsley flakes and onion soup. Add chicken livers, pan drippings and enough water to make moist dressing. Pound steak; cut into serving pieces. Place 2 tablespoons dressing on each piece of steak. Roll up; secure with toothpicks. Roll in small amount flour; brown quickly in 1/2 inch hot fat. Arrange rolls in baking dish; mound remaining dressing in center. Mix mushroom soup, wine, salt and pepper; pour over top. Cover. Bake for 45 minutes in 350-degree oven. Yield: 6 servings.

Mrs. Shirley Evers
Alpha Gamma, Story, Wyoming

ROAST BEEF AND YORKSHIRE PUDDING

1 5-lb. standing rib roast
Salt and pepper
1 c. sifted flour
2 eggs
1 c. milk

Rub roast with salt and pepper to taste; place on rack in baking pan. Bake at 450 degrees for 25 minutes. Reduce oven temperature to 300 degrees; bake for 16 to 18 minutes per pound longer. Sift flour with 1/2 teaspoon salt; stir in eggs and milk. Beat until smooth; refrigerate batter for at least 1 hour. Remove roast from oven. Increase oven temperature to 450 degrees. Spoon 3 tablespoons beef drippings into 12 x 8-inch pan; heat pan in oven until drippings are smoking. Pour in pudding batter. Bake for 15 minutes or until puffy and browned. Cut in squares and serve immediately. Yield: 6 servings.

Loyce Cartwright
Pi Gamma, Dickinson, Texas

TENDERLOIN WITH MUSHROOM STUFFING

1 3-lb. beef tenderloin
1/2 sm. onion, chopped
1 4-oz. can mushrooms
1/4 c. butter
1 1/2 c. soft bread crumbs
1/2 c. celery, diced
Salt and pepper to taste
4 slices bacon

Have tenderloin split and flattened at market. Brown onion and mushrooms lightly in butter; add bread crumbs, celery and enough hot water to moisten. Season; spread over half the beef. Bring second half over; fasten edges together. Season; place on rack in baking pan. Arrange bacon over top. Bake at 350 degrees for 1 hour. Yield: 6 servings.

Mrs. Kenneth H. McChesney
Kure Beach, North Carolina

STEAK DIANE

2 3/4-in. thick boneless sirloin steaks
6 tbsp. butter or margarine
2 tsp. dry mustard
1/2 tsp. salt
2 tbsp. sliced green onions
2 tbsp. olive oil
1 tsp. freshly ground pepper
1 tbsp. Worcestershire sauce
2 tbsp. lemon juice

Pound steaks well with mallet or edge of saucer. Melt 4 tablespoons butter in large skillet. Stir in mustard, salt and green onions; saute for 1 minute. Press 1 tablespoon olive oil into steaks; sprinkle with half the pepper. Cook, oiled side down, for about 2 minutes, spooning pan juices over steaks. Rub remaining oil and pepper into uncooked side of steaks; turn and cook for 2 minutes or to desired degree of doneness. Remove from skillet. Add remaining butter, Worcestershire sauce and lemon juice to skillet drippings; blend and heat. Pour over steaks just before serving. Garnish with chopped parsley. Yield: 4 servings.

Mrs. Mary C. Pittman
Xi Beta Delta, DeFuniak Springs, Florida

ELEGANT BEEF WELLINGTON

1 4 to 4 1/2-lb. beef filet
Salt to taste
Pepper to taste
Butter Pastry
Duxelles
1 egg
Sesame seeds

Place beef on rack in shallow baking pan. Sprinkle with salt and pepper. Bake at 425 degrees for 30 minutes. Let stand until cool. Trim off all fat. Roll pastry to rectangle large enough to wrap around beef, about 3 inches longer than roast and 12 to 13 inches wide. Press cool Duxelles into pastry, leaving an inch uncovered on all edges. Place beef on pastry. Moisten pastry edges; enclose beef, pressing edges firmly together. Trim off excess pastry from ends so single layer covers ends of roast. Place roll, seam side

down, on shallow baking pan. Cut decorations from pastry trimmings; place on top. Brush pastry with egg beaten with 1 tablespoon water. Sprinkle with sesame seeds. Bake at 400 degrees for 30 to 35 minutes until browned. Let stand for 15 to 20 minutes before slicing.

Butter Pastry

3 3/4 c. sifted flour
1 tsp. salt
1 c. cold butter
2 tbsp. shortening
3/4 c. (about) ice water

Combine flour and salt. Cut in butter and shortening until particles are fine. Add water, 1 tablespoon at a time, to make stiff dough. Shape dough into square. Cover and chill.

Duxelles

1 lb. mushrooms, finely chopped
1/4 c. chopped green onion
1/4 c. butter
1/2 tsp. salt
1/2 tsp. marjoram
2 tsp. flour
Dash of pepper
1/4 c. beef broth
2 tbsp. chopped parsley
1/2 c. finely chopped cooked ham

Saute mushrooms and onion in butter until liquid evaporates. Stir in salt, marjoram, flour, pepper and broth. Cook, stirring constantly, until mixture comes to a boil and thickens. Remove from heat; stir in parsley and ham. Cool.

Tomatoes With Horseradish Cream

8 sm. tomatoes
1/2 c. whipping cream
1 tbsp. horseradish
1/2 tsp. Dijon mustard
Dash of salt

Cut tops from tomatoes; hollow out slightly, scooping out seeds. Drain upside down. Whip cream until stiff; fold in horseradish, mustard and salt. Fill tomatoes with cream just before serving. Serve around Elegant Beef Wellington. Yield: 8 servings.

CHRISTMAS DAY STANDING RIB ROAST OF BEEF

1 standing 4-rib beef roast
Salt
Freshly ground pepper
1 crumbled bay leaf
4 to 8 med. potatoes
Cooking oil or shortening

Have butcher remove chine from roast and cut ribs short. Sprinkle with salt, pepper and bay leaf. Insert meat thermometer so tip is in center of roast. Bake at 325 degrees until meat thermometer reads 120 degrees for rare, 140 degrees for medium rare or 150 degrees for well done. Remove from oven; cover. Let set for 20 minutes before carving. Peel potatoes; cut with spiral French cutter. Fill deep fat fryer about one third full with oil; heat to 360 degrees on thermometer. Place potatoes in single layer in fryer basket. Lower into hot fat; cook until potatoes are tender but not brown. Remove from oil; drain well on paper towels. Keep at room temperature until almost serving time. Reheat oil to 375 degrees. Fry potatoes until golden brown. Drain; sprinkle with salt. Place on tray around roast; garnish with watercress.

VEAL CUTLETS A LA BOLOGNAISE

2 to 2 1/2 lb. veal, sliced
Lemon juice
Salt and pepper to taste
Grated Parmesan cheese
2 eggs, beaten
Bread crumbs
1/2 stick butter
1/2 can beef or chicken broth

Pound veal thin. Mix juice of 2 lemons, salt, pepper and small amount of cheese. Spread mixture over veal; let stand for 1 to 2 hours. Dip veal in eggs; coat with crumbs. Let stand for 1 to 2 hours. Melt butter in ovenproof skillet. Brown veal lightly on one side. Turn veal; top with cheese. Bake at 300 degrees until tender. Heat broth; stir into pan juices just before serving. Sprinkle veal with lemon juice. Yield: 4 servings.

Mrs. John J. Ross
Beta Sigma Phi Intl., Kansas City, Missouri

MARINATED PORK ROAST

1 6 to 8-lb. pork loin
4 cloves of garlic, slivered
1 tsp. thyme
1/2 tsp. salt
1/2 tsp. parsley flakes
1/4 tsp. powdered ginger
1/4 c. olive oil
1/2 bottle dry white wine
Paprika
Coarsely ground pepper

Make small slits in surface of pork; insert garlic in slits. Rub thyme, salt, parsley flakes and ginger over surface of pork; rub gently with oil, being careful not to rub off seasonings. Place pork in shallow roasting pan; pour wine over pork. Cover pan with foil.

Marinate for 12 hours, turning several times. Remove from marinade; sprinkle with paprika and pepper. Return pork to marinade, fat side up. Bake at 325 degrees for 4 hours to 4 hours and 30 minutes, basting frequently with marinade. Remove pork from pan; let stand for 15 minutes in warm place before slicing. Strain drippings into saucepan; skim off as much fat as possible. Add 3/4 cup water to drippings; heat and use as sauce.

Mrs. J. G. Gemmill
Huntington, Beach, California

BEEF AU JUS FOR CHRISTMAS

1 6 to 8-lb. standing rib of beef

Let beef stand at room temperature for 1 hour before roasting. Place, fat side up, on rack in shallow pan. Insert meat thermometer so tip will be in center. Bake at 325 degrees for 18 to 20 minutes per pound or to 130 degrees on thermometer for rare. Let roast stand for 20 minutes in warm place before carving. Cut into thin slices across grain.

VEAL WITH LEMON SAUCE

2 lb. thin veal cutlets
2 or 3 eggs, beaten
Cooking oil
2 tbsp. butter
2 c. water
Onion salt to taste
Garlic salt to taste
Juice of 1 lemon
1 tbsp. minced parsley

Season and flour veal; dip into eggs. Brown veal lightly in oil; arrange in baking dish. Melt butter in saucepan; add 1 tablespoon oil. Blend 1 tablespoon flour and small amount of water to a paste; add remaining water. Stir into butter mixture in saucepan. Simmer, stirring, until smooth. Add salt, pepper, onion salt, garlic salt and lemon juice; simmer for about 45 minutes longer. Spoon small amount of sauce over veal. Bake at 350 degrees for 45 minutes. Pour in remaining sauce; sprinkle with parsley. Bake for 5 minutes longer. Yield: 8 servings.

Mrs. Raymond J. Fontana
Longmeadow, Massachusetts

CHICKEN IN WINE SAUCE

Flour
Salt to taste
2 boiling hens, cut in 10 pieces
Butter or margarine
Paprika
6 med. onions, sliced
2 c. water
1 can consomme or chicken stock
1/2 to 3/4 c. cream
1/2 c. white wine or sherry
1/2 lb. mushrooms, chopped
1 green pepper, cut in rings

Season flour with salt; roll chicken in flour, reserving any remaining flour. Brown chicken well on all sides in butter in large skillet. Place chicken in single layer in baking pan; sprinkle generously with paprika. Spread onion over chicken. Melt small amount of butter in skillet drippings; blend in about 3 tablespoons reserved flour. Add water; cook, stirring, until thickened. Stir in consomme; heat through. Reduce heat; stir in cream slowly. Add wine; pour mixture over chicken. Bake for 3 hours at 325 degrees. Saute mushrooms and green pepper lightly in butter. Remove chicken to serving platter; pour pan liquid over chicken. Garnish with mushrooms and green pepper.

Greta Jackson
Beta Xi, Haney, British Columbia, Canada

CHICKEN HARPIN

1 chicken
1 9-oz. can pitted ripe olives
1 6-oz. can mushroom bits
1/4 c. butter
6 tbsp. flour
1 1/2 tsp. salt
1/4 tsp. pepper
Pinch of mace or curry powder
1 c. heavy cream
5 thin slices buttered toast
Paprika

Place chicken in large kettle; add water to cover. Bring to a boil; reduce heat and cover kettle. Simmer chicken for 30 minutes. Drain chicken, reserving 3 cups broth. Slice chicken meat from bones; arrange in 12 x 8-inch baking dish. Slice olives; scatter olives and mushrooms over chicken. Melt butter in skillet; blend in flour, salt, pepper and mace. Stir in reserved broth and cream, a small amount at a time. Cook, stirring, until thickened; pour sauce over chicken. Bake at 325 degrees for 35 minutes. Cut toast into triangles; arrange over chicken. Sprinkle with paprika and bake for 10 minutes longer. Yield: 6-8 servings.

Mary Lawrence
Zeta Psi, Champaign, Illinois

ROAST TURKEY WITH FRUIT DRESSING

4 c. toasted bread cubes
2 c. diced celery
3 tbsp. grated grapefruit peel
1/2 c. raisins
1/2 c. crushed pineapple
1/4 c. chopped nuts
1/3 c. melted butter
Salt
Hot water or broth
1 8 to 10-lb. hen turkey
1 or 2 cloves of garlic
1 med. grapefruit, halved

Combine bread cubes, celery, grapefruit peel, raisins, pineapple, nuts, butter and 1 teaspoon salt. Toss mixture lightly with enough water to moisten. Rub turkey inside and out with garlic and salt to taste. Fill turkey with stuffing mixture; do not pack stuffing. Close and secure cavity opening; tie legs to body. Grease turkey well with fat; arrange, breast down, on rack in baking pan. Cover loosely with aluminum foil. Bake at 325 degrees for 3 hours and 30 minutes. Turn turkey; squeeze half the grapefruit over turkey. Bake, uncovered, for about 20 minutes. Cut tie holding legs to body; squeeze remaining grapefruit over turkey. Increase oven temperature to 375 degrees; bake, uncovered, until turkey is browned. Yield: 10-12 servings.

Mrs. Anne Stafford
Xi Lambda Exemplar, Columbus, Mississippi

TURKEY IN A BAG

1 12-lb. turkey
1 tsp. salt
1 stick butter, melted
1 24-oz. loaf bread, crumbled
Chopped onion to taste
Sage to taste
Pepper to taste
1 c. chopped celery tops
1 egg, beaten

Preheat oven to 325 degrees. Rub inside of turkey with salt; spread outside with butter. Combine bread, onion, sage, pepper and celery tops; stir in egg. Add enough hot water to moisten. Stuff turkey lightly, spreading any remaining stuffing in casserole. Close and secure cavity opening; tie legs to body. Place turkey in large brown paper bag, making sure seam of bag is at top. Place on broiler pan. Bake for 3 hours without opening bag. Remove turkey from bag. Pour small amount of drippings over stuffing in casserole. Bake stuffing for 30 to 35 minutes until browned. Use remaining drippings to make gravy. Yield: 15 servings.

Janie L. Crosswhite
Marshall, Missouri

ROAST TURKEY WITH TROPICAL RICE STUFFING

1 13 1/2-oz. can pineapple tidbits
1 10 1/2-oz. can chicken consomme
1 c. rice
1 5-oz. can water chestnuts
1/4 c. butter
1/2 c. chopped green onion
1/2 c. thinly sliced celery
1 tbsp. soy sauce
1 10-lb. turkey

Drain syrup from pineapple; combine syrup with consomme. Add enough water to make 2 cups liquid. Stir in rice; heat to boiling. Cover; cook for 15 minutes or until liquid is absorbed and rice is tender. Drain water chestnuts; slice. Lightly mix in pineapple, water chestnuts and remaining ingredients. Stuff in turkey. Bake as desired.

ROAST TURKEY IN BLANKET

1 recipe stuffing
1 turkey or capon
4 c. (or more) all-purpose flour
1 1/4 c. water

Place stuffing in cavity of turkey, grease turkey with small amount of fat. Place on rack in baking pan. Bake at 425 degrees until brown on all sides. Remove from oven. Mix flour and water to make stiff dough. Roll out on floured board 1/2 inch thick. Cover turkey with dough, tucking straight down. Do not allow dough to extend below rack into drippings. Press dough gently to seal. Reduce oven temperature to 325 degrees; bake until turkey is tender. Lift blanket from turkey. Test for doneness by pressing flesh of leg with fingers; turkey should be soft and pliable.

Mrs. Hazel K. Bieber
Poland, Ohio

BAKED QUAIL

Quail
Salt
1 pkg. dry onion soup mix
1 can cream of mushroom soup
1 can cream of chicken soup
1 can cream of celery soup

Soak quail overnight in salted water. Place quail, breasts up, on large sheet of heavy-duty aluminum foil in roasting pan. Sprinkle onion soup mix over quail. Mix mushroom soup, chicken soup and celery soup; pour over quail. Fold foil up and over quail, sealing edges well. Bake at 350 degrees until quail are tender. Serve with wild rice if desired.

Mrs. Walter W. Ross, III
Beta Sigma Phi Intl., Kansas City, Missouri

QUAIL IN WINE

1/2 c. butter or bacon drippings
2 sm. onions, minced
1 tsp. whole cloves
1 tsp. peppercorns
2 cloves of garlic, minced
1/2 bay leaf
6 quail, cleaned and trussed
2 c. white wine
1/2 tsp. salt
1/2 tsp. pepper
Few grains of cayenne pepper
Chopped chives to taste
2 c. cream

Melt butter in large skillet; add onions, cloves, peppercorns, garlic and bay leaf. Cook, stirring, for several minutes. Brown quail in onion mixture, turning to brown all sides. Add wine, salt, pepper, cayenne pepper and chives; simmer for 30 minutes or until quail are tender. Remove quail to hot serving dish. Strain sauce into saucepan; blend in cream. Heat just to boiling point. Serve sauce over quail or in gravy boat. Yield: 6 servings.

Mrs. John R. McClure
Beta Lambda, San Antonio, Texas

GOOSE STUFFED WITH SAUERKRAUT

1 goose
1 lge. can sauerkraut
1 potato, grated
Salt and pepper to taste

Arrange goose on rack in baking pan. Bake at 400 degrees for 20 minutes. Combine sauerkraut and potato in saucepan; bring to a boil. Reduce heat and simmer for 20 minutes. Sprinkle cavity of goose with salt and pepper; stuff with sauerkraut mixture. Reduce oven temperature to 300 degrees. Bake goose until done.

Mrs. Sadie Mundt
Owen, Wisconsin

HOLIDAY BOAR'S HEAD

1 10 to 12-lb. ham, with rind
1 c. brown sugar
1 tsp. dry mustard
3 tsp. honey
1 can sliced pineapple
1 red apple
2 stuffed olives
Orange peel
Cranberries

Slit ham at shank end, forming boar's snout; insert small measuring cup in slit to hold slit open. Cut slice from bottom of ham to level ham during baking. Arrange ham on rack in baking pan. Bake at 325 degrees for 3 hours to 3 hours and 40 minutes. Remove ham rind, reserving 2 pieces rind. Mix brown sugar, mustard and honey for glaze; spread glaze over ham. Drain pineapple, reserving syrup. Increase oven temperature to 350 degrees; bake ham for 45 minutes longer, basting occasionally with reserved pineapple syrup. Remove measuring cup from slit in ham; insert apple in slit. Impale olives on toothpicks; insert in ham, forming boar's eyes. Fasten reserved rind to ham to simulate ears and form curly tail from orange peel. String cranberries and hang around boar's neck. Yield: 10 servings.

Deanna Johnson
China Lake City Council, China Lake, California

SHRIMP ELEGANTE

2 tbsp. minced onion
2 tbsp. butter
1 lb. cleaned shrimp
1/4 lb. mushrooms, sliced
1 tsp. salt
1/8 tsp. pepper
3 tbsp. chili sauce
1 2/3 c. water
1 1/3 c. instant rice
1 c. sour cream
1 tbsp. flour
1 tbsp. chopped chives or parsley

Saute onion in butter until golden. Add shrimp and mushrooms; cook, stirring, until shrimp are pink. Combine salt, pepper, chili sauce and water; add to shrimp mixture. Bring to a boil; stir in rice. Reduce heat and cover; simmer for 5 minutes. Blend sour cream and flour together; stir into rice mixture. Heat gently; sprinkle with chives. Yield: 4 servings.

Mrs. Garvis White
Pi Zeta, Vidor, Texas

SHRIMP STROGANOFF

1/4 c. butter
1 tbsp. flour
1 lb. cleaned cooked shrimp
2/3 c. mushrooms
1 tbsp. onion flakes
1 tbsp. Worcestershire sauce
1 tsp. salt
Dash of pepper
1 c. sour cream
3 tbsp. catsup

Melt butter in saucepan; blend in flour. Add shrimp, mushrooms, onion flakes, Worcestershire sauce, salt and pepper. Heat gently, stirring frequently, until shrimp and mushrooms are coated with butter and mixture is heated through. Add sour cream and catsup; heat gently, but do not boil. Serve in party shells. Yield: 6 servings.

Mrs. T. Lane Ormand
Alpha Xi, Monroe, North Carolina

BRUSSELS SPROUTS WITH CHESTNUTS

2 tbsp. butter
2 tsp. flour
3/4 c. warm chicken broth
Salt
Pinch of white pepper
1/4 tsp. basil
3 lb. Brussels sprouts
1 1/2 c. sliced cooked chestnuts

Melt butter in top of double boiler; blend in flour. Cook, stirring, until bubbly. Add chicken broth, small amount at a time, stirring until smooth. Season with 1/4 teaspoon salt, pepper and basil; keep warm over hot water. Cook Brussels sprouts in boiling salted water until just tender; drain well. Arrange Brussels sprouts in serving dish. Stir chestnuts into sauce; pour sauce over Brussels sprouts. Yield: 8 servings.

Meroe E. Stanley
Northville, Michigan

CREAMED ONIONS WITH PECANS AND CHEESE

20 sm. onions
1/2 c. water
1 1/2 tsp. salt
1/4 c. butter or margarine
1/4 c. flour
1 1/2 c. milk
1 c. shredded cheese
1/2 c. chopped pecans

Place onions, water and 1 teaspoon salt in 1 1/2-quart saucepan. Cover and bring to a boil. Reduce heat; simmer for 15 minutes or until onions are tender. Drain. Melt butter in saucepan. Blend in flour; stir in milk and remaining salt. Cook over medium heat, stirring constantly, until thick. Add cheese; stir until melted. Add onions and heat through. Place in serving dish; sprinkle with pecans. Yield: 4-6 servings.

Mrs. Juanita Patton
Inola, Oklahoma

SWEET POTATO CUPS

2 lb. sweet potatoes
2 tbsp. butter or margarine
2 tsp. grated orange peel
1/2 tsp. salt
Orange juice or milk
1/2 c. dark or golden raisins
6 lge. oranges
Marshmallows

Cook sweet potatoes in small amount of boiling salted water for about 20 minutes or until tender. Cool slightly; peel and mash. Add butter, orange peel and salt. Beat until fluffy, adding small amount orange juice if potatoes seem dry. Stir in raisins. Cut slice off top oranges. Cut and scoop out pulp with grapefruit knife. Heap potato mixture into orange shells. Top with marshmallows. Bake at 350 degrees for 20 minutes or until thoroughly heated. Yield: 6 servings.

GALA BEETS

2 1/2 c. diced or sliced beets
2 tbsp. butter
1 c. thinly sliced onions
1/4 c. chopped celery
Salt and pepper to taste
1 tbsp. chopped parsley

Drain beets, reserving 2 tablespoons liquid. Melt butter in saucepan; add beets, reserved beet liquid, onions and celery. Cover and simmer for 12 minutes or until onions are tender. Season with salt and pepper. Sprinkle with parsley before serving. Yield: 4 servings.

Mrs. Evelyn Johnson
Bottineau, North Dakota

ASPARAGUS BEARNAISE

2 pkg. frozen asparagus
1 1/2 tsp. monosodium glutamate
3 egg yolks
2 tbsp. lemon juice
1/4 tsp. minced onion
1/4 tsp. minced parsley
1/2 tsp. dried tarragon
Dash of cayenne pepper
1/2 c. butter

Prepare asparagus according to package directions; drain. Season with monosodium glutamate. Blend egg yolks, lemon juice, onion, parsley, tarragon and cayenne pepper together. Melt butter; blend into egg mixture, stirring or beating constantly. Serve immediately over hot asparagus. Yield: 8 servings.

Mrs. Ruth B. Marsh
Millersville, Pennsylvania

SPINACH DELIGHT

1 pkg. frozen spinach
1 tbsp. butter
1 tbsp. flour
1/2 c. sour cream
1/2 tsp. minced onion
1/4 tsp. monosodium glutamate
1/2 tsp. salt
1/4 tsp. pepper

Cook spinach until tender; drain well. Melt butter in saucepan; blend in flour. Add sour cream; cook, stirring constantly, until thickened. Add spinach, onion and seasonings. Heat through over low heat. Yield: 4 servings.

Mrs. Muriel F. Richards
Battle Creek, Nebraska

SOUR CREAM SCALLOPED TOMATOES

1 No. 2 1/2 can tomatoes, drained
1 c. chopped onions
1/2 c. cheese cracker crumbs
1 1/2 tsp. sugar
1/2 tsp. monosodium glutamate
1/2 tsp. salt
3/4 c. sour cream
3 slices bread, cubed and toasted
1 tbsp. melted margarine

Break tomatoes into pieces with spoon. Layer tomatoes, 1/2 cup onions, cracker crumbs, sugar, monosodium glutamate and salt in greased 1 1/2-quart casserole. Cover with remaining onions; top with sour cream. Sprinkle bread cubes over sour cream; brush with margarine. Bake at 325 degrees for 20 minutes or until heated through. Yield: 6 servings.

Judith G. Collins
Albany, New York

CHESAPEAKE CRAB IMPERIAL

Butter
2 tbsp. chopped onion
1 tbsp. chopped green pepper
2 tbsp. flour
1/2 tsp. salt
1/2 tsp. celery salt
Dash of pepper
1 c. milk
2 tbsp. sherry
Dash of pepper sauce
1 egg, slightly beaten
1 lb. crab meat
1 tbsp. minced parsley
1 chopped pimento
1/4 tsp. grated orange rind
1 c. bread cubes
Paprika

Melt 1/4 cup butter in saucepan; add onion and green pepper. Blend in flour, salt, celery salt and pepper. Add milk gradually; cook until thickened, stirring constantly. Remove from heat; add sherry and pepper sauce. Blend small amount of cream sauce into egg; return to saucepan, blending well. Fold in crab meat, parsley, pimento and orange rind. Toss bread cubes in 1 tablespoon melted butter. Place on top of casserole; sprinkle with paprika. Bake in 375-degree oven for 15 to 20 minutes. Yield: 6 servings.

Lenore Eckstrom
Psi Delta, Los Gatos, California

BAKED HOLIDAY RICE

1 c. rice
1 med. onion, chopped
1/2 stick margarine
2 cans consomme
1 sm. can sliced mushrooms, undrained

Brown rice and onion lightly in margarine. Place in 2-quart casserole. Add consomme and mushrooms; mix well. Bake, uncovered, at 350 degrees for 1 hour. Yield: 8 servings.

Marinelle Click
Xi Phi X-1601, Concord, North Carolina

MUSHROOM-RICE CASSEROLE

1 med. onion, finely chopped
1/2 green pepper, finely chopped
1/2 c. finely chopped celery
1 8-oz. can chopped mushrooms
1/2 c. butter
3 c. instant rice
2 10-oz. cans beef consomme
Salt and pepper to taste
Paprika

Cook onion, green pepper, celery and mushrooms in butter slowly for 15 minutes. Add rice, consomme, 1 consomme can water, salt and pepper; mix thoroughly. Pour into buttered 2-quart casserole. Let stand overnight; stir occasionally. Add water if rice absorbs all moisture. Bake for 1 hour to 1 hour and 30 minutes at 350 degrees. Sprinkle with paprika. Yield: 8-10 servings.

Elaine Elliot
Xi Beta X0791, Halifax, Nova Scotia, Canada

MACARONI FIESTA

1 3/4 c. macaroni
1/2 c. minced green pepper
3 tbsp. butter
2 tbsp. flour
2 c. milk
1 tsp. salt
1/4 tsp. pepper
1/2 tsp. dry mustard
2 c. grated cheese
1/2 c. sliced stuffed olives
2 c. corn flakes

Cook macaroni until tender; drain. Cook green pepper in 2 tablespoons butter until soft; stir in flour. Add milk gradually; cook, stirring, until thickened. Add seasonings and 1 cup cheese. Fold in olives; add macaroni. Pour into baking dish. Melt remaining butter; toss corn flakes with butter. Sprinkle over macaroni; top with remaining cheese. Bake at 350 to 375 degrees for 20 minutes or until heated through. Yield: 12 servings.

Clella Rogers Minor
Xi Upsilon X 1157, Norton, Virginia

VERMICELLI-CHEESE CASSEROLE

1 c. (scant) broken vermicelli
Salt
2 eggs
1/8 tsp. red pepper
1/4 tsp. dry mustard
Pinch of oregano
1 c. evaporated milk
5 oz. sharp cheese, grated

Cook vermicelli in boiling salted water for about 5 minutes; rinse in cold water. Drain. Beat eggs with 1/4 teaspoon salt and remaining seasonings; pour into casserole. Stir in milk and 1 cup water. Add vermicelli and cheese, mixing with fork. Bake at 350 degrees for 45 minutes. Yield: 5 servings.

Patty Cubbedge
Zeta No. 599, Atlanta, Georgia

MOTHER'S ICEBOX ROLLS

2 pkg. yeast
1/2 c. lukewarm water
2 eggs
2/3 c. sugar
2 tsp. salt
3/4 c. shortening
1 c. mashed potatoes
1 c. scalded milk, cooled
6 c. sifted flour

Dissolve yeast in lukewarm water. Place eggs, sugar, salt and shortening in large electric mixer bowl; beat well. Add potatoes, milk and yeast mixture; beat until blended. Work in flour, by hand, one cup at a time, to make stiff dough. Place dough in greased bowl; turn dough to grease well. Cover; let rise for 2 hours and 30 minutes or until light and doubled in bulk. Work dough down; shape into rolls with floured hands. Place in greased pan; cover and let rise again until doubled in bulk. Bake for 15 minutes in preheated 400-degree oven. Any unused rolls may be wrapped and frozen. Reheat to serve.

Judy Yates
Delta Xi No. 6292, Gastonia, North Carolina

CHRISTMAS TOWERS

2 pkg. yeast
1 c. warm water
6 c. sifted all-purpose flour
1/2 c. butter, softened
1 c. crunchy peanut butter
3/4 c. sugar
1 tsp. salt
5 eggs
1 4-oz. jar cut citron
1 c. light raisins
1/3 c. chopped glace cherries

Sprinkle yeast over water in large bowl of electric mixer; stir to dissolve. Add 3 cups flour, butter, peanut butter, sugar, salt, 4 eggs and 1 egg yolk. Blend together on low speed; beat on medium speed for 2 minutes. Add remaining flour and fruits; beat in with wooden spoon. Turn out on floured board; knead until smooth. Place in lightly greased bowl; cover with towel. Let rise in warm place, free from draft, for about 2 hours or until doubled in bulk. Punch down; knead until smooth. Place in 3 greased and floured 1-pound coffee cans. Let rise for 30 to 45 minutes or until doubled in bulk. Score top of loaf. Bake in 350-degree oven for 1 hour to 1 hour and 30 minutes or until bread tests done, brushing with egg white and sprinkling with additional sugar about 45 minutes before end of baking time.

CHRISTMAS STOLLEN

1 pkg. dry yeast
1/2 c. sugar
1/2 tsp. salt
4 eggs
Margarine
3 1/2 c. flour
1/2 c. blanched almonds
1/4 c. chopped citron
1/4 c. candied cherries
1/4 c. raisins
1 tbsp. grated lemon peel
Confectioners' sugar frosting

Measure 3/4 cup warm water into large warm mixing bowl. Sprinkle in yeast; stir until dissolved. Add sugar, salt, 3 eggs, 1 egg yolk, 1/2 cup softened margarine and half the flour. Beat for 10 minutes; scrape bottom and sides of bowl frequently. Blend in remaining flour, almonds, fruits and lemon peel. Cover; let rise in warm place for 1 hour and 30 minutes or until doubled in bulk. Beat batter 25 strokes. Cover tightly; refrigerate overnight. Turn dough onto well-floured board; divide in half. Press each half into 10 x 7-inch oval pan; spread with 2 tablespoons softened margarine. Fold over twice lengthwise; press edges firmly. Place on greased baking sheets. Beat egg white lightly with 1 tablespoon water; brush onto dough. Let rise in warm place for 1 hour or until doubled in bulk. Bake at 375 degrees for 20 minutes or until done. Frost with confectioners' sugar frosting. Decorate with whole almonds, citron and candied cherries if desired.

Diana Adams
Phi Beta Xi P-2375, Kansas City, Missouri

ANGEL BISCUITS

5 c. flour
1 tsp. soda
3 tsp. baking powder
1 tsp. salt
3 tbsp. sugar
1 c. shortening or lard
1 pkg. dry yeast
2 tbsp. warm water
2 c. buttermilk
Melted butter

Mix flour, soda, baking powder, salt and sugar; cut in shortening. Dissolve yeast in warm water; stir into buttermilk. Add to dry ingredients; mix lightly. Turn dough onto floured surface; shape into smooth ball with hands. Roll out to thin rectangle; fold in half and roll again lightly. Cut with biscuit cutter; place biscuits in greased pan. Brush tops with melted butter; let rise until light. Bake in preheated 450 degree oven for 12 to 15 minutes. Dough will keep for several days in refrigerator.

Billie Roberts
Iota Upsilon No. 6712, Fort Walton Beach, Florida

GOLDEN CAKE BREAD

1 pkg. yeast
1/4 c. warm water
1 c. scalded milk
1/2 c. butter or margarine
1/2 c. sugar
2 eggs, lightly beaten
2 tsp. vanilla
1 tsp. salt
4 to 4 1/2 c. sifted all-purpose flour

Dissolve yeast in water. Combine hot milk, butter and sugar in large mixing bowl; cool to lukewarm. Stir in eggs, reserving 1 tablespoon egg. Add vanilla, salt and yeast. Add flour gradually, beating well after each addition. Cover; let rise in warm place for 1 hour or until light and doubled in bulk. Beat down; let rise again for 45 minutes or until doubled in bulk. Turn into 2 well-greased 9 x 5 x 3-inch pans; let rise in warm place for 45 minutes or until light. Brush with reserved egg. Bake in 350-degree oven for 25 to 30 minutes. Yield: 2 loaves.

Cathy McKellar
Gamma Nu No. 6612, Jasper, Alabama

CANDIED FRUIT BREAD

1 3/4 c. sifted flour
4 tsp. baking powder
1/2 tsp. salt
1/4 tsp. cinnamon
3/4 c. sugar
1/4 c. chopped citron
1/4 c. seedless raisins
2 tbsp. chopped candied cherries
2 tbsp. candied lemon peel
1/4 c. chopped blanched almonds
1/4 c. chopped pecans
2 eggs, beaten
1 c. milk
3 tbsp. melted butter

Sift flour with baking powder, salt and cinnamon. Add sugar, fruits, lemon peel and nuts; mix well. Combine eggs, milk and butter; add to dry ingredients. Stir just enough to blend. Turn into greased 8 x 5 x 3-inch pan. Let stand for 20 minutes. Bake at 375 degrees for 1 hour in center of oven. Turn out onto wire rack; cool for several hours before slicing.

Rose A. Kristian
Sigma, No. 3146
Prince George, British Columbia, Canada

CRANBERRY BREAD

Grated rind of 1 lemon
Grated rind of 1 orange
3 tbsp. lemon juice
2 tbsp. shortening, melted
Orange juice
2 c. flour
1 1/2 tsp. baking powder
1/2 tsp. salt
1 1/4 c. sugar
1/2 tsp. soda
1 tsp. nutmeg

1 egg, beaten
1 tsp. vanilla
1/2 tsp. almond extract
1 c. chopped nuts
1 c. halved cranberries

Mix lemon rind, orange rind, lemon juice and shortening; add enough orange juice to equal 3/4 cup liquid. Sift flour, baking powder, salt, sugar, soda and nutmeg together. Add orange juice liquid, egg, vanilla and almond extract; stir only to moisten dry ingredients. Fold in nuts and cranberries; spoon batter into loaf pan lined with greased paper. Bake in 350-degree oven for 1 hour to 1 hour and 10 minutes. Cool loaf and cut in thin slices.

Evelyn Strickland
Xi Delta Lambda X2677, Jacksonville, Florida

CHRISTMAS PUDDING

2 3/4 c. day-old bread crumbs
1 c. diced figs
1 1/2 c. seedless raisins
3/4 c. mixed candied fruit
1/2 c. dried currants
1/2 c. toasted filberts, chopped
2 c. ground suet
1 1/2 tsp. salt
3/4 tsp. cinnamon
1/2 tsp. mace
1/4 tsp. cloves
1 c. scalded milk
1/2 c. (packed) dark brown sugar
4 eggs
2 tsp. brandy flavoring
2 tbsp. orange juice
Hard Sauce or Lemon Sauce

Coat greased 2-quart mold with 3 to 4 tablespoons bread crumbs. Combine fruits, filberts and suet in large bowl. Mix remaining bread crumbs, salt, spices, milk and brown sugar together; stir until sugar dissolves. Add eggs, brandy flavoring and orange juice; beat until well blended. Stir into fruit mixture. Pour into prepared mold; cover tightly. Place mold on rack in bottom of large pot or roaster; fill with enough boiling water to cover 2/3 of the mold. Cover and steam pudding for 5 hours, adding water as needed. Pour off any excess fat from top of steamed pudding. Cool for about 1 hour before unmolding. Serve warm with Lemon or Hard Sauce. Pudding may be made ahead; reheated in mold before serving.

Hard Sauce

1/2 c. butter
1/2 tsp. vanilla
1 c. confectioners' sugar

Beat butter and vanilla together until smooth. Add confectioners' sugar gradually; beat until fluffy. Chill.

Lemon Sauce

1 tbsp. cornstarch
1/2 c. sugar
1/4 tsp. salt
1 tsp. grated lemon peel
1/4 c. lemon juice
2 tbsp. butter

Mix cornstarch, sugar and salt together in saucepan. Stir in 1 cup water. Bring to a boil; cook for 1 minute, stirring constantly. Add lemon peel, lemon juice and butter; stir until butter melts. Serve hot.

CANDLELIGHT HOLIDAY RAISIN CAKE

1 1/4 c. shortening
1 1/4 c. honey
6 eggs, well beaten
2 1/2 c. sifted flour
1 tsp. salt
1 tsp. baking powder
1 tsp. cinnamon
1/2 tsp. nutmeg
1/2 tsp. ginger
2 c. dark seedless raisins
2 c. golden seedless raisins
1 c. halved candied cherries
2 c. candied pineapple pieces
2 c. mixed diced candied fruits and peels
2 c. pecans

Beat shortening and honey together until creamy and well blended. Blend in eggs. Sift flour with salt, baking powder and spices into batter, stirring until smooth. Blend in fruits and pecans. Turn into greased 10-inch tube pan lined with 2 thicknesses greased heavy brown paper. Bake at 250 degrees for 4 hours to 4 hours and 30 minutes with shallow pan of water in bottom of oven.

Photograph for this recipe on cover.

CHARLOTTE RUSSE

12 ladyfingers
2 env. unflavored gelatin
1 c. sugar
1/4 tsp. salt
4 eggs, separated
2 1/2 c. milk
2 tsp. brandy flavoring
1/3 c. chopped cherries, (opt.)
1/4 c. chopped nuts, (opt.)
1 c. heavy cream, whipped

Split ladyfingers; cut off one end to stand upright. Place around sides of 8-inch springform pan. Mix gelatin, 1/2 cup sugar and salt together in 2-quart saucepan. Beat egg yolks and milk together; add to gelatin mixture. Place over low heat; heat, stirring constantly, for about 6 minutes or until gelatin is dissolved. Remove from heat; add brandy flavoring. Chill until mixture mounds slightly when dropped from spoon. Beat egg whites until stiff but not dry. Add remaining sugar gradually; beat until very stiff. Fold in gelatin mixture. Fold in cherries, nuts and whipped cream. Turn into prepared pan; chill until firm. Release spring unmold; remove sides of mold carefully. Garnish with additional whipped cream, shaved chocolate, angelica or citron, chopped nuts and pieces of maraschino cherries. Yield: 12 servings.

CHRISTMAS FRUIT PUDDING CAKE

2 c. sifted flour
1 1/2 c. sugar
2 tsp. soda
1/4 tsp. salt
2 eggs, beaten
1 17-oz. can fruit cocktail, undrained

Sift flour, sugar, soda and salt together; add eggs and fruit cocktail. Mix well; pour into greased and floured 8 or 9-inch tube pan. Bake at 300 degrees for 1 hour or until toothpick inserted in center comes out clean. Cool for 10 to 15 minutes. Remove from pan.

Icing

1/2 c. butter
1 c. powdered sugar
1/2 c. evaporated milk
1 egg yolk
1 tbsp. vanilla
1 c. shredded coconut
1/2 c. chopped nuts

Place butter, powdered sugar, milk and egg yolk in heavy saucepan; bring to a boil. Cook for 2 minutes, stirring constantly. Add vanilla, coconut and nuts, mixing well. Cool slightly; spoon onto warm cake. Cherries and mint gumdrops may be arranged on top for festive Christmas decoration. Yield: 10-12 servings.

Charlene McPherridge
Gamma Alpha Iota No. 6459, Upland, California

BEER CAKE

2 c. sifted flour
1/4 tsp. soda
1 tsp. cream of tartar
1/4 tsp. salt
1/4 tsp. allspice
1/4 tsp. cloves
1/4 tsp. mace
1/4 tsp. nutmeg
1 tsp. cinnamon
2/3 c. currants
2/3 c. raisins
1/2 c. chopped dried figs
1/3 c. candied citrus peel
Grated rind of 1/2 lemon
1/2 c. butter or margarine
1 1/2 c. (firmly packed) dark brown sugar
1 egg plus 1 egg yolk
1/2 c. flat beer

Sift dry ingredients together; add fruits, candied peel and lemon rind. Mix until fruits and peels are well coated. Beat butter and sugar with electric beater until creamy. Add egg and egg yolk. Beat until light. Add beer; beat in well. Fold beer mixture into fruit mixture until just blended. Spoon into buttered and floured 9 x 5 x 3-inch pan. Bake in 350-degree oven for about 1 hour and 15 minutes. Test with wire cake tester for doneness. Remove from oven; let stand for 5 minutes. Loosen edges with dull knife. Turn onto waxed paper-covered wire cake rack. Cool. Slice 1/2 inch thick; serve. Cake may be topped with hard sauce.

Marjorie Sargent
Xi Gamma X0300, Bronxville, New York

WHISKEY-RAISIN CAKE

1 c. raisins
1 c. cold water
3/4 c. sugar
1/2 c. butter
1 egg
1 1/2 c. flour
1 tsp. soda
1/2 tsp. baking powder
1/2 tsp. salt
1/2 tsp. cinnamon
1/2 tsp. allspice
2/3 c. chopped walnuts
2 tbsp. whiskey

Cook raisins in water for 10 minutes; drain raisins, reserving 1/2 cup water. Cream sugar and butter; beat in egg. Sift dry ingredients together; add to creamed mixture alternately with reserved raisin water. Stir in raisins and walnuts; add whiskey. Pour batter into layer cake pans. Bake in 350-degree oven for 25 minutes. Cool layers.

Frosting

1/4 c. butter
3 c. powdered sugar
1 egg
1 tsp. vanilla
1/4 c. whiskey

Cream butter and powdered sugar; add egg, vanilla and whiskey. Beat until thick and smooth. Spread Frosting between layers and over cake.

Nota Le Spencer
Exemplar Preceptor Alpha Mu XP470
Santa Clara, California

FESTIVE LOUISIANA YAM PIE

2 c. mashed cooked yams
1 c. (packed) brown sugar
1 c. light cream
1/2 c. milk
3 eggs
1/2 tsp. salt
1 tsp. cinnamon
1 tsp. nutmeg
1/2 tsp. ground ginger
1 11-in. unbaked pastry shell
2 c. sour cream
1/4 c. sifted confectioners' sugar
1/2 tsp. vanilla

Combine yams, brown sugar, cream, milk, eggs, salt, cinnamon, nutmeg and ginger in large mixing bowl. Mix well. Pour into pastry shell. Bake in 350-degree oven for 1 hour or until knife inserted in center comes out clean. Cool. Mix sour cream, confectioners' sugar and vanilla together. Serve with yam pie. May bake in two 8-inch pastry shells for 50 minutes if desired.

WEXFORD RAISIN JEWEL CAKE

1 c. butter
1 1/4 c. (packed) light brown sugar
6 well-beaten eggs
3 c. sifted flour
1/2 tsp. baking powder
1 tsp. salt
1/2 tsp. cinnamon
1 c. whiskey
2 1/2 c. dark seedless raisins
2 1/2 c. golden seedless raisins
1 c. candied pineapple chunks
1 c. halved candied cherries
1 c. finely chopped walnuts
2 tsp. vanilla
Glaze or icing

Line 9-inch tube pan with heavy brown paper; grease well. Beat butter until soft; beat in sugar gradually until light and fluffy. Beat in eggs. Sift flour with baking powder, salt and cinnamon; add alternately with 1/2 cup whiskey. Stir in fruits, walnuts and vanilla. Turn into prepared pan. Place pan of water on bottom rack of oven. Bake at 275 degrees for 3 hours or until cake tests done. Remove from oven; brush with 1/4 cup whiskey. Cool in pan. Peel off paper; brush with remaining whiskey. Wrap in foil or store in airtight container. Glaze cake before serving. Decorate as desired.

Glaze

1/4 c. (packed) brown sugar
3 tbsp. corn syrup
1 tbsp. lemon juice

Combine brown sugar, light corn syrup and 3 tablespoons water. Boil for 2 minutes. Remove from heat; add lemon juice.

Photograph for this recipe on page 211.

SANTA'S PUMPKIN PIE

2 c. pumpkin
3 eggs, separated plus 1 egg white
1 c. brown sugar
1/4 tsp. salt
1/2 tsp. nutmeg
1/2 tsp. ginger
1/2 tsp. allspice
1/4 tsp. cinnamon
3 c. scalded milk
1 unbaked pie shell

Combine pumpkin, egg yolks, brown sugar, salt and spices; add milk. Beat 3 egg whites until stiff; fold into pumpkin mixture. Brush pie shell with remaining egg white; pour in pumpkin mixture. Bake at 450 degrees for 10 minutes. Reduce oven temperature to 325 degrees; bake for 30 minutes longer or until pie tests done.

Kathy Heden
Psi, Bettendorf, Iowa

MERINGUE DESSERT

6 egg whites
1/2 tsp. cream of tartar
1/4 tsp. salt
1 1/2 c. sugar
1 pkg. lemon pudding mix
Whipped cream
Chopped nuts or shaved chocolate

Preheat oven to 400 degrees. Whip egg whites, cream of tartar and salt until stiff. Add sugar gradually. Spread in greased 13 x 9-inch pan. Place in oven; turn oven off. Let stand in oven overnight; do not open oven door. Cook pudding mix according to package directions; cool. Spread thin layer of whipped cream over meringue. Top with pudding. Add remaining whipped cream. Sprinkle nuts over top. Yield: 15 servings.

Darlene Brown
Oneida No. 5415, Duluth, Minnesota

BLACK FOREST WALNUT TORTE

14 eggs
2 c. sugar
12 oz. walnuts, ground
1/2 tsp. vanilla
1/2 lb. unsalted butter
1/2 lb. milk chocolate, melted

Preheat oven to 325 to 350 degrees. Separate 12 eggs. Place egg yolks and 1 1/2 cups sugar in small electric mixer bowl; beat for 15 minutes, until stiff. Add walnuts and vanilla. Beat egg whites until stiff but not dry; fold into yolk mixture. Pour batter into 3 springform pans or 9-inch cake pans with scraper. Bake for 1 hour or until cake tests done. Remove pans from oven; invert onto cake racks until cool. Remove cake from pans. Place butter, chocolate and remaining sugar in small bowl; beat until blended. Add remaining eggs; beat until of spreading consistency. Spread between layers and on sides; assemble cake. Sprinkle top with additional ground walnuts. Yield: 10 servings.

Jean Delzell
Gamma Alpha Iota No. 6459, Ontario, California

CHRISTMAS CANDY CANE COOKIES

3 c. sifted all-purpose flour
1 tsp. baking powder
3/4 tsp. salt
1/2 c. shortening
1 1/2 c. sugar
2 eggs
1 1/2 tsp. vanilla
1 tbsp. milk
1/2 tsp. red food coloring

Sift flour, baking powder and salt together. Cream shortening and sugar until light and fluffy; beat in eggs, one at a time. Stir in vanilla and milk; work in flour mixture. Divide dough in half; tint half the dough with food coloring. Wrap each half in waxed paper and chill for 2 hours. Shape dough in 6 x 1/4-inch rolls on lightly floured surface. Place plain roll and tinted roll together and twist to form cane. Place on baking sheet. Repeat with remaining rolls. Bake in preheated 375-degree oven for 8 to 10 minutes. Remove to rack with spatula immediately.

Mrs. Sally Broccoli
Beta Omicron, Waterbury, Connecticut

ENGLISH WASSAIL

1 3/4 c. sugar
1 qt. water
2 whole cloves
4 cinnamon sticks
4 whole allspice
2 tbsp. chopped ginger
2 c. lemon juice
2 qt. apple cider
3 c. orange juice

Place sugar and water in saucepan; boil for 10 minutes. Add spices and ginger; cover and let stand in warm place for 1 hour. Strain syrup into large kettle; stir in lemon juice, cider and orange juice. Bring to a boil; serve hot. Float sliced oranges on top if desired.

JoAnn Bonner
Delta No. 5652, San Francisco, California

HOT SPICED GRAPE PUNCH

1 tbsp. whole cloves
1 2-in. stick cinnamon
1 qt. grape juice
1/2 c. water
3/4 c. orange juice
1/4 c. lemon juice

Tie cloves and cinnamon in small cloth bag. Place grape juice, spice bag and water in saucepan; bring to a boil. Remove from heat; remove spice bag. Stir in orange juice and lemon juice. Yield: 10 servings.

Yvonne Louthan
Epsilon No. 6482, Montesano, Washington

CRANBERRY EGGNOG

6 eggs, beaten
1 pt. heavy cream, whipped
3/4 c. sugar
2 pt. cranberry juice

Combine eggs and whipped cream; fold in sugar. Stir in cranberry juice; serve. Yield: 12 servings.

Mrs. Clarence H. Kemp
Oakland, California

EGGNOG SUPREME

12 eggs, separated
1 1/2 c. sugar
1 qt. apple brandy or whiskey
2 qt. milk
1 pt. light cream
1 pt. heavy cream
Nutmeg

Blend egg yolks with sugar. Add brandy. Stir in milk and light cream. Beat egg whites until soft peaks form. Whip heavy cream until fluffy. Fold egg whites and whipped cream into yolk mixture. Chill. Serve sprinkled with nutmeg. Yield: 40 servings.

Mrs. C. W. Hassler
Chicago, Illinois

BUBBLING CHRISTMAS PUNCH

1 pkg. lime gelatin
1 c. hot water
2 c. cold water
1 6-oz. can frozen lemonade
1 c. pineapple juice
1 qt. ginger ale

Dissolve gelatin in hot water; add cold water, lemonade and pineapple juice. Mix well. Stir in ginger ale just before serving. Pour over ice in punch bowl. Sherbet balls may be floated on top if desired. Yield: 15-20 servings.

Florence Brennan
Xi Beta Nu No. 2589, Joseph, Oregon

SNOW PUNCH

3 c. mashed ripe bananas
1 c. lemon juice
2 c. sugar
2 c. light cream
6 7-oz. bottles lemon-lime carbonated beverage
1 pt. lemon sherbet
1/3 c. flaked coconut

Beat bananas, lemon juice and sugar together; chill well. Pour banana mixture into punch bowl; stir in cream. Pour in carbonated beverage slowly. Float spoonfuls of sherbet in punch. Sprinkle coconut on top. Yield: 40 servings.

Maud Heilman
Xi Nu Alpha X3032, San Jose, California

SPICED ORANGE WEDGES

4 oranges
2 c. sugar
1/2 c. vinegar
12 whole cloves
3 pieces stick cinnamon

Place whole oranges in saucepan; add 1 quart water. Bring to a boil; boil for 20 minutes. Drain oranges and cut into eighths. Combine sugar, 1 1/4 cups water, vinegar, cloves and cinnamon in saucepan; stir over low heat until sugar is dissolved. Bring to a boil; add oranges. Reduce heat; simmer for about 20 minutes. Cool; cover and store in refrigerator. Remove cloves and cinnamon before serving.

Mrs. Margaret Meigs
Montgomery, Alabama

FRESH CRANBERRY RELISH

1 pkg. fresh cranberries
1 med. apple
2 med. oranges
1 1/2 c. sugar
1/2 c. walnut pieces

Grind cranberries through coarse blade of food grinder; grind apple and oranges through medium blade of grinder. Mix cranberries, apple and oranges; add sugar and walnut pieces. Refrigerate for about 24 hours before serving. Yield: 6 servings.

Ruth Phelan Jahimiak
Preceptor Epsilon XP243
Swartz Creek, Michigan

PEAR PICKLE

1 gal. pears
6 c. sugar
4 c. vinegar
2 pieces gingerroot
2 sticks cinnamon
2 tbsp. whole allspice
1 tbsp. whole cloves

Peel pears; cut in halves or quarters. Remove cores; place in large kettle. Cover with cold water; bring to a boil and cook for 20 to 30 minutes. Mix sugar, vinegar and 2 cups water in large kettle. Tie spices in small bag; add to vinegar mixture. Bring to a boil and cook for 10 minutes. Drain pears and place in syrup; let stand overnight. Bring to a boil; reduce heat. Cook, stirring, until pears are tender. Pack pears into hot sterilized jars. Cook syrup until thickened; pour over pears. Seal jars. Process for 5 minutes in hot water bath. Test seal. Yield: 6-7 pints.

Mrs. Jesse Risener
Union Point, Georgia

Weddings, Anniversaries, and Birthdays

Weddings, anniversaries, and birthdays — three of the most festive occasions in everyone's life. Each of us cherish memories of special birthday parties, pre-wedding festivities, and anniversary celebrations. The food served on these happy occasions is so important in making precious memories.

Special and important events seem to bring out that creative something in all of us. And here, in this chapter featuring foods for weddings, anniversaries, and birthdays, you'll find the all-time favorite foods from creative cooks — those extra-special foods they serve for a real celebration. In the following pages, you'll find all the recipes you need for a perfect formal engagement dinner, a delightfully casual bachelor's brunch, a sweet and light bridesmaids' luncheon, an unforgettable anniversary reception, and birthday parties for both the younger set and teenagers.

Just browsing through this chapter is an enchanting adventure. It's packed full of hints about serving and party decorations. Best of all, it is a treasure chest of the time-cherished favorite recipes from families all over the country. These recipes represent generations-old favorites and bright new ideas, combined to promise you — today's hostess — the most memorable of all parties on these most special of all occasions.

Joyous pre-wedding days when love and laughter abound! Someone is going to be married and everyone shares in the joy of this very special occasion. Excitement begins as soon as the engagement is announced and builds through the following months until it is at fever pitch on the wedding day. A big part of this excitement is the many parties which honor the bride-to-be and her prospective groom.

These happy days begin with the announcement of the forthcoming wedding. Today, as has been the custom for generations, this announcement is usually made at an engagement dinner — an old-fashioned but still-beloved custom. Remember your engagement dinner? The thrill of just a few people knowing your great news until someone — your father, brother, or uncle, perhaps — called for attention and proposed a toast to you and your fiance. What excitement!

Now, it's your turn to hostess an engagement dinner. For such an occasion, you'll want a menu featuring dishes which have long been the standard of excellence for formal dining. Icy-cold pink shrimp nestling in tangy grapefruit halves offer an appetizer with an unusual combination of flavors and textures. Sirloin, broiled with mushrooms, is a simple but superb entree. Follow with twice-baked potatoes with Roquefort — these can be made ahead and heated just before serving time — and green peas

Weddings

with tiny pearl onions. For a delicious salad — and a bright note of color — try tomato aspic with mayonnaise. Fragrant, hot cloverleaf rolls with butter are the perfect finish to this palate-pleasing main course.

Top this delightful engagement dinner with fresh strawberry parfaits — a tasty and light treat well matched to your filling main course. Follow with coffee, tea, and mints.

The happy-engagement news provides ideas for party decorating. "Daisies tell" might be your theme. Bouquets of daisies around the house and on the dining table will set the tone, and a daisy-decorated cake with the words "daisies do tell" will let your guests know that a surprise is in store.

Or, you may choose to hint at the news with ring cakes. Bake your favorite cake in two ring molds, and cover them with a white icing. Use silver dragees as "diamonds" and put the initials of the bride-to-be on one cake, and the groom-to-be on another. Serve the cakes, and let them announce the forthcoming wedding.

Sweetheart cookies are another nice way to announce the happy news. Cut your favorite sugar cookies into heart shapes. Make a small hole in the top of each cookie before baking. After baking, put the bride's initials on half the cookies with decorative icing. The groom's initials go on the other half. Then tie pairs of initialed cookies together with a ribbon threaded through the holes and present them to your guests.

Whatever your choice of ways to announce the engagement, the dinner itself should be elegantly formal. This is the occasion to use your most cherished linen and very best silver, crystal, and china.

If an engagement dinner is in the very best formal tradition, the bachelor's brunch certainly personifies the casual tradition. Usually planned for the morning after the bachelor's party, this brunch should feature foods men love best — the hearty steak-and-potatoes fare.

An ideal appetizer for the morning after the big party — Bloodless Marys, a mixture of tomato juice, lemon juice, and Worcestershire sauce. The brisk combination of flavors is sure to wake up even your sleepiest guest! And a main course of hearty flavorful brunch pudding with crisp sausages, plenty of lean and meaty Canadian bacon and an unusual — and irresistible — Quiche Lorraine will satisfy the biggest appetite. To round out your menu, offer tomatoes broiled with Parmesan cheese and baskets piled with hot, fluffy biscuits. Top this meal with a tangy fresh fruit compote, and you'll satisfy even the hungriest of your bachelor guests!

While you'll want masculine fare for your bachelor guests, the theme is sweetness and light for a bridesmaids' luncheon. If your luncheon is scheduled for warm weather, you may want to use the patio or garden to capitalize on the loveliness of sunshine and blooming flowers. Cover small tables for two or four, with gaily colored tablecloths.

Whatever your decorating scheme, you'll want to pick a luncheon menu that's light and bright. Vichyssoise — the delectable cold soup Americans borrowed from the French cuisine — is a perfect appetizer. And lobster mousse, light yet flavorful, is a main dish certain to please your luncheon guests. Add hot and fragrant Parker House rolls, and you'll have a delightful and easy main course sure to fill but not stuff.

Dessert — what else but peach meringues, a cloud-light combination of flavors. Just what you need to end your bridal luncheon. With this lighthearted meal, be sure to have plenty of flavorful punch.

In the pages that follow, you'll find all-time favorite recipes perfect for each of these dishes — from the sirloin with mushrooms suggested for the engagement dinner through the peach meringue dessert for the bridesmaids' luncheon. Each recipe is the tried-and-true favorite of the homemaker who submitted it. And each has been successfully served at innumerable engagement dinners, bachelor's brunches, and bridesmaids' showers through the years. So, relax and enjoy yourself during the festivities for this happiest of all occasions — a wedding!

Engagement Dinner

STEAK WITH MUSHROOMS

1/2 c. butter
1 1/2 lb. 1/4-in. thick sirloin steak
6 peppercorns
1/4 c. chopped onion
1 tsp. Worcestershire sauce
2 tbsp. vinegar
1 4-oz. can mushrooms, drained

Melt butter in skillet; add steak, peppercorns and onion. Cook steak for about 1 minute on each side; remove to platter. Add Worcestershire sauce, vinegar and mushrooms to skillet; heat for about 5 minutes, stirring constantly. Return steak to pan; heat for 1 minute. Serve immediately. Yield: 4 servings.

Mrs. Edward F. C. Arndt
Malta, Illinois

TOMATO ASPIC WITH MAYONNAISE

4 c. tomato juice
2 pkg. lemon gelatin
2 tbsp. lemon juice
Dash of hot sauce
1 tsp. Worcestershire sauce
1/4 tsp. salt
Dash of pepper
1 c. chopped celery
1/2 c. sliced stuffed green olives
1 c. sliced cucumber
1/4 c. chopped green onions
Mayonnaise

Heat 2 cups tomato juice in saucepan; stir in gelatin until dissolved. Stir in remaining tomato juice, lemon juice, hot sauce, Worcestershire sauce, salt and pepper; chill until partially congealed. Stir in celery, green olives, cucumber and green onions; turn into oiled mold. Chill until firm. Unmold onto lettuce; serve with Mayonnaise. Yield: 12 servings.

Mayonnaise

3 egg yolks
2 tbsp. lemon juice
1/2 tsp. salt
1/4 tsp. dry mustard
1 1/2 to 2 1/4 c. olive or salad oil

Bring egg yolks to room temperature; beat until thick and creamy. Add lemon juice, salt and mustard; beat moderately fast for 1 minute. Add olive oil by drops, beating constantly until mixture thickens to consistency of heavy cream. Continue adding olive oil by tablespoonfuls, beating constantly until mixture thickens to desired consistency. Beat in additional seasoning, if needed. Store in refrigerator. Yield: About 2 1/2 cups.

Mrs. Elmo Henderson
Arrington, Virginia

TWICE-BAKED POTATOES WITH ROQUEFORT

4 med. baking potatoes
Shortening
1/2 c. sour cream
1 oz. Roquefort cheese, crumbled
1/4 c. milk
4 tbsp. butter or margarine
3/4 tsp. salt
Dash of pepper
4 slices bacon

Rub potatoes with shortening. Bake in 400-degree oven for 1 hour or until potatoes are done. Remove from oven; cut lengthwise slice from top of each potato. Scoop out inside of each; mash. Stir in sour cream, Roquefort cheese, milk, butter, salt and pepper; beat with electric mixer until fluffy. Spoon mixture lightly into potato shells. Place on baking sheet; return to oven for 15 minutes or until heated through. Fry bacon until crisp; drain well. Crumble; sprinkle over potatoes. Serve immediately. Yield: 4 servings.

Mrs. James F. Hayes III
Richmond, Virginia

SHRIMP IN GRAPEFRUIT HALVES

2 grapefruit, halved
1 can sm. shrimp
Celery slices
Chopped pecans
Mayonnaise or salad dressing

Scoop out fruit sections from grapefruit halves; reserve. Remove membrane from shells. Return reserved sections to shells. Combine shrimp, celery and pecans; moisten with mayonnaise. Pile over grapefruit sections. Yield: 4 servings.

Mrs. Helen E. Reigel
Harrisburg, Pennsylvania

PEAS WITH PEARL ONIONS

1 c. diagonally-cut celery
1/2 c. slivered blanched almonds
1/2 c. melted butter
1 sm. can whole onions
1 10-oz. package frozen peas, cooked
Salt and pepper to taste

Cook celery in boiling salted water until crisp-tender; drain. Brown almonds lightly in butter. Add onions, peas and celery; season with salt and pepper. Serve hot.

Mrs. Marie M. Hubbard
Providence, Rhode Island

FRESH STRAWBERRY PARFAIT

2 pt. fresh strawberries, halved
1/2 c. sifted confectioners' sugar
2 c. sour cream
3/4 tsp. almond flavoring
Mint

Mix strawberries with confectioners' sugar; chill. Combine sour cream and almond flavoring. Place strawberries in parfait glasses or serving dishes; top with sour cream mixture. Garnish with mint.

Mrs. J. W. Browning
San Diego, California

Bachelor's Brunch

BROILED TOMATOES WITH PARMESAN CHEESE

4 lge. tomatoes
1 c. fresh bread crumbs
1/4 c. melted butter
2 tbsp. grated Parmesan cheese
1/2 tsp. Italian herb seasoning

Wash tomatoes; remove stems. Slice; place in large broiler pan. Combine bread crumbs, butter, Parmesan cheese and seasoning; spoon mixture over tomatoes. Broil 10 inches from source of heat for 4 to 5 minutes or until tomatoes are hot and crumbs are browned. Serve at once. Yield: 4 servings.

Mrs. Barbara Hammerberg
Hortonville, Wisconsin

QUICHE LORRAINE TARTS

1 pkg. pie crust mix
1 tbsp. poppy seed
1 1/3 c. coarsely shredded Swiss cheese
2/3 c. chopped salami
1/3 c. sliced green onions
4 eggs, slightly beaten
1 1/3 c. sour cream
1 tsp. salt
1 tsp. Worcestershire sauce

Preheat oven to 375 degrees. Prepare pastry for 2-crust pie according to package directions, stirring poppy seed into dry crumbled mix. Roll out as thin as possible on lightly floured board; cut into 3-inch rounds. Fit rounds into 2 1/2-inch muffin cups. Combine Swiss cheese, salami and green onions; spoon into pastry. Combine eggs, sour cream, salt and Worcestershire sauce; pour about 1 tablespoonful into each muffin cup. Bake for 20 to 25 minutes. Yield: 36 tarts.

Mrs. Arnold F. Boehnke
Leadville, Colorado

FRUIT COMPOTE

Fresh fruit
1 1/2 c. sugar
Grated rind of 1 orange
Grated rind of 1 lemon
Grated rind of 1 grapefruit
Brandy flavoring to taste
Rum flavoring to taste

Prepare enough fruit for 12 servings. Combine sugar and 2 cups water in saucepan; cook until syrupy and translucent. Add grated rinds; stir in brandy and rum. Pour over fruit; chill. Yield: 12 servings.

Mrs. William Pride
Wilmington, North Carolina

SLICED CANADIAN BACON

12 1/4-in. thick slices Canadian bacon
6 thin onion slices
6 orange slices, peeled
2 tsp. sugar
1 tbsp. cornstarch
1 c. orange juice
1 orange, peeled and sectioned
2 tsp. grated lemon rind

Preheat oven to 300 degrees. Arrange 6 slices Canadian bacon in greased, shallow 1 1/2-quart baking dish. Top each with onion slice, orange slice and another bacon slice. Bake for 30 minutes. Mix sugar and cornstarch together in saucepan; blend in orange juice, mixing well. Cook, stirring constantly, until thickened and clear. Stir in orange sections and lemon rind; heat thoroughly. Serve orange sauce over Canadian bacon. Yield: 6 servings.

Mrs. Twila Shankland
Westminster, Colorado

BRUNCH PUDDING WITH SAUSAGES

3 pkg. frozen corn in butter sauce
2 tbsp. flour
1/2 c. light cream, scalded
2 eggs, separated
1/2 tsp. salt
1/4 tsp. pepper
1/4 c. frozen chopped onions
1/4 c. frozen chopped green peppers
1/4 c. diced pimento
12 pork sausages, cooked

Heat pouches of corn in boiling water according to package directions. Separate butter sauce from corn by emptying pouches into strainer or colander over saucepan. Blend flour into butter sauce; add cream, stirring to blend. Beat egg yolks with salt and pepper; add to sauce. Mix corn with onions, green pepper and pimento. Whip egg whites until stiff; fold into sauce mixture. Stir in vegetables gently; pour into buttered baking dish. Bake for 30 minutes at 350 degrees. Serve hot with pork sausages. Yield: 6-8 servings.

BLUEBERRY MUFFINS

1/2 c. milk
1/4 c. salad oil
1 egg, beaten slightly
1 1/2 c. flour
1/2 c. sugar
2 tsp. baking powder
1/2 tsp. salt
1 c. well-drained fresh blueberries

Stir milk and salad oil into egg. Sift dry ingredients together; add to milk mixture. Stir just until flour is moistened. Fold in blueberries; batter should be lumpy. Fill greased muffin cups 2/3 full. Bake for 20 to 25 minutes at 400 degrees. Yield: 12 servings.

Mrs. Ronald Higerd
Colby, Kansas

Bridesmaid Luncheon

PEACH TORTE

6 egg whites
1/4 tsp. salt
1/2 tsp. cream of tartar
1 1/2 c. sugar
1 1/2 tsp. vanilla
6 med. fresh peaches
2 tbsp. fresh lemon juice
1/4 c. sugar
1 env. unflavored gelatin
2 tbsp. water
Vanilla Whipped Cream

Preheat oven to 400 degrees. Place egg whites, salt and cream of tartar in large mixing bowl; beat with mixer until eggs have doubled in bulk. Beat in sugar, 1 tablespoon at a time, beating well after each addition; beat in vanilla. Spoon into buttered 8-inch springform pan; make depression in center about 5 inches wide and 1 inch deep, using back of tablespoon. Place in oven; close door. Turn off heat; let stand in oven for 12 hours or overnight. Do not open oven door. Remove pan from oven; run spatula around side to loosen torte. Release spring; lift off side gently. Slide torte onto serving plate carefully. Peel and slice peaches; sprinkle with lemon juice and sugar. Soften gelatin in water; dissolve over hot water. Blend with peaches; chill until juice has partially congealed. Pile into torte. Top with Vanilla Whipped Cream; garnish with slices of peaches and mint leaves. Serve at once. Yield: 6 servings.

Vanilla Whipped Cream

1/2 c. heavy cream
1 tbsp. sugar
1/4 tsp. vanilla

Whip cream until stiff, adding sugar and vanilla gradually.

Mrs. James Shaw
Medford, Wisconsin

LOBSTER MOUSSE

3 3-oz. packages cream cheese
1 can tomato soup
2 tbsp. gelatin
1 c. cold water
3/4 c. chopped celery
2 tbsp. chopped green onion
1/2 c. chopped green pepper
1 1/2 c. chopped lobster
1 c. mayonnaise
Salt and pepper to taste
Hot sauce to taste
Worcestershire sauce to taste

Combine cheese and soup in saucepan; heat and stir until smooth. Soak gelatin in cold water; dissolve in cheese mixture. Chill until partially congealed. Stir in celery, green onion, green pepper and lobster. Add mayonnaise and seasonings to taste. Pour into 2-quart fish mold; chill until firm. Unmold on serving plate; keep chilled until ready to serve.

Mrs. Everett Holstrom
Washington, D.C.

VICHYSSOISE

4 or 5 leeks
1/4 c. butter
3 c. thinly sliced potatoes
1 c. hot water
4 chicken bouillon cubes
3 c. milk
1 tsp. salt
1/8 tsp. white pepper
1/8 tsp. paprika
1 c. cream
2 tbsp. finely chopped chives

Slice leeks thin, using only white and very light green portions to measure 1 1/2 cups. Melt butter in large, heavy saucepan. Add leeks; cook and stir until transparent but not brown. Add potatoes, water and bouillon cubes. Cover; cook over moderate heat until tender. Press through fine sieve or puree in blender; return to saucepan. Add milk; stir rapidly to blend. Stir in salt, white pepper and paprika. Add cream; heat only to serving temperature. Serve hot with garnish of chives or chill quickly and serve cold. Sliced onions may be substituted for leeks; parsley may be substituted for chives. Yield: 6 servings.

Mrs. Paul Lang
Leachville, Arkansas

PARKER HOUSE ROLLS

1 pkg. yeast
1/2 c. warm water
Sugar
1/2 c. milk, scalded
3 tbsp. butter
1 tsp. salt
1 egg, beaten
3 c. flour
Melted butter

Mix yeast, water and 1 teaspoon sugar together. Combine milk, 3 tablespoons sugar, butter and salt; cool. Stir milk mixture, egg and flour into yeast mixture; mix well. Place in greased bowl. Cover; let rise until doubled in bulk. Roll out on floured board to about 1/2 inch thick; cut with 3-inch roll cutter. Brush with melted butter; fold in half with butter on inside. Pinch edges together; brush tops with melted butter. Place on greased baking sheet. Cover; let rise until doubled in bulk. Bake at 350 degrees for about 15 minutes or until browned. Yield: 16 rolls.

Mrs. S. F. Glasser
Winter Haven, Florida

PINEAPPLE-MINT PUNCH

1 c. green mint jelly
3 c. boiling water
1 c. canned pineapple juice
1 c. orange juice
1 12-oz. bottle pale dry ginger ale
Lemon slices
Cucumber slices

Heat jelly in boiling water till dissolved; cool. Add fruit juices. Add ginger ale just before serving. Fill each glass half full of ice; add lemon slices and cucumber slices. Fill with punch. May increase quantity; serve in punch bowl with ice. Float slices in punch. Yield: 8 servings.

Mrs. H. S. Dunning
Ridgefield, Connecticut

ASPARAGUS AND CARROT CASSEROLE

2 c. sliced carrots
2 cans asparagus
1 c. slivered almonds
3/4 stick margarine
1 can mushroom soup
1/2 c. water
1 1/2 c. cheese cracker crumbs

Layer half the first 4 ingredients in casserole; repeat layers. Mix soup and water; pour over layers. Bake for 30 minutes in 350-degree oven. Top with cracker crumbs; bake for 7 minutes longer.

Mrs. Eleanor Hunt Bishop
Greenville, South Carolina

Recapture the joy and excitement of your wedding day with a special wedding anniversary party. Let the anniversary set your party theme. If it's a first anniversary, use paper as your motif — brilliant paper flowers, and easy-to-use paper plates for example. You might even want to experiment with the new paper aprons and dresses! Your fifth anniversary features wood and is the perfect time for a picnic. Your wooden salad bowls, wooden ice-cream freezer and many of your wooden accent pieces are perfect to hold picnic foods. And the tenth — tin — could be fun with a tin plate party. Let your imagination run free, and you're sure to have unforgettable anniversary parties.

One of the happiest anniversaries is the silver anniversary, the 25th. This occasion, above all others, demands a very special party.

Here's a fabulous silver anniversary wedding reception. Your guests can choose their favorites from bite-sized watercress sandwiches, tiny chicken salad sandwiches, or the unusual flavor and texture blend of cream cheese and olive sandwiches. To complement these tasty sandwiches, tiny puff shells filled with a delicious crab mixture. Add colorful bowls of marinated shrimp, and you'll have a menu to remember.

Continue the delicious variety theme by offering a wide selection of desserts. Petit fours — perhaps decorated with silver dragees in honor of

Anniversaries

the silver anniversary — miniature eggnog and lemon tarts, a tangy flavor combination sure to please your guests; and cool, refreshing lemon ice. Cap this gala reception menu with divinity, mints, and punch.

Both your invitations and your party decorations can take advantage of the silver anniversary theme. Perhaps you will want your invitations to be printed or written in silver ink. Or, you may want to reproduce the original wedding invitation, and write the anniversary party invitation on the inside.

In decorating for the party, you'll want to use as much silver as possible, especially on the reception table. An arrangement of silver balls and seasonal greenery makes a lovely centerpiece. Or you may decide to swag your table with silver net. Using the glow and gleam of silver as your theme, you're sure to come up with elegant and memorable party decorations.

To make the party food just as memorable as your decorating, here are favorite recipes perfect for the simplest or most lavish parties. And using these recipes, you're sure to have an anniversary reception every bit as memorable as the original wedding reception!

Reception

WATERCRESS SANDWICHES

1 loaf thin-sliced bread
1 3-oz. package cream cheese, softened
1 c. slivered almonds, toasted
2 tbsp. finely chopped watercress
1/4 tsp. salt
Sprigs of watercress

Trim crusts from bread; flatten slices with rolling pin. Beat cheese until fluffy. Add almonds, watercress, and salt; spread 1 teaspoonful on each bread slice. Roll as for jelly roll; place seam side down on cookie sheet. Cover with waxed paper; refrigerate until serving. Tuck a sprig of watercress in end of each sandwich; serve.

Mrs. A. C. Bowes
Burlington, North Carolina

PETITS FOURS

1 1-lb. 3-oz. package white cake mix
1 pkg. fluffy white frosting mix
Food coloring
Chocolate shot
Toasted coconut
Chopped nuts
Candied cherries
Currant jelly

Preheat oven to 350 degrees. Line bottom of ungreased 15 x 10-inch jelly roll pan with waxed paper. Prepare cake batter according to package directions; pour into pan. Bake for 25 to 30 minutes or until cake tests done. Cool cake in pan for 5 minutes; turn out onto wire rack. Remove paper; cool completely. Cut cake into five 2-inch strips lengthwise; cut strips into seven 2-inch pieces on the diagonal or square. Prepare frosting mix according to package directions; frost cake pieces. Decorate with remaining ingredients as desired. Yield: 35 pieces.

Mrs. D. K. Layman
Honolulu, Hawaii

EGGNOG TARTS

1 3-oz. package pineapple gelatin
3/4 c. boiling water
2 eggs, separated
1 pt. vanilla ice cream, softened
1 1/2 tsp. brandy extract
10 baked pastry tart shells
Nutmeg

Dissolve gelatin in boiling water. Beat egg yolks; stir in hot gelatin mixture gradually. Add ice cream; stir until melted. Blend in brandy extract. Beat egg whites until stiff but not dry; fold into gelatin mixture. Chill until partially congealed. Spoon into tart shells; chill until firm. Sprinkle with nutmeg before serving. Yield: 10 servings.

Mrs. Elmer Harris
Seattle, Washington

CHICKEN SALAD SANDWICHES

1 1/4 c. chopped cooked chicken
2 tsp. minced green pepper
1/8 tsp. salt
1/2 c. finely chopped celery
1 tbsp. lemon juice
3 tbsp. mayonnaise
Buttered bread slices
Crisp lettuce leaves

Combine first 6 ingredients; chill. Spread chicken mixture between bread slices, placing lettuce in each sandwich. Chopped stuffed olives may be substituted for green pepper if desired.

Mrs. Frank J. Zadow
Early, Iowa

LEMON ICE

2 1/2 c. water
3/4 c. corn syrup
1 c. sugar
1/4 tsp. salt
1 tbsp. grated lemon rind
2/3 c. lemon juice
Yellow food coloring

Combine water, corn syrup, sugar, salt and lemon rind in saucepan. Cook and stir over low heat until sugar is dissolved. Bring to a boil; boil for 5 minutes without stirring. Cool. Add lemon juice; strain syrup to remove lemon rind. Add several drops of food coloring to tint syrup a delicate yellow. Pour into refrigerator tray; freeze until firm. Remove to chilled bowl. Break into lumps; beat until light and creamy. Return to refrigerator tray; freeze until firm.

Dixie Lindsay
Jackson, Tennessee

LEMON TARTS

1 stick margarine or butter
1 3-oz. package cream cheese
Flour
1 egg
1 c. sugar
Juice and grated rind of 1 1/2 lemons
1 tbsp. melted butter

Blend margarine with cream cheese. Add 1 cup flour; mix thoroughly. Shape into small balls; press into small muffin cups. Beat egg; add 1 tablespoon flour and remaining ingredients. Pour into pastry shells; fill 2/3 full. Bake at 350 degrees for about 20 minutes or until filling is almost set. Reduce oven temperature to 250 degrees; bake for 10 minutes longer or until filling is firm. Cool in muffin cups.

Mrs. B. J. Ahlin
Lynchburg, Virginia

CRAB SALAD IN PUFF SHELLS

1 c. crab meat, flaked
1/4 c. mayonnaise or salad dressing
1/2 c. finely chopped celery
1 tbsp. sweet pickle relish
1 tsp. grated onion
1 c. chopped hard-cooked eggs
Salt and pepper to taste
36 1-in. puff shells

Combine all ingredients except shells; chill. Remove tops from shells; fill with crab mixture. Replace tops and serve.

Helen Schott
Kodiak, Alaska

DIVINITY

4 c. sugar
1 c. light corn syrup
Food coloring
3/4 c. cold water
3 egg whites, stiffly beaten
1 tsp. vanilla
1 c. chopped nuts

Combine sugar, syrup and food coloring in heavy saucepan; cook and stir until sugar is dissolved. Cook, without stirring, to soft-ball stage or 245 degrees on candy thermometer; remove from heat. Pour slowly into egg whites, beating constantly. Beat until candy holds shape and loses gloss. Add vanilla and nuts; drop by spoonfuls onto waxed paper.

Mrs. Don H. Clausen
Takoma Park, Maryland

STRAWBERRY PUNCH

3 boxes frozen strawberries
3 lge. cans pineapple juice
1 sm. bottle vanilla
1 lge. bottle ginger ale
3 c. sugar
3 cans frozen orange juice
1 sm. bottle almond extract
3 pkg. strawberry drink powder mix
3 pt. pineapple sherbet

Combine first 8 ingredients in large punch bowl; add enough water to make 3 gallons punch. Add sherbet to punch just before serving. Yield: 100 one-cup servings.

Mrs. Maye Donaldson
Oakland, Mississippi

CREAM CHEESE AND OLIVE SANDWICHES

1 3-oz. package cream cheese
1/2 c. chopped pimento-stuffed olives
1/2 c. chopped walnuts
2 tbsp. mayonnaise
12 thin slices sandwich bread

Combine cream cheese, olives, walnuts, and mayonnaise; spread on 6 slices of bread. Cover with remaining 6 slices. Trim crusts; cut each sandwich into thirds.

Mrs. Raymond B. Hill
Kansas City, Kansas

SHRIMP ARNAUD

1/4 c. vinegar
1/4 c. salad oil
1/4 c. chili sauce
1/4 tsp. garlic salt
1 tsp. prepared mustard
1 lb. shrimp, cooked

Combine vinegar, salad oil, chili sauce, garlic salt and mustard. Add shrimp; toss to coat with sauce. Cover; marinate overnight. Insert a toothpick in each shrimp; serve in sauce.

Elizabeth Woodward
New London, Ohio

MINT RECEPTION PUNCH

1 46-oz. can pineapple juice
1 46-oz. can orange juice
1/2 c. lemon juice
12 7-oz. bottles lemon-lime carbonated drink
1 c. sugar
Sprigs of fresh mint

Chill first 4 ingredients. Combine sugar, 1 quart water and about 20 sprigs of mint in saucepan; simmer for 5 minutes. Let stand for several hours or overnight. Strain into punch bowl; stir in fruit juices. Pour in lemon-lime carbonated drink slowly. Add ice cubes; garnish with sprigs of mint. Yield: 40 servings.

Mrs. Bradford Clark, Jr.
Haxtun, Colorado

PASTEL SHERBET CREAM PUNCH

2 1/2 c. canned pineapple juice, chilled
1 pt. lime, lemon or raspberry sherbet
1 pt. vanilla ice cream
1 12-oz. bottle chilled sparkling water

Combine pineapple juice, sherbet and half of the ice cream; beat until smooth. Add sparkling water. Spoon remaining ice cream into punch. Serve immediately. Yield: Fourteen 1/2-cup servings.

Birthday parties are wonderful fun for everyone, young and old! For children they're the most excitement-packed occasions ever. Whether your child is a party-loving six-year-old or a teenager beginning to try his wings, he is sure to look forward to his birthday party with excitement.

For youngsters from five to ten, a "let's go to the farm" party is guaranteed fun. Their favorite sandwiches — yummy tuna salad, tangy pimento cheese, or the all-time favorite, peanut butter and jelly — will draw excited exclamations from your small guests when you serve them cut in the shapes of farm animals.

To satisfy young children's endless appetites, you'll want at least two kinds of cookies! Peanut butter drop cookies are a must! And farm animal cookies will echo your party theme.

The high point of every child's party is cake-and-ice cream time. Vanilla is the best ice cream for young children — everyone is sure to like it, and it's less apt to stain if there should be accidental spills. But it's the cake that will excite the most interest. For this "let's go to the farm" party, try a yellow sheet cake, covered with tinted icing — perhaps a green to suggest farm grass. You can make a farm fence using birthday candles as posts with licorice whips or hard candy sticks as the fencing.

Birthdays

A "let's go to the farm" party is fun for the young set, but hardly suitable for your teenager and his friends. For these hard-to-please young people, a party where they can "do their own thing" is ideal. Here's a menu designed just for a teenager's patio party.

Huge bowls of delicious dip with a variety of crisp, fresh vegetables would be sure hits with your guests. For the main course, let them build their own beef kabobs. Fill bowls with beef chunks, sauces, onions, peppers, tomatoes, pineapple, lemon — providing ample opportunity for your guests to make their own flavor combinations. A hearty and delicious green bean casserole will complement the kabobs.

Cake-and-ice cream time can continue the "do-it-yourself" theme. Offer a variety of ice creams, sauces, nuts, syrups, cherries, bananas — all the makings for scrumptious sundaes so beloved by teenagers. And, be sure to have plenty of milk on hand — they can mix milk, ice cream and syrup to make their own milk shakes — a favorite teenager's drink. Another teenaged favorite is the birthday cake — a yummy double chocolate cake with chocolate frosting. And birthday candles, of course!

In the pages that follow, you'll find favorite recipes for each of the suggested dishes. These flavorful favorites are sure to please party-goers of all ages — and to make birthdays memorable special occasions.

Let's Go To The Farm

MINTS

1 egg white
2 c. sifted confectioners' sugar
Dash of cream of tartar
12 drops of oil of peppermint
9 drops of food coloring
2 tbsp. butter

Combine egg white, confectioners' sugar, cream of tartar, oil of peppermint and food coloring; mix thoroughly. Add butter; mix until smooth and creamy. Shape into roll; slice. Peppermint mixture may be pressed through cookie press to form mints.

Geraldine I. Meyer
New Orleans, Louisiana

PIMENTO-CHEESE SANDWICHES

1 4-oz. jar pimentos, minced
2 hard-cooked eggs, diced
1/2 lb. hoop cheese, grated
3 tbsp. salad dressing
1/2 tsp. sugar
Salt to taste
2 tbsp. sour cream
1 loaf sliced bread

Combine all ingredients except bread; refrigerate for 30 minutes. Remove crusts from bread; cut slices with animal cookie cutters. Spread pimento-cheese filling on half the bread animals; top with remaining animals.

Mrs. A. L. George
Beaumont, Texas

SUGAR COOKIES

2 c. sugar
1 c. shortening
2 eggs
1 c. milk
Flour
1 tsp. soda
4 tsp. baking powder
1 tsp. salt
Pinch of cream of tartar

Mix sugar, shortening and eggs together with electric mixer. Add milk; stir in flour to make a soft dough. Add soda, baking powder, salt and cream of tartar; mix well. Refrigerate for 1 hour. Knead part of the dough at a time on floured board until soft and easy to handle. Cut as desired; place on cookie sheets. Bake at 400 degrees for 10 to 12 minutes. Yield: 60 cookies.

Mrs. J. F. Hawk
Chicora, Pennsylvania

PEANUT BUTTER COOKIES

2 egg whites
1 c. sugar
1 c. crunchy peanut butter
1/2 tsp. almond extract

Beat egg whites until stiff; fold in sugar, peanut butter and almond extract. Drop by spoonfuls onto greased cookie sheet. Bake for 15 minutes at 350 degrees.

Carol Bird
Salt Lake City, Utah

PINEAPPLE-ORANGE PUNCH

1 6-oz. can frozen orange juice
1 pt. pineapple sherbet

Reconstitute orange juice according to label directions, using chilled water. Stir into sherbet until smooth and creamy. Serve immediately. Yield: 8 servings.

Mrs. D. C. Mitchell
Newport News, Virginia

TUNA SANDWICH SPREAD

1 loaf thin-sliced bread
1 sm. can flaked tuna
1 med. apple, chopped fine
1 hard-boiled egg, diced

1 sm. onion, chopped fine
2 sweet pickles, diced
1/2 c. finely chopped pecans
1/2 c. diced celery
1/2 c. (or more) mayonnaise

Trim crusts from bread; flatten slices with rolling pin, if desired. Cut slices with animal cookie cutters. Combine remaining ingredients, adding enough mayonnaise for spreading consistency. Spread tuna mixture between bread animals.

Mrs. Arthur A. Behrens
San Saba, Texas

ICE CREAM TREATS FOR THE YOUNG

Flower Pot

Ice cream
Candy sucker
Green gumdrop leaves

Fill heavy paper cup with handle with scoops of ice cream; stick sucker in center of top scoop. Stand candy leaves upright on either side of sucker.

Ice Cream Cart

1 pt. brick ice cream
Animal cookies
Sm. round flat cookies

Cut ice cream into quarters or thirds. Arrange each slice on chilled plate to 1 side of center; freeze. Stand 2 animal cookies in front of each slice; arrange 2 round cookies on each side ice cream for wheels of cart.

Ice Cream-Sandwich

Ice cream squares
Graham crackers
Chocolate shot or sm. candies

Place square of ice cream between 2 graham crackers. Dip sides in chocolate shot. May top with ice cream sauce if desired.

PEANUT BUTTER-HONEY SUPREME

1/3 c. peanut butter
1/4 c. cream cheese
2 tbsp. honey
Bread or toast

Mix peanut butter, cream cheese and honey together until well blended. Trim crusts from bread; cut slices into animal shapes, using cookie cutters. Spread peanut butter mixture carefully on half the bread animals; top with remaining animals. May be covered and refrigerated until ready to serve.

Mary A. Powers
Conifer, Colorado

Teenage Patio Party

VEGETABLE DIP

1 c. salad dressing
1 tsp. Worcestershire sauce
2 tsp. celery, chopped fine
2 tsp. vinegar
1/2 tsp. garlic salt
2 tbsp. minced onion
2 hard-cooked eggs, chopped

Combine all ingredients; mix well. Serve with carrot and celery strips, cauliflower, green peppers or other vegetables.

Mrs. Luther Mylander
Oak Harbor, Ohio

TASTY TIDBITS

2 1/2 c. margarine
1 tsp. (heaping) garlic salt
Savory salt to taste
Celery salt to taste
6 tsp. Worcestershire sauce
2 tsp. hot sauce
1 box corn puffs
1 box oat puffs
1 box bite-size toasted rice cereal
2 cans peanuts
1 can mixed nuts
1 sm. box pretzel sticks

Melt margarine in a large roaster; do not brown. Add seasonings; mix well. Add cereals, nuts and pretzels; toss to mix well. Bake at 250 degrees for at least 1 hour, stirring often. Store in glass or tin containers in cool place; mixture will keep indefinitely.

Mrs. Avery L. Cox
McAlester, Oklahoma

GREEN BEAN CASSEROLE

2 pkg. French-style frozen beans
1 c. sliced water chestnuts
1 can bean sprouts, drained
1 lge. can sliced mushrooms
1 med. onion, chopped
2 c. medium cream sauce
Salt to taste
Grated cheese to taste
1 can French-fried onions

Thaw green beans. Layer half the beans, water chestnuts, bean sprouts, mushrooms and onion in 2-quart casserole. Cover with half the cream sauce; sprinkle lightly with salt and cheese. Repeat layers. Bake at 400 degrees for about 20 minutes. Top with onions; bake for 10 minutes longer or until bubbly. Cream of mushroom soup may be substituted for cream sauce; sherry may be added. Casserole may be prepared a day ahead and refrigerated. Yield: 8 servings.

Mrs. Carroll McColpin
San Raphael, California

CHOCOLATE CAKE WITH CHOCOLATE FROSTING

3/4 c. butter
1 1-lb. box light brown sugar
3 eggs
3 sq. unsweetened chocolate
2 tsp. vanilla
2 1/4 c. sifted cake flour
3/4 tsp. salt
2 tsp. soda
1/2 c. sour milk
1 c. boiling water

Cream butter, brown sugar and eggs together until light and fluffy. Melt chocolate. Add chocolate and vanilla; mix well. Sift flour, salt and soda together; add to chocolate mixture alternately with sour milk. Stir in boiling water. Pour in 2 layer cake pans or one 9 x 13-inch pan lined with greased waxed paper. Bake at 350 degrees for 35 to 40 minutes. Remove from oven; let cool in pans for several minutes. Turn out on cake racks to finish cooling.

Chocolate Frosting

1 1-lb. box powdered sugar
4 sq. unsweetened chocolate
1/4 c. butter
1 egg, beaten

2 tsp. vanilla
Pinch of salt
1/4 c. (about) hot water

Sift powdered sugar; melt chocolate. Cream powdered sugar with butter; stir in egg. Add vanilla, salt and chocolate; mix well. Add hot water slowly, stirring constantly until frosting is of desired spreading consistency. Beat until light and fluffy. Spread between layers; frost top and side of cake.

Mrs. John A. Burns
Honolulu, Hawaii

KABOB MARINADE

1 1/2 c. salad oil
3/4 c. soy sauce
1/4 c. Worcestershire sauce
2 tbsp. dry mustard
2 1/4 tsp. salt
1 tbsp. freshly ground pepper
1/2 c. wine vinegar
1 1/2 tsp. dried parsley flakes
2 crushed garlic cloves
1/3 c. fresh lemon juice

Combine all ingredients; mix well. Use to marinate meat chunks or brush kabobs while grilling. Yield: 3 1/2 cups.

Mrs. Joseph Black
St. Louis, Missouri

MINCEMEAT TOPPING FOR ICE CREAM

1/2 c. sugar
1/2 c. water
1 tsp. grated orange rind
1 c. canned mincemeat
1 1/4 c. chopped nuts

Combine sugar, water and orange rind in saucepan; boil for 5 minutes. Add mincemeat; boil for 5 minutes longer. Stir in nuts; serve warm on ice cream. Yield: 6 servings.

Mrs. D'Anne Kohl Nesbitt
Mt. Pleasant, Iowa

CARAMEL CREAM SAUCE FOR ICE CREAM

1 egg
1 c. whipping cream
2 c. light brown sugar
2 tbsp. butter

Beat egg slightly; pour in top of double boiler. Add remaining ingredients; cook and stir until thick. Pour into serving dish. Cover; refrigerate until ready to use. Yield: 10-12 servings.

Mrs. T. O. Van DeGrift
Nampa, Idaho

ALMOND FUDGE FANCY

1/2 c. whipping cream
1 tbsp. sugar
1/4 tsp. rum flavoring
1 c. milk chocolate fudge topping
Vanilla ice cream
Sliced almonds, toasted

Whip cream in small bowl until stiff, adding sugar and rum flavoring. Fold in chocolate fudge topping. Serve over ice cream; top with toasted sliced almonds. Yield: 2 cups.

Mrs. Janet May
Red Wing, Minnesota

VANILLA ICE CREAM

4 eggs
2 c. (heaping) sugar
2 tbsp. vanilla
1 1/2 pt. coffee cream
3 1/2 qt. milk

Beat eggs; add sugar gradually. Beat until sugar is dissolved. Stir in remaining ingredients; mix well. Pour into ice cream freezer container to 1 inch from top. Freeze according to freezer directions. Fresh sweetened peaches or strawberries may be added, if desired. Yield: 1 gallon.

Martha Morrin
Dayton, Ohio

Festive events are those very special occasions which delight us with their appearance throughout the year. A festive event may be the day to commemorate mother or father . . . graduation . . . a long-awaited trip . . . that most-important game . . . or a host of other happenings. Whatever the occasion, festive events are best celebrated with festive parties. Nothing contributes to the joy of these events quite so much as a gala party with all the trimmings.

In this section, you'll find suggested menus for nine such parties. And in the pages that follow, there are favorite recipes for all of these festive party foods. As you browse through these suggestions, let your imagination run free. You may find your all-time favorite foods in several menus. Why not mix and match dishes to create a party that is uniquely yours. After all, that's half the fun of a party, isn't it?

Parties are exciting! Remember the excitement of Mother's Day when you were a

Festive Events

child? Your plans for that "surprise" breakfast or dinner . . . the carefully bought and hidden gifts . . . the joy of having the kitchen all to yourself. Even today, Mother's Day is the one day of the year when Mother can really relax and enjoy herself. Nothing contributes to that relaxation quite so much as being freed from cooking — and cleaning up afterwards.

Here's an almost-foolproof menu Dad and the kids can have fun preparing. It's easy, quick, and calls for an absolute minimum of fuss and pans. It begins with Barbecued Ham Slices — succulent slices of ham in their own rich barbecue sauce. A tangy Mixed Green Salad with Creamy Garlic Dressing and Garlic Cheese Loaf contribute their own special flavors to this family meal. And for dessert,

tart and delicious Apricot Nectar Cakes tastes like anything but the cake mix it is!

Just as Mother has her day, so Dad has his — Father's Day. This is the occasion to serve all his favorite foods. Cool, tasty Shrimp Cocktail with a tongue-biting sauce that men love so well. And what else but Prime Ribs of Roast Beef — cooked just the way he likes it and served in its own rich juices. Add Corn on The Cob — dripping with melted butter and salt — and tangy Asparagus Amandine, and you'll have the man in your life beaming with satisfaction. For dessert, the family's favorite Lemon Meringue Pie — cool, tart and the perfect accompaniment to this Father's Day Party dinner.

You can add to the party atmosphere by waiting until his big dinner to present his gifts. And be sure to decorate the dining area with a typically-male color scheme — strong shades of green, brown, and gold, perhaps.

If spring is the signal for Mother's and Father's Day, it's also the signal for Derby Day. Whether you watch the running for the roses from a trackside seat in Louisville or from the comfort of your living room, the Kentucky Derby is certainly a festive occasion. More than that, it's an American tradition. What better way to celebrate this day than enjoying Louisville's typical Old South breakfast. Build your party decorating scheme around the rich colors and masses of flowers so typically Southern. And be sure to build your menu around the best-loved Southern foods. For this hale and hearty breakfast — the same one eaten in Louisville homes just before the great race — you might begin with Old Virginia Ham and Red-Eye Gravy. Candied Apples bring a rich and colorful note to your breakfast table. For a light and delicious dish, try Cheese and Egg Souffle. And don't forget the Biscuits — no Southern breakfast would be complete without them! Top this meal with Fresh Strawberries and Peaches with Brown Sugar and Sour Cream, and your guests will think they're back in the antebellum South!

As American as the Kentucky Derby is Election Night. Whether it's a local, state, or national election, American families eagerly await election returns, pencils poised, comparing their predictions with the outcome. And whether your candidate wins or loses, Election Night is the perfect occasion for a party.

You'll want a menu you can prepare well in advance so you can share in the excitement of watching the returns come in. Spicy Chicken Tetrazzini is sure to bring compliments from your guests. Add Scalloped Green Peas and Onions, and you'll have an unbeatable flavor combination. Crusty Rolls are a must with this menu — they're good served as they are or piping hot. Introduce a welcome note of cool lightness with Lemon Icebox Cake.

You might decide to carry out your Election Night theme with place mats made from election posters. And be sure to provide your guests with plenty of paper and pencils so they can take part in predicting the outcome.

If Election Night predictions are an American tradition, so is The Game. Whether your preference is football, basketball, hockey, baseball, or soccer, after the game suppers are great party times. Your guests are sure to bring with them the excitement of watching their favorite team. Capitalize on that excitement with party decorations that echo the game — clusters of miniature footballs or basketballs.

What's better for a late evening after-the-game party than a pancake supper? Cottage Cheese Fruit Pancakes offer your guests a delicious taste treat. Don't forget the delightful Apple Pancakes or the Banana or Blueberry variety. And a Corn Bread Jelly Roll presents an old favorite in new dress. Cap this delicious meal with Strawberry Hot Cakes, then sit back and listen to the compliments pour in.

Almost as exciting as the night of the big game is Graduation Night. Coming in June as it usually does, it's the perfect occasion for a swim supper party. Swimming is a good way to raise an enormous appetite, and Fried Chicken Legs — crispy crunchy outside and delicately delicious inside — are sure to satisfy that hunger. Marinated Green Bean Salad will add a note of color — and the unusual flavor will be welcomed by your young guests. Tuna Salad Cups are another teenage favorite. And be sure to have plenty of Cheese Potato Strips on hand — they disappear like magic when young people are around! To quench the parching thirst energetic swimming raises, bypass the usual sweet soft drinks in favor of Iced Lemonade. Its tart taste does more to quench thirst than do any of the soft drinks — and it's better for you.

Summertime may be the occasion for delightful graduation parties, but it's also the time when friends depart for far-away places. Or perhaps this is your year for that long-awaited trip. Whether it's your trip or that of friends, it's an occasion for real celebrating. For many of us, trips abroad are once-in-a-lifetime events that deserve extra special parties . . . like this Bon Voyage Party that features taste-tempting dishes from the major countries of Europe.

From Greece come Feta Cheese Turnovers — an unusual melt-in-the-mouth appetizer. Spanish Gazpacho is a flavorful soup sure to bring compliments from your guests. Roast Beef with Yorkshire Pudding — typically English in its elegant taste — is a classic way to prepare beef. Eggplant Parmigiana is piquantly Italian in its combination of flavors. And Salade Nicoise will taste as delightful in your home as it does on the Cote d'Azur of France. End this international meal with the most elegant of all desserts — Peach-Cream Kuchen from Germany. Express your party theme with welcome signs in many languages, place mats made of maps, and centerpieces commemorative of the places to be visited — a wooden shoe full of flowers, for example.

Back on this side of the Atlantic, there are two almost universal American pastimes — playing bridge for the ladies and poker for the men. There are few things as relaxing and enjoyable as gathering with friends around a card table for several hours of enjoyable companionship. These are always occasions for delightful parties.

Poker parties are traditionally male — perhaps no other festive event except Father's Day features a party menu so full of the foods men love. Take advantage of the casual atmosphere that's an integral part of the poker game to serve great thick Reuben Sandwiches and fragrantly delicious Hot Potato Salad. Add plenty of their favorite beverages, and lots and lots of pretzels, and your poker party is sure to be a success. Skip the usual party decorations, but be sure you have plenty of matches, ash trays, and decks of cards.

Bridge parties lend themselves to many wonderful themes. For example, you may decide to go Italian with brightly-colored woven placemats, wooden table decorations, and tinted goblets. Antipasto is a superb appetizer for such a party. And Lasagna — the layered main dish combining pasta, rich tomato sauce, and cheese — will bring compliments from your guests. Italian Breadsticks and Vegetable Salad Mold are the perfect additions to this dish. For dessert, introduce a welcome note of color — and light flavor — with Pistachio Ice Cream and Brownies. Your guests will praise your party for weeks to come.

These are only nine of the most common festive occasions. There may be many more you would like to commemorate with a gala party — Mardi Gras, May Day, your state's holidays, etc. Use this section as a guide to planning the most delightful party ever. It takes planning . . . delicious food . . . eye-appealing decorations . . . and you, the hostess with verve, imagination, and the ability to turn every festive event into a memorable party occasion!

Mother's Day Dinner

Barbecued Ham Slices

Mixed Green Salad with Creamy Garlic Dressing

Garlic-Cheese Loaf

Apricot Nectar Cake

Pink Lady Punch

MIXED GREEN SALAD WITH CREAMY GARLIC DRESSING

1 head romaine, torn
1 head Bibb lettuce, torn
1/2 head iceberg lettuce, torn
1/2 lge. cucumber
1 c. halved cherry tomatoes
1/2 c. sliced green pepper
1/4 c. sliced ripe olives
3 slices bacon
1/4 c. grated Parmesan cheese
Creamy Garlic Dressing

Combine romaine, Bibb lettuce and iceberg lettuce in large bowl. Pare and slice cucumber; arrange cucumber, tomatoes, green pepper and olives on lettuce. Fry bacon until crisp; crumble coarsely. Sprinkle over salad; sprinkle with Parmesan cheese. Toss with Creamy Garlic Dressing; serve immediately.

Creamy Garlic Dressing

1 c. bottled Italian salad dressing
1 c. mayonnaise
1/4 c. shredded Cheddar cheese
1 tsp. anchovy paste

Combine all ingredients; beat until well mixed. Chill until ready to use.

Marie Bell
Rockaway, Oregon

GARLIC-CHEESE LOAF

1/2 c. butter
1/4 tsp. garlic powder
2 pkg. refrigerator biscuits
1 c. grated sharp cheese

Combine butter and garlic powder in saucepan; heat until butter is melted. Cut biscuits into quarters; dip pieces in butter then in cheese. Arrange in greased bread pan. Bake in 400-degree oven for 25 minutes or until crispy brown. Yield: 6-8 servings.

Barbara Matte
Plato Center, Illinois

BARBECUED HAM SLICES

1 c. brown sugar
3 tbsp. catsup
1 tbsp. soy sauce
1 tsp. dry mustard
1 c. crushed pineapple
2 tbsp. green pepper flakes
1 1/2 tbsp. cornstarch
3/4 to 1-in. thick ready-to-eat ham slices

Combine 1 cup water and brown sugar in saucepan. Add catsup, soy sauce, mustard, pineapple and pepper flakes. Bring to a boil; simmer for 10 minutes. Dissolve cornstarch in 1/4 cup cold water; add to sauce. Cook, stirring, until sauce is clear and thick. Cook ham on grill over hot coals for about 8 minutes, basting frequently with sauce. Serve with additional sauce.

Claire Collins
Trenton, New Jersey

APRICOT NECTAR CAKE

1 pkg. yellow cake mix
3/4 c. cooking oil
Apricot nectar
2 tsp. lemon extract
4 eggs, separated

1 1/2 c. confectioners' sugar
2 tbsp. lemon juice

Combine cake mix, cooking oil, 5 1/2 ounces apricot nectar, lemon extract and egg yolks in electric mixer bowl. Mix at low speed for 5 minutes. Fold in stiffly beaten egg whites; place batter in greased tube pan. Bake at 350 degrees for 35 to 40 minutes. Let cool slightly; remove from pan. Combine 2 tablespoons apricot nectar and remaining ingredients; beat until smooth. Spread over hot cake. Yield: 12 servings.

Mrs. Walter Wenzel
Kerrville, Texas

PINK LADY PUNCH

4 c. cranberry juice cocktail
1 1/2 c. sugar
4 c. pineapple or grapefruit juice
2 qt. ginger ale, chilled

Mix cranberry juice and sugar until sugar is dissolved. Add pineapple juice; chill. Pour into punch bowl; add ginger ale. Yield: 32 punch cup servings.

Mrs. William H. Junghans, Jr.
Philadelphia, Pennsylvania

Father's Day Dinner

Shrimp Cocktail

Roast Prime Ribs of Beef

Corn on the Cob   Asparagus Amandine

Lemon Meringue Pie

SHRIMP COCKTAIL

Desired amount of cooked shrimp
Desired amount of celery, finely chopped
1/2 c. chili sauce
1/3 c. catsup
2 tbsp. horseradish
1 1/2 tsp. Worcestershire sauce

Clean shrimp, removing black line from back. Chill. Add celery; mix well. Season. Place 4 to 6 shrimp in lettuce-lined cocktail cup set in ice for each serving. Combine remaining ingredients; mix and chill. Serve over shrimp.

Mrs. Arnold Boehnke
Leadville, Colorado

ASPARAGUS AMANDINE

2 10-oz. packages frozen asparagus spears
1/3 c. butter or margarine
1/2 c. slivered blanched almonds
Juice of 1/2 lemon

Cook asparagus in small amount of salted water for 8 to 10 minutes or until tender. Drain; arrange in warm serving dish. Combine butter, almonds and lemon juice in saucepan; heat until butter is melted. Pour over asparagus; serve immediately. Yield: 8 servings.

Mrs. Hiram Fry
Corvallis, Oregon

ROAST PRIME RIBS OF BEEF

1 2 to 3-lb. rib roast
Seasoned flour

Wipe roast with clean damp cloth; rub with seasoned flour. Place fat side up in roaster. Roast, uncovered, at 300 degrees for 15 minutes per pound for rare, 20 minutes per pound for medium or 30 minutes per pound for well done. Remove to hot platter; garnish with parsley. Serve with a red Bordeaux wine, if desired.

Donna Meyerhoven
Maitland, Florida

CORN-ON-THE-COB

6 ears of corn
2 tbsp. salt
Butter

Remove husks and silks from corn; wash. Drop carefully into kettle of salted boiling water; bring to a boil. Boil for 7 minutes; drain. Season with butter; serve immediately. Yield: 6 servings.

Jewel Mitchell
Centreville, Alabama

LEMON MERINGUE PIE

1 1/3 c. sugar
3 tbsp. flour
1 tsp. salt
Grated lemon rind to taste
3 eggs, separated
Juice of 1 lemon
1 c. boiling water
1 tbsp. butter
1 baked pie shell

Combine 1 cup sugar, flour, salt and lemon rind. Beat egg yolks; pour in saucepan. Stir in lemon juice. Add sugar mixture; mix well. Stir in boiling water. Cook until thickened, stirring constantly. Add butter; stir until melted. Pour into pie shell. Beat egg whites until firm peaks form, adding remaining sugar. Spread over lemon filling. Bake at 325 degrees for 20 minutes or until golden brown.

Anna Terry
Weaverville, California

Derby Day Brunch

Old Virginia Ham with Red-Eye Gravy

Egg and Cheese Souffle

Candied Apples — Biscuits

Fresh Strawberries and Peaches With Brown Sugar and Sour Cream

OLD VIRGINIA HAM WITH RED-EYE GRAVY

1 lge. center-cut ham slice,
1/2 in. thick
1/8 tsp. salt
1/2 c. strong coffee

Slash fat on edge of ham in several places. Place ham in hot skillet; brown quickly on one side. Turn; brown lightly on other side. Simmer for 15 minutes or until tender. Remove from pan; place on heated platter. Sprinkle salt in hot skillet; add coffee. Boil for 2 minutes. Pour over ham. Serve with biscuits. Yield: 4 servings.

Mrs. Martha Henegar
Jellico, Tennessee

EGG AND CHEESE SOUFFLE

3 tbsp. butter
3 tbsp. flour
1 c. milk
1/2 tsp. salt
Pepper to taste
3 eggs, separated
1 c. grated cheese

Melt butter in saucepan; stir in flour to make a smooth paste. Add milk; cook, stirring constantly, until thick. Add salt and pepper. Pour a small amount of the white sauce into egg yolks, stirring constantly; stir egg yolks into white sauce. Add cheese; cook and stir until cheese has melted. Remove from heat; fold in stiffly beaten egg whites. Pour into greased baking dish. Bake at 350 degrees for 45 to 50 minutes.

Mrs. Joseph F. Yurso
Charleston, South Carolina

CANDIED APPLES

6 apples, peeled and cored
1 8-oz. package red cinnamon hearts
1 tsp. nutmeg
4 oz. cottage cheese

Place apples upright in baking dish. Dissolve cinnamon hearts in 1 cup water over low heat. Add nutmeg; pour cinnamon mixture over apples. Bake at 300 degrees for 40 minutes. Remove from oven; fill apple cavities with cottage cheese. Serve immediately.

Mrs. Charles Livick
Kingston, North Carolina

BISCUITS

2 c. sifted all-purpose flour
1 tbsp. baking powder
1 tsp. salt
1/4 c. shortening
2/3 to 3/4 c. milk

Sift flour, baking powder and salt together; cut in shortening until mixture is crumbly. Add enough milk to make a soft dough. Turn out on lightly floured board; knead for 30 seconds. Roll dough out to 1/2 inch thick; cut with floured biscuit cutter. Place on ungreased baking sheet. Bake at 450 degrees for 10 to 12 minutes or until lightly browned. Yield: 12 biscuits.

Mrs. Walter Jones
Atlanta, Georgia

Election Night Supper

Chicken Tetrazzini

Scalloped Green Peas and Onions

Crusty Rolls — Lemon Icebox Cake

Hot Spiced Percolator Punch

LEMON ICEBOX CAKE

1/2 lb. butter
2 c. powdered sugar
4 eggs, separated
Juice and grated rind of 1 lge. lemon
1 c. pecans, chopped fine
1 tsp. vanilla
1 1/2 doz. ladyfingers, split

Cream butter and powdered sugar; stir in well-beaten egg yolks. Add lemon juice, rind, pecans and vanilla; mix well. Fold in stiffly beaten egg whites. Line bottom of springform pan with half the ladyfingers; spread on half the filling. Add remaining ladyfingers; top with remaining filling. Refrigerate overnight. Serve with whipped cream.

Mrs. Jerry Jones
Marbury, Alabama

HOT SPICED PERCOLATOR PUNCH

2 1/4 c. pineapple juice
2 c. cranberry juice
1 3/4 c. water
1 tbsp. whole cloves
1/2 tbsp. whole allspice
3 sticks cinnamon, broken
1/4 tsp. salt
1/2 c. (lightly packed) brown sugar
Tea bags (opt.)

Pour pineapple juice, cranberry juice and water in bottom of 8-cup percolator; place remaining ingredients in top. Perk for 10 minutes. Serve hot in mugs or punch cups. Yield: 8 servings.

Mrs. E. B. Caraway, Jr.
McMinnville, Tennessee

SCALLOPED GREEN PEAS AND ONIONS

1 10-oz. package frozen peas
1/4 c. butter
1/4 c. flour
1 tsp. salt
1 tsp. seasoned salt
1/4 tsp. pepper
2 c. milk
1 lb. small white onions, peeled
1 lb. potatoes, sliced
1 c. shredded Swiss cheese

Partially thaw peas; break apart. Melt butter in saucepan over low heat; blend in flour, salts and pepper. Add milk, stirring constantly. Cook and stir until sauce is smooth and thickened. Arrange 1/2 of the peas, onions and potatoes in buttered 1 1/2-quart shallow casserole. Spoon 1/2 of the sauce over vegetables; sprinkle 1/2 of the cheese over sauce. Repeat layers. Bake at 375 degrees about 1 hour or until vegetables are tender. Yield: 6 servings.

CRUSTY ROLLS

1 c. lukewarm water
1 tbsp. sugar
1 1/2 tsp. salt
1 pkg. yeast
3 1/2 c. (about) all-purpose flour
2 tbsp. salad oil
2 egg whites
Whole sesame seed
1 egg yolk

Combine water, sugar, salt and yeast in large bowl; stir until yeast is dissolved. Add 1 cup flour; mix well. Add oil; beat until batter is smooth. Beat egg whites until stiff but not dry; fold into batter. Add remaining flour; mix to moderately stiff dough. Turn out onto lightly floured board; knead until smooth. Place in greased bowl. Cover; let rise until doubled in bulk. Punch down; let rise for 15 minutes. Punch down; shape into 18 rolls. Dip in sesame seed; place on greased baking sheet. Cover; let rise until doubled in bulk. Beat egg yolk with 1 tablespoon water; brush rolls with egg yolk mixture. Bake at 400 degrees for 15 minutes.

Gloria Eighorn
Melrose, Montana

CHICKEN TETRAZZINI

1 c. diced celery
1 c. diced green pepper
1/2 c. diced onion
1 sm. can mushrooms
1/2 c. butter
1/4 c. flour
1 c. milk
1/2 lb. sharp cheese, grated
2 tsp. salt
1/4 tsp. pepper
1/4 c. pimento
1 clove of garlic, crushed
2 tbsp. Worcestershire sauce
2 c. diced cooked chicken
1/4 c. sherry
1 8-oz. package spaghetti
3/4 c. Parmesan cheese

Cook celery, green pepper, onion and mushrooms in butter until onion is transparent. Blend in flour; add milk, stirring constantly. Blend in cheese, salt, pepper, pimento, garlic, Worcestershire sauce, chicken and sherry; stir until cheese is melted. Cook spaghetti according to package directions. Mix sauce with spaghetti. Place in casserole; sprinkle with Parmesan cheese. Bake at 350 degrees for 15 to 20 minutes. Yield: 8-10 servings.

Mrs. Henry McCoy
Guntersville, Alabama

After-The-Game Pancake Supper

Apple Pancakes

Banana Pancakes   Blueberry Pancakes

Cottage Cheese-Fruit Pancakes

Corn Bread Jelly Roll   Strawberry Hot Cakes

BANANA PANCAKES

2 to 3 ripe bananas
1 1/2 c. buttermilk
2 eggs
2 tbsp. sugar
2 c. self-rising flour
1/4 tsp. soda
2 tbsp. melted butter or oil

Mash bananas. Add buttermilk, eggs and sugar; blend well. Add flour and soda; beat thoroughly. Add melted butter. Pour onto greased hot griddle; cook on both sides until brown. Serve with butter and powdered sugar. Yield: 8-10 servings.

Eleanor Fulford
Tampa, Florida

STRAWBERRY HOT CAKES

2 c. cake mix
1 egg
1/2 c. water
1/3 c. flour
1/3 c. chopped nuts
Sweetened strawberries
Whipped cream

Combine cake mix, egg and water; beat until smooth. Stir in flour and nuts. Preheat grill. Drop from tablespoons onto lightly greased surface. Cook on both sides until done. Spoon strawberries over hot cakes; top with whipped cream. Serve immediately. Yield: 6-8 servings.

Marlene Caszatt
Whitehall, Michigan

COTTAGE CHEESE-FRUIT PANCAKES

3 well-beaten eggs
1 c. cream-style cottage cheese
2 tbsp. salad oil
1/4 c. sifted flour
1/4 tsp. salt
Raspberry jam
Confectioners' sugar

Preheat grill. Combine eggs, cheese and salad oil; mix well. Sift flour and salt together; add to egg mixture. Beat only until blended. Bake 4-inch cakes on lightly greased griddle. Place about 1 tablespoon jam in center of each cake; bring edges of pancake together and roll. Sprinkle with confectioners' sugar. Serve at once. Yield: 8 cakes.

Mrs. Arthur H. Raasch
Lake Oswego, Oregon

CORN BREAD JELLY ROLL

1 pkg. corn bread mix
2 tbsp. cooking oil
1 c. berry jam
3/4 c. powdered sugar

Prepare corn bread mix according to package directions, adding 1/4 cup more liquid and 2 tablespoons cooking oil. Mix only until moistened. Pour small amount batter at a time on hot greased griddle. Bake on both sides until done. Place about 1 tablespoon jam in center of each griddle cake. Roll tightly; secure with toothpick. Roll in powdered sugar; serve hot. Yield: 12 servings.

Mrs. Charles S. Carlisle
Pearl Harbor, Hawaii

APPLE PANCAKES

2 c. flour
2 tbsp. sugar
4 tsp. baking powder
1 tsp. salt
2 c. milk
2 eggs, separated
2 tbsp. melted butter
1 c. grated peeled apple

Combine flour, sugar, baking powder and salt in mixing bowl. Combine milk, well-beaten egg yolks and butter in small bowl; mix well. Add to flour mixture; beat until smooth. Stir in apple; fold in beaten egg whites. Grease hot griddle for first pancakes only. Pour batter by 1/2 cupfuls onto griddle; cook until puffy and bubbly. Turn; brown other side. Serve with syrup.

Mrs. Ralph Niccum
Aberdeen, Indiana

BLUEBERRY PANCAKES

1 c. sifted flour
1 1/2 tsp. baking powder
1 tbsp. sugar
1/2 tsp. salt
1/4 tsp. cinnamon
2 tbsp. melted butter
1 egg, separated
3/4 c. milk
3/4 c. drained blueberries

Sift flour, baking powder, sugar, salt and cinnamon together. Add butter to beaten egg yolk; stir in milk. Add to dry ingredients, mixing just enough to moisten. Fold in stiffly beaten egg white. Add blueberries; mix lightly. Pour batter on hot greased griddle. Bake on both sides until done. Serve with butter. Yield: 8 pancakes.

Patricia Wissinger
Windber, Pennsylvania

Graduation Swim Supper

Miniature Drumsticks

Marinated Green Bean Salad

Tuna Salad Cups — Cheese-Potato Strips

Pineapple-Apricot Shrub

Individual Strawberry Shortcakes

TUNA SALAD CUPS

6 sm. ripe tomatoes
1 can water-pack tuna
1/2 c. drained mushroom pieces
1/2 c. drained canned peas
1/4 c. chopped stuffed olives
Salad dressing
Salt to taste
Celery salt to taste
Lettuce

Cut tops off tomatoes; scoop out pulp. Drain. Drain tuna; flake. Combine tuna, mushrooms, peas, olives and enough salad dressing to moisten. Mix well. Season with salt and celery salt. Fill tomato shells. Place on lettuce. Garnish with salad dressing and olive slice. Yield: 6 servings.

Ethel Anderson
Smyrna Mills, Maine

MINIATURE DRUMSTICKS

3 lb. broiler-fryer chicken wings
1/2 c. flour
1/2 c. grated Parmesan cheese
1 tsp. monosodium glutamate
1 tsp. salt
1 tsp. paprika
1/8 tsp. pepper
1/2 tsp. oregano

3/4 c. buttermilk
Oil or shortening

Cut wings in half; remove wing tips. Blend dry ingredients together in shallow dish. Dip wing pieces in buttermilk; shake to remove excess. Roll in dry ingredients. Heat oil in electric fryer to 365 degrees. Fry 5 minutes. Drain on absorbent paper.

Rose Woodward
Toledo, Ohio

CHEESE-POTATO STRIPS

5 med. potatoes
2/3 c. milk
1/2 tsp. hot sauce
1 1/2 tsp. salt
1 tbsp. butter
1/4 lb. American cheese, grated
Paprika

Peel potatoes; cut into strips as for French-fried potatoes. Place in greased shallow baking dish. Combine milk, hot sauce and salt; pour over potatoes. Dot with butter. Cover. Bake in 425-degree oven for 40 minutes or until potatoes are tender. Top with cheese. Bake, uncovered, for 5 minutes longer. Sprinkle with paprika.

Mrs. Sam Knox
Johnson City, Tennessee

MARINATED GREEN BEAN SALAD

2 lge. Italian onions
1 can water chestnuts, drained
2 cans green beans, drained
1 No. 2 can peas, drained
4 c. 1-inch celery pieces
1/2 c. sliced stuffed olives
1 pkg. slivered toasted almonds
Juice of 1 1/2 lemons
Juice of 1 1/2 oranges
2 buds crushed garlic
1 c. salad oil
1 tsp. Worcestershire sauce
3/4 tsp. pepper
1 tsp. salt
3/4 c. powdered sugar
1 tsp. dry mustard
1/2 c. vinegar

Slice onions; separate into rings. Slice water chestnuts. Combine onions, water chestnuts, beans, peas, celery, olives and almonds in large bowl. Combine remaining ingredients for marinade; mix well. Pour over vegetable mixture. Marinate for 24 hours or overnight, stirring occasionally. Salad keeps indefinitely in refrigerator.

Helen Nelson
Tacoma, Washington

INDIVIDUAL STRAWBERRY SHORTCAKES

2 c. flour
3 tsp. baking powder
1/2 tsp. salt
6 tbsp. (about) sugar
1/2 c. butter
1 egg
1 c. milk
Sliced sweetened strawberries

Sift flour, baking powder and salt together. Combine sugar, butter and egg; mix until creamy. Add milk; beat well. Add dry ingredients; stir well. Pour into small individual pans. Bake at 375 degrees for 15 to 20 minutes or until light brown. Spoon strawberries over warm shortcakes. Serve with whipped cream or milk. Yield: 8-12 servings.

Mrs. Betty Custer
Garrett, Indiana

PINEAPPLE-APRICOT SHRUB

1 8 1/2-oz. can crushed pineapple
1 tbsp. lemon juice
1 c. apricot nectar
2 c. cracked ice

Combine all ingredients in blender container. Cover; blend for about 30 seconds or until smooth. Serve in tall glasses. Top with maraschino cherries, if desired. Yield: 3 servings.

Nancy B. Goshin
New City, New York

Bon Voyage Party

Spanish Gazpacho

Feta Greek Cheese Turnovers

English Roast Beef with Yorkshire Pudding

Italian Eggplant Parmigiana

French Salade Nicoise

German Peach – Cream Kuchen   Viennese Coffee

FETA GREEK CHEESE TURNOVERS

1 lb. feta cheese, crumbled
5 tbsp. grated Parmesan cheese
2 eggs
Pepper to taste
1/2 lb. filo or strudel dough
Melted butter

Mix cheeses, eggs and pepper together. Stack several sheets filo, brushing each sheet with butter. Cut sheets in 4-inch squares. Spread half of 1 side of each square with cheese filling; fold unspread half over filling. Press edges firmly together; brush with butter. Place on baking sheet. Bake at 375 degrees for 20 to 30 minutes or until browned. Serve hot. Yield: 8 servings.

Mrs. Spiro Babalis
Detroit, Michigan

FRENCH SALADE NICOISE

5 tomatoes, quartered
1/2 onion, finely sliced
1 green pepper, sliced
5 or 6 radishes, sliced
4 stalks celery, chopped
8 anchovy fillets
2 hard-cooked eggs, quartered
10 black olives
1 clove of garlic, crushed
1 lge. can chunk tuna, flaked

Chill all ingredients well. Place in large salad bowl in order listed.

Dressing

2 tbsp. wine vinegar
6 tbsp. oil
Pinch of fresh basil

Combine all ingredients in jar; shake well. Pour over salad; mix gently.

Mrs. Coleman Smith
Boise, Idaho

ENGLISH ROAST BEEF AND YORKSHIRE PUDDING

Flour
6 tbsp. butter
1 tbsp. dry mustard
1 tsp. paprika
1/4 tsp. pepper
1 6-lb. standing rib roast
2 eggs, well-beaten
1 c. milk
1/4 tsp. salt

Place 1/4 cup flour into heavy skillet; place over moderate heat. Stir until lightly browned; remove from heat. Cream butter; add browned flour, mustard, paprika and pepper. Blend well. Place roast, standing on bones, in roasting pan. Spread flour mixture over roast. Bake at 325 degrees until of desired doneness. Combine eggs and milk; add 3 tablespoons drippings from roast. Add 1 cup sifted flour and salt; beat until smooth with rotary beater. Pour into greased cups. Bake at 450 degrees for 25 minutes or until well browned. Yield: 6 servings.

Mrs. David Nash
Pt. Muga, California

SPANISH GAZPACHO

1 clove of garlic, crushed
1/2 tsp. salt
2 tbsp. olive oil
5 ripe tomatoes, chopped
1 chopped onion
1/4 tsp. pepper
1/4 tsp. paprika
1 1/2 tbsp. vinegar
1 1/2 c. cold water or bouillon
1/4 c. dry bread crumbs

Mix all ingredients together except bread crumbs; refrigerate for at least 1 hour or overnight. Grind in food mill or mash through coarse sieve; add more salt, if needed. Add bread crumbs just before serving; pour into soup bowls. Place 1 ice cube in each bowl; serve with croutons, chopped green peppers and chopped cucumbers. Yield: 4 servings.

Mrs. Fred Euhus
Yuma, Arizona

GERMAN PEACH CREAM KUCHEN

2 c. sifted flour
3/4 c. sugar
1/4 tsp. baking powder
1 tsp. salt
1/2 c. butter or margarine
1 No. 2 1/2 can peach slices, drained
1 tsp. cinnamon
2 egg yolks, beaten
1 c. sour cream

Sift flour, 1/4 cup sugar, baking powder and salt together; cut in butter until mixture resembles fine crumbs. Press firmly against bottom and side of lightly greased 9-inch springform pan. Arrange peaches evenly over crumbs. Combine remaining sugar and cinnamon; sprinkle over peaches. Bake at 400 degrees for 15 minutes. Blend egg yolks and sour cream. Spoon over peaches. Bake for 20 minutes longer or until golden brown. Serve warm or chilled. Yield: 8 servings.

Mrs. Victor Kendall
Norfolk, Virginia

ITALIAN EGGPLANT PARMIGIANA

1 lge. eggplant
2 eggs
1/4 c. milk
Parmesan cheese
1 tbsp. chopped parsley
Garlic salt to taste
Salt and pepper to taste
1/2 c. oil
Flour
2 c. tomato sauce
Mozzarella cheese, sliced thin

Slice eggplant into 1/4 to 1/2-inch slices. Beat eggs with fork; add milk, 2 tablespoons Parmesan cheese, parsley, garlic salt, salt and pepper to taste. Heat oil in frypan. Coat eggplant slices with flour; dip eggplant slices into egg mixture. Fry on both sides until golden brown. Drain on absorbent paper. Place layer of eggplant in baking dish. Add layer of tomato sauce; sprinkle with Parmesan cheese. Repeat layers. Top with mozzarella cheese. Bake for about 20 to 30 minutes in 350-degree oven until sauce starts to bubble and mozzarella is slightly browned. Yield: 8 servings.

June Carosia
Newark, New Jersey

VIENNESE COFFEE

1/2 c. heavy cream
1 tbsp. confectioners' sugar
1/2 tsp. vanilla
3 c. hot strong coffee
1/2 tsp. grated orange peel
4 cinnamon sticks

Combine cream, confectioners' sugar and vanilla; beat with mixer until stiff. Pour hot coffee into 4 coffee mugs. Spoon whipped cream on top. Garnish with orange peel; place 1 cinnamon stick in each cup. Serve at once. Yield: 4 servings.

Mrs. Virginia Lettie
Ajo, Arizona

Poker Party Snack

Pretzels and Potato Chips

Hot Potato Salad **Reuben Sandwiches**

Gold Coast Coffee

HOT POTATO SALAD

6 lge. potatoes
2 tbsp. pickle relish (opt.)
1 onion, chopped
4 stalks celery, chopped
Salt and pepper
2 or 3 eggs, beaten
1/2 c. sugar
1 tsp. dry mustard
2 tbsp. flour
1/2 c. vinegar
2 tbsp. butter
4 hard-boiled eggs

Cook potatoes; let cool. Peel; dice. Mix potatoes, pickle relish, onion and celery; season with salt and pepper to taste. Cream beaten eggs and sugar; add mustard, 1 teaspoon salt and flour. Blend; add vinegar, 1 1/2 cups water and butter. Cook until thick, adding 1/2 cup water if needed. Pour over potato mixture. Slice or dice hard-boiled eggs; add to salad. Salad is good served hot or chilled. Dressing may also be used over dandelion greens, endive or garden lettuce. Yield: 6 servings.

Betty Lou Huffman
Harrington, Delaware

GOLD COAST COFFEE

1 c. instant cocoa
1/3 c. instant coffee
4 c. boiling water
1/2 pt. heavy cream, whipped
Nutmeg

Mix cocoa, coffee and boiling water in large pan. Cover; heat. Pour into coffee urn of coffee service. Serve after dinner in demitasse cups. Top with whipped cream and dash of nutmeg. Yield: 6 demitasse servings.

Mrs. George Phillip Case
Portsmouth, Virginia

REUBEN SANDWICH

2 c. drained sauerkraut
1/2 tsp. caraway or dillseed
1/8 tsp. garlic powder
16 slices round bread
1/2 c. Russian dressing
1 lb. thinly sliced corned beef
1 lb. Swiss cheese slices
Melted butter or margarine

Toss sauerkraut with caraway seed and garlic powder; set aside. Spread bread with dressing. Top 8 slices bread with corned beef, sauerkraut, cheese and remaining 8 slices bread. Brush melted butter on both sides of sandwiches. Grill in skillet or electric sandwich toaster until cheese is melted.

Bridge Buffet

Antipasto Relish
Lasagna
Vegetable Salad Mold
Italian Breadsticks
Pistachio Ice Cream with Brownies

ANTIPASTO RELISH

1/2 sm. head cauliflower
2 carrots
1 green pepper
2 stalks celery
1 4-oz. jar pimento strips
1 3-oz. jar pitted green olives
3/4 c. wine vinegar
1/2 c. olive oil
2 tbsp. sugar
1 tsp. salt
1/2 tsp. dried oregano
1/4 tsp. pepper

Break cauliflower into flowerets; slice. Cut carrots and green pepper into 2-inch strips. Cut celery into 1-inch pieces. Drain pimento and olives. Place all ingredients in large skillet; add 1/4 cup water. Bring to a boil, stirring occasionally. Reduce heat; cover. Simmer for 5 minutes. Cool. Refrigerate for 24 hours. Drain well before serving.

Mrs. William A. Chater
Charlotte, North Carolina

LASAGNA

3/4 lb. ground beef
1/4 lb. bulk sausage
1 sm. onion, minced
1/2 clove of garlic, chopped
1 sm. can mushroom pieces
1 bay leaf
1 tsp. salt
1/2 tsp. pepper
1 tsp. mixed Italian spices
2 sm. cans tomato paste
1 pkg. lasagna
1 carton ricotta cheese
12 oz. sliced mozzarella cheese
Grated Parmesan cheese

Brown ground beef, sausage and onion in skillet; pour off excess fat. Add garlic, mushroom pieces, seasonings and tomato paste. Rinse each tomato paste can with 3 tablespoons water; stir into meat mixture. Simmer for 45 minutes, stirring occasionally. Cook lasagna according to package directions. Alternate layers of lasagna, meat sauce, ricotta, mozzarella and Parmesan cheeses in greased oblong baking dish. Repeat layers. Bake in 325-degree oven for 45 minutes.

Elsie Hale
Scottsdale, Arizona

VEGETABLE SALAD MOLD

1 pkg. lemon gelatin
1 1/2 c. hot water
1/2 c. sour cream
1/2 tsp. salt
1/2 c. diced cucumbers
1/2 c. sliced radishes
1/4 c. sliced green onions
1/2 c. diced celery
1/4 c. diced green pepper
1 pkg. lime gelatin
2 c. hot water

Dissolve lemon gelatin in hot water. Chill until thickened. Blend in sour cream and salt. Chill until partially set. Add vegetables; pour into 6-cup mold. Chill until firm. Dissolve lime gelatin in hot water. Chill until thickened. Pour over vegetable mixture. Chill until firm. Yield: 10 servings.

Mrs. Eldore Messerschmidt
Marshfield, Wisconsin

BROWNIES

4 sq. baking chocolate
3/4 c. melted butter or margarine
6 eggs
3 c. sugar
2 c. sifted flour
1/2 tsp. salt
1/2 c. chopped nuts
2 tsp. vanilla

Melt chocolate in butter. Beat eggs well; add sugar. Beat until well blended. Sift flour with salt; add to sugar mixture. Add chocolate mixture, nuts and vanilla; mix well. Turn into 2 greased 10 x 14-inch pans. Bake in 450-degree oven for 12 to 15 minutes. Place under broiler flame to brown. Cut into squares while warm. Yield: 48 brownies.

Carol Ramsay
Waveland, Indiana

AMBROSIAL CHIFFON CAKE

2 1/4 c. sifted cake flour
1 1/2 c. sugar
3 tsp. baking powder
1 tsp. salt
1/2 c. corn oil
6 eggs, separated
3/4 c. orange juice
2 tsp. vanilla
1/2 tsp. cream of tartar

Sift flour, sugar, baking powder and salt in mixing bowl. Make well in center; add oil, egg yolks, juice and vanilla. Beat with spoon until smooth. Beat egg whites and cream of tartar until stiff peaks form. Fold flour mixture into egg whites gently. Turn batter into ungreased 10-inch tube pan. Bake at 350 degrees for 1 hour and 15 minutes or until cake tests done. Invert pan over funnel; cool. Remove from pan when cold. Place on rack. Slice crosswise into 3 equal layers. Place top third, crust side down, on cake plate. Spread with Fruit Filling. Cover with center layer. Spread with Creamy Cake Filling. Top with bottom layer. Frost top and side with White Cloud Frosting.

Fruit Filling

1/2 c. chopped candied cherries
1/2 c. chopped candied pineapple
1/2 c. chopped white raisins
1/2 c. chopped nuts
1/2 c. flaked coconut
1/2 c. orange juice
3 slightly beaten egg yolks
1/3 c. sugar
2 tbsp. margarine
1/4 c. Creamy Cake Filling

Combine fruits, nuts, coconut and orange juice. Marinate for 2 hours. Combine egg yolks, sugar and margarine in saucepan. Cook over low heat, stirring constantly, until slightly thickened. Stir in fruit mixture. Cool. Fold in Creamy Cake Filling.

Creamy Cake Filling

3 tbsp. sugar
4 1/2 tsp. cornstarch
1 c. milk
1 tsp. vanilla
1/4 c. whipping cream, whipped

Combine sugar and cornstarch in top of double boiler. Blend in milk, a small amount at a time. Cook over boiling water, stirring constantly, until thickened. Cover; cook for 10 minutes longer, stirring occasionally. Remove from boiling water; stir in vanilla. Cool; chill. Beat with rotary beater until creamy. Fold in whipped cream.

White Cloud Frosting

3 egg whites
1/4 tsp. salt
1/3 c. sugar
1 c. white corn syrup
1 1/2 tsp. vanilla

Beat egg whites and salt until soft peaks form. Add sugar, 1 tablespoon at a time, beating until smooth and glossy. Beat in syrup, a small amount at a time, blending thoroughly after each addition. Beat until stiff peaks form. Fold in vanilla.

Photograph for this recipe on page 261.

INDEX

PHOTOGRAPHY CREDITS: Cling Peach Advisory Board; National Cherry Growers and Industries Foundation; Corning Glass Works; California Raisin Advisory Board; Standard Brands Products: Fleischmann's Margarine, Planter's Peanut Oil; South African Rock Lobster Service Corporation; Olive Administration Committee; Anderson Clayton and Company: Seven Seas Dressing; Florida Citrus Commission; California Avocado Advisory Board; Florida Fruit and Vegetable Association; Washington State Apple Commission; National Macaroni Institute; Pickle Packers International, Inc.; The Quaker Oats Company; Ocean Spray Cranberries, Inc.; United Fresh Fruit and Vegetable Association; Fostoria Glass Company; Pet, Inc.; California Raisin Advisory Board; California Beef Council; U. S. Bureau of Commerical Fisheries; General Foods Kitchens; American Lamb Council; Oregon Filbert Commission; Campbell Soup Company; Brussels Sprouts Marketing Program; The Borden Company; Best Foods: Division of Corn Products Company; American Home Foods; National Dairy Council; National Kraut Packers Association; Louisiana Yam Commission; R. C. Bigelow Tea Company; Peter Pan Peanut Butter; International Chicory Institute; Artichoke Advisory Board; Dried Fig Advisory Board; Filbert/ Hazelnut Institute; Kraft Foods; Pineapple Growers Association; The McIlhenny Company; Grandma's West Indies Molasses; Knox Gelatine; Diamond Walnut Kitchen; National Peanut Council; North American Blueberry Council; Angostura-Wuppermann Corporation; National Pecan Shellers and Processors Association; Keith Thomas Company; National Livestock and Meat Board; Evaporated Milk Company; National Biscuit Company; and National Association of Frozen Food Packers.